THE MILLIONAIRE Mindset

Awakening Through Divine Touch

BORIS VENE – NIKOLA GRUBIŠA

THE MILLIONAIRE
Mindset
Awakening Through Divine Touch

Copyrights © Inisa d.o.o. 2007

INISA

First Edition, August 2007

ISBN 81-7899-88-1

Published by
Sai Towers Publishing
23/1142, V L Colony, Kadugodi, Bangalore 560 067, INDIA
www.saitowers.com

All rights reserved. This book may not be reproduced in whole or in part, or transmitted in any form, without written permission from the publisher, except by a reviewer who may quote brief passages in a review; nor may any part of this book be reproduced, stored in a retrieval system, or transmitted in any form or by any means electronic, mechanical, photocopying, recording, or other, without written permission from the publisher.

A CATALOGUE RECORD FOR THIS BOOK IS AVAILABLE FROM THE BRITISH LIBRARY.

Printed and bound in India by Vishruti Prints

Sri Sathya Sai Baba
is one of the greatest spiritual leaders of our time.
He has signed the original (short) version of this book
and his signature is facsimiled here.

Warning

The book you are holding carries a very strong initiative energy. This means that, on the basis of the information that you will become aware of while reading this book, a karmic process could be touched off within you. The consequences are: quicker and more intensive development of events, a feeling of a lesser ability to influence events, and the beginning of solutions to jammed, abandoned or completely new situations, or even in areas with which you were not occupied until now. The goal of this process is the soul's growth.

So you can choose to stay in present positions and energies... or move ahead into a **new reality**. If you want to move on, **reading this book can give you a big boost** and bring about a dynamic changes, and perhaps even aid in alleviating the crisis. This is because with a step forward comes as a result – **in dealing with (difficult) situations** from how you have dealt with them in the past.

If you ask God, for example, for love, you will not wake up next morning full of love. However, you will likely **find yourself in a situation where you will have an opportunity to evoke and awaken all the love that is within you.** (Read: You will stick with one of the most unloving people you can imagine... and be compelled to deal with this situation.)

We should know that as long as we do not relate with a certain situation, person or event, then we do not **resonate** with it, and so **the energy in**

relation to it remains foreign and unimportant to us. So energy does not touch us, but passes by, which is why we can persist in old habits, related to this experience, **without a feeling of additional responsibility.**

But when we identify with the person or experience, we may no longer be capable of ignoring this information, and we will **begin to be aware of the consequences and responsibilities we carry within ourselves.** That way **the "intuitive code" within us, will trigger new dynamic energies and change events around us.**

Therefore we begin to realize, the ways we previously thought and worked limit us and we will no longer be capable of performing them superficially, because we realize what they will bring us or where they will lead us. For this reason – we will begin to either **abandon** them, or **continue with our old habits** while **feeling badly when doing so.**

So if you believe that it is not yet time for change, it is perhaps recommended that you put this book aside and continue with your daily routine.

On the other hand, you need not fear that **anything will happen – except that which serves the growth of your soul.** However, we must realize that the growth of the soul can be an **unpleasant experience for our ego or personality,** which works according to routine patterns of behavior and life habits and does not want change.

> *The Millionaire Mindset Awakening Through Divine Touch* was selected as one of the best books ever written and was awarded second place in the prosperity category.
>
> Source: *The Greatest Money-Making Secret in History* by Dr. Joe Vitale, USA 2003, pages 107-108

How This Book Changed My Life

Foreword by Dr. Joe Vitale

You never know what your e-mail will bring you. In August of 2001, I received the following message. **It changed my life.**

"I am an owner of a web services company in Slovenia, Europe.

"One of my Slovenian business partners (my off-line business is located in Slovenia, my country of origin), who has not only become a European MLM (multilevel marketing) legend, but is also a member of many international negotiating groups on both business-to-business and national levels, is a speaker at many international conventions, and the author of the best-selling book "The Millionaire Mindset".

"Mr. Boris Vene coauthored this book with Nikola Grubisa, another internationally acknowledged marketer. It is difficult to explain how well this book did in Slovenia just by sheer numbers. It has sold 10,000* hard cover copies in a market of 2,000,000 (the population of Slovenia) without any direct marketing, only by word-of-mouth and articles of praise that were printed in Slovenian newspapers.

"2,000 of these 10,000 copies sold were purchased by Slovenian businessmen, who chose to present the book to their business partners as a gift. It's also at the top of *Amway's recommended* reading list, but the book

---

* Today (2007), **more than 150,000 copies** have been sold in Slovenia alone. This book has also been made available in other languages.

itself is not on multilevel marketing. We are also in the process of preparing an electronic version of the book for the Slovenian market, and the hard copy is just entering its third release with 1,000 preorders!

"**This book undoubtedly has great potential for the U.S. market. Based on Slovenian sales, we could even expect between 1,000,000 to 1,600,000 hard copies to sell in the US.**

"But, we need a publisher for the print and e-versions…"

And that is why they were writing to me. They were hoping I would want to publish this successful book.

Was I interested? Was I? Of course! With the numbers he gave in that e-mail, I wanted to see the book. So I asked for a copy.

I read it. And **I was stunned**. Here was a book with how-to techniques, a positive philosophy, uplifting message, and practical too! It talks about human nature, as well as business, and even spirituality. **It is like the best of every business and self-help book I have ever seen while still being entirely fresh, new, inspiring, and practical.**

And this book sold where? In Slovenia? I have never heard of it. I'm told it's a small country right above Italy. Well, if it's near Italy, it's got to be good.

I quickly decided that I wanted to be the one to bring this book to Americans. After nearly a year of translating the book, refining some of the book's messages to be clear for the Western audience, and settling on our deal, I'm proud to say the e-book version is done.

You're now looking at it. **Read it slowly. Savor it.** This is a huge book. It's not to be read lightly like a novel. It's to be chewed and digested. **It's a fine meal with nourishment for your body, mind, and soul.**

But something else is also wonderful about this book.

> **It has been blessed.** The famous spiritual teacher, **Sri Sathya Sai Baba**, signed the front of it. You will see his digitized signature in the book. In a sense, he infused the book with his own magical power. That alone, for a book touted to be pure business, is rare.

Any way you look at it, you are about to read a treasure. Let it touch your mind, stir your soul, and awaken the millionaire mindset within you.

Dr. Joe Vitale[**]
President, Hypnotic Marketing, Inc.
#1 Best-Selling Author: "Spiritual Marketing"
and "The Attractor Factor"
www.mrfire.com

[**] Besides being one of the five top marketing specialists in the world today, and the world's first hypnotic writer, Joe is also a certified hypnotherapist, a certified metaphysical practitioner, a certified Chi Kung healer, and an ordained minister. He also holds a doctorate degree in Metaphysical Science and another doctorate degree in Marketing.

The Enlightened Millionaire's Time Has Arrived

Or the revised edition of *The Millionaire Mindset: How to Tap Real Wealth from Within* harmonized with the energies of the new millennium

> "When you declare Love for God... then God will manifest His power through that Love."
>
> (Stephen Turoff, psychic surgeon)

Every age is marked by certain energies. We have now finally moved out of the age characterized by the search for balance **between war and peace**. It started two thousand years ago when Jesus suggested that we should love our enemy and God, as much as we love ourselves.

In this age lasting until the end of the previous millennium, we should have **calmed our passions and reconciled**. But not just on the outside. The greatest peace should have happened **within**, when we should have risen above all conflicts, judgments, and stances, and begun **accepting ourselves, as we are**.

When this happens, we **accept everything else**. That is why we **no longer compare ourselves to others** or have to **prove** ourselves to others. Because, we are directed inwards and toward **our personal development**, this task is more important than what kind of car the neighbor drives, which seaside resort the relatives vacationed at, or how much more money our neighbor, John (a businessman), makes.

When Money Replaces the Heart

Our development does not mean that we have renounced materiality... quite the contrary. Everyone who wants to reach a certain level of spiritual growth

must accept the energy of money. Otherwise, this energy ("How nice it would be if I didn't have to work, could travel the world, and buy whatever my heart desires." "Oh! More bills!" "Maybe we don't have as much money as the neighbors have, but we're better people because we focus on spirituality.") will **hold individuals back** and **prevent them from growing in other areas**.

This does not mean that everyone wanting peace within has to get rich, but that one **must first create complete and perfect harmony with the energy of money**. In that way, the person will **no longer be controlled by money**.

So our goal is to **perfectly manage our life energy**, which can only happen when we **derive from our inner selves** – heart and intuition. When this becomes our identity, and therefore more important than anything else, we will simply **allow experiences in all areas of our lives to happen** – in our inner world of feelings and thoughts (mind), in relations with partners, parents, children, money, God, and even in relations with neighbors and enemies.

This energy of the new millennium is literally up in the air and **very different from the old energy, which supported other habits, patterns, and stances**... when materiality alone was the measure of success. In the past, millionaires, above all, scrambled for money and everything related to it.

Enlightened millionaires respect the soul, heart, and intuition. Everything else takes second place and is born out of these energies, rather than the other way around (as it has been until now).

Mark Victor Hansen, coauthor of the remarkable *Chicken Soup* series, launched a new movement in America with his release of the Enlightened Millionaire concept as described in his book (coauthored with Robert Allen), *The One Minute Millionaire*. His goal is not just to sell a billion copies by the year 2020, but to also make the world a better place by donating **500 million dollars to charity**. This is now a vision... and a **world trend**.

Considering that businessmen, with their financing, hold the world in the palms of their hands, there is the promise of good times. We have the chance to be among the first to join the trend, which is supported by the **entire Universe**.

The Entire Universe Supports Enlightened Millionaires in Their Experience

Enlightened millionaires are aware of this and look forward to the experience because it will enable them to reach their goal even more quickly. We are in the millennium of searching for the Truth, and everyone who sets out to look for it can count on **infinite help**.

We should ask ourselves: What is the Truth? It is time to recognize who we really are, admit it to ourselves, and then begin living this energy.

The Truth is, **we are spiritual beings created in God's image**. We are God's children to whom the will has been given to decide freely. And we are the soul, found on Earth in the School of Mysteries, looking for the path to infinite happiness, peace, and perfection.

Enlightened millionaires are set apart from others because they are seekers of Truth, rejecting no energy that comes their way, but learning to deal with it and consequently accept it. This remains the **only path left to us** if we want to get back to Wholeness.

How did we get to this point? It is the **mobile of growth**.

Wise Men and Holy Men Throughout History

Buddha, who lived around 500 B.C., said that the **energies of the mind must be harmonized**.

So, first put the things in your mind in order and choose **the middle path rather than extremes** – not by denying or giving in to extremes, but by overcoming them.

At around the same time, there lived various **philosophers** who presented the typical expression of the mind and contributed wonderful theories. However, neither the heart nor the **experience of living in and from the heart** was predominant in these theories.

During that time, the very progressive Pythagoras lived and was already teaching the necessity of **moving from the mind into the heart**. The students of his school lived in silence, dressed alike, and were not permitted to use any kind of cosmetics or anything that would differentiate them from others.

In this way, Pythagoras clearly showed that **the essence is inside a person and not in the person's exterior.**

Later came Jesus, who had the task of **showing people a clear path for moving into the heart**. At the same time, He spread the message that **God is within you and that you are directly linked to God when you live in and from the heart**. Everyone can do this right now (not when we die), if he or she decides to... and persists on that path. "On that day you will realize that I am in my Father, and you are in me, and I am in you." (John 14:20)

Jesus gave us two thousand years to move into the energy of the heart, to discover that we have everything we are looking for outside of ourselves (happiness, joy, abundance, etc.) hidden within.

One must come to this realization through experience – likely by experiencing all extremes and everything in between, which leads to the realization that what we feel inside is most important – and finally, **choose Love**. This means that we move from the energy of self-importance, self-sufficiency, and self-indulgence in habits and deeply rooted patterns into unconditional energies, where we are not against anyone, but only **create, develop, and grow**.

Wisdom comes from knowledge and experience – repeated perhaps numerous times until we become consciously aware of it. Wisdom leads to **cognition** and **real-I-zation** (the cognition of your true God-self)... followed by **Love, peace, and freedom**.

> "A revolution is called for, certainly, but not a political, economic, or a technical revolution. We have had enough experience of these during the past century to know that a purely external approach will not suffice. What I propose is a **spiritual revolution**." (Dalai Lama)

A Time When It Is Necessary to Separate Truth From Illusion

So the time has come for us **to begin distinguishing the truth from illusion**. Pythagoras explained this by instructing his pupils to look into the mirror. He told them that the images they saw reflected in the mirror were mere illusion and that the cause behind it – the energy they could not see – was the **Truth and what really existed**.

It is our **true world of energies** that we experience. Everything else that we can see as a result in the material world is only the result and **consequence of accepting, experiencing, and processing of these energies**.

We can feel the Truth after we have – at least to some degree – **moved into the heart**, because Truth does not come to us through our sensory world (five senses linked to the mind), **but through our soul**.

As long as we are in the energies of the mind, we are **so preoccupied with the energies of comparing, proving, and affirming** that we fail to understand the difference between Truth and illusion. In other words, it is not even important to us because our **identity** – the strongest energy that guides our processes and expressions – is burdened with fears such as what others will think of us.

When our consciousness – or concentration of life's energy – moves into the heart, it is no longer what happens outside of us that is important, but **what is happening inside**. And we automatically begin to distinguish between Truth and illusion.

That is when we notice that we are increasingly more devoted to working from the heart… and performing things that (further) open our heart. This also becomes our **biggest passion, joy, and mission**; everything else – money, friends, and reputation – **follows on its own**.

Now that time has come.

The Energy of a New Era: Example, Not Words

"Hands that help are holier than lips that pray."
(Sri Sathya Sai Baba)

The Universe gives us the chance to co-create with energy so that we **do not have to repeat any (unpleasant) experience**, but can learn from it by accepting and recognizing the message it carries… and by deciding to conclude the lesson. That is how we get through ordeals without pain and suffering. **When our hearts manage our lives, we are guided through lessons by a clear and decisive energy – love – and not fear, revenge, ignorance, or denial.**

We are less and less susceptible to various theories and philosophies. Also, the more we are in the heart, the more important **example** becomes to us. If, while living with the mind and working outwards from there, directions and rules are important, then for the heart, only example is our teacher and motivator. The remarkable Indian wise man, Sai Baba, said that **children cover their ears to sermons and open their hearts to experience.**

Today it is **no longer important what we have... but rather what we are**. Sai Baba long ago proclaimed: **"My life is my message."** Like it or not, the time has come when this statement applies to everyone. It is not how we want to portray ourselves to someone that is most important, but what **our actions – and especially the energy that accompanies them – are saying about us all the time.**

Every Moment Is Important

Every moment, we are creating in ourselves a certain energy state or vibration, which spreads like radio waves among others and **attracts certain people, situations, and events into our lives**. In this way, we are literally **creating our environment**.

And so, in a way, we are attending to our karma and creating our destiny.

"Then you will know the truth, and the truth will set you free." (John 8:32)

Therefore, it is important to realize that **no time of the day is more important or more spiritual than another**. If, for instance, we meditate every morning and evening for two hours, but are at work in between, where we feel sorry for ourselves, curse God, and look for ways and opportunities to get even with our boss, **we have not moved anywhere**. (These things are explained more precisely later in the book.)

Our true spiritual growth is known when we come home and take off all masks.

One of the first challenges we meet will be **harmonizing thoughts, words, and actions**. If we do not master this, we will not be giving any positive example. The next thing, as we mentioned, is to begin to accept ourselves as we are.

Denying some energy internally shows up in denying everything **that expresses a similar vibration outwards and vice versa.**

The time has come to become aware of what is going on inside and to discover that it is the **beauty of our inner world that makes us happy**.

The time has also come when the old covenant of *The Holy Bible* – Moses' story – has long been fulfilled. The new covenant, Jesus' story, has **also been fulfilled**. This is the time when **we ourselves are apostles looking for gurus and teachers within our hearts and not outside of ourselves.** Jesus predicted this time saying, "The stone which the builders rejected, became the chief cornerstone." (Matthew 21:42)

Let us explain it.

> *Sai Baba said that children cover their ears to sermons and open their hearts to experience.*

It is our **heart** that our personality (the builder) rejected when, instead of building life around the foundation stone, it built on some other cornerstone: materiality, outside appearance, social worth, religion, teachers, teachings, etc.

The Universe will no longer allow us to build our lives on anything but the energy of our hearts. If we continue, the temple will be destroyed over and over again until we choose the heart as our foundation rock – the foundation of our lives.

It is time to learn **how to build a strong temple on a rock and on the right cornerstone,** so **no storm will destroy it... and it will be eternal.** At the same time, it will provide not just shelter in turbulent times, but will inspire you with joy, wisdom, motivation, and inspiration – so that you will find everything you are looking for at home. And so you will discover that you **do not have to go anywhere because everything is waiting for you – within yourself.**

That way the final bonds will fall to the wayside and you will be able to say aloud, "Home – in my heart – is really the best."

After this big step, you will be able to **realize beauty everywhere around you** and with your example show others how to build temples, which will be indestructible and unrepeatable.

You will become an enlightened millionaire who controls his or her life in all aspects.

Finally, we will together realize that all people built for themselves the most beautiful temples while affectionately accepting, loving, and respecting everything (read: the temples of others) around them.

Only this energy will finally free us because this is the Truth.

Upon the Release of *The Millionaire Mindset Awakening Through Divine Touch* in 2007

In 2004, the entire book was **rewritten in a different vibration**; only the basic idea and outline remained of the old book.

The rest of the content was supplemented, upgraded, and harmonized with the **Five Laws**, which are **valid for the Mystery School on Earth**. And so the book now expresses even greater strength and more of heart's energy.

If you have the previous edition of the book (*The Millionaire Mindset: How to Tap Real Wealth from Within*), the book you are holding in your hands is **something completely different**. You may not realize it in the text itself, but there is a significant difference in the approach and the **vibration**. Now the reader often subconsciously reaches for deeper secrets than those hidden in the original *Millionaire Mindset*.

Before you sink your teeth into reading, here is some advice from other readers.

You may come to a point where you will want to put the book down, skip a few pages, or you may feel that you cannot concentrate or focus on the content. Stop reading at that point and return when you feel the urge. Read the book gradually with a pencil close at hand. Come back to the chapters that are of particular interest to you. Think about what is written even if it takes weeks.

Compare it with your own life until you are completely convinced that what is written is the Truth – because this is the only way to believe and change yourself. The idea is to **adopt certain thoughts, which are good and that will help you**.

Some readers also suggest that you **close the book, and with your eyes closed, open the book to a random page**. Begin reading the part of the page that interests you. It is usually the title or subtitle of a particular chapter, but does not have to be. Continue reading until the energy has been set free. The page to which you opened by chance may contain a certain message for you to which you should pay **special attention**.

Another thing: Some people use the book as a kind of advisor during crisis. When they have a problem, while their eyes are closed, they ask to open to the page where they will find the answer written. They say it works. Feel free to try it.

Contents

Warning vii

How This Book Changed My Life
(Foreword by Dr. Joe Vitale) ix

The Enlightened Millionaire's Time
Has Arrived xiii

1. Born to Win: Ideas for Winning the Game of Life 1
2. The Principles That Control Your Destiny 30
3. Your Conscious and Subconscious Minds 127
4. The Next Step: Self-Acknowledgement 202
5. If You Want to Change Your Life, Make a Different Choice ... 255
6. Living a New Life 291
7. About Money 328
8. The Basics of Working With People and Why Learning
   the Basics of Selling is Vital to Success 377
9. You Always Have the Opportunity to Choose 419

P.S. The Story of a Boy Who Achieves Everything...
or Miracles Do Happen! 421

Glossary of Concepts and Expressions in the
Context Used in this Book 466

About the Authors and Their Works 476

1. Born to Win: Ideas for Winning the Game of Life

The Foundation of Success

Every year, publishers release hundreds of new guidebooks and **most of them end up sitting on store shelves**... and that is a fact. Most of them do not have the **energy to attract readers**.

Some of them are hugely successful. The next logical question we ask is, "Which of these books is suitable for me and could be beneficial to me on my path of development, success, and happiness?" Are they worth reading? Are they worth buying and reading repeatedly?

This is where things get complicated. Oftentimes, the following is true:

In most books, authors describe the personal experiences that helped them in life – and then proclaim that the lessons learned from those experiences will apply to anyone in any situation.

But this is true in most of the cases. **Many authors write books for themselves.** This means that the advice given in their books really does work, **but only for a handful of people who find themselves at exactly the same point in their paths in life, have similar outlooks on life, find themselves faced with a similar dilemma, and have very similar experiences and desires** (or similar **life missions**).

How do we know this? Let us take a look at the advice itself – how various authors suggest **healing serious illness**.

In addition to traditional methods – visiting a doctor and/or surgeon – some recommend drinking only water, and that is all. Others advocate fasting and unprocessed foods. Some rely on very specific healing methods, such as homeopathy. While others suggest adding special additives to foods, some suggest prayer and meditation. Still others, suggest natural healing herbs, some suggest exercise and attention to personal hygiene.

We could probably list hundreds or even thousands of other ways people cured exactly the same problem (serious illness, for instance). The fact is that these methods are **very different** from each other – some of the patients who took particular steps completely recovered... while others who took similar steps did not recover.

What does this tell us?

There are lots of methods, **but no one can tell you what is good for you**. Only when your heart flutters and you feel motivated, gaining strength (through the energies of **faith, hope, and trust**... or simply Love) – while thinking of a solution to the problem – is it a sign that you have found your path, which can be similar to or even the same as someone else's path.

So do not blindly listen to individuals guaranteeing that their path is the only right one. If you are unable to **accept it completely** and **dedicate yourself to it with all of your heart and soul, it surely is not**. Only when you feel it, rejoice in it, and have a sense of **heart expansiveness** when you think of it, it is suitable for you. And this is the best guarantee you can get.

When you find such a path, do not look any further. A lot of people get lost on the way and give up when looking for alternatives, instead of investing the energy into **solving the problem**.

But how do you recognize which path is right for you?

You do not have to wait for your mind to explain, justify, and demonstrate it – **your heart will show it to you**. You will feel that you can dedicate yourself to it, and you will be ready to do anything that this path requires of you. Nothing will be too much for you, and you will gain **faith, hope, and trust whenever you think about this path**.

Only then you have to **act and trust**. Otherwise, you will be lost and stuck in searching, comparing, and proving.

So open your heart and your mind. Free them both of all the beliefs that do not serve you on your journey to success, wealth, and happiness. Prepare yourself to consider and adopt new ways of thinking, feeling, and living, and apply them everyday to every part of your life.

How to Turn Lead Into Gold

Does this mean that we cannot be happy because we cannot achieve, let us say, as much as our neighbor? Absolutely not, because **true happiness is always connected to our internal world, which is unraveling within us**, and not with the activities in which we are involved on the outside world (money, etc.). Everyone can fulfill the **wishes of his or her soul**, which makes him or her **happier than everything else in the world**.

Many people look for the magic formula for turning lead into gold. They are often caught in a trap when they begin looking for treasure outside of themselves... when it is actually hidden in **their hearts**. They would rather imitate others who succeeded and try to be like them because **they trust the paths of others more than their personal intuition**. As mentioned earlier, this path of confirming, proving, and following others (whom we admire) – while denying our heart's wishes – does not represent our path to happiness, but is the path to pain and suffering and, in the end, disappointment.

Does this mean that God is punishing us when He does not let us succeed by following someone else's footsteps? It is exactly the opposite – this is the **mercy of the Universe**. Because we are all individuals, walking a certain path with the soul's growth as the goal, life **calls our attention or even guides us** to the specific path – most suitable for our soul's growth – at every moment.

We have to remember that **Earth is only a School, where we reclaim our true nature – spiritual** and **divine**. What is the point in going to school if not to listen to the material and learn?

The purpose is same: **to redirect us into our hearts, where miracles happen and we are God**. That is why **everything on Earth is second to the growth of the soul**, which is based on certain "tests" that can differ greatly from person to person. Until we realize what that is – indicated in a person's life's mission – we can **perceive this growth as pain and suffering**.

But when we direct our consciousness inward and realize that every day we are closer to our goal – eternal happiness – this suffering changes into contentedness. "And ye shall be sorrowful, but your sorrow shall be turned into joy," said the Master. (John 16:20)

Our Life's Mission

Let us review for a moment. We discovered that a lot of people **try in similar ways, but only some are successful.** For instance, a lot of people read the same books and follow the advice to the letter – and some succeed while others do not. You have probably experienced this, or at least noticed in your surroundings someone trying to copy (closely mimic) someone else but **not succeeding.**

What is worse is that the experience can lead the person to **pain, suffering, and even crime.**

The pattern lies in the so-called **life's mission**, which we have already mentioned. Namely, every person is born with a specific mission, which he or she is **supposed to fulfill.** Thomas Keller, a world-famous counselor, said that we could ask all of our angels, gurus, and teachers for help, or turn to religion, philosophy, or whatever. But from all of these, we can only get the knowledge, courage, and strength to help us complete our task. **No one – not even divine beings – can do anything for you, or instead of you.**

> *The lucky thing is that our heart's desires show us the path to freedom and everlasting contentedness. So by listening to our hearts, we will not only be fulfilling our deepest desires, but completing our life's missions, as well.*

That also means that we as people do not have **free will**, but rather the chance **to choose** – to decide between various possibilities. Jesus shared this Truth in this way: "Are not two sparrows sold for a cent? And yet not one of them will fall to the ground apart from your Father. But the very hairs of your head are all numbered. So do not fear; you are more valuable than many sparrows." (Matthew 10:29-31)

The lucky thing is that **our heart's desires show us the path to freedom and everlasting contentedness.** So **by listening to our hearts, we will not only be fulfilling our deepest desires, but completing our life's missions, as well**.

Life's Internal and External Experiences

These are certain tests or ordeals through which the path to happiness leads – and **there is no other path**. That is why **no one can take responsibility for our actions or show us an easier path or shortcut**.

These lessons or life's experiences are always very intimate and completely personal going on **inside the individual**; even if someone in such a situation is in a group – among other people – he still experiences the situation very personally and perhaps in a completely **different way than everyone else**. What usually happens is that individuals experience some outside situations (i.e., events) in **completely unique ways – in their individual ways** inside, like **their personal realities** that they create from minute to minute – with comprehension, thoughts, emotions, and expressions.

We all live **double lives**: one on the **outside** – in the physical world through meetings, events, etc.; and the other **within** – through experiencing, feeling, thinking.

That is why someone can succeed beyond all boundaries – if this arises from the task they choose to complete in this lifetime, or from a person's life's mission – while someone else may try very hard but not succeed. The latter **may even attain similar material successes, but will not be as relaxed, content, or happy** as the first person, who was literally **born with the intention to know – and consequently able to harmonize with – this energy**.

This thought always raises a new question: **Is it more important to achieve success externally so that it is visible to all, or to be happy and content within?**

Here we encounter another Universal rule, the **Law of Vibration**, which states that every thing – animate or inanimate – "vibrates" on a certain specific frequency or vibration, which determines that thing.

The great thinkers and spiritual teachers proved that the Universe is full of **countless vibrations**. With his work, Einstein became aware that what we perceive to be a solid substance is actually **space with a pattern of energy running through it**. Modern physics supports this; it has been discovered that even solid material is actually **condensed energy**. This means that **we are also waves or vibrations in the Universe**; each individual emits a specific field of energy.

can also imagine that each person has a built in radio transmitter and receiver, which **transmits and receives at a precise frequency**. And when we transmit a certain message, people on the same wavelength accept this message. That is why the "better" we become, the "better" the people we attract into our lives are.

We, as human beings, are lucky that we can **change** this vibration within. A content, calm, respectful person who trusts in life and is grateful for everything lives in a completely different vibration than someone who is scared or worried and has the feeling that he is a victim, merely enduring or experiencing life's challenges as punishment.

Every moment, we are either creating a new vibration or fortifying the old one. As already mentioned, this is happening on two "fronts" (or levels):

- The first level is our outside experience, **or external life**.
- The second level is our internal experience (of generating and processing thoughts, feelings, emotions, and other energies), or **internal life**.

So what is more important – what is going on around us, or within? Let us explain it by taking a look at what happens, for example, at your workplace.

If You Hate Your Work

Did you know that nearly 90% of the world's workforce hate their jobs? That means that people everywhere are spending an average of fifty hours every week **doing something they do not like while trying to become joyful and wealthy doing it**.

This does not work. **You can only be successful and content in life if you are doing what you enjoy.**

> *You can only be successful and content in life if you are doing what you enjoy.*

Because, as we already know, this vibration attracts new experiences into our lives like a magnet. **If the vibration is high, then we will experience life as pleasant and we will attract experiences, events, and people that are in the same vibration.** The same is true if we experience energies of lower vibrations such as sorrow, helplessness, victim-like feelings, denial of beauty, stress, etc.

This is our inside world, which **causes and influences** – wi vibration **through the process of resonance – what will happen in outside world**... and **not the other way around**. The process is alw such that by **working on ourselves, we influence the outside world a thus change it**.

Many people believe the opposite to be true – that outside success should bring satisfaction within. That is to say, we believe that the **outer goal or achievement itself will influence and therefore guarantee our internal emotions of joy and satisfaction**.

In this way, we are looking to satisfy internal feelings through the outside world. Or in other words, **we use the external occurrences to generate pleasant emotions within us**. (If we believe this, we will constantly be trying to build a **world of happiness around us**, which includes **controlling others**.)

This process – described in detail later in the book – generates a **big problem**. When these outside conditions and circumstances do not follow (support) our expectations, our vibration drops and we feel **bad**. For example, we are happy when our bosses tell us that we are good employees and give us good salaries... but when they behave differently, for whatever reason, we are disappointed. (What most likely follows is a **fight for the external conditions** that bring us internal satisfaction... which is always a painful task and impossible to win.)

Here is another thought to consider. Oftentimes, we discover that the **path itself** – accompanied by the high vibration of joyful expectation – **which led us to the goal, was a much greater experience than the end result**. As an American businessman said, "I enjoyed my car the most the day before I bought it."

The reason for this lies in the **process of creation**. When we create, **we express ourselves**, which is the **highest vibration possible**. During this, we experience **an energy boost**; we need less food, less sleep, less support from others, etc. In fact, we **literally generate energy** and direct it into the external world's projects; i.e., painting, creating something at work, playing an instrument, repairing something, cultivating our garden, etc.

When we finish the project, we **stop generating this energy of high vibration** (in ourselves) – that was coming directly from the heart and intuition – and consequently **stop directing energy from the inside out**.

And we feel that **energy decreases**.

How to Live a Fulfilling Life

When we stop generating energy and experience a lack of it, we want it back. So we often start **searching for it (in the wrong place) in the outside world**. We want this energy from **other people**. Here is what happens.

If we want to get energy from others – possible only through the **process of resonance** – we **have to be in harmony with the energy source**; in this case, with the other person. (But this also applies to any other source. For example, the Eternal Source – or God – as we have seen in the previous example. When we harmonize with our soul [through our heart and intuition], we get energy from there.)

Sometimes we try so hard to harmonize with another person's vibration that **we totally forget and deny ourselves… and literally assume the energy from the other person**. (A part of the Law of Energy states that when two subjects are in the same vibration, energy flows freely from higher to lower potential.)

In this way, we identify ourselves with **other people's vibrations and feel their desires, standpoints, worries, goals… as our own**. We may even think, "This is my heart and intuition."

The secret is that we **cannot discern whether we are feeling someone else's desires rather than our own, because we always sense them as our own**. Namely, whatever we assume **becomes ours**. And later, we can hardly distinguish whether they were ours. For example, has it ever happened that you felt the desire for, let us say, a new car, but then after a while realized that it was actually the desire of a friend who had talked about his new car to you a few hours earlier?

That is how the transfer of energy works. Here is another example.

When we trace other people's achievements, we want to **be like them**, but when we **calm down, relax, and awaken our heart's energy, we realize that it would not make us content and happy and that we are on exactly the right path with what we are doing right now**. Although we may not be as successful, famous, or rich as we would be on the other path by which we were tempted, we are **richer and calmer inside** and have a feeling of **completeness and fulfillment**… and we know that we are **moving forward in life**.

Here is a similar problem, which is not related to others, but rather to our **promises from the past**. We often drag with us **desires from the past**, which are completely unsuited to us here and now.

For example, in our youth we may have said to ourselves that we would have the best car on the block. Today's stand (vibration) **do not support this**, and it is good to separate what was suitable then from what suits us now. (Here we can encounter a new problem – if we made a lot of promises in the past, we will have a **feeling of guilt** and our conscience will badger us if we do not fulfill these promises.)

Falling Into Another Person's Energy

Let us look at an example of how we fall into someone else's energy and then how we disconnect from this experience. Let us take the relationship between two people in **network marketing**, which is an excellent laboratory for learning about one's self.

Imagine the situation where you are in the role of a potential new member in door-to-door sales (network marketing), but you do not feel any special affection or attraction toward this kind of work.

It has probably happened that a friend visited you with the opportunity to cooperate in product sales or new member acquisition. When you listened to how enthusiastically he explained all of this, it all seemed quite clear, logical, and exciting. You even **started thinking in the same way, approving these things your friend presented**.

But when you were alone and thought objectively about everything, you realized that this is far from what makes your heart flutter. You temporarily **surrendered to dreams, perhaps even greed, and the desire to get results with as little effort as possible. You had forgotten that you have your specific path, which you feel inside and which always brings you the greatest feeling of fulfillment, peace, contentedness, and trust.** (When you are calm, you can clearly perceive this path inside.)

So you come back to your true energy with no desire for this experience at all.

If you come to that point of real-I-zation (through observing, comprehending, and guiding your consciousness into high vibration –

your heart and intuition) and persevere in it, while not fighting for it or denying any other path, you **may not need the experience (the physical event** – work in network marketing) where you would not be content.

On the other hand, those who succumb to the energy, and feel an urge to try to do what successful people do and follow in their footsteps, must physically go through the experience to discover that they **surrendered to desires, which were not in harmony with their life's missions.**

If they become aware of what has already happened, they gain wisdom from the experience and can move ahead. If not, they can repeat this experience – with some variations – numerous times, **until they become consciously aware of what they do.** And only then can they disconnect from it, redirect their life energy somewhere else, and move to the next level of development.

Here is a question that might arise for you. Does this mean that we cannot become rich, appreciated, and respected, if we feel deep inside that MLM – or whatever we see as a golden opportunity – does not suit us?

Of course not. **Most people who invest a certain amount of energy into achieving these goals will probably – at least to some degree – reach that goal.**

However, it should be known that **only some who achieve this goal will be really happy** and feel that they have taken a step forward – those whose life's missions are related to this goal. The others will one day discover that they **want to return to the old ways** because this new experience was only an **escape from their current life's cycles.** Also, sometimes life itself will – without any help whatsoever from the person – literally throw the person back to his or her old path to settle accounts.

But do not worry. If there is a great enough desire for material wealth within you – not just when you are in the company of such people or when conversation leads to this topic, but when you are relaxed and calm (which means that this energy is coming from within and you did not assume it from others) – then it is **your life's mission to experience this energy of abundance.**

This can be done, as we have already said, in two ways:

- By **tasting material wealth.**
- By going through this experience in such a way that you come to the realization – without physically experiencing material wealth

– that it **does not bring you ultimate satisfaction**. Then you can give up your wish for enormous material wealth and free all the energy related to it so that you can move forward to encounter new experiences.

In both cases, you will take a big step forward. From that point on, **you will control** this energy rather than **being controlled by it**. Also, you may stay in that vibration (surrounded by wealth) for a very long time, or only for some months, weeks, or even days.

The only goal is to **harmonize with this energy** – to overcome fears of (not having) money or, on the other hand, to overcome an admiration for money... and rather become its friend. That is when you will not worry about money anymore, but **redirect your energy somewhere else** – such as, into fulfilling your heart's wishes and desires.

And so you will be able to turn inwards where you will find true satisfaction and happiness.

The common question that follows is, "Is there any shortcut to this final step?" Yes, there is. If you **recognize your life's mission, identify with it, and stick to it**, you will not have to go through all the turbulences and dramas.

But this does not mean that you must sit down, close your eyes, and meditate all day from now on... not at all. You must **harmonize the energies** that you have chosen to deal with in this lifetime – most likely through **experiences**, or **conscious awareness** of them at least.

Another question is: "How do I determine whether a certain (future) experience represents my life's mission?"

The first step is to completely calm down and relax, disconnect yourself from everything on the outside, and go within. This is the state that is located beyond the senses in the outside world, which is why we feel no worries or fears. The result is that we are completely neutral and unbiased; we are not nurturing any expectations, which always evolve out of **fears, worries, and concerns.**

When we achieve this state of higher consciousness, we think about the future experience (of a possible life's mission). The **feeling**, which takes over us, shows us the **"energy line"** – the direction in which the experience will unravel.

If we are consumed by **joyful and supportive feelings, especially a feeling of fulfillment and growth,** the experience will point us further – if we complete it in this energy of high vibration.

If we do not feel contentedness or fulfillment while thinking of the future experience, then it is more about an ego trip and recognition than the soul's growth or the raising of a vibration.

We can also face another problem. While we are in this meditative state, we can feel this experience as **growth,** but when we return to the real (material) world, we may look at the entire situation differently.

Obviously, you then have to decide **what is more important to you –** growth or the status quo.

In the next chapters, we will reveal even more background concerning why things happen the way they do. We will explain **the basic Laws of the Universe** and their practical applications in our daily lives.

The Answers to the Greatest Questions

You now hold in your hands the tool that will provide you with practical examples and give you insight into some of the greatest questions controlling your success. Why are some poor and others rich? Why are some happy with little money and others miserable with millions of dollars? What makes one person popular and their company sought after, another despicable and avoided at all cost? What is the truth behind "positive thinking" and how can it help you? (Fact: The conventional understanding of "Positive Thinking" and its techniques, misunderstood and misused by the masses, often **produces the opposite of what you seek to bring about.**) What other traps await you under the names of spirituality, wealth, and success? What makes most people hide from their problems, and how can you overcome your fears?

There is no universal principle that decides your happiness for you… or even instead of you. However, **there are Universal Laws you must heed on the path to your happiness, wealth, and success,** the path which is uniquely yours.

How the Universe Supports Your Own Path

In *The Holy Bible* we find four Gospels: Matthew, Mark, Luke, and John. There exists another besides these – ***The Gospel of Thomas,*** which has – in original form – been preserved to this very day. Stephen Turoff, a remarkable English healer, even says that this Gospel represents **the only real truth about Jesus**.

It contains a very interesting statement, which Jesus made, **"For there are five trees in Paradise for you. They do not change, summer or winter, and their leaves do not drop. Whoever knows about them will not taste death."** (*The Gospel of Thomas*, saying 19)

It is important to remember that Jesus spoke in parables. And so these five trees may represent the **Five Laws** – or Five Truths – which command the **secrets of life** (" …he who recognizes them will never die") and they are valid **always, everywhere, and for everyone** ("…they do not change… their leaves do not drop.").

Immediately, there is a problem because we have an array of various "laws," which are sometimes valid, like the universal Truth – valid **always, everywhere, and for everyone** – but most often are not and change depending on the surroundings.

Let us say that it is the five main basic Laws, which conceal many other lesser Laws or Sub-Laws.

Two of these Laws are:

- **The (Sub)Law about Life's Mission – or (Sub)Law of Life's Mission**, which governs a person's life's mission. This Law represents a small part of the basic Law, the **Law of Living on Earth**, but we will refer to it as a separate entity in this book.

- The **Law of Vibration**, which we already touched on a little.

The third is the **Law of Resonance**, the fourth is the **Law of Energy**, and the fifth is the **Law of Critical Mass**, which commands every event, thought, and situation.

Let us examine the last one closer.

It is simply the **principle of balance**. Something can happen when the mass (energy) on one side outweighs the other mass (energy), which is on the opposite side. For instance, if we focus our energy on achieving some goal, it is necessary to supply enough energy so that this side will be **stronger than the other side**, which represents the **opposite of achieving the goal** –

things that deter us from this experience: fears, excuses, lack of time or motivation, and so on.

Said simpler, if we **believe** – we do not necessarily have to be very convinced about this – we cannot succeed at something, this thought represents the opposite side of the balance. When this is the case, the other side of the scale will have to be **loaded with a very strong opposite thought** ("I can succeed!"), so that the previous unsupportive thought will be weaker in comparison.

Everything happens according to this principle. When some energy – or energies – is focused toward a goal outweighing the opposition, the experience can happen.

How can we tip the scales in our favor? Just like with a real scale – we **place a heavy weight** on it. In our case, this means that we must master a **very strong opposing (supportive) thought** with which we can tip the scale in the desired direction.

This is often quite difficult because our **existing way of thinking does not allow for such strong new standpoints**. And we cannot just eliminate a strong unsupportive thought, which is anchored deep within us, at a moment's notice.

We can do the following (like with a real scale): Instead of placing a heavy weight on it all at once, we **gradually add grains of sand to it**.

These grains represent more subtle thoughts, which we can adopt and, with **long-term perseverance**, yield excellent results.

The Law of Critical Mass states that the energy that materializes is the one that will be stronger in the long-term. It may come either all at once in a package or by droplets. In the latter case, **perseverance** and **consistency**, which we attain through faith, hope, and trust, are very important.

Sometimes we may also notice that the strongest energy may manifest at some moment, but **last only for a short time**; if the opposing forces are still working, they can gradually prevail over it.

We can illustrate this very clearly with the effect of pouring water on hot asphalt. One force – the sun – is always at work heating the asphalt. When we pour a bucket of water on it, a puddle forms. If the sun were to set at that time, the temperature would fall, and the puddle would **last a long** time. But as the sun continues to shine (opposing force), the heat will gradually predominate and the **puddle will disappear under the influence of this energy**.

If we want it to reappear, we have to invest **additional energy** (tip the scales in the opposite direction) by **pouring another bucket of water**.

We can describe a lot of events in our lives with this example.

Namely, the **achievement of every goal will require our attentive cooperation** and the **constant maintenance of energy in the direction toward goal achievement**. The easiest way to do this is by focusing energy on achieving goals, droplet by droplet, for a longer period of time. This requires – among other energies – **trust** that it will have a (positive) result because we **will not be able to see any result** until critical mass is reached.

This is important, so let us look at it in greater detail.

We can imagine that there is an enormous weight on the left side of a scale and we want to tip the scale in the other direction. We put heavier or lighter weights on the right side. The fact is that, **until the very last moment when the scale tips to the right side, we will not see the end result** – until we reach critical mass. No result will be visible until that moment.

The same happens with our thoughts and energy: Sometimes we cannot see results until they appear out of the blue – like with the scale. Although the right (supportive) side has not moved an inch, we know that with every new weight we place on the right side, we are closer to our goal. Until then, we have to **believe, persevere, and be active**.

So **do not give up**! Even if the result is not visible yet – maybe one more grain of sand is all that is needed to tip the scales in our favor.

How can we take advantage of this behavior to achieve our goals? Let us look at a new concept, which will reveal our potentials, which are hidden within us and can be awakened **immediately**.

We will discuss **ideas that come to each of us**.

How to Achieve Goals Easily, Without Suffering

Let us begin with the **first step**, which we all experience: **All of a sudden we come up with a remarkable idea, which appears out of nowhere.** Now we are faced with the challenge of whether to do something with this idea. **Every realization of an idea requires a special process for it to happen.** If we do not follow it, two things – which we probably will not like – can happen:

- We **discard** an idea with a lot of potential.
- We realize the idea in reality, but **"suffer" (do not feel well)** while doing so.

We are going to learn the recipe for what we need to do within, in order to be able to move from looking for **reasons against the realization of some idea** (excuses, apologies, etc.) to a situation where **we motivate ourselves** to perform the activities the idea requires. We are also going to take a look at the right time for realization and how to tackle such things with greater joy.

If we analyze the situation when a new idea awakens within us more closely, we could also say that when a **new idea comes to mind, our patterns, habits, and old standpoints resist to accept it**... and within seconds gives us a multitude of reasons against the idea's realization.

This is a natural process, which we have mastered over the years. It is the **mind at work**, comparing the new idea with **past experiences** and the **necessary amount of investment in energy**. It also looks for the **possibility that something could go wrong**. (We have to overcome this resistance, but that comes gradually during the process, as we will see later.)

An important question is how do we know which idea is the right one? Through our **feelings**. As said before, **if we feel joy, high-spiritedness, expansion, and that it is a step forward on our life's path, then it is right for us**. And the time is also right; maybe not for the final realization, but certainly **for the beginning** of (some) action.

Of course, these pleasant feelings, which possess us upon thinking of the new idea, will not last very long. If we are not careful, the mechanism of our mind kicks in, "Aha, a new idea. Oh dear! I don't have the time, money, or knowledge to see it through. It's a **good idea, but not for me**." And the issue is resolved.

This is one of the biggest mistakes that we can make when it comes to moving forward in our lives... or for the mastering of new truths on higher levels.

Let us examine it closer. Actually, we will look at the whole process of realizing ideas.

The Process of Carrying Ideas Out

As said earlier, we are in a situation where we got a new idea and our mind said that we do not have all the requirements to make it happen. In this way, we immediately put it away: **"I know this now, but I'll wait for better conditions – then maybe I'll do something with it."**

For many people, this represents the **first and last thought** concerning these ideas. They **never come back to them** or never begin to really pursue the realization of these ideas.

With this kind of thinking – "I don't have the requirements to make this idea happen… maybe later." – we literally **turn away** from the idea, which becomes just another mental concept in our head. Only a remarkable change will restore our strength and inspiration to return to the idea.

When we hear about this idea again, our brain points out that **we already know and have considered this idea and discovered that it cannot be realized**. And so we do not consider it anymore, but store it away thinking, "I've already heard it. I already know this. I will look for something that is more useful at this moment."

When we hear this idea – or read it, or it comes to mind – for perhaps the tenth time, we say to ourselves, **"Everyone already knows this."** We may even **get angry** when someone enthusiastically mentions it to us, and think: "What are you talking about, this is nothing new – I've known this for months!"

So we are in a situation where the same idea appears before us, **but we do not engage ourselves with it because, on a previous occassion, we discovered that it was not the right time for its realization.**

Said differently, **we do not allow ourselves to review the current situation, which may be different than it was last time we received this idea**. We do not employ ourselves with the idea, or give it new energy, or add a few grains of sand to the right side of the scale, but only automatically store it away saying, "I already know this – it's not worth bothering with."

In this way, when we do not allow an idea to be expressed **anew each time** or stimulate **current thinking**, we have taken away the idea's enormous potential. We have established a **pattern of reactions in ourselves** so that we perceive the idea as merely an **inconvenient – or even annoying – thought**.

In other words, **when we classify an idea in the "I already know this" category, we are automatically depositing it in the storage place of inactivity**. Or differently – the "I know this" reply becomes an **excuse or apology to keep from physically carrying out the idea**. This is an elegant mind game that robs us of experience...

If we do not want this to happen, the first step is to become **consciously aware** of the idea's potential. Or to be attentive enough that when we are taken by that unbelievable feeling, "Hey! This is the answer!" we can say to ourselves, "Aha, this is my new idea. If I'm not careful, it will pass me by. I won't let that happen."

This is very important because an idea shows us both a new direction and goals, and is most often the **answer to our prayers and questions**. It **has not come to us coincidently**, but is a **clear sign** of the path we should travel. **Ideas are the motive power of development.** Every day we have them, but most of them just pass by.

So when an idea comes to mind over and over again, it is good to **feel it anew and always rethink about it**. Perhaps you may say, "I have already heard this. Why does it keep coming up? There is obviously something in it that needs to be carried out... the concept is good – I agree! But I don't have all the possibilities to finally execute it. **Has anything changed since the last time I heard it?** Are conditions now such that I can do something – anything – in relation to this?"

That is all that needs to be done. In this case, we do not automatically turn away from the idea or remain passive, but we continue to "chew it over" somewhere in our subconscious. We have **created an energy line** through which we are now linked to the idea.

This is a requirement for successful functioning. And another thing – establishing this energy line consumes the most energy, everything following requires progressively **less energy**.

This concept of willfully recognizing an idea and not permitting it to be stored and forgotten, but beginning to actively work on it – in any way – represents the **second step**.

As we can see, things are quite simple... if we **decide on them and have the desire to realize them**.

We could say that the second step is marked by thinking like: "This could be useful. Maybe the step forward or answer to my problems is hidden somewhere here within." Or in other words: **"I agree with this concept. This could turn out to be the right path!"**

If we support an idea long enough – so that we think about that concept, which is feasible, but we may not be able to carry it out at that very moment – we will move forward to the **third step: "This would be really good… for me, too!"**

Or **"Yes, this is the right path!"** Now we have come far enough that the **idea cannot simply fade away**. We know that it is useful, we just do not, as of yet, know how we are going to bring it about.

And if we persist in this energy – and try to imagine the successful realization of the idea, looking for answers to the questions about who can help us and what would bring us to realization most quickly, etc. – we will come to the **fourth step**, which is felt like, "Yes, this could be the right path and the solution to my problem… I am ready to try it out."

Everything moves according to the **critical mass principle – what we are aiming for becomes ever larger.**

Now we are already very close to realization. In this situation, when we truly feel that this is our path, we will probably no longer look for excuses as to why the idea is not possible, but will begin looking for reasons, which **support** the idea's realization; how to realize it most quickly. In this phase, we are even prepared to **defend our idea before others** because we **see the path**. It may still be hazy, but we clearly see the potential the idea possesses.

The next **fifth step** – if we do not give up beforehand – is thinking in the sense: **"I know – or am certain – that this is the only path for me."**

Here we are strong enough to **find motivation within ourselves and no longer require outside approval**. Usually, there is sufficient energy that, from this point on, we are accompanied by a feeling of **fulfillment and rapture**. By the way, this kind of energy – the opposite of suffering – is what Saints experienced while performing their life's missions.

To summarize – the chain of feelings driving us to successful realization can occur if we **do not allow a new idea, which we feel can lead us further in life, to be misguided into the "I am familiar with this"** category, where an idea becomes "Something that I know, but don't have the requirements to fulfill," but we begin to work with it, even if only in our thoughts.

This "I am already familiar with this" concept is as if a housewife had just collected her five hundredth recipe, which she had been clipping out of various cooking magazines for years and years, but would still prepare the same dishes week after week, as she had done for the past ten years: meatloaf on Monday, steak on Tuesday, stew on Wednesday, etc.

This was one way to use The Law of Critical Mass for goal achievement. You can read much more about it – and the other four immortal Laws and their practical use – in the book, *Charisma, Self-Confidence and Personal Power*.

In the next chapters, we will see some other basics that will help us understand – and then build – the life we want.

Entering the New World

Every day, more and more people become successful, achieve their life's goals, and perhaps even enter the elite society of millionaires – or even billionaires.

The question you need to ask is: "What do all successful people have in common?"

Your education, skin color, age, gender, or even your profession or measured intelligence do not determine whether you become an enlightened millionaire.

Here are some basic ideas:

- **Successful people listen to their inner voices, feelings, and hunches.** In short, winners rely on their own inherent wisdom because they already know that **they have the path to their unique success within them.**

- **Successful people see opportunity where others see only defeat.** If you read biographies of successful people, you will discover that they saw opportunity in the challenges before them, whereas others saw only insurmountable obstacles.

- **Successful people become involved in the process of success instead of focusing on the destination of wealth.**

- **Successful people do what they love, and money, happiness, peace of mind, etc. follow.** Those achieving true financial freedom, who really make it big, do so by doing what they love and what they feel they were born for, rather than focusing on the money it will bring them. Successful people concentrate on bringing their ideas to fruition; making money is merely the logical consequence of realizing their dreams. In other words, **money is not the dream,** but merely follows because successful people live their dreams and do what they love.

Their grand prize, as well as motivation, was their **passion for creation**. Doing something that no one had done before. Moving the boundaries of the believable and achievable further, expanding their awareness about life itself, researching the unknown… and discovering a new world. During all of this, they enjoyed themselves beyond belief and even occasionally felt like children – joyful and playful. The outside world was not as important to them as it is to many of us. **They simply enjoyed every moment and lived it like a boundless gift from the Creator;** their real world was happening within them.

- **Successful people take responsibility for their lives.** They do not make excuses. Circumstantial excuses have no connection with the actions that result in your success. **People become wealthy and fail in exactly the same circumstances.** For example, growing up in the ghettos of the world produces just as many winners as losers. The difference is all in what you do with what you already have inside.

- **Successful people know that the best way to ensure their success is by giving away, not taking in;** such as, **helping other people become successful**… and feeling great about it.

We can easily perceive how the lives of some people are connected only to **creating material wealth, achieving fame, and gaining respect from others** (or **directing energy into the outside world**), which has become their **identity**. This is not the ultimate goal…

The great mathematician Pythagoras researched the secret of materialization more than two thousand years ago and came up with ten steps necessary for any creation. He announced the remarkable secret of passage from satisfaction in the **material world** to **satisfaction within people themselves.**

The Millionaire Mindset

> **We cannot reach satisfaction in ourselves until we harmonize with the material world.**

This link or passage is exactly what we are all searching for – not nice houses, yachts, and a villa in the hills – but **satisfaction on all levels,** including the material. What is interesting about this finding is that satisfaction within every person is usually **conditional, on the realization of experience in the material world.**

In other words, we **cannot reach satisfaction in ourselves until we harmonize with the material world.** Some people believe that they will come to enlightenment and similar states of consciousness by taking a shortcut to **avoid the material world.**

Well, the fact is just the **opposite**: Only after we settle our relationship to the material world, do we become mature and turn inward. If we do not go through this step, the outside material world will always **limit** us: Our search for happiness in our inside world – while denying the external material world – will represent **an escape from what we are not ready to handle.**

Namely, bills will still come, and we will be forced to go to work to earn money to finance our spiritual development (and there will never be enough money because we will feel dependent on it), desires for material objects will be great, and so on.

All this disappears when we harmonize with the material world.

So **do not run into the inside world to escape the experiences life brings**; rather first settle your outside life so that you will not be burdened when you journey within.

Here is another thought to consider. A lot of people say, "When I get rid of my boss and my problems at work, when my partner deals with his or her karma, when my children become responsible, when my parents start listening to me instead of being stubborn and persisting in their ideas (because I know what is best for them)... **then I will have the time and opportunity to meditate, turn inward, and become spiritual."**

The truth is: **The very things that you want to run away from are your opportunities for spiritual growth and your very path to it.** They can literally make you become spiritual – when you are able to **accept them and harmonize with them.**

The Best of Both Worlds

Here is something else to keep in mind. We have to be careful about how some information – for instance, from books – **is directed exclusively toward the achievement of goals in the material world, while other information is directed exclusively toward the achievement of goals in the spiritual sphere.**

In both cases, the **rejection of the other sphere can often be observed**. For instance, a lot of books about the acquisition of material wealth do not explain that this is not the ultimate goal and that certain values must be maintained all the while.

Likewise, books talking about spiritual growth, often do not mention that **we can only reach this state when we have completely settled our relationship to the material world** – either by gaining so much wealth that we no longer have to think about money, or by having gone through these experiences in a way that money and the material world really no longer interest us and experiencing modesty represents the greatest happiness.

So if we are in a situation, where we want to settle both areas, **the information in such books and lessons will not be of very much help to us** unless we have already settled the other area – material or spiritual – on our own. For this reason, a book on (solely) personal growth and spirituality would be very beneficial to, let us say, a businessman who has reached the level where he is completely unburdened materially and is now highly motivated to turn inwards. For everyone else in the situation where both areas – the material world and spiritual growth – must be settled, such advice would represent **only a partial view of the situation** (and if identifying with it, the risk of **denying or undermining the other area**).

What Is True Wealth?

While it is true that financial success is a consequence of true wealth, having money does not in itself indicate true wealth. **Truly wealthy people** are those who are **not burdened by money** and who live their lives according to their wishes, dreams, and desires. They do not allow their finances, employment status, time constraints, family pressures, which may be trying to force them into compromises etc., to control their lives or paths to success.

> **Truly happy is the person who can maintain contentedness in soul, peace in mind, and love in heart.**

In other words: **Truly happy is the person who can maintain contentedness in soul, peace in mind, and love in heart – in any circumstances.** And this can be done with very little money... and sometimes cannot be done even with millions in your bank account.

As said before, some people feel they do not need to harmonize with material wealth (any longer) for their happiness... and maybe they really do not. But this is not true for everyone. It is much more important to take **another step towards our goal**, rather than create the impression of being enlightened... while suffering within.

A spiritually aware person knows that and would not impose his or her personal preferences in life on anybody else. He/she understands that your – and everybody else's – journey is your own unique path that you have to travel at **your own pace**, which only you know.

You will never meet a greater or wiser teacher than your heart. Therefore, statements like "You don't need money!" are often just excuses made by those claiming to be spiritually aware.

Only people who have money – or had it and gave it away, or harmonized and reconciled their relationship with money the other way – can teach you about money. Even then, they can only tell you the **truth that is valid for them**.

Would you believe a homeless person telling you that having a home is not important? They may truly believe that within – if not, their opinion has no validity at all – but this does not mean this is the right path for everyone.

For example, Mother Theresa insisted on sleeping on the floor wherever she went. Even when a hospital had been donated to her, she **threw out all the furniture**, put blankets on the floor (to sleep on) and only then was she happy. Her reason for doing so was to live life under the same conditions as the poorest people she worked with.

So her **purpose** was clear and she persisted on her path, no matter what. That standpoint made her **powerful and known worldwide**.

But that was her – **and only her** – path. That is to say, you can throw all your furniture and sleep on the floor, but that **will not make you powerful**, happy, or content.

People are planets in and of themselves. Unless you **feel exactly like someone else** – which is almost impossible because your vibration is always unique – your path **cannot be the same.** So **do not try to achieve someone else's dreams**... achieve your own instead.

You will find your purpose in life, not in giving up, but in searching for fulfillment of your soul's dreams.

Some religions teach, "You must not have desires." At least, that is how we may understand their message. Thomas Keller offers a better philosophy: **"It is better not to have desires unsatisfied."** That means do not deny them or close your eyes to them; you have to **deal with that energy in some way.**

You have to either (literally) **satisfy** them – through an experience, – or **energetically harmonize with them within.**

Unsatisfied wishes themselves are often the very cause for the battles taking place within individuals and in their relationships with others. The most correct explanation for the ultimate goal, as far as wishes are concerned, is the following: **to reach a situation where we ourselves choose and influence the events around us rather than having the feeling that we are forced or pushed into them.**

Stephen Turoff proclaims: "You must have at least one very strong desire – to **meet and experience God."**

But this can only happen when **we release ourselves from everything and have no particular expectations**. Said another way: when this becomes our true goal and even identity. Before then, it is an escape. Let us explain.

Our attachment to certain results provokes certain expectations. If these expectations are not fulfilled, unpleasant feelings such as sadness, anger, weakness, melancholy, etc. are aroused within us.

Getting to the state, which we also call the **state of complete integrity** (integrated with one's true self), when we are free of all expectations, requires that we build our own identity on the basis of our internal world of feelings and not the outside material world.

In other words: **What is happening within us – what we are becoming – has to be more important to us than what is going on around us** (or what we have or acquire).

When achieving these internal wishes becomes our identity, we feel **very motivated** by them.

Our Identity Shows the Way

> Our identity usually represents the area where we invest the most energy.

Let us say a word or two about identity. Our identity usually represents the **area where we invest the most energy**. Or as *The Holy Bible* states, "For where your treasure is, there your heart will also be." (Luke 12:34)

Your identity is what you choose as the **expression of yourself** and how **you want to be seen and known**, so you support and defend it. You take pains to build your life, or at least part of it, around this. **It is on this basis that you want people to notice you, recognize what is within you, and appreciate you.**

Identity can change very quickly or remain the same for decades depending on how much we move forward in life, how much it benefits us, or how harmonized it is with our goals, vision, and philosophy of life.

Depending on what your identity supports, you do your best to realize it either inwards or outwards, so in the inside or outside world.

When your identity is related to your inside world, what you feel in yourself becomes more important than how others perceive you. In this case, you are **liberated from expectations**, for example, how you would be accepted in some circles – and so **these people, who will (not) accept you, no longer have any influence over you**.

This is **the only way to have your life's energy under control**: to direct it towards your inside world.

But we sometimes exaggerate in these activities. We either want to **take a shortcut**; for example, we want to make an impression that we are focused inwards and accept all life from the outer world while… what people think about us is still very important to us.

Or we use our internal world as an **escape from existing problems** on the outside.

How do we know when we are running away from problems or taking shortcuts?

When we notice that we want to **run away from some particular event, person, or situation, or deny or hide something, we are not accepting the situation.**

If we notice that this is going on in our lives, the next thing we have to do – if we want to move forward in our lives – is to **stop perceiving ourselves as victims or feeling sorry for ourselves**. Instead, we should accept the situation and think, "OK, now I see how I deal with energies. I recognize that this is not what I want… and I want to change it."

You cannot move on without accepting your current conditions. And you cannot accept something unless you become **consciously aware of what you are doing**… and then disconnect from it and redirect your energy somewhere else.

We can even say that we become mature enough, and ready to build our identity on the basis of what we truly are and not what we have or possess, when we **can accept the outside world, and at the same time feel that it is not important enough to invest much energy on it**. That is, when our own contentment within represents greater happiness and means much more to us than being liked or pleasing others. In other words, when we stop comparing ourselves to others, proving ourselves, and arguing for our standpoints.

Believe in Yourself

The biggest achievements that people have achieved through history – famous sculptures, paintings, songs and symphonies, factories, business empires, etc. – **were not linked to the external world, but internal**.

Expressions in the outside material world were just **their paths to raising their vibration within**. Everyone can do the same… and you do not need to be famous to achieve it. Well, you could become famous, but need to be.

You can achieve happiness in life, but only you have the **power to make it happen**. You have to listen to your internal wishes, accept them, and persist in fulfilling them.

Do you remember receiving your first bike as a child? No doubt you were excited, but the first time you held the handlebars in your hands and sat on the seat, your first thoughts may have been, "I will never get the hang of this. I'm going to fall down and hurt myself." Was your fear confirmed? No… You kept practicing, and you

> *The biggest achievements that people have achieved through history were not linked to the external world but internal.*

did get the hang of it. Not only that, even if you have not ridden a bike in years, if you go back today, you would still remember how to ride. **If you do not try, you will never know the satisfaction of accomplishment, the vibration of winning, or the amazing energy of your own success.**

Also, do not deny the reality of the world around you… but do not fall victim to it either. This is critical: If, in every circumstance, you do not betray who you are inside, but only experience something new, you literally **create a vibration of love** that flows through your work and everything you create. If instead, you feel as though you are betraying your true self – are out of harmony with the person you are – then you will probably create instead a **lower vibration of resentment and contempt.**

Your vibration is who you are – your essence and what others see and feel when they meet you.

There is nothing more powerful or attractive than the vibration of **pure love. Such harmony is the substance that true wealth is born of.**

What the Future Holds for You

So you have to be oriented toward high vibration. Can you achieve it by doing what you are already doing? It depends on **how much the energy of your heart and intuition enter into your daily thoughts and expressions** of yourself. If you find out that it is not enough, a change is necessary.

Because if you continue your present path, which you are not satisfied with, you will not need a fortune-teller to reveal your future – it will continue to be exactly as it is now. **If you want a different future, you must change your current path, and that begins with seeing, accepting, comprehending, thinking, and acting differently.** Playing out the same losing pattern repeatedly, while expecting a different result each time, is just one illustration of madness.

Rejecting and denying a change often means rejecting and denying true growth.

The most important step you must take now is to **decide to believe in yourself.** And yes, it is a decision that requires no judgment on your part whether you are worthy of that belief. You must first **accept with all your heart** that **you are a unique person** – a being that deserves only the best in life including love, wealth, and everlasting happiness. **Then miracles will happen.**

From this point, people will see you in a whole new light – a brighter one. Others will listen to you, want to spend more time with you, and even choose you as their role model. Your newly discovered self-awareness will get you started on the most amazing adventure of your life.

You will discover the secrets for which humankind has been searching thousands of years. Also, you will discover a **new deep well of fortune – your heart**.

Rejecting and denying a change often means rejecting and denying true growth.

This was an introduction; a taste of what you will read from here on. We will repeat many things to **fortify your knowledge** and maybe even **give birth to wisdom**. Also, we will activate your intuition because with new cognition, your thoughts will explore deeper and deeper realities.

2. The Principles That Control Your Destiny

In this chapter, you will discover some basic influences over events in your life. As unbelievable as it may sound, what is remarkable is that **it does not matter if you believe in them or not; they are valid and you cannot ignore their impact on the events in your life**.

So if we do know about these influences, we can learn how to incorporate them into our lives to work for us, rather than against us.

The five fundamental Laws cause these influences. For instance, the statement "What you give is what you get" is the **reflection of the combination of all Five Laws**. But this book addresses only the most important influences on our lives, so you do not have to know the aforementioned Laws.

Here are some practical examples that will encourage you to think about what entities, seen and unseen, affect your life:

- A plane crashes, and most of the passengers perish. Yet, some of them survive though nothing tangible connects them.
- A man divorces for the second time and then remarries, thinking that at last he will be happy. But yet again, another divorce awaits him.
- A worker labors hard to make enough money to get ahead of his or her bills, yet always falls short and thus continues to struggle just to pay monthly bills. The worker's neighbor does not work half as much, or nearly as many hours, and enjoys a lifestyle of leisure and wealth.

- A successful executive loses almost everything with one wrong investment. He starts again from scratch, and in a few years, he is once again a wealthy man.

1. Everything That Happens to You Depends on You Alone

Who or what is responsible for your current circumstances in life? You? Someone else? Pure chance? Is your current situation the result of circumstances beyond your control? Can you influence the events that touch your life?

Many prefer to blame God, their employer, family, spouse, or even the political system they live in for their current circumstances and failures in life. Unfortunately, most of them never realize the role their past decisions and actions have played in bringing them to their current position in life.

> *You make your own choices and thus everything that happens to you, depends on you alone.*

Whether actively or passively, consciously or unconsciously, **you make your own choices** and thus everything that happens to you, **depends on you alone**. (But you should not blame yourself for any bad choice from your past – you **needed all those experiences** for your soul's growth.)

For example, you buy the car you want to drive and work at the job you have accepted. You have developed precisely the personality you produced in your mind and brought it into being through your beliefs and actions. You associate with certain people, distance yourself from others, read the books of your choice, and watch the television programs you want to see. Even the newspaper you read is a choice you have made.

Every choice you have made has had an impact on your view of the world, other people, and especially yourself. It is also true that **every choice you make today will have a profound impact on your tomorrow**.

But there are also some situations and activities you **did not choose consciously** or even had the chance to influence because they are the result of your **karmic past**. Namely, your **karma is represented through your environment's influences** and how they related to and consequently affected you.

The Millionaire Mindset

The way you look at or perceive the thoughts, circumstances, and events that surround you is highly important. It can even happen that you do not have the **conscious possibility to choose** because you already made your choice – **by directing your consciousness into the vibration you are currently in** (and everything that happens is a **consequence of this vibration**).

For example, if you are really happy and joyful, you will see happiness wherever you look; think about lottery winners or people in love. And if you are in a bad mood – i.e., you have to pay bills, but have no money – you will not recognize a sunny day, kind word, or even a gift from a loved one, etc.

But this does not mean that you do not have any influence on your life. Your vibration is usually (kind of) neutral – that means somewhere around the average – and this allows you to notice people, situations, and events **neutrally**... and then **choose the prism** you want to see them through.

For example, when we see half a glass of water, we **have a choice** to view the glass as, optimistically, half-full, or, pessimistically, half-empty. The optimist will be glad he or she still has half a glass of water to drink, while the pessimist will whine about having only half a glass of liquid left. The latter's sorrow prevents him or her from even enjoying the remaining half.

When considering your career or job, you can choose to see only obstacles, or you can choose to view each challenge as a new experience and unique adventure. **The way you think raises pleasant or unpleasant emotions within you, which reflect in your general beliefs, the words you speak, and the actions you perform.** Others, who come into contact with you, **feel your energy and behave in harmony with it**, regardless of how strongly you want to conceal what is happening within. Usually, the energy is even visible on the outside – through an expression on your face, body language, tone of voice, and so on.

Let us see an example.

For instance, a new coworker joins your office team. He is young and energetic, having just completed his university degree, and is eager to impress you with his newfound knowledge. Someone – another coworker – may think, "I don't need another greenhorn wise-guy trying to teach me all the theory he has just learned in college." As a result, this unfortunate person sticks to this viewpoint and disapproves of any suggestion the newcomer makes, trying to make him look incapable and his performance worse than his. This person sees the newcomer as a **competitor** who could **steal his or her promotion or even his or her job**.

What is the result of all that kind of unsupportive thinking? This person's performance begins to slip; **too much of his or her energy is tied up in considering his or her miserable position and the threat of the newcomer**. In the end, after so much energy has been wasted thinking about and even putting down the newcomer, this person is surprised, even astonished, when he or she does not receive the long-awaited promotion.

The outcome could have been so different if the coworker had taken an optimistic stance and chosen to view the newcomer in a different way; like taking action, adding the newcomer's knowledge to his or her own learning and self-improvement.

We will explain how to achieve it, but we have to know some more facts first. We will now reveal important background for all of our choices, and continue with this story afterwards.

Duality Causes Us Problems

You must understand that **everything seemingly "bad" has something good in it**. Actually, "good" and "bad" exist diametrically, which means that one does not exist without the other tied to it. In some circumstances, there is but a thin line that separates the two.

All this happens because we have let ourselves get caught in the trap of **duality**. This is a world where we **take stances**, and thus **support or negate energies**: if we like what we see, we support it; if not, we negate, criticize, deny, etc. If we live in this world of opposites, we really cannot be happy because **whenever we choose one position, we automatically deny** (or reject or negate) **its opposite**. For example, if we say we like John's car most, we **lessen the importance (or credit) of all other cars** with that sentence. Or if we believe that it is nice if someone brings us flowers, we feel good if we get them… and bad if we do not get them.

Here is another example: If we think that being nice means not turning down any invitation and accepting whatever people want from us, we will have a feeling that we are a good person who pleases others. But if we do not respond or want to have time for ourselves, we will feel bad.

This is a battle we cannot win.

What is above all that appreciation and negation? The Rule of One or Oneness, when we **accept the world just as it is and do not take any positions**.

But this can be done only when we **reach a certain level or critical mass of unconditional energy**. In other words, when **our consciousness moves into and stays in that vibration no matter what**. That way, when you take a look at your problem **from and with that vibration**, your consciousness will not drop into a lower energy state (i.e., sadness), but **will remain in higher vibration and literally embrace the sadness**. In that case, **sadness will disappear**, just as the darkness disappears when we switch the light on.

> *A person's true self is pure love that everyone — including you — holds in his or her heart.*

This does not mean you have to avoid unpleasant emotions like anger, disappointment, sadness, and such. If you think that way, you will **hide and suppress your true emotions**. It is better to recognize, accept, and love them for what they are. **These are energies that need our attention and love**, but we usually do just the opposite — we reject them.

It is usually the same way with people: **The less love they deserve, the more love they need.**

How to Deal With Fears and Unsupportive Emotions

So how will you treat your unpleasant emotions?

The Unsupportive Emotions serve a purpose, like trying to **protect** you, warn you, or show you something you need to change. They are not there to make you crazy or a bad person.

Can you just be grateful for that? Can you love your emotions for how they try to help you? On the other hand, can you also recognize that these emotions are not **who you really are deep inside**?

A person's true self is pure love that everyone — including you — holds in his or her heart.

Focus on this and embrace your fears with love. If you can inject a vibration of love into your unpleasant — or protective — emotions, you will discover **there is nothing to be afraid of**... because **love is much stronger than any fear or unpleasant emotion.**

Love can influence fear, but fear cannot influence true, unconditional love. Why? Because **unconditional love accepts everything without judgment**. Therefore, when any fear appears, love just embraces it like it embraces everything else.

When this happens, **fear loses its power because there is nothing to struggle with and no source to give it energy**. Your fear feeds on the energy you give to it. Only when you can **accept and love** it, rather than be **consumed by it**, can you strip away the power it has over you.

> A different view of this is, **when dealing with any emotion, staying in your high, pure vibration of love gives you the ability to influence that emotion** or anything else you direct your pure vibration towards, **and it will change**. This principle is Universal and holds true for people, animals, everything! However, if you decrease your energy, lower your vibration, and allow this emotion to affect you – by allowing your consciousness to drop and **resonate** with a lower vibration, thus feeding it – you succeed only in making this lower vibration **stronger**.

We **intensify** and make **stronger** any thought or content on which we concentrate more. This is how the energy world works: **Whatever we think of expands**. You have probably experienced this with your fears: The more you thought of it, the greater this fear seemed to be.

The next time around, it will be even more difficult to influence this (lower) vibration with a higher one because you have just **added another particle of critical mass to the vibration itself, and now it is stronger**. The more often you do this, the harder it becomes to affect and change it. Nevertheless, it is not impossible! Sometimes you just have to be **patient and persistent**. (And in some extreme cases – if you still cannot affect it – you will need a **shock** to put this energy out of the current framework. But **you will still need to embrace it with love** later on. If not, it will **come back** very soon in the same form or in a slightly different one.)

In addition to this, **keep in mind that you are making progress**. Nobody knows when he or she will reach critical mass, and the pendulum will swing in the other direction.

However, if you know what you are doing and can trust the process, you will find the time and energy to deal with it.

Be Careful What You Ask For...
and Listen to the Answer

Let us take a look at other factors that are important when it comes to making good decisions.

One of the primary secrets to getting the best answers and solutions in your life is to **draft the right questions** – because you always get an answer to every question you ask. For instance, ask yourself: What is the **positive side** of my job? The answer that comes to you will **give you new power and energy**. However, if you are in the habit of only asking about what is bothering you, or what is wrong with your job, then just the opposite will happen. Your answers will come, but they will not be empowering or filled with positive energy... they will be depressing and will do nothing to support you.

In both cases, the answers you receive to the questions you have just asked will affect how you view your workplace. (But this is only possible if we deal with things that we do **not identify with** [too much] – when we are **neutral** about them and ask questions from and with **neutral energy**. Namely, if we are chained to a certain position or perception, we will always try to support, rationalize, and justify what we **have already decided to believe**. Therefore, if we want neutral answers, we have to **disconnect from this one-sided stand first and then ask**.)

Let us get just a little more personal. You could ask yourself about your spouse, "How is my partner **unique from anyone else I know**? What does he or she gives me that I enjoy and that I cannot give myself or get from anyone else? What does my spouse – or significant other – do for me that makes my heart sing?"

The answer that comes to you is certain to be a supportive and pleasant one. On the other hand, walking down the street, admiring someone you pass, and questioning **what is missing from your relationship** will only bring about unpleasant emotions regarding your partner.

One viewpoint gives you pleasure and motivational energy to give more love, attention, and care for your partner, while the other brings only grief, sorrow, and a depressing outlook on your life. Furthermore, **whatever mindset you wind up in attracts more of the same**. Can you see how much faster your relationship will improve by focusing on supportive and pleasant energies, and how quickly it will go downhill if you bury yourself in unpleasant details and relive everything you do not like about it?

But it is most important that you do not **pretend to feel supportive and pleasant energy in some areas if you do not truly feel it**. The urge for awakening higher vibration energy – or directing your consciousness into it – should come from your heart and soul. Otherwise, you will only **run away from (unpleasant) reality into "positive thinking,"** which usually **brings even more energy of lower vibration**, and so you only **intensify the vibration you are running away from**.

So the fastest way to true progress is by acting from your **current vibration**, no matter how high or low it is, and then **accepting it and moving on**.

> *We will find that we must be in a constant state of learning if we want to become real experts in our fields.*

With that in mind, let us find the **advantage** of having the newcomer (remember the story above?) join our office team. First, once the new person is trained, he will take on some of our obligations, which means the workload will **decrease for others**. Second, we have a unique **opportunity to learn the latest theories** taught in our field without spending a dime or having to go to college ourselves.

Connecting our real-life experiences with new and applicable theories will provide new solutions to our old problems. At the very least, we should find confirmations for either changing the course of current projects or continuing our work along the same path. Perhaps the newcomer can indirectly address any doubt we might have about the current direction of our projects or challenges by adding the insights of their theoretical education, which we can put to good use.

Having a new coworker on the team, who may also be competing for our job, will surely keep us on our toes. This gentle reminder will encourage us to better ourselves and improve the quality and performance of our own work. **We will find that we must be in a constant state of learning if we want to become real experts in our fields.** In fact, the new coworker will have a very positive and supportive effect on our motivation and self-improvement.

Even more, their presence may motivate us to improve ourselves and reach a height where there are no other obstacles – to an executive position, if not in our current company, then someplace else.

Who Is in Charge of Your Life?

All great people know they create their own everyday life, and their choices create their performances. They have the courage to take responsibility for everything that happens in their lives. They do not criticize others when something goes wrong; they simply find the best and most efficient course of action to correct the situation and learn from the unexpected circumstances they find themselves in.

This happens because their identity is connected to their **urge to create something new**, not against anybody or to prove anything to anyone.

How do we know that taking responsibility is something all successful people do? Because if they blamed other people or circumstances – their boss, partner, children, lack of time, government, or others – for their setbacks or failures, they will never do anything to **improve themselves**. How will they improve, when the blame falls somewhere else?

Leading psychologists and psychiatrists have found, not surprisingly, that **most people**, in fact, **do not want to change**. Not that they resist change or prefer not to change, but rather that they do not want to change. In fact, most people crave for comfort and relief; they want to hear they are not guilty for what is happening to them. They prefer to believe they have no control over the events in their lives… believing instead that they cannot do anything to change them. They want to feel that they are not responsible for their current situation or the circumstances they find themselves in.

Change demands **determination, persistence, and continuing action** to "…**get up from the warm bed of habits and commonplace and go towards the unknown**," as Anthony DeMello said. When you realize that your choices and their resulting actions are behind everything that happens to you, you can pose the following question in a nurturing way and be ready to receive the wisdom of the answer that comes to you: **"What happened to produce this unexpected outcome? What can I learn from this, and how can I quickly move beyond it?"** Not, "Who can I blame for it?" or "Why did I fail?"

Focus on the question which will bring you the answer that will move you forward.

An even more appropriate question, which comes from an even higher vibration is, "How can I accept this situation unconditionally… without judging, blaming, or criticizing anyone or anything?"

As we already know, posing the question properly is the only way to receive the supportive response that allows you to **learn, grow, and harmonize with the situation**. Ask a question from your heart, and you will get a supportive answer. That way, you will **keep your consciousness in higher vibration**.

> When you think in such a way, you will automatically improve your character and personality, and you will avoid being stuck in the blame game that prevents you from ever moving forward. Shake the habit of blaming others, and you will soon discover that emotions like anger, jealousy, sadness, and disappointment all go away.

How does this contrast to what the average person does?

Average people take responsibility for all the good events that happen to them, but they "forget" to take responsibility for everything else that did not turn out according to expectations or was not as successfully planned and carried out. Instead, they **blame others**. For example, if their car breaks down, they blame the dealer who sold it to them or the mechanic who worked on it last. Let us take a look.

A car dealer surprises you with a $2,000 discount on a used car. You have your doubts and get a mechanic to do a little checking under the hood, and he tells you that the car is great and that you are getting it for a steal. You had nothing to do with the dealer's pricing, yet you tell all your friends that you negotiated a great deal, not that the salesperson offered you that deal. In other words, **you are taking responsibility for this positive event**, even though it was not the direct result of your actions.

Two weeks pass and you discover the purchase was not as astonishing as you first thought. You find hidden problems with the car, and the repairs cost you more money than you initially saved in the deal. What now? Do you say, "I bought the car and made a big mistake in assessing its value?" No, now your story is a little different: **"That crook of a car dealer tricked me into buying this lemon!"** Or maybe, "That lousy mechanic I took this car to made me buy a real piece of junk!" Of course, the latter responses are the responses of the person who is never to blame.

The Truth Behind the Rational World

It is true that sometimes some irrational thought, which we cannot explain, compels us to do something or drives us to something. Even when everyone around us tries to persuade us that something is not right, we will not listen because inside we feel that this path has to be taken.

Oftentimes, it is the (Sub)Law of Life's Mission as we already know: It indicates the actions **we have chosen so that we can experience them in this lifetime**, and all events and thoughts will direct us and lead us towards these actions.

Said another way – these energies are about our **karma and destiny**. Let us take a closer look at these terms.

Karma is marked by energy, which is dependent upon our previous decisions. According to the principle: Sooner or later you have to pay for your actions. We can feel this debt as an **unresolved energy**. We always feel it when we are thrown off track and not able to stay in our vibration. In other words, **the situation, which we do not control, but are controlled by, is the one we must (sooner or later) settle**. That way, we sometimes have the feeling – or we have been told – that we are karmicaly linked to some person.

But this is not the case. We are linked on the basis of The Law of Resonance. For instance, if someone's consciousness is located in the same vibration as yours – generally or in some particular area of life – you both will have similar lessons and experiences to explore. Therefore, you will be **mutually attracted.**

> *Karma is marked by energy, which is dependent upon our previous decisions.*

It is likely that you will awaken these common energies, which will surface at your first meeting or at a later one. That way, you will have **an opportunity to deal with the energies** that have gotten stuck and consequently harmonize them (if you are ready and willing to do so).

And so you are not solving a common jam, but your own jam; each person completes his or her own lesson. So it may happen that you use this experience to break free while the other person remains exactly where he or she was.

This individual problem solving, when a person can come to the answer regardless of how others will complete the test, shows us the truth that **our karma is solely our own** and that we do not need anyone else to help us solve it… we only need a "push." For example, a specific conversation or situation with another person will lift this energy to the surface so we can clearly notice it and become consciously aware of it. Well, if it does not work the first time, this experience is repeated as many times as needed. And this is all we need from the other person.

After that initiation, the other person has **nothing else to do with our dealing with these energies**.

Even if a situation is solved together with the other person, or even with more persons (as in a group), the experience the individual gains in such a situation is very **intimate and personal**.

Let us answer another question that might have arisen.

Where do the roots of the trials in which we are stuck today come from? From our **past**. We brought into the world with us a code, which contains the source of our life's mission. With the help of our **parents**, who reminded us of this unsolved energy within us, patterns and habits are formed. This vibration now **represents our learning material**. But again, this is a gift because **the sooner we relieve this energy, which is not harmonious, the sooner we will be liberated of all fears**.

On the other hand, this karmic code is linked to our **destiny**: it represents **future actions**, which relate to resolving karmic lessons. We could say that **karma is the reflection of our previous experiences while destiny indicates how the situation will unravel** or how we will solve this karma. We can influence everything greatly with our **choice to either solve the aforementioned matters** or postpone them for another time.

The motivation to tackle these matters is the prize that follows – **the state of complete command of our life's energy**. That is when we are completely free of expectations, fears, and worries, and only enjoy the moment here and now. This is the state of Heaven on Earth as Jesus described it, "I tell you, on that night there will be two in one bed; one will be taken and the other will be left." (Luke 17:34)

> This Heaven is not a physical place, but a **state of consciousness**. And this can absolutely be achieved in our lifetime and not when we die. Actually, Jesus **never once said that it is necessary to physically die to enter the Promised Land** or Heaven. Quite the **opposite** – He said, "The kingdom is inside you and outside you." (*The Gospel of Thomas*, saying 3) However, it is necessary for our old habits, patterns, and the positions we have taken in duality to die in order to awaken **the heart**.

Dealing with karmic issues certainly brings us advantages that serve us in the highest good, although we often do not see that. Everything that happens to us serves the **growth of the soul** and helps free us from the shackles of fears, dependence, and attachment.

But we have a choice, so we can also use events and energies around us for the **growth of the character** – that is how we raise a certain person, thing, or situation above others, praising and idolizing it so that we **separate it from everything else**... which is how all fears and problems arise.

This also means that the goal of experiencing some situation, where we achieve great results (according to the outer world perspective) – like having a lot of money – not to appear to be better or more than others.

The goal is in **the adjustment and harmonization with the energy** the situation carries, so that fears can vanish and we can untangle and liberate ourselves, and in this way, move forward.

And so the goal is to **liberate attachments from the situation itself** so that we can **release this energy and neutrally experience the situation** – enjoy it and accept it unconditionally.

That way, the following similar situation, which happens to us or anyone else, will not influence change in our consciousness or throw us into another vibration, but we will **maintain our energy under control**.

That is Heaven on Earth.

Such experiences can be very unpleasant because this energy of Oneness does not support bragging or the energies of comparing, judging, and proving. Our heart and soul do not care who is better, wealthier, or has the better reputation, etc., and that usually **hurts our ego and personality**.

If we focus the majority of our life energy towards our spiritual growth or **our inside world** – and build an identity upon it – we will **welcome** such a situation. If we are busy comparing, proving, and affirming ourselves before others and are turned toward the **devil's principles**, which are displayed in **self-sufficiency, self-importance**, and **self-indulgence**, we will be **hurt and disappointed**.

In any case, sooner or later, it will be necessary to come to a situation where we must turn inside and **build our temple on the fundamental energy of our heart**.

Jesus also spoke about this as we indicated in the introductory chapter. He said, "Do you see these great buildings? Not one stone will be left upon another which will not be torn down." (Mark 13:2) Also, "The stone which the builders rejected became the chief corner stone? Everyone who falls on that stone will be broken to pieces; but on whomever it falls, it will scatter him like dust." (Luke 20:17-18)

Perhaps some advice about reading *The Holy Bible*: Wherever the word Jesus is written, we can replace the name with the phrase **Living Love**, which will give the text a whole new dimension. (The majority of *The Holy Bible* is written in parables or else it would not have been preserved until today.)

And so it is in our case that Jesus, the person, did not lay the foundation, which incidentally took forty-six years to build, but what He was referring to is our lives: **When we decide to build our temple – our lives – on the basis of the energy of the heart, we will come to the goal very quickly** – much more quickly than had we built on the other energies we usually use.

Even the passage about the corner stone refers to the same thing. Most people choose things, which are **outside of themselves** for the foundation – or corner – stone of their lives although **the real corner stone is the heart**. So if they have selected anything else for the corner stone, the builder – the mind or personality – will have rejected the corner stone. Jesus said that the **very foundation stone** (the heart), **which the builders rejected, would sooner or later become the corner stone**.

What will happen if we insist on the chosen foundation stone, which is not the heart? As we have said, the temple built on these energies will be "...razed to its foundations; not even one stone will remain atop another." Or "Every plant which my heavenly Father did not plant shall be uprooted. Let them alone; they are blind guides of the blind..." (Matthew 15:13-14) We can read similar quotes in holy documents of eastern religions.

This does not mean that we have to change our direction overnight and forget our achievements in the material world... quite the contrary. As we already know, every new experience enables us to grow if we accept it unconditionally, which is why we cannot deal with it accidentally or even by mistake.

Every time we turn our heads away from any experience, we are **denying our true selves and our lives.**

In life, it is never about denying anything, but completing the very experiences we do not like with love.

That is **always an accomplishment and a major victory.**

And so it follows that it would be good to **involve our own hearts** in all of our activities – especially in acquiring wealth. Or said another way, **our aim and goal should not be for money in and of itself, but for the unconditional realization of creativity and strengthening the energies of trust in life, faith, other people, and in our selves.** All of these unconditional energies always come from intuition, the heart, and the soul.

Let the money that follows be **a result** or **a prize** for such an approach.

In this case, we will build our house on a rock, while **not being attached to money, and so we will be able to unconditionally – and without expectations – enjoy it.** That is true wealth.

2. Nothing Comes by Itself: You Cannot Win the Lottery if You Do Not Buy a Ticket

If fate intended you to be rich, then all you have to do is just wait for the business of the century, money, a spouse, health, and wealth to fall into your lap. Right?

Most people understand destiny as something static – as if there were a message written in the stars that said, "This is the way it's going to be, and it's not up to you." No wonder **passive lives develop from this attitude,** lives where people wait for their fate to find them and just happen.

Years go by before they realize that in all this time they have not experienced anything and have virtually slept through most of their days in a monotonous routine of work, lunch, dinner, occasional entertainment, television, and rest. Each day is the same boring routine until the days become months and finally they stretch into years. Not to mention that they have probably been struggling for money and possibly survival, experiencing health and relationship problems and such. It is not surprising that in the end, all this leads to the final conclusion that "I am not intended to live the good life."

We Are Situated on Different Levels

It is a process, where people must first free themselves of everyday pressures in order to relax and understand what their soul wants. This is only possible when we are not loaded down by work, worries, and the like.

The fact is that a thirsty man wants water – not money or fame. The same is true for the person who, for example, experiences his or her daily job as a living hell, which does not even bring him or her enough money to cover day-to-day expenses. He or she wants to find a new job, where he or she will feel better and earn more money.

If, for instance, we mention a **higher goal**, our **life's mission**, or **enlightenment** to this person, he or she will only stare at us blankly. We all know that we have to achieve our goals with due priorities.

Actually, there is a **clear "plan"** that indicates what kind of experiences will likely happen to us… and what choices we have at hand.

We are on **various levels. Our view on life depends on where we are, and even our goals are adjusted to this level.** How can we confirm this? Imagine winning the largest prize in the lottery and, at that very moment, solving most of the financial, material, and work-related problems that trouble you.

Will not life – have a completely different meaning?

This is where it will be necessary to decide **where we will direct our growth** – either towards (more) comparing, proving, and affirming ourselves, or **inward towards our spiritual growth.**

And because this energy within us is **more important than that which we achieve outside of ourselves**, it is necessary – if we really want to grow spiritually – that we begin building our identity on these energies, as we have already discovered.

We all cannot do this the same way because we are, as we mentioned, situated on different **levels of development**. It is the **five levels**

phenomenon, in which each of us is located at one of the levels. Sometimes the levels also intermingle, or we move from one to another very quickly.

While we can move from one level to the next, **we cannot skip a level**, with the exception of the second, which will be explained later.

How can we move to the next level most quickly? When we **accept where we are right now, invoke the heart's energy, persevere in that state of consciousness,** and move toward the next level with **faith, hope, and trust**. In this way, we will be doing **the most that we possibly can for ourselves**.

Let us take a look at these five levels and explain them briefly.

First level: consciously doing things that we know will cause us ill will and suffering.

For example, this is the case when people go to a job they hate (or are at least dissatisfied with), attend gatherings where everyone gets on their nerves, and so on. The emphasis here is on the fact that **we know that this is not good for us, but we do it anyway... because we feel it is necessary and that we have no choice, feeling that we are always the victims.**

We remain passive and wait for others to change our lives. So we are nice to everyone because we are **afraid of what others will say about us.** And we expect others to be nice to us, as well.

This is a little game we play: Because **we want peace on the outside, we never argue or stand up for ourselves.** We are always nice, polite, and "positive" while battles rage within us.

But **we do not trust in life enough to get off this train and turn elsewhere.**

Second level: looking for one's identity in the material world of affirming, comparing, and proving.

At this level, we have somewhat managed to pull ourselves out of the belief that we are victims and are now trying to **build our own identity** on the basis of the things we **show outwardly**. It is still not how we feel that is important, but how others **perceive us**. So we build our opinion of ourselves on the basis of rules and **what other people think of us**. For this reason, how we are accepted and what people think of us is so important to us.

At this level, we do stand up for ourselves: **We put ourselves before anybody else** and take destiny into our own hands (read: become smarter than God). We also believe that **everything can be done with persistence and determination**; so when we do not get results, we just **try a bit harder.**

Third level: releasing tension.
This is the only level to which we can advance directly from the first, or normally from the second level. The reason is that the first two levels express the two **opposite sides of the coin**, which means that they represent opposite energies... but are on a **similar energy level** (vibration), thus they bring the **same results**: disappointment, pain, suffering, and so on.

The first two levels are very wearying because we are so burdened. Particularly at the first level, we feel powerless. At the second, we use vast amounts of energy following the events around us so that we know how to behave. And we put **enormous energy into achieving results** – no matter what.

At the third level, we come to the point when **we only want peace – nothing else**. Most of our time at the first or second levels – or both – is spent dreaming and striving for third level activities: **walks in nature, weekends on the coast, travel**, etc.

This is clearly because we feel that we have **lost part of ourselves**. This is what has literally happened: We lost our heart and soul – and this causes imbalance or discord within us. When we set off on a nature walk, for example, we feel that we are **full of energy**. Really, we are just disconnecting from existing problems and filling the critical mass of the heart (or the other side of the scale). We **tune ourselves to nature's vibration, which is the unrepeatable expression of the Creator**. This process is felt as **relaxation**.

And so what might to happen, if we spend most of our time at the first two levels, is that **we see this relaxation or tension releasing as our final life's goal**. But this usually is not the case. Nevertheless, the fact is that to people at the first or second level, tension releasing **represents the achievement of a goal or the most that they can imagine at that moment**.

Another thing – we talked about **network marketing**. Some people subconsciously know that the majority of people are at the first or second levels. That is why the leaders of network marketing are able to attract new coworkers by offering them a **lifelong vacation** or the idea that **they will never have to work again**. People like this because it represents their current dream.

But what happens after people release tensions? That is when **they touch their true nature and tune themselves to the heart's vibration** (passage to the fourth level), because Christ in us – Love and unconditional energies – can be born only from a virgin nature (Virgin Mary). That means we have to **release everything that is not pure and unconditional** (the beliefs, positions and standpoints that we take on at the first two levels) if we want to move into the heart… which is the next, fourth level.

But this does not mean that they will just glide into it. No, this is where a lot of people get **caught in a trap**. Let us look at an example.

A successful businessman is overwhelmed with work. He has a lot of problems getting through, but he is wise enough to **reserve a two-week vacation on the most beautiful beach**. He also orders all the extras: pleasure trips, massages, a doctor's examination, and so on. In short, he makes sure that his vacation will be one big joyful experience.

When he comes to this piece of paradise, he is **enraptured for two days**. On the third day, when all the stress, ill humor, tension, and rashness go away, he suddenly gets **a new business idea**. (A characteristic of intuition is that it only works if we allow it to. That is, only when we are so relaxed that the mind is at rest and out of the way, can we even become aware of and notice the flash of intuitive thought.)

But that is not all. All of a sudden, the businessman wants to **go back – to work!** In other words, he is again tempted to go back to the first or second level where he was trying to escape to get some peace. (This is a good illustration of the **concept of experiencing two extremes**, which we repeat over and over again, until we realize that happiness is somewhere else entirely… and that **your final goal is not to establish the environment where you freely jump from one side to its opposite** and thus balance your life; although this can be a big step ahead.)

And so it often happens that a person does not even enjoy his or her vacation, but literally **rushes back to suffering**. This is also the case with our businessman, who finds himself at the first or second level… **and the cycle begins all over again.**

The more often we repeat this process, the harder it is for us to move to the next level. The critical mass principle tells us that **the more often a habit is repeated, the more deeply it is embedded within us and the more difficult it is to overcome**. This means that more and more energy will be necessary to move forward. **So if we repeat this cycle – levels one to three – often enough, this way of life becomes our pattern and habit**... and we cannot easily disconnect from it.

Sadly, **most people are trapped in this cycle** – the first two levels (the first, second, or both), releasing tensions, and back again and again and again.

Fourth level: searching for your own potentials.

Sometimes we successfully exceed the critical mass of repeating this pattern and **look beyond** or **past it**. For this level, which can only follow tension releasing, it is typical to **turn inwards**. Now it is no longer what others think of us that is important to us, but **how we ourselves feel while doing something**. Are we content? Does it open our hearts? Do we feel that we are growing and developing?

At this level, we search for and choose only things that **enrich us inside**.

Of course, these things are related to performing things in the outside material world, but **we do not strive for external conditions** that will give us a sense of contentment in order to feel good inside – what we were doing in the second level – but we **build these feelings and emotions inside**.

To us, external conditions represent only **circumstances** – or environment – and the **opportunity to express our true nature**.

This means that our motivation no longer comes from trying to be like someone, belonging to someone, or even opposing something, but that we only wish to **express the creative potentials**, which we awaken within us.

Entering the heart also awakens our creativity, which **gives us creative power**; unlike the tiresome work of the first two levels where we **search for** and **use** energy – usually in/of other people – (instead of generating it by creating and expressing our self), so energy is **chronically lacking**.

Fifth level: fulfilling your life's mission.

This level is the logical continuation of the one before it.

Now we have discovered the activity, or combination of activities that make us happiest and lead us forward; when we have come this far, **we decide to do only this** – regardless of finances, other people's opinions of us, and so on. We **dedicate our lives to the idea**, which now represents our only **identity**, and infinitely trust that the Universe will stand by us.

Typical examples of people who were at this level are Mother Theresa, Einstein, Gandhi, Nikola Tesla, Pythagoras, Da Vinci, Mozart, and so on. They are all known for having dedicated their lives to ideas representing their creativity and not opposition, spite, or searching.

But these things were not just given to them. They had to go through their own **crucifixion**, which Jesus symbolically illustrated with His life's story. **Crucifixion is not a death experience, but the passage from one developmental level to another**... just as Jesus did not die, but **lived in peace ever after**.

This means that **at some moment, all of these great people had to decide, choose, and then persist in this energy – no matter what**. This was the time when they needed to **unplug from everything that did not support their vision**... depart from their old life and carry on with their new life (although maybe no one supported them).

This is what awaits us here: We can either succumb to fears, or listen to our heart and intuition, and step into the unknown.

We can also say that if we do not turn inward at that time, we will block our development. We know that expressing the talents, skills, and other potentials that we are given in the external world, leads to only **part of success** in life – **outer (external) success**. Strength, courage, and the dedication to listen to our heart, and follow it with faith and trust, leads to the fulfillment of **every dream**.

What Level Are We On?

Remember these five levels because we will refer to them throughout the book. They are very important, so let us explain things related to them in more detail.

Many times we do not even know if we are already on the fifth level because we cannot tell the difference between the energies appearing on the first, fourth, and fifth levels.

Let us consider a practical example to examine how we distinguish these energies. For instance, think about a situation when we are deciding what to do with a certain item, money, etc. We are considering whether to **keep the item** (or money) for ourselves or give it to someone else as a present.

At the first level, we will ask ourselves about **the consequences this action brings** us or **the opinion others will have of us** in either case: If we discover that by giving gifts we can "buy love" (this is what we are aspiring toward at the first level), we present the item as a gift – and at the same time expect return energy: thanks, appreciation, a return gift, affection, and so on.

If we get what we are expecting in return, we are **satisfied**. But if we do not, we will **point our finger at the person we presented the item to and complain that the world today is cruel and people no longer have conscience or compassion.**

If we are at the fourth level, we will no longer think about how the other person will react, but place ourselves first. For instance, we will think: "Does this serve me? Do I really need this item or money? Will I miss it? No, **I can easily live without it.** Therefore, I will give it to somebody and feel good inside."

As we see, we took into consideration our inner feelings, **but put ourselves before everybody else**.

At the fifth level, we act completely differently. Well, maybe inside – for a moment and with a small part of our consciousness – feel passion, desire, or attachment to the thing we would present as a gift, but we are aware that this is **merely the wish of our personality or ego,** and that this wish comes **from fear and not Love.**

At the same time, we **treat all including ourselves alike, and listen to our heart**, which is telling us what to do with the item. It is like we **disconnect from our personality** and then take a look at the situation.

Let us say that we feel that we will make someone (not necessarily a particular person) very happy with this gift – so we give it freely. Namely, **we do not give ourselves preference over others**, but we relate to our personality-self the same as we relate to other people.

We feel great in this energy because it represents true satisfaction, fulfillment, and growth. Actually nothing else can make us happier.

This is how we will feel the whole time when we are at the fifth level. This is why we will not hesitate with our heart's decision, but nurture this energy all the time, no matter what. Because we have reached the critical mass of this high vibration – which is where we are now based and the point from which we are looking out at life around us – **fear and doubt neither appear at the decision-making moment** (while deciding to whom to give the item) **nor later**.

Also, we persist in the energy of high vibration because once we feel in our hearts that we want to make a gift of something, the subject is closed and **nothing will detract us from this purpose.**

As already mentioned, this can only change if we slip from this level to a lower one.

There is another indication that we have reached the fifth level: After this act, we will **never again relive** the experience of having done a favor for someone or look for energy in return, much less mention the deed to someone or **expect anything in thanks**. If we relive this experience, it will be to reawaken the unconditional energy within us and so that the thought of this event will always **fill us with Love**.

Said another way: With this giving, **we are not giving up the item** or sacrificing for someone else, but only fulfilling our greatest desire. The **heart's desire prevailed over the character's desire**, so giving this object to someone in need now becomes our true joy.

The Prison We Live In

Jacob Needleman, a philosophy professor at the University of San Francisco and author of many philosophical, religious, and medical books, sometimes compares life with a jail cell, where institutionalized prisoners no longer remember their previous – internal – life of freedom. Instead, their only goal becomes poor attempts to improve their living conditions (if they can) within the prison walls.

They may paint the walls with the vivid colors of nature, or hang posters or magazine pictures to cover the ugly walls that surround them. They may also dream about a better life all the while and envy other prisoners for sparse privileges above their own.

The Principles That Control Your Destiny

The strange thing is that their cells are **wide open and nobody is forcing them to stay in the prison**: they are free to go and experience a new exciting life.

Instead, they refuse to believe that a better life (focusing inward) awaits them somewhere. No, they prefer to put another poster on the wall (improve their external world) – and continue to **dream about a better life** rather than take the chance of moving towards it – afraid they will end up disappointed.

> *Many people live in a mental prison, which is as strong and confining as a real prison with bars.*

For a prisoner to survive behind bars within the prison system, he or she must engage in a wide range of mind games. The most important one is to **forget a better life outside the walls**. Unfortunately, this is also the most dangerous game of all because playing it successfully means **you must become satisfied with the limited life you have now** and **give up searching**.

If a new prisoner comes in with grand tales of life outside, the rules of the game force the prisoner to reject them; not because he or she does not believe them, but because **he or she does not want to believe**. Namely, believing the messenger might elicit talking, thinking, and dreaming of escape (taking action and turning inward)… and this is **not suitable for them**. It takes **courage, strength, and trust**, which require **action, to change present circumstances**. This way, the prisoner has **no more excuses and apologies for his or her desire to continue living in prison**, which makes living the restricted and limited life inside prison unbearable.

And the prisoner simply "can't afford" for that to happen…

Many people live in a mental prison, which is as strong and confining as a real prison with bars. They have all the freedom in the world, but exercise none of it because, like the prisoner, they are afraid to think that a better life can be theirs. They know that **it takes energy** to change their lives, break old patterns, change old habits, and rebuild their mental infrastructures. It is easier to stay where they are, blame others, and tell themselves, "No, this is too hard. Who am I to think that I can make it happen? What if I fail? Right now, I have something; maybe it isn't what I wanted or even what I like – but it's something! If I lose this…"

Are you thinking that you cannot make it happen? Are you living in a prison without bars? Maybe it is time to start thinking about escaping…

Paths to Success

Let us think about **who is destined for success**.

Look at the successful people around you. Do you know anyone who relies on fate to throw heaps of money at them? **Think about your future.** If you are waiting for someone to come knocking on your door and offer you the deal of a lifetime, you should prepare for a long wait indeed. Even if such a person did come knocking on your door, you can be sure that their primary interest would be personal gain and personal profit. **They do not care (much) about you – that is your job.**

Do you really believe that such an excellent deal would be so graciously offered and so widely promoted? That would be like someone finding a map for a hidden treasure and then asking unknown people all around to help him dig it up.

Perhaps you are not one of the passive ones we spoke of above, playing the "waiting for your fate to kick in" game – or are you? Even a woman who dreams of a prince on a white horse to sweep her away on a journey filled with adventure and gifts, does exactly that – she waits and **shifts responsibility for her life on the prince** (or fate).

Success requires making a decision, taking responsibility for it, and following that path – not passivity.

Lack of Time and Opportunity

The most common excuse among passive people is lack of time and opportunity. However, research shows that there are more opportunities available every day for people to develop their abilities, and achieve success through, than ever before. On the other hand, research also shows that people with excuses far exceed those that choose to take action on their own behalf. Look at the next real-life examples.

> *Success requires making a decision, taking responsibility for it, and following that path – not passivity.*

An acquaintance of mine, a waitress who had been living with her mother, had suddenly decided to move to Australia, her dreamland. While she had been failing at home, once in Australia, she landed an excellent job and could afford a nice apartment. Some time ago, she returned home to finish some business, and I asked her if she now felt that she had fulfilled her dreams. She told me it surprised her to discover **how easy it was to live her dream and succeed**. Together, we discovered that the turning point was her **decision** to board the plane and go for her dream.

You do not need much money to begin living your dream. My friend only needed the plane fare to get to Australia. Being on her own in a new country forced her to get a good job just to survive, and surprisingly, it was not all that hard, once she abandoned her old viewpoints and left her excuses behind her. **She simply acted.** And also, **she did not care anymore about what other people thought** – which is the second most common reason for delaying or refusing to take action to change our lives.

You see, when faced with a situation that is not **urgent**, it is easy to make excuses and never change. However, when faced with a potentially life-threatening set of circumstances, where we simply have to do something to survive, all excuses disappear, and we become creative and successful in our problem-solving efforts.

> *You do not need much money to begin living your dream.*

Further querying my friend, I asked her about her situation in her hometown. She admitted that she could have found the same opportunities here that she had found in Australia – if she had both looked for them and then acted to obtain them.

In fact, she returned back some years ago, finished school, found a good job, and – for the first time in her life – established a loving and fulfilling relationship with a really nice guy.

What was different? **She now knew she really could be a success...**

Over the years, I have worked with many door-to-door salespeople. Most sales reps blame outside circumstances for their failures to sell products. It's always something: the location wasn't right, their prospect isn't interested in their product, some even cite their own lack of intelligence or money, and on and on and on. Those of you who are familiar with sales and marketing know exactly what I am talking about.

Years ago, I had the pleasure and opportunity to show a group of people how they alone build barriers in their minds. One of the groups I was lecturing sold household products door-to-door. First, I listened to the salespeople complain and rant, and then I decided to run an interesting test.

The Millionaire Mindset

I selected a new sales representative, John, because he was new to the business and **was not yet burdened with the self-inflicted problems of his colleagues**. I also made sure to sequester him from the other reps to prevent him from hearing any gossip about how difficult some specific region was to sell.

What I had in mind was to send him to a region that every other salesperson was avoiding because in their words it was impossible to sell anything at all there. However, I told John something much different. I said, "John, today I'm sending you to a neighborhood that is a great place to learn, especially for new salespeople. You know, there really is a **lack of our salespeople and products there**... so **you will have no competition** and people won't tell you, 'Thanks, but your friend with the same product was here yesterday.'"

After specifically training John to respond to rejections and combat his fear of the unknown, I sent him on his way to the area. For three days, I repeatedly sent him to areas his colleagues described as impossible to sell.

The results he achieved were not just above average, but were **far better than the results of the average salesperson while selling there**. John was ecstatic – in those three days, he made more money than he did at his previous company in three weeks!

After that, I met with the whole group of sales reps and introduced John to the others. When I told them what he had achieved, much to John's amazement, they applauded and congratulated him enthusiastically. However, this was not the real – or only – miracle. It happened a week later...

As I eagerly anticipated how the group would react to John's amazing success, I immediately organized a motivational seminar. John's example was perfect to demonstrate the truth that I wanted the other reps to discover: The essence of their success is often in their minds. **Two-thirds of the sales representatives voluntarily returned to the "Devil's Area"** where John had experienced such incredible success: 58% achieved average results, 8% were below average, while 34% were more successful than they had ever been, anywhere.

What changed? The prospects did not. Neither did their buying habits, nor the products the reps sold. **The change took place in the mind of each** salesperson... a change that ultimately determined his or her failure or success.

> **Opportunities exist and will always exist. The question is whether we are able to see them and accept their challenge in time – before they fade away.**

Also, luck is not a note that falls only on the ears of those destined to hear it; it exists everywhere and always in the music going by. Luck does not hit the ground three feet from you, like lightning. **It is the bird flying overhead that you reach out for and catch with both hands.**

There is a joke about a poor farmer who, during the last moments of his life, complained to God: "I have always trusted You. I have prayed to You that I might win the lottery. I respected all of Your commandments and yet never received a cent in my life." God answered: "Yes, what you say is true, but you **never bought a lottery ticket..."**

If you do not take advantage of an opportunity when it is offered to you, it passes you by as if it had never existed at all. Mark Twain said that **those who buy books but do not read them have no advantage over those who do not know how to read.**

One of life's truths says that **people are so burdened with the unimportant stuff that they do not have the time – or the opportunity – to earn money.**

Here is a perfect example.

One of my friends, an architect, was constructing a new office building a few years back. He dug gutters, carried mortar, plastered walls, etc. Although he usually makes $100 per hour, he wasted his precious time doing work that paid him **ten times less**... just because it was his building, and **he thought he was saving a few dollars.** He never lacked architectural work, so he could have been financially more productive by hiring bricklayers and similar professionals to do the physical work. He would then have the time to do the work his experience and training qualified him to do, which paid ten times more.

Had my friend been doing the work, which he enjoys most, instead of trying to save a buck by doing the labor himself, everyone would have benefitted. The bricklayers would have had work, he would have contracted more jobs, and the building would have been finished sooner and possibly been crafted better. Additionally, my friend's burdens, the added worries he encountered by doing the work himself, would have been far less.

The Truth About Being Lucky

So who are the successful people who recognize opportunity and then turn it to advantage? **Do you think their success and wealth are based on luck?**

A well-known millionaire once gave this answer, **"I have been working hard for fifteen years to become lucky and succeed overnight."** Gary Player, one of the best golfers of his time, gave a different answer, **"The harder I work, the luckier I am."**

Do you have this winning attitude about your life?

> *The harder I work, the luckier I am.*

So **do not rely on luck**. At any moment, a situation can change, and what we once thought was lucky can backfire and turn out to hurt us even more than the lack of luck did to begin with!

It is all about **expectations and taking things for granted**. Disappointment arises as a consequence of directing **energy into something and expecting a return (that never comes)**: if expectations are not fulfilled, unpleasant emotions will occur, and we will get the feeling that, yet again, **life became hard**.

There is an old Chinese tale that speaks about being lucky. Dr. Walter Doyle Staples, in his amazing book, *Think Like a Winner!*, tells the following tale:

In a small village, there was an old man who had everything – a loving son, all the material wealth he needed, and a valuable racehorse, which all his neighbors admired. One day, his horse jumped over the fence and got lost in the woods. His most valuable possession was gone in an instant. Hearing about the accident and feeling sorry for the old man, the people in his village said, "You lost your horse, what a terrible tragedy for you. Oh, what bad luck..." As they each offered their condolences, his reply was always the same: **"Bad luck, good luck... how do you know it is a tragedy?"**

A few days later, knowing there was food and water at the old man's barn, the hungry horse returned to the old man but not alone; the horse brought **twelve other beautiful wild horses with it**. When the old man's neighbors heard about his great fortune, they all thought he was extremely lucky and told him so. The wise old man simply replied, "Bad luck, good luck… **how do you know it is good luck?**"

The next day, his son saddled and tried to ride one of the new horses. The horse threw him from the saddle and the fall injured him badly. Doctors said the boy was incurably lame. Farmers from the village came to offer their condolences to the old man, saying: "Oh, your only son, disabled forever, what a tragedy, what bad luck…" The old man replied, **"How do you know it is bad luck or a tragedy?"**

Months passed into years, and war broke out. They recruited men and boys from every city to join the army and drafted soldiers from every village, but the crippled boy, unable to fight, remained with the old man. The following week, the news came that a great battle killed all the soldiers from their village.

An important lesson: **You never know what is bad luck or good luck… so never rely on luck to get you closer to your goals.**

Believe instead in yourself, life, and God. A lot of times, we do not know what experience is hiding within because we only see immediate results that show up in our external world. We do not see how our **soul grows from the experience – which is most important**. As we know, it often happens that **when personality and ego suffer, our soul rejoices**… and when we recognize this, we notice how **"our greatest joy comes from our greatest sorrow"** as Master Jesus said.

Do not rely on circumstances outside yourself: the goodwill, sympathy, or gratitude of others. **Rely on yourself** – on your talents, your heart, and your worthiness.

Do not take this the wrong way; most people are kind and many are grateful, but **responsibility for your happiness lies only within you**. If you expect others to take care of you, then you place your life and happiness in their hands, as we said earlier. When that happens, and your wishes and desires are not fulfilled, energy of lower vibration takes over your mind, and you will feel like a miserable victim of fate, living your life as others dictate.

Make your own luck by invoking your heart, accepting life, and trusting in tomorrow. Learn how to recognize and use an opportunity to move ahead.

Think about someone who succeeded in a business you refused to try. Is he or she successful because they are **more capable than you**? Probably not...

They succeeded because they opened their hearts to recognize that opportunity. They embraced fears with the energies of love, trust, and joyful expectation... and acted! They succeeded because they made their own luck and took their lives and fate into their own hands. What you feel in your heart is **God's will – what He wants you to do**.

This is what life's mission is about. It is a great opportunity that will fill you with good feelings and help you move forward. But you have to be **conscious enough** to become **aware of it**, or the opportunity will slip away. Then you have to **act**.

Thomas Keller told a story about well-known healer, Elizabeth Kübler Ross. Once upon a time, she was very tired from her work, and during meditation in the garden **turned to God to give her a shoulder to lean on**. Surprisingly she heard a very clear answer,

"No!"
"What about a hand?" she asked.
"No!"
"A palm?"
"No!"
"Just a finger?"
"No!!!"

Because the woman was very energetic and truthful about her emotions, she answered, "Then the hell with you! **I'll do it myself!**" In that moment, she **rose from the ground** and in this levitational state was carried floating into the house.

When you decide on something – if it is in harmony with your life's mission (that is, you feel it in your heart) – **the entire Universe stands by you**: You get everything, not just a shoulder to lean on.

Sacred Scriptures say that **God helps those who help themselves**.

Beyond Luck

Oftentimes, our comprehension of luck is related to **people's typical reaction to a certain situation**. So it is **not our action that makes us happy, but the** reaction of others. (Searching for one's identity in other people's reactions to our actions is **very typical for the first and second levels** of personal development, which we already talked about.)

As said, it is necessary to come to a situation where we will be able to **assume an active role in life.** If we are situated at the first level, where we feel like unlucky victims of destiny, this will seem very hard to us. That is why we must **gather the will and courage to move forward as soon as possible.**

We first ensure that we will release tensions as much as possible if we feel that we are burdened. (Relaxation techniques such as meditation and, to an extent, sports and other hobbies can be very useful to this end.) It is in this state of relaxation that we will be able to notice our true path.

Then **do not get frightened, but act as your heart dictates.**

Oftentimes, we will go through various unpleasant situations – such as fears – but when we arrive at our destination, we regret having chosen this path... quite the contrary! **We will begin to build life inwards and will have more control over it than we do on outside circumstances.** This is the key step in our path to success.

Two "Kinds" – or "Types" – of Destinies

On the basis of everything said up to now, we could also say that **every person has two destinies,** just as we noticed that we all have two lives (one external and one internal). Our first destiny is based on and linked to our external life. This destiny, which is shown **outwards** and is expressed in the material world, is called **external destiny** or **secondary destiny.**

The other is the very intimate one, which each individual experiences deep inside. It is connected to our internal life, and we call it **internal destiny or primary destiny.**

A person's two destinies can either **intertwine or exclude each other.** For example, a successful businessperson can be scared and hurt within, regardless of the material success he or she experiences.

Which of these is more important? As we have mentioned a number of times, it is absolutely **the one we experience inwards,** which represents the **vibration we carry within us.** This energy represents our **true identity** that stays with us even if we – outwardly – have, do, or possess nothing. This is also the energy, which others intuitively feel about us when they know nothing of us in advance. Have you ever experienced feeling a certain way about a person, but when you were told about this person, your relationship or impression **completely changed** – for the better or for the worse?

Our first reaction to him or her was how we perceived or felt his or her **internal energy state**. The second reaction was based on his or her **expression in the material world** or on his or her creative abilities, which we **perceived through our own character filters**.

If we respect these qualities, our relationship to this person changed accordingly. On the other hand, if we do not approve of the qualities that we have been told about this person, we immediately lose interest in him or her.

We often give the expression of energy in the material world precedence over that which a person is in reality. In other words – **what a person has achieved (or created) or what he or she owns is more important to us than what is actually going on within him or her or what his or her vibration is expressing.**

What Is Happening Inside of Us

The fact is that within, **we are constantly creating certain energy states (emotions, for example), which influence our thinking, comprehension, method of processing data, and output.**

As we have already mentioned, every person is **constantly creating his or her vibration**. It can be **prevailing** or **predominant** – meaning that it dominates most of the time – or it can be **momentary** so that it gradually yields and the dominant vibration comes to the forefront again. We illustrated this with the example of pouring water on hot asphalt.

We also mentioned that it is exactly that vibration that **motivates us to certain activities**: Our vibration **attracts certain people and events into our lives**. To a great extent, it is related to our **life's mission**.

This life's mission, correlated with a vibration, operates as if we were carrying a **certain code** that is **triggered at only certain moments** and literally throws us into some activity... even though we ourselves may not know why.

That is why various theories in the sense, "Do exactly as I did and you will succeed." **do not work**, as we mentioned at the beginning. **Everything** is dependent upon the **(Sub)Law of Life's Mission.** The business, method, or activity, which would work for all people and in which everyone would be equally successful, does not exist. Only when a **person needs the experience for his or her soul's growth** can it happen. Nothing in life happens to us by coincidence or by mistake.

In this way, absolutely every moment brings us potential for growth – if we recognize the gift and include it in our vibration through conscious observation, comprehension, and acceptance.

It is necessary to look into your heart to find the answer for everything. Books, tapes, motivational speeches, etc. can be a **basis** or **starting-point** from which we check if what has been said resonates with us. But these tools, for example, cannot guarantee you success simply because something worked for your neighbor.

Every individual's life depends only on the choices (decisions) available to him or her and not his or her free will to do whatever he or she wants.

Still, we have nothing to worry about. The **choices available to us bring us the greatest happiness, growth, and feeling of fulfillment.** We would not be as happy, fulfilled, or even successful with anything else we would try.

That is why **we listen to our hearts and in this way achieve the most, taking into account both destinies** – external and internal. This is how we will achieve the most **outside** ("for show") and feel that we have more trust in our lives, and that life is **more joyful, peaceful, and entertaining.**

3. Life Is a Discovery... and Growth

Are we born with a certain innate knowledge or do we acquire everything we know through experience? Do we have to experience many failures and mistakes before we can finally come out on top?

There is not just one answer to this question. On the one hand, everyone probably knows people who were, as we say, successful from the get-go. These people did not have to invest much effort or endure many rejections in comparison to someone else who took years to finally succeed.

This means that obviously **not everyone has to go down the same path of thorns, and that some people are just born to succeed.** If we look at family businesses, we can find a number of children who inherit a polished moneymaking machine such as a restaurant, production or service company, etc. So they find themselves **in the middle of a well-established system**... and they do not have to do (almost) anything, but count money.

There are also cases where the opposite is true: Under the management of a new owner or director, the company went bankrupt or folded in a few years, although it was prospering beforehand.

> *Nothing in life happens to us by coincidence or by mistake.*

Again the question of **what true success is to us** is born. Is it only about earning money (external or secondary destiny) or the feeling when we are at peace, satisfied, enjoying every moment (internal or primary destiny), or perhaps the **two together**?

Those who have had the chance to experience everything will probably agree that success is not (just) money; success is supposed to be **liberating and unburdening**. Many people with money only manage to place **new burdens** on their shoulders, sometimes unnecessarily, while someone else in the same situation would sit back and enjoy themselves. So success is also related to our **personal experience of the situation** and not just the situation itself.

So what is the answer to the question? Are we born with certain innate knowledge or do we have to acquire it (through experiences)?

None of us received a map of life's hidden treasures at birth. Born salespeople, born winners, or even born losers do not exist. But it is true that everyone has certain hidden abilities, which they must **discover and develop**, or they will remain forever dormant inside and thus useless.

Some people are more gifted than others in certain areas, but that gift is never the whole cause of success. Research has proven, in the vast majority of cases studied, that **only 10% of success is talent, and the remaining 90% is made up of plain old hard work and a positive attitude**.

Of course, this does not apply to very specific matters that depend on certain constant factors like the shape of our bodies. For instance, a person weighing 220 pounds can forget about a career in the 100-meter dash.

We will find the answer to everything if we look at the (Sub)Law of Life's Mission. Well, even our body, like everything in our surroundings, is shaped to **enable, motivate, and help us perform our life's mission**. For instance, if your body does not allow you to run very quickly, success in the **100-meter dash is not connected to your life's mission,** no matter how much you want to persuade yourself into believing it. Also, if you tried to get into it, you would not feel good inside. You might be able to achieve some kind of career there, but that would only represent **searching for opportunities;** sooner or later, you would find that this is **not what you really want to do in life.**

On the other hand, if you decide to do what **enables your soul's growth,** everything will **support the tasks.**

Let us take a look at a "born winner" to explain this.

What does a born salesperson look like? Jason, as a young boy, was always hanging around the corner store. In his free time, while his friends played football, which he was not interested in because he was short for his age, **Jason enjoyed watching salespeople work their magic.** He would watch them for hours, fascinated by their interesting dialogue and the skill they displayed in the various techniques they used to sell as much as possible to their customers.

As a young man, Jason liked to watch movies, especially ones about merchants and people **succeeding against all odds.** All these events **influenced the way Jason thought, spoke, and acted.**

When he was a bit older, he got a summer job at the local grocery. He jumped at every opportunity to mimic the techniques he witnessed when he was young, but he was not selling anything yet because he did only unskilled work and was not allowed to serve customers. However, he dreamed about **one day becoming a great salesperson.**

Always in action, he enjoyed practicing and portraying himself as the successful negotiator, salesperson, and business entrepreneur in front of his friends. Of course, his friends complained because they were still playing football and having fun.

In secondary school, his passion became stronger and he discovered that there were classes he could take to learn more about business and sales. He liked what he was studying so much that he spent his free time reading books about all the great businesspeople and how they made and kept their fortunes. He went deeper and deeper into his art, listening to seminars on tape, reading articles, and comparing the experiences and wisdom of all who had gone before him.

The Millionaire Mindset

Finally, Jason landed a job, and it was time to prove that he was good at selling and negotiating.

Everyone was astonished at his immediate success. His friends envied him and comforted themselves saying, "That Jason... he is just a born salesman."

Is Jason a born salesman?

No, **he just developed skills based on his interests and what he loved**. He read everything he could get his hands on and practiced his technique for years. His interests led him to discover a hidden ability, a talent he developed and cultivated into an art and successful business. A tremendous amount of effort – though it never felt like effort to Jason because he loved what he was doing – willpower, determination, self-confidence, time, and other "investments" were necessary for him to reach his present status of a successful salesman.

In this story, we again encounter the (Sub)Law of Life's Mission. What made the young boy, even at a young age, to get attracted to everything related to this profession? Obviously there was some motive – a code – **inside of him**, which was not artificially created, but in its purest, most genuine form.

This was the only way the boy could have had the motivation to research further. He noticed that code, took it into consideration, and had the strength and courage to follow this inner call.

And we are all in this kind of situation day after day. We feel something (a call for action) inside, but we need **determination to listen and follow** that hint. Otherwise, we will find a lot of excuses concerning why it is best for us not to follow it.

It is important to remember that we have to go through this process by ourselves. No one can guarantee, promise, or take responsibility for our action. **We have to decide.**

Because if someone tries to impose something on us, we perceive it as something forced and experience the action as **suffering**. But if the motive comes from within us, it is **wish fulfillment**.

Well, sometimes it can happen that an outside wish sneaks in. For example, a father, who is a specialist in his field, wants his son to have the same education and do what he does, but the son is not interested in it. Occasionally, after a certain amount of time – according to the critical mass principle – when the son tries it himself and is employed with it for some time, a spark can fly, and the son discovers that he could actually enjoy doing this for a living.

We ourselves constantly experience this, perhaps not as obviously, when we listen to friends go on about how fun it is, for example, to play tennis... and we believe them: even if we are not interested at first, they convince us to try... and we discover that it **could be fun** – if we knew how to play the game. We also discover that, until we are able to get the ball over the net, it is not even reminiscent of fun.

So first, **we have to get to the stage where we have mastered enough technique that we are not preoccupied with technique and can start to have fun.**

The key factors in whether we will **persist** in learning tennis long enough to master the basic techniques, and the game will actually become fun, are our **faith, hope, and trust**, which are shown in the **love, passion, and attention** with which we set about something. (This is true for every activity we carry out; even meditation or searching for God.)

So, many times the key is in **trusting in a successful solution**: If we have a **vision** where we see ourselves as successful, we will be able to derive from this vision the **strength, motivation, and inspiration** to overcome obstacles. If we do not see ourselves as successful, we will find ourselves faced with a big problem when we experience failure or when things are not going our way. Where do we get the motivation then?

If we do not get motivation, strength, and inspiration from a vision, which drives us over obstacles even in situations when things are not going smoothly, we will seek motivation in existing experiences and the current environment.

This means that we will be motivated and full of energy **as long as everything goes smoothly**... but when it does not, it will also bring an end to our enthusiasm.

(You can read more about success in sales and working with people, especially how to sell with love and an open heart following the energies of faith, hope, and trust, in the book, *The Enlightened Salesperson*.)

Here is something else to consider.

Are we **certain within that we are even capable of learning** (whatever)? If we are not certain, our **motivation will drop**, and love, passion, and attention will turn into responsibility, denial, and suffering.

But if we are really certain, then the step forward is just a **question of time**: If we persist in loving energy and enthusiasm, we will reach the critical mass of what we want to achieve. This applies to every new activity we undertake.

Let us not forget that it is **our emotion and not the physical action that creates our vibration**. If, for instance, we are learning tennis (or doing anything else) with love, **we are – according to the critical mass principle – strengthening and multiplying the highest vibrations within**, which can bring us to the point where this energy becomes our **prevailing vibration**. This means that we will **build our life** on the energy of joy, passion, trust, peace, and so on.

When we feel lower energies like anger, stubbornness, suffering, and so on, we also fill the critical mass of that vibration in the same way. It may happen that **we project our consciousness into these vibrations and look at our entire life from them**. This means that the entire time, and in all opportunities, we will understand and accept – according to the principle of resonance – **only these and similar energies**.

A Power That Drives Success

If the power of your interests and desires is strong enough, nothing you have to do to achieve your goal will feel hard. Everyone can endeavor to be an expert in his or her field. Fortunately, not everyone has the same dreams, interests, and goals. It is essential to do what you really want to do in life. **Desire is the catalyst that transforms work into contentedness.**

Something else is also important: In persevering to achieve a goal – is it genuine **perseverance** or **stubbornness** and **being rash and reckless**? The secret is again hidden in each individual. Each person knows how much energy and motivation each activity that turned out differently than expected takes from him or her, or how he or she views the situation in the end. Do individuals remain **motivated from the heart**… or do they just want to do what they promised to themselves or others?

If they have the feeling that they are suffering, but they still persevere, it is a question of what the result will bring regarding their vibration. Maybe just an end to the suffering… Must one really suffer first in order to appreciate and be grateful for the ordinary things that he or she has?

Here is another look at how to treat our wishes and desires.

You can always choose to:

- Try to **restrain** them, which will adversely, even traumatically, affect your future experiences.
- Consciously decide to fulfill them and **work hard on them**.
- **Wait for the proper time to fulfill them, trusting you will know when that is** (by getting an impulse or "a sign").

This is the common conflict between **being active** and **staying passive** – **letting life be**.

Namely, successful businesspeople say they work more than ten hours each day. They insist they are more successful because of this rigorous schedule, which serves to keep them active, engaged all the time. On the other hand, various philosophies, religions, and nations defend the state of being; letting your life flow, being in a passive mental state.

A combination of the second and third choices is right.

First, **wait for the right moment**. The act of **trusting**, in both your future and to fulfill your goals, sends clear instructions to your subconscious to bring you the solution for how to achieve your goal.

Your subconscious will let you know (through your intuition, which is the primary secret weapon of all successful people) when the ideal time for realization has arrived – you **merely need to recognize and believe in the message your intuition sends you**.

So pay attention to the many signs – impulses from the outside and from the inside – along the way.

When you feel the time is right, **take the best action**.

So the truth is, **both standpoints are correct and the best answer is between both extremes**. You have to let it go… until you get a strong urge for action. Then, and **only then**, your dreams and desires will become a reality.

> *If the power of your interests and desires is strong enough, nothing you have to do to achieve your goal will feel hard.*

Nobody can succeed by just watching TV day after day, or by madly doing everything that comes to mind. Surrendering does not mean waiting and hoping for something to happen or even knowing that something will happen. It means **you have to clear out blockages and let life – intuition, love, and peace – in.**

Then – **act**! You have to be an active participant in your life.

All those who have succeeded, in any area, have trusted both in themselves and the future. Does this mean that **they never feared anything**? Not at all. But their **trust in the glory of life** (and therefore in the future, as well) was greater than fear. So they probably experienced mixed emotions, but trust prevailed.

If you live consciously in this moment, you can also feel this everlasting and omnipresent Love: **You have everything you need in this very moment**. Only when you direct your energy **outside of yourself** (in comparison with others, for example, or in the past or the future), you **establish an environment for fears**.

So this is also how you can recognize when you are in vibration of trusting: **The energy state of trusting the future – and therefore living fully in the present moment – is a mental state free of fear in the moment.**

We can even say it this way: **When we are momentarily overwhelmed with love, we are unable to let fear in**. And this vibration of love, trust, and faith makes the **perfect surroundings** for your subconscious to **deliver you a supportive and uplifting message.**

Remember that sometimes you will get a message to do something you did not expect, if you want to get what you have imagined. That way, you will receive an answer to your wishes and prayers, but in a **completely different manner**. But if you look at that solution with your heart open, you will notice that **this is even better than what you had in mind**.

We always have a choice: **Do we trust God and His solutions more… or our conscious mind**, which has doubts about the future and often prevents us from taking the next step to realizing our goals?

The solutions to your problems and challenges come from the same place as your dreams and desires – from the infinite wisdom.

They all come in one package. So if you decide to resonate with dreams and desires, do yourself a favor and **let in the other part of the package**.

Adjusting or Denying?

There is another way to check the line between perseverance and stubbornness. As long as we have the feeling that **we are adjusting** to the situation – still following the basic vision with faith, hope, and trust or love – it is **perseverance**. When we feel that we have moved into a situation, where we are **denying ourselves** – our heart and inner hopes – for the goal, we have crossed the line and are **forcing** something.

If we listen to ourselves, we will behave so that **we neither try, force, nor hinder (block) an experience**.

If we know our values, wishes, and the goal that we are trying to achieve, we can discover if the three are in **harmony**, and either **interweave and complete** or **exclude** each other.

> If you realize that what you are doing does not suit you, it is time to make a decision: you can persist... or **turn away and follow your heart**. But if you decide to choose the latter, then as we already know, **courage, strength, and trust are necessary**.

Know and Trust Yourself... and Persevere in Your Purpose

There is a well-known story in which a high-society woman approached Pablo Picasso, who was already a famous and reputable painter at the time, and asked him to draw something on her napkin. "I will pay whatever you want," said the woman. Picasso took a pen and made some lines. The woman was quite enthusiastic until she heard the (heavy) price. "What? Thousands of dollars for just a couple of minutes of work?!" Now she was quite angry.

Calmly the painter replied, "This is not for a couple of minutes of work, my dear madam, but for **long years of schooling and experience**, which allowed me to draw this in just a couple of minutes."

Picasso was aware of how much energy he had invested in the past so that today he could show the expression of his personal creation, which he cared for and shaped for years and years until it became his trademark.

Well, sometimes such traits seem strange and inappropriate to us mortals, depending on our perspective.

When we experience growth, our values also change, and so also does our view of ourselves, others, and the world in general. For instance, a well-known singer does not want to give an interview for a renowned magazine free of charge... **unless the journalist donates a certain – fairly high – amount of money to a charity or hospital.**

What is this about? Depending on our point of view, we can perceive this as cold-heartedness, revenge on the media, or **maturity** when an individual realizes that **the newspaper will, because of the interview, earn a lot** and increase its reputation and circulation. **Why should a piece of the pie not be given to someone who really needs the money?**

A similar thing happens when a rich businessperson agrees to lunch with a journalist and in the end calmly allows the **journalist to pay for everything.** This most often is not about being cheap, but **respect for his or her own integrity.** Because the businessperson is aware that the journalist (or printing house, television, magazine, etc.) has **much more to gain**, it seems normal that the journalist **repay the businessperson for his or her time and wisdom by at least treating him or her to lunch.** After all, this was all at the request of the journalist.

But this stance is only possible when we reach a certain stage of development and **outgrow fears.**

All successful businesspeople, scientists, and even artists have behind them **many years** in their field, which allow them to arrive at the important decisions, discoveries, and techniques that are the foundation upon which they have built their success.

They too have had their failures and setbacks – many more than most.

Another story is told how reporters once asked Mr. Kashogi, presumably one of the wealthiest people in the world at the time, to reveal the secret of his extraordinary success. "No problem," smiled the rich man, "I can tell you in two words – **good decisions.**" Reporters, who were expecting some magic formula, looked at one another. They were not satisfied with his answer.

A second reporter mustered up the courage and asked, "I understand, but can you tell us how you were able to make such good decisions?" The businessman smiled again and answered, "Of course, I can tell you how in one word – **experience.**" Still frustrated, a third young reporter piped up, "Fine, Mr. Kashogi, good decisions, experience... we can understand all that, but what interests us is your background. What is **behind** that? How and where did you get it? How did you treat it?" Still in a good mood, Kashogi answered, "This even my grandmother could tell you; learning is the basis for good decisions... and **we gain experience by making many mistakes.**"

Do not discount your unsuccessful attempts because they will eventually bring you to your success. Part of the magic formula of success is **learning by our mistakes**. "He who works, makes mistakes," says an old proverb, which we have all heard. It is a good proverb to remember.

A successful person who has always done what is right and best for him or her at the moment does not exist in all of history.

The successful person learns a lesson from his or her unsuccessful action. The unsuccessful person does not learn anything, repeats the same mistakes again and again, refuses to listen to advice, and **does not** get out of **this cycle**.

Step, for a moment, into the shoes of a young student just coming home from a dance, refused once again by a **young woman he is fond of and has been asking to dance for nearly a year**. After coming home, he thought, "The first time she refused to dance with me because of the way I dressed, so I learned how to dress better. Then she refused me because I didn't know how to dance well, so I learned how to dance better. Tonight, she refused me because she wasn't sure I was her type of man. I asked her what that meant and during our conversation, she told me all the things she liked, and even said that I was an interesting person. Well, tomorrow, I will invite her to the theater. I will dress well and bring her flowers because now I know everything she likes and doesn't like! **And all that makes me happy and is great fun.** In truth, she inspires me to try new things that I've never had the chance, courage, or time to do, but wanted to deep inside. **Isn't life beautiful?**"

How would you react after three refusals – in business, by a friend, or from someone you are attracted to? Would you declare failure and give up... or would you persevere and not let them discourage you?

Well, this is where stubbornness often steps in.

And this leads us to the beginning of this discussion: Often the important question in all this chaos is whether **our** activities are still **accompanied by the same contentedness, with which they** were at the start... or has the initial (primal) motivation, which came from researching and creating something new, turned into **stubbornness, proving oneself, and (coercively) persevering** – not because we feel it as an achievement, as we did in the beginning, but because we **simply cannot afford to not reach what we have announced**.

Although we may perceive this activity as achieving the goal, the **goal in and of itself becomes the purpose**.

This often happens – like some other unpleasant things we have already mentioned – when our **identity is related to realization in the physical world**… with anything happening **outside of us**. Because we now have certain **expectations**, things must progress as we imagined them if we want to be happy. And because we **cannot influence** all the factors that govern the achievement of our goal, we are often **disappointed**.

The reason for everything that happens here is focusing on **external activities** (in the material world), giving them the power **to prevail over our own feelings**.

Here is the conclusion. When we stubbornly persist on some path and consciously register all the rejections – according to the "That which doesn't kill you makes you stronger" principle – **we really have no advantage over someone who withdrew at the first obstacle** or rejection. Neither the person from the first scenario, nor the person from the second scenario, will **achieve the real (main) goal**, which is always related to the growth of the soul – **raising the vibration within**.

Whoever stubbornly persists to the bitter end will have something to show outwardly. But is that really **all that we want**? Outwardly successful people have their own saying, "Wealth is accompanied by loneliness."

If we want to have **everything**, it is **necessary to include the heart** and energies of higher vibrations – contentedness, dedication, compassion, etc. – in the achievement of each and every goal and allow this energy to guide us and lead us into a state of higher consciousness. Or as Sai Baba said,

> **"The end of wisdom is freedom.**
> **The end of culture is perfection.**
> **The end of knowledge is love.**
> **The end of education is character."**

Knowledge of the Higher Worlds

We learned that successful people do not consider bad decisions to be a waste of time, money, or energy, but an **important sign**. Rejection does not bother them much. They could actually be happy because they identified a misunderstanding, or caught a mistake early in the game when it is easier to correct, so they spent less energy heading in the wrong direction.

Another way to look at it is: If you do not know the hard times, how can you ever fully appreciate the best times? We appreciate pleasure because our day is not filled with it. Success is always sweeter when contrasted by our failures. A person that rises from rags to riches appreciates his new lifestyle in a way nobody who has grown up with wealth ever can.

Eastern religions know there is no good without evil, no beauty without ugliness, no success without failure. It is the world of duality where two extremes, opposite each other yet part of each other, perfectly balance any system and make it work.

This is Yin and Yang. Without a beginning, there is no end, and there can be no beginning without an ending first. Day and night follow each other in an endless cycle of dawn and dusk, each known only by the other – white is known only through black as one absorbs all color and the other repels all light. Silence is broken by sound, and sound can only be heard distinct from silence.

Successful people embrace both extremes and perceive them as equal parts of the same whole – learning their characteristics to raise their awareness and accept them as part of themselves. They **raise the vibrations** of these extremes and then **embrace the wholeness** from a **higher vibration**.

This is the way masters approach the problem: They do not identify with the problem or a partial (one-sided) solution that does not bring Love to everyone. Rather they **redirect their focus into the highest energy possible and then look at the problem from that perspective**. The result is a solution that is for the **higher good of everyone**.

Follow the Masters

Part of your journey will be complete **when you return from the life of duality** (polarity) where you fight for everything – because the only way back is to **decide for or against**. This is, by the way, where **all pain, suffering, wars, and even crime begin**: If you are not for me, then you are against me.

We have to move towards **the everlasting whole of Unity or Oneness, where there is no right or wrong, good or bad, black or white – everything simply is**… and where everyone is free to express himself or herself the way he or she wants.

So this Unity or **Oneness does not represent the opposite of some pole,** but **embraces** everything that is – including these **good and bad extremes**. For example, we have in duality the energies of **fear** (one extreme) and **courage** (the opposite of fear). Unity represents **surrendering to the situation and unconditionally accepting**, when we neither push or force, nor hinder or block anything.

Fear indicates the **hindering of something**, and courage the **proving**. A **level above this – Unity – is coming from ourselves** and **performing the things dictated to us by our heart**, which never judges and does not care how something will look on the outside, and that is why it neither hinders nor forces. We often call this path the **middle way**.

Can you accept such a perception of life? Can you accept a view that means the end of pain, envy, and sorrow? The perception that **all is one** and everyone supports everyone else?

The Concept of Unity Versus Duality

Since we talk a lot about the concepts of Unity and duality, let us examine them closer.

As we already know, energies are always divided into two groups – **not into two poles, but two groups**. One group of energies comes from so-called Unity, Oneness, or unconditionality, while the other falls into the world of opposites or polarities.

Unity does not have an opposite. This is also, among other things, the state of our **soul, heart, and intuition**; or the state of our consciousness during meditation, surrender to creativity, appreciation of nature, or other beauties. The most well-known – and most celebrated – representative of these energies is **Love**. Not the kind of love that hides attachment in the sense of, "I love you as long as you behave the way I like" (which is very typical for the extreme or conditional energies of duality), but the

unconditional energy, which only accepts all there is – no matter what. True Love is forever, and nothing can force it to change into anything else, such as hatred.

The state of Unity does not represent the opposite of any of these poles, but **rises above them**; it is the concept, when the energy of one or the other extreme **does not even reach us** because we are not coming out of it, so we are **not attached to it in any way**.

Which are the energies of Unity? All those **expressing high vibration** – not conditioning anything – **coming directly from the heart and intuition** and not as a reaction to the outside world.

So if we want to try unconditional energies, we must always raise our vibration (go to the heart), which neither judges nor compares – typical of the energies of polarity – but only **accepts** and **lets Life be**. Or in other words, in the state of Unity we just love... everything and everyone unconditionally.

On the other hand, "human love" as most of us know and experience it, **comes from polarity**. It is not unconditional energy, but trade: **If you give me something, I will give you something else in exchange**. We could say that it is the **reaction to a certain situation**, which we sometimes call love and at other times call something else; for example, **attachment** to a certain person, activity, relation, energy.

This trade goes something like this: As long as someone is kind and obliging, we "love" them, but when they are no longer like that, we don't love them. (More on this is described in a special chapter about love.)

Here is something else we should consider: Sometimes when a person expresses a certain energy state, **we cannot tell if this energy derives from Unity or from polarity**.

For example, this means that a person can be in a **good mood**, but this mood comes out of either a state of unconditionality or a state of polarity. We can find out in the following way: If happiness was brought about as a reaction to some event, situation, thought, etc., it is the energy of polarity. It is typical for this happiness to change – or disappear – when the event, thought, or situation changes. This is **conditional**: We are happy as long as...

> *Unity is everything that does not have an opposite.*

Besides that, laughter and attempts to impress others with jokes and a person's good mood often express stages of **tension releasing** or **searching for identity**. Some people **look for resonance with others** in this way and, for example, want to be **recognized** among people for their jokes.

On the other side, **if a person's happiness and contentedness come from within, and not as a reaction to some other energies or attempt to get something, they are unconditional and will last**. No matter what happens around them, their state of contentedness will not be influenced because **it did not originate outside and therefore does not depend on anything outside of them**.

This is what we are trying to come to and what has been called **enlightenment: being in high vibration regardless of the situation around us**. In this way, we will persevere in joy, happiness, peace, satisfaction, compassion, harmony, and so on, **in every situation**. But if we want to achieve that state, we have to **change our identity** – from appreciating the external world into **appreciating unconditional energies**… or **Life itself**.

As we have already stated, Jesus described this state nicely in *The Gospel of Thomas*, "Rather, the (Father's) kingdom is inside you and outside you." And also, "There is light within an enlightened person, and it shines on the whole world." (*The Gospel of Thomas*, saying 24)

We also said that **this means that Heaven is a state of consciousness** and not some place we go to when we die… if we have done everything right or followed the rules. As Jesus said, "If your leaders say to you, 'Behold, the kingdom is in the sky,' then the birds in the sky will get there before you. If they say to you, 'It is in the sea,' then the fish will get there before you." (*The Gospel of Thomas*, saying 3)

The Difference Between the Heart and Emotions

Let us explain one more thing concerning conditional and unconditional energies: the difference between the heart and emotions.

First, energy of the heart – Love – is **pure energy in its original form**. Emotions do contain this energy… but have something added to them: a **personal perception** (or a **specific meaning**, which the mind attached to neutral energy). That "added material" – i.e., description of some event, person, idea – now governs the whole process: The more this description is important to us and the more we identify with it, the **more powerful the emotion**... and the more we are influenced by it.

So emotions are always **conditional**, which means that they **have an opposite** and are always related to or react to some other energy that conditions the emotion. For example, we will become angry if **something specific happens**, and this very anger can, in a certain situation, change – become harsher or milder. The same is true for all other emotions.

As we have already mentioned, in the world of duality we always have two **opposite polarities**.

The source of conditional energies is our **mind**, which also **creates emotions** (by attributing a certain meaning to an experience or neutral feeling) and so polarizes the experience through judgment, comparison with similar experiences, and its expectations for the future.

For instance, our mind believes that it is nice to greet an individual on the street. In the event that someone close to us does not greet us in passing, the mind will attach an **unpleasant and unsupportive meaning** to this experience. That way, it will create an **emotion: This experience will hurt us.**

The same happens with "positive" emotions: When the mind recognizes something as supportive and pleasant for us, it creates an uplifting emotion.

So when we designate something as left or right, right or wrong, and so on, we are already in polarity or comparing, proving, and affirming, which leads to **fears, pain, and suffering** (as the repetition and strengthening of painful experiences).

The heart, intuition, and other unconditional energies never compare or judge. So if we catch ourselves categorizing, judging, and comparing, it means that we have already **closed our hearts**. Jesus said, **"No one can serve two masters."**(Mathew 6:24)

He meant that **you cannot be in the heart while judging**. For instance, you cannot love one and at the same time not love the other. **You are either in this vibration and are proceeding from it, or are reacting (nicely) to outside influences**, which is **far from being in the heart**.

So if we do not love a person who is perceived as incapable and unworthy of giving or receiving love, we do not know what Love is – we just respond to the kindness coming to us from the outer world.

Jesus similarly said, as we already mentioned, "**If you do good to those who do good to you, what credit is that to you? For even sinners do the same.** If you lend to those from whom you expect to receive, what credit is that to you? Even sinners lend to sinners in order to receive back the same amount." (Luke 6:33-34)

Behind the Concept of Love

For a long time – through the Ten Commandments, Jesus' stories, and the other lessons of world religions – we have been taught to **look at ourselves, open our hearts, and love everything unconditionally**. How do we know when we really love and are not just being nice to someone who is nice to us?

We are in a vibration of Love **when we stop differentiating between whom we love and whom we will not**. Also, we react to all energies the same. That means we treat **everyone** – whether he or she is our best friend, a stranger, or even an enemy – the same.

Once the consciousness is located in love's vibration, it understands and accepts everything around it and looks at things from and with this vibration. Love resonates or communicates and connects with a **similar vibration of love**.

Fortunately, this vibration is **in every person** because **we all carry all vibrations** – from greed and anger, etc., to unconditional love – **within**.

It is true, however, that **we do not show or express all of these vibrations**. The one that is presently expressed is the one in which our consciousness is located – for a long time or only for a moment. And so by guiding our consciousness, for example, we can achieve the skill to **come into and remain in a certain energy – regardless of all outside motivations**.

Our entire **view of the world** around us depends on this principle, on the basis of which the various energies – momentary or general (or prevailing) – within us are activated. The vibration of anger, for example, cannot resonate with joy, but only with anger.

These two facts – **everyone carries all vibrations within, and every vibration can only communicate with a similar or at most a lower vibration** – explain why one person can see beauty in everything while another sees only desperation, worry, and fear in the same thing.

We can say all this in another way: We can react to outside impulses (vibrations), or we can **proceed only from our own consciousness and not allow anything outside to come near us** and consequently affect us.

So when are we proceeding from ourselves and **not reacting to outside circumstances**?

When we **take off our masks and free ourselves of all mechanisms**, scenarios, and little tricks with which we defended and protected ourselves up until now... and begin consciously and lovingly accepting all these experiences.

If this energy is really within us and we express it outwardly, we are not just doing things that **look good outwardly** while feeling resistance within, but are enjoying performing them.

So our goal is to **focus inward** – for instance with meditation – **and awaken a very high vibration**. Then we have to perceive and **carry our consciousness into it...** and so **fill our consciousness with the vibration until it reaches critical mass**. When this happens, we will be able to **proceed from it**, regardless of outside influences. This is the only way to move into the heart and find both strength and happiness.

We can have outside help on this path, but **every individual must go through the process within himself or herself**. (The whole process is further explained in other books, such as *Charisma, Self-Confidence and Personal Power*).

Successful People Throughout History

Once again, we return to the question, "**What do successful people have that unsuccessful people don't?**"

Do they know more theory? We can find theory in a book. Do they know more people? Most started without knowing anyone. Did they have a lot of money to start with? Once again, most had nothing in the beginning.

It must be something that relates to wisdom and/or **experiences**.

So let us talk a bit about experiences.

We could say that successful people **remain goal-oriented all the time** because their goal – derived from the heart and intuition – never changes. They do not push or hold anything back, nor do they need to do so. If a goal carries the heart's energy within, people around this person will feel that energy and **support him or her spontaneously**.

The Millionaire Mindset

One of the ways to recognize individuals who chose following the heart's goal is this: The individual **no longer goes to extremes or repeats past experiences**.

That path is most often connected to:

- A very **personal approach** to the well-known activity.
- The person having added **something new** to the classical method.

In both cases, this person **creates something new**, so both paths express **creativity**, which is one of the **clearest signs of energies of the heart**. So if we want to succeed, the classical method, which someone else passed through, must be **improved** or **changed**, or we must find a new way. For instance, if we want to improve our business, we will have to improve a client approach or find a new one, perhaps introduce a new way of performing an established process, improve logistics, and so on.

If we only blindly follow something, we often will not make a step forward, at least not in primary (internal) destiny, which is, as we have already mentioned many times, the **most important**.

Beside that, external success is also very hard to attain if we only repeat existing activities. After all, there are a lot of people who do the same as their mentor or role model, but do not get anywhere. The secret that determines success is hidden in **resonance with business** (product, market, buyers), **time, and space**. If we are not in harmony with the vibration around us and do not follow our heart, we will **step out of the creational process** and start to **adjust to something outside of us**.

Or better said – we will adjust to **somebody else's creative process and want to beat him**; we will **follow the leader** and want to **overtake** him, which is not possible.

We have to **add our own vibration to the process.**

If we look back in history, we will find a lot of creative minds that have followed their hearts and, more or less, succeeded outwardly; but they all succeeded inwardly in a bigger way.

Here is an outline of the events of one "successful" person's life:

He was two years old when his infant brother died.

When he was seven, he almost drowned.

The Principles That Control Your Destiny

His mother died of milk sickness when he was nine.
When he was ten, a horse kicked him, and he nearly died.
He was sixteen years old when he took a job to support his impoverished family.
He was nineteen when his older sister died in childbirth.
Lost his job at twenty-three.
Defeated for state legislature at twenty-three.
Failed in business (a grocery store) at twenty-four.
Elected to state legislature at twenty-five.
Overcame the death of his sweetheart at twenty-six.
Reelected to state legislature at twenty-seven.
Had a nervous breakdown at twenty-seven.
Turned down in a marriage proposal at twenty-eight.
Defeated for Speaker at twenty-nine.
Reelected to state legislature at twenty-nine.
Reelected to state legislature at thirty-one.
Filed bankruptcy at thirty-one.
Filed bankruptcy again at thirty-three (but spent the next seventeen years paying back a debt he had borrowed to lend money to a friend with the purpose of starting a new business).
Lost a congressional race at thirty-four.
Elected to congress at thirty-seven.
Lost renomination at thirty-nine.
Rejected for land officer at forty.
When he was forty-one, his son died.
When he was forty-two, his father died.
Lost a senatorial race at forty-five.
Defeated for nomination for Vice President at forty-seven (received only 110 votes).
Lost a senatorial race at forty-nine.
Elected President of the United States at age fifty-two and reelected for a second term at fifty-six.

His name was Abraham Lincoln – known as one of the **greatest** presidents of the United States of America.

4. Your Thoughts Influence and Even Create Your World

How important is what and how we think? Is it true that everything that happens to us in our lives is a product of our thoughts?

Scientists say that events that influence our condition are only a small percentage of what accounts for where we are in life, and it is **our reaction** to certain events that has a significant impact on our present condition. We can choose to allow certain events to influence us... or not.

Said differently, it is about our **vibration** in combination with the external energy's **level of absorbability**. As we know, we can be oriented inwardly and persevere in our internal state of consciousness, or we can **search for energy** and resonate with surroundings, remaining open to the outside world, **absorbing whatever comes our way**.

If that happens, we will be **influenced by the energies of the external world**. But we always have another choice: If we reach critical mass – concentrating on our internal state of consciousness and maintaining (high) vibration, no matter what – external energies cannot throw us from that equilibrium.

Another Way

Again, we can see how the **external and internal worlds intertwine**. As long as we are trapped in duality, things actually happen as described. When we move away from it and rise above it in our hearts, we reach the state **when the outside world does not influence us, but we influence it**.

That depends, as already described, on **how much energy we absorb** from the outside world and how much energy we **direct into it**. The more we are energetically connected to this world (and try to get energy from it), the **more we will search for our identity in it** and the more this world will **control** us. Jack Canfield, American motivator and co-author of the *Chicken Soup* series of books said, **"What you are identified with controls you."**

So when **we identify with the world of unconditional energies** – the soul, heart, and intuition – and search there for identity, the external world of duality no longer influences us. That way, all pain, suffering, and other conditional energies, which come from the search for resonance in a world of duality, will disappear.

If we look at enlightened people such as Mother Theresa, we will discover that they did not submit to anything from outside, but **created around them the world they lived in**. And this energy is so determinate and powerful, it can easily **master the material world**.

For instance, Mother Theresa was constantly around people who were seriously ill and even had fatal and highly contagious illnesses, **without fear that she would become ill**. She created the world around her and was not subject to the influences of the outside world.

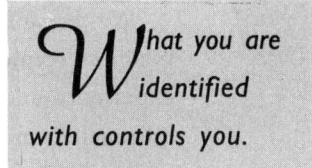

> *What you are identified with controls you.*

That does not mean that she denied everything else she did not like... quite the contrary. She accepted everything, and that was **the key to creating a new world**. When you do not want to oppose anything but merely **enrich it with a vibration of Love, everything opens to you and wants to be influenced by you**.

But if we are coming from the conditional world or just moving within it, we will always encounter contradictions: We will expect certain activities to happen – to make us happy; and when they do not, we will be hurt... and pain and suffering will also arise.

But we must not forget the **crucial factor** that governs the influence of thought on action – the (Sub)Law of Life's Mission. This is always **above the mind**, and we cannot escape or outwit it.

So thought can influence our actions – as long as it is in harmony with our **life's mission**, which we recognize when we enter the heart. **Our greatest wishes will express and describe our life's mission and motivate us to begin to realize it**.

How We Choose Our Way

In an earlier chapter, we were talking about a new coworker and how his employment affected our work. Let us take a look at another situation happening at work: We expected to get promoted, but someone else got the promotion. Here is a chain reaction happening within us.

We have our heart set on a promotion we have been working towards for a long time, so we entertained certain expectations about it. When someone else receives the promotion, we – disappointed and even a little bit angry – try to **find out and rationalize why they were chosen over us**.

But we are not impartial because we feel offended and cheated. In this way, our consciousness is in a certain (lower) vibration, so we see everything around us **from that vibration.**

What do we see?

We certainly discover new information. One, our colleague must have business connections that are far superior to ours. Two, we have more experience and a better education than our colleague, so we assess the information and **begin to think,** "This is proof that the system I work in prefers young, fresh employees for the top positions." It even makes us think that our company **appreciates the work of others over our own.**

Now we are more than a little angry. Our self-talk, the thoughts that arise inside our mind, says things like, "They don't respect me. My work isn't worth anything. Nobody sees what an important team player I am. I will never be able to achieve my goals in a company that prefers younger employees for top positions."

That leads us to the conclusion that **there is no point in trying again.** In fact, it does not matter how hard we try because **we will not be successful anyway.**

We now **see ourselves in a hopeless situation.**

The next step is that we **become depressed and short-tempered... and come to work in a bad mood every day.** Where we used to see coworkers, we now see only competitors and backstabbers. Angry all the time, we no longer see our future in this company.

What comes out as a result of that kind of processing (thinking)?

Obviously, **we are no longer enthusiastic about our job.** We have a lack of interest (motivation) in our line of work. Our energy level has decreased dramatically, and we display an attitude of indifference in everything we do. All these things, without a doubt, **stomp our productivity into the ground and destroy our effectiveness on the job.**

We are now in a really hopeless situation that will **never allow a promotion.** And if we continue to work like mediocre people do, we will probably **never again find the edge and creativity that put us so close to the top.**

But we must know that this is what is going on inside of us and **most of it is not real,** but based on fear. Fear is by definition a **fantasy about a** future event, but we can make it real – in our mind. We can actually **live in that (fantasy) world**… so this fear **becomes very real** to us.

We have to **disconnect from that kind of thinking,** "change gears," and take a look at our jobs and ourselves from a **neutral position**. Why not try a different, more supportive approach to the event that has just occurred in your life?

Before we explain that kind of approach, let us examine the truth behind it and the Mercy of the Universe that supports us at every step we take.

The Esoteric Truth Behind Suffering

Because all experiences are designed for the **growth of the soul**, sometimes life – if we do not become aware of this in a nice way – will serve an experience where we will be literally **thrown into a new situation**.

It is the situation we have mentioned once before: we should be moving forward, but are so stuck that a shocking **push** is necessary to destroy existing **patterns and habits** and release certain energy so that we can get unstuck and move a step forward.

This is where a cruel situation, like suddenly being fired, can happen – if we do not sooner sense that **it is time to move into a new experience**, if we want to follow our life's mission.

These passages into new experiences can be harsh, especially if we do not recognize them on time with the help of intuition and "signs" that we get along the way, but instead **behave like a child, who has decided to stay in the third grade** because he or she particularly liked this year… rather than **successfully completing exams and moving on to the fourth grade**.

It is the Mercy of the Universe that does not let us stay in one place, but regardless of our ignorance, **pushes us into growth**. This happens so that we can get to the state when we will be able to enjoy life unconditionally inwardly and outwardly as soon as possible and **enjoy every moment**, which is our goal. ("Lead us not into temptation, but deliver us from evil," was how Jesus described this mercy in the *Lord's Prayer*.)

If we look at the experience of growth only through the eyes of the external world, we experience everything as **pain** and a **conspiracy** where everything turns against us.

But we have to know that **nothing that does not benefit our soul's growth can ever happen**.

If we have our identity linked to the soul's growth, we will experience every such passage not as suffering, but as a **step forward**.

Herein lies the secret of enlightened or self real-I-zed people. Let us illustrate this by recalling Mother Theresa's lifestyle.

We said once before that she slept on the floor wherever she went. This was not with the intention to suffer, but with a very clear purpose: **She wanted to live exactly as her brothers and sisters** (the poor people she treated) **did in order to get close to them in this way, so that she could understand and then help them**. This was her **vision**, like someone else's vision is to buy a yacht.

It is energy, which is **far from suffering or rejection** if we look at the matter from the right perspective. As long as we are burdened – or have linked our identity – with luxury, soft cushions, and the like, we will perceive Mother Theresa's path as rejection and suffering.

In essence, she **did not want to be doing anything** other than that which she was doing. Actually she was living – if you look at it from this standpoint – the dream life because she had **fulfilled all her wishes, which served her in the achievement of her goal**.

Our Focus Determines Our Perceptions

Let us get back to our story about being rejected at work and see how we can use this "bad" situation for growth.

First, we should try to find out why – the true reasons – they chose the other candidate. So we should, for example, ask our supervisor **what we could have done differently that might have swayed them to choose us instead**. There are times when others see that something is going on with us, which **we do not recognize at all**. In other words, there is a gap between how they see us and our work and how we see ourselves.

Then we need to sit down, be frank, and admit to ourselves any "bad" choices we have made.

Perhaps we have been late or often absent. Perhaps they feel we lack initiative or do not take enough calculated risks to put the company in front. Maybe they feel that our work is not our top priority or that we are not loyal enough; maybe they do not perceive us as enthusiastic enough about the company, our job, and so on.

The Principles That Control Your Destiny

All or any of these or other reasons may have kept us from getting the promotion we wanted. **We should find out, if we can, and improve our performance in those areas**... if this is our heart's desire, of course.

Even if we never discover the real reason behind another person's perception of us, our **self-assessment** will lead us to areas in which we can improve. This gives us the opportunity to take a huge leap forward and higher. In fact, we can view losing the promotion as a clear sign for self-assessment, so we can **realize the difference between our own view of our performance and that of our company's view and expectations**. Then we also have to reevaluate our goals, vision, and purpose, and decide what to do: change something regarding our performance at work or leave our current workplace.

If we decide to persist there and change for the better, we will now have **a reason and the motivation** to learn more, educate ourselves further, take better care in fulfilling expectations from business partners and coworkers, and in so doing, **improve our images, reputations, professionalism, and our capacity to lead and do business with others**.

> *True professionals and successful people always find another job opening.*

Had we received the promotion, our motivation to further educate and improve ourselves would have **gone**. Seeing the situation that way, our **competitor did us a great favor** – a favor that will eventually **allow us to achieve much more than we were previously able to, given the limits of our past knowledge**... even if we do not stay at our present company. **True professionals and successful people always find another job opening!**

Here is my story. It so happens that I once took part in a financial project for which I expected a far different outcome than happened in the end. Although I really tried very hard, my work was not perceived as good – because I did not follow the ordinary rules, but instead tried a lot of common sense approaches that could work. (The problem was that the company **did not have a sales system**, but wanted us to establish it while using their unsuccessful and unproductive instructions.)

My sign to leave the project came when I saw an amount five times smaller than I expected in my paycheck. **I left the project the very same day.**

The Millionaire Mindset

Once alone, I found myself in a crisis with circumstances so unexpected that even my own survival was in question. Even so, I also knew that, up to that point, I had not found a business that I could see myself working in for long and be joyful doing. I was yet to discover a business that I enjoyed as much as, say, my favorite hobbies. I asked myself, **"What do I want to do today, and what would I like to be doing twenty years from now?"** In writing out the answers that came to me, I began to discover my areas of interest and skill and even ways that I could put them to work to profit from them, or at least make a living. Soon, the path began to appear all by itself.

I "accidentally" stumbled across the address of an organization that did consulting business. I called them and offered my knowledge and experience because that is something I have been doing for years – advising people how to profit from their current circumstances – but until now, I had provided this counseling free. **After the second interview, they hired me to run their seminars.** It is funny how well we clicked right from the beginning.

I knew this was my chance and I prepared, as thoroughly as possible, for my first session. The results were more than excellent! I gave my first independent seminar to a house packed so full that the company decided **I should give a repeat session as soon as possible**.

In the beginning, I only conducted a few seminars each month. However, it was not long before I was able to **choose** when, with whom, and for whom I will work. I felt **this was it** and even today, I feel that way.

I will never forget the people and events that helped me make this happen, including the financial project, which seemed like a disaster and God's punishment at the time, that got me started on my correct path. Since then I have realized **how much knowledge I gained from that failed project**.

In fact, I could never be where I am today without it. My decision to join – and later leave the financial project – was right for that moment and among the best business choices I have ever made.

> **Always look at life as an opportunity to grow and move on... even if your company fires you.** You will see that a lot of times God closes the side door in order to open the main gate.

So a lot depends on our **understanding** and **processing** of the external world and energy (internal) world. And because we can influence and direct our thinking, we can also direct the **course of our life's energy** and predict the kinds of actions and experiences to which this will lead us.

5. Your Past Choices Brought You Where You Are Today; Your Choices Today Will Form Your Immediate Future

Do you want your future to be the same as your present? Nothing is easier – **just continue to do everything the same way you have done in the past**. If you want to have a different future, you must first realize that **nothing new comes without change**.

Most people want from their future more than they have today. The only logical conclusion is **if they want different results, they need to change their thinking and actions and they need to sustain this change every day of their life**.

Since our thinking influences our actions, it only makes sense to begin with the reasons we think the way we do – the external change for the better first requires an internal one.

You have to disconnect from certain unsupportive thinking patterns – some call them "negative" – that may have been part of you for years. But there could be one more thing going on that is not in our favor... and you have to consider it as well.

Namely, some people think that supportive means everything that is **pleasant to others and ourselves**, such as happiness, joy, good health, and smiling faces.

That thinking can lead to another decision, "If I want others to see me as a good person, I will have to hide my true emotions when I don't feel that way... and show only what others perceive as being pleasant emotions." In this moment, we have already begun to **hide our true selves, give away our power, and aim our life energy at pleasing others**.

What is supposed to be "positive" now turns against us. As the critical mass of that pretended energy builds up, we create a bigger and bigger gap between who we really are and what we express. Thus, **the energy we really feel about ourselves when we try to please others** – denying our true nature in the process – is **the energy we are now filling ourselves with**.

That way, we feel more and more **guilt** and **shame** deep inside us, which only **strengthen those lower vibration energies**.

Moreover, we then **live a double life**: one inside of us and the other public. And we have to carry on this drama indefinitely.

That means we will **have no choice** but to **hide our true selves** from now on, pretending to be someone or something that we are not, living to please others.

This is **the biggest self-denial we can experience**.

> *Nothing new comes without change.*

So everybody has to choose: Will you please yourself or please others? Will you live according to your wishes and desires... or the expectations of others? (The sad story is that usually **others do not even have the kinds of expectations we assume they have** – and live by – so while carefully pretending and being someone we are not, we are not really pleasing anyone. Like when, for example, we assume our guests need a bed to sleep over, so we always make our bed available for them, while we sleep on an uncomfortable sofa.)

Another truth is: If you please yourself, you will please others because you will show them that this is the right path for you. By doing so, you show them how to treat you and also **give them permission to do the same for themselves**. In this way, you will represent a **role model they can look up to** (important if you have kids).

If you please everyone but yourself, nobody will be happy. They will feel that you compromised your **honesty, integrity, and true identity** in the process, and those are the very qualities we seek most when it comes to friends. Maybe this could work for you short-term, but not in the long run.

Every time you try to please others by denying yourself, you are acting against your true nature and power. And when you cannot express your true nature, you feel pain deep within you.

This does not mean you do not have to help friends... but it means that before doing so, ask yourself if you want to help him or her... or are you "selling out" for his or her good opinion of you.

Therefore, if you want to be "positive," you have to change your perception of what positive is. Here is the truth: **If you can love yourself** whoever you are – **especially your shadows** (the characteristics, habits, etc., which you are not proud of and do not want others to know about) – **you are the most positive person on Earth!**

Being positive means loving and accepting everything. However, we are not talking about pretending here, but about sincere feelings. Maybe you want to ask: "But how can I love feelings and whatever else that causes me pain?"

That is the point. **Not loving and consequently denying and hiding these emotions causes you the most pain.** When you try to – falsely – protect yourself from the pain by not being true to the person you are inside, you create pain. The reason is that **the energy from the emotions that engulf you reaches a critical mass** and your consciousness drops into this energy state of lower vibration, so now you perceive your entire life from that vibration... and feel even worse. This is how we usually create more defense mechanisms (more excuses, apologies, rationalizations, etc.) concealing our true selves from others.

That leads us to the question, "What can I do about the bad thoughts that may already be present in my mind?" We are talking about thoughts like: "Money is dirty and spoils people. I'll never succeed – nobody in my family did. If I work fewer than ten hours per day I won't earn enough to live on, etc."

First, try not to **identify with these thoughts**, but see them as something that belongs to you rather than something that is you. The next step is **building energy of high vibration and reaching its critical mass** by focusing your consciousness on something you do believe in and accept. When the critical mass of that energy is reached, you will have no problem accepting and embracing your shadows.

Here is a common self-help method that you can always use in the process. You can shift your consciousness into another direction with **affirmations**. These are supportive and uplifting thoughts that bring you good feelings about yourself.

So let us try replacing unsupportive thoughts with more pleasant thinking patterns, like the ones below, which remind you that **you deserve success and are worthy of it**. (However, bear in mind that this is a quick and temporary fix, not a long-term solution. If you want to be free, you will have to **accept everything**.)

"I gain more and more experience every day."

"With everything I do, my work gets better and better."

"I'm good at what I do – I've succeeded in the past, and I can do it again today."

"I use each waking moment to learn something new."

"Just being alive is a success because each moment enriches me with a new realization worth more than money alone."

"I believe in myself and know that I am trustworthy."

Most importantly, these affirmations will work for you only if you **strongly and unconditionally believe in them**.

But how do you know if you believe them? Repeat them in your mind and then **pay close attention to any feedback or comments your mind responds with**. If you find yourself voicing an affirmation, and an immediate and contrary argument arises in your mind, then you do not believe the affirmation you are saying.

There is a special technique, which will show you how you can change your present perception of reality with affirmations, which we will cover later. For now, you have to remember: **If you repeat what you believe in over and over, you will reach the critical mass of the energy the affirmation evokes inside you**. This energy will affect your future thinking and actions.

On the other hand, if you say something you do not believe, your mind will immediately kick into an argumentative state. What happens then? As we already mentioned, **the energy of the unsupportive response will create a state that better reflects what you are really feeling – resentment, sadness, bad feelings, and so on.**

So use affirmations as reminders, not thought builders.

Be aware that it has taken many years of unpleasant self-talk to implant your current thought patterns. Your self-talk and thinking patterns are what make you choose what you do and act the way you do. They represent themselves as habits, the iron rule, traditions, business or religious dogma, etiquette, and so on. Your parents, society, teachers, community, religion, etc. all play a part to instill these patterns of thought. Some of them are so strong that they easily provoke certain thoughts and emotions just by thinking about them.

You have to learn to distinguish your true self from your thought patterns. Thought forms affect your view of the world both outside and inside you, as well as the way you deal with these – external and internal – worlds.

You can change thoughts, actions, and habits, if you so desire. Again, the ultimate way is to **love and thus accept them**… and to realize that nothing is bad in and of itself, just **different**. If you hate them, you give them too much of your energy – and **bond them even stronger to yourself**.

When you love them and give them **no special treatment**, they become less and less important… until you can just drop them, or they fall away from you.

Automatic Responses Can Hinder Our Growth

Many times the reason for being stuck in life is derived from **automatic responses**. It is most important to remember: **When you act automatically, as in habitual behavior, you close all other options (responses) that were open to you.** Doing so means that you will experience certain feelings, which "you shouldn't have to," either the way you feel about them or your mind says to, because they are tied to the automatic response.

These responses happen unconsciously, and **we become aware of them only after they occur**. For example, if a messenger rings your doorbell and says, "I have a telegram for you," what is the first thought – automatic response – that crosses your mind? Most people immediately think that there is something wrong, perhaps someone has died; especially if you are part of the Baby Boom, or earlier generations, when a telegram almost always announced a death or an unexpected tragedy. Receiving a telegram sends chills down the spines of most people.

Most of these reactions **feel like they happen without your choosing them**, which is why they continue to happen and are difficult to change (and that is why we think we **cannot** affect them).

So the first step in changing them is this: **You must first be aware that something is happening**. Therefore, if you do not pay attention and become aware of these ingrained patterns, you run a real risk of sleepwalking through your life.

We are talking about the energy of **conscious awareness** that is crucial in that phase.

After **accepting** what is going on, you have to firmly **decide** to change these unsupportive energies.

A supportive approach (self-confidence, a positive outlook and taking responsibility for your actions) is not all you need. Exercising **self-discipline** is equally important. Once you develop your plan – stick to it. Follow it strictly... **and take all necessary action**. To do this, you need motivation.

Here is how it works in practice. Let us take a real life example.

> *When you act automatically, as in habitual behavior, you close all other options (responses) that were open to you.*

Do you have a challenge with your weight? If so, it is not hard for you to remember that horrible feeling of being stuffed and the anger at yourself that followed, especially when you could not need to eat that much, right?

One of the hardest times for most people who overeat is watching television or any other time their body is idle or sedentary. For some reason, sitting in front of the TV brings on all the feelings of missing something – as if getting through the program requires potato chips, a can of pop, or a sandwich. At that moment, however, to the overeater there is nothing better in life than a comfortable seat, a good movie, and a bowl of popcorn or sweets. Even more – the commercials we watch are specifically crafted to turn on the snack-craving mechanism in our brain as we mindlessly tread a path between the refrigerator and the couch.

A lot of people try to overcome this automatic response, but they just can't break the habit. Their body opposes consuming more and more (junk) food, but their mind usually wins... and something inside them lifts them up and carries them to the refrigerator.

Here is one way you can change this: After deciding to stop this agony, you have to make a battle plan. **Rid your cupboards of snacks that are easy-to-grab-in-a-daze and make sure that whatever food you do have takes just long enough to prepare** that it discourages you from eating during your high-trigger moments. You could also put up photos of how you would like to look – a slender woman or athletic man – right on the refrigerator or cupboard, so you see them every time you enter the "danger zone." Post a note underneath which reads, **"If you want to look like this, turn and walk away."**

On the other hand, maybe a little **reverse psychology** would work better for you. Post a photo of someone who is grossly overweight on that forbidden door – a photo of what you do not want to look like – with a note underneath saying, **"Open this door, and this is how you will end up!"**

The above mentioned techniques will help you when your willpower is weak and you are unable to resist temptation; that is, when you find yourself in front of the refrigerator with the usual excuse, "Ok, just this last time, but then that's it… I will start my diet tomorrow. I promise!"

We just described the **first part of the battle plan** – we have broken the chain that automatically unravels. Now we are in the next phase, where we have to **create a new habit**: watching TV without snacks, or eating fruit and drinking flavored tea. Here we also need **willpower** and **perseverance**.

It is very important that we do not experience this as suffering because then we will – as we already know – build up this energy (of the vibration we feel deep inside): suffering, denial, and so on. That is why it is a good idea to remember the **benefit we will reap**, think about the results and the **basic wish and motivation** that drove us to do this.

When you begin to see progress, **reward yourself with something** (but not with food): a great book, a bicycle (so you can begin a healthier lifestyle), or anything that makes you feel good about your progress.

All of this sounds simple; so simple, in fact, you may even be thinking, "I don't need to do all that. All I need to do is have more willpower and tell myself 'No!'" Unfortunately, that is what most people do, and that is why most people fail.

Also, you will not experience any progress if you deny or try to hide anything. **If you are not strong enough to stick to the plan, you should admit it first…** and then **establish the circumstances that will motivate you to achieve your goal.**

How to Change Anything You Want

As we said, **if you want to change something, you just have to love it first.**

This does not mean you must fall in love with something you want to change, only that you cannot harbor bad feelings about it. Whatever is not important to you will simply fall away or disappear. **Whatever is important for you or to you – no matter if its importance is about something "good" or "bad" – is chained to you.**

This is analogous to a child who wants attention. He or she will get it by exhibiting either good or bad behavior. If you accept the bad behavior without fighting against it, you do not reinforce that behavior. And if you pay attention to the good behavior, you reinforce it.

Therefore, the more you need or the more you hate something – the more you are bonded to it. Free yourself from the **identity linked to it**, and you will be able to redirect your energy somewhere else (and thus change a habit, pattern, etc.).

But we must, nevertheless, be prepared to discover the truth. We will not get far if we tackle a habit or pattern too quickly or lightly with too little **energy of determination** and **dedication** and too little **energy of the heart**. Here we cannot achieve anything with force; quite the opposite, we will need a lot of love and patience.

Three Phases

If we think about all the life experiences that happen to the majority of us, we can see that we basically **go through three different stages**: We may **fight for ourselves** (one extreme), **give power away to others** (the other extreme), or **work from the heart with no exceptions** – equally for everyone, including ourselves (higher level).

Let us explain these three steps; we will call them phases.

Phase 1: "The **doormat**" – here we give our power away and want to please others... so that they will like us, and thus we will feel good.

Phase 2: **Sticking up for yourself** – we have had enough of using all our time and energy for others... where do we come in? Who ever gives us anything? Here we put ourselves first, but in such a way that we push everything else – which does not support our growth and is perceived as energy draining, parasitism, or at our expense – aside.

> *If you want to change something, you just have to love it first.*

Phase 3: **Working from the heart** – when we have spent enough time in the second phase, we realize that we have just gone to another extreme: in the first phase, we put all our energy into others, while in the second phase we kept all energy within, but we feel that neither of these two phases is the right one. We want to be connected to others, but in such a way that we all benefit – through harmony and the heart's energy.

We do not want to make anyone more or less important than anybody else because we want to create relationships on a joyful and loving energy… with everyone. That way this loving energy becomes a generator and the trademark of these relationships. It is no longer important who gives what and what he or she gets because we realize that the goal is always in harmony between giving and taking, and the more we give something from the heart, the happier we will feel. Because when we invoke the heart's energy in ourselves, we gain the most.

As we see, these three phases coincide with the **five levels** we have already mentioned; except that here we skip the **tension releasing** (third level), which would be between the second and third phases, and we **unite the fourth and fifth levels into the third phase**.

We do not necessarily go through these phases in numerical order. Sometimes we do not go from phase one to phase two and on to the third phase, but **start the experience in the second phase** and then go to **phase one** and then proceed.

We usually do not just breeze through the first two phases to the third one, but either **get stuck in one of them** or **repeat the cycle** (many times): first phase, second… and then the first again, and again the second, and so on.

Another thing: We can be in one particular phase in one area and in another phase in another area, but the goal is to get to the end (phase three) in every area of our life and in every situation; **where we will work from the heart and act the same towards others and ourselves**. In other words, when we understand and accept life and live it from **high vibration outwards**.

But do not rush. When we feel that the time has come, we begin thinking about it. **Why would a mole think about what it would be like to have wings?** It would be a **waste of time** and **denial of his own self** if this thinking and his **new wishes made him feel badly on his own journey**.

Remember these three phases. Actually, this concept is the simplest, yet a very effective description of what energies are going on in our lives and where to move (the next step) for the quickest progress.

How to Heal Body and Soul

Whatever we do, and however we want to skip the phases, we just cannot skip the experiences that we are meant to go through. Well, we can try and skip them for some time, but we have to come back and do the work we abandoned.

In other words, if we want to move faster than what is natural for the experience to develop and take place (read: before critical mass is formed), we are actually turning away from that existing energy and **denying the present experience**.

Here is an interesting review about this.

Together with Boris Vene, in the book, *The Beauty is Within*, Dr. Marjan Fabjan, specialist in plastic surgery, writes about the experiences of people who have decided to change their outer appearances.

Analyzing changes to a person's outer appearance shows that outside changes (plastic surgery), which will bring the person satisfaction and a new life, only **follow changes on the inside**. This means **a person is mature enough to change his or her outside appearance** only when **he or she has achieved a new vibration and self-image on the inside**. Only in this case will the patient be happy and content.

Upon examination of his statistics of the most satisfied and most disappointed patients, Dr. Fabjan discovered that **patient satisfaction does not depend on the (level of) technical perfection** of the operation. He learned that some people, who even had **complications** during and after the operations, were **extremely satisfied** in the long run, not just with their appearances, but with **the doctor and staff**, as well.

On the other hand, there were also people who were **disappointed** despite the surgeon's excellent work. In this way, Dr. Fabjan determined that **the grounds for satisfaction were not in how well he completed his work, but whether the patient's new appearance was an expression of his or her** (higher) **consciousness**, which the body was not able to follow, or if it was merely an attempt to escape from his or her own self, which never works.

In the latter case, there are a lot of complications. The patient expected to like himself or herself more because of the surgical procedure, but because **his or her consciousness and self-acceptance cannot rise above the vibration in which they are located** – a universal rule, valid always and everywhere – they cannot forcibly or artificially raise it in this way. That is why the person **remains in the same vibration even after the operation**, and as the patient describes, "The operation didn't produce the desired results," regardless of how perfectly the surgeon performed his or her work.

The problem arose because the person was thinking along these lines, "I don't accept myself the way I am. If someone tells me that I look fine, I don't believe them because **I know exactly how good I am (or am not) and what I'm worth**. I can accept myself to this point, but no further. **If someone tells me that I am good or deserve more, I don't believe him or her**... maybe this person is even laughing at me. But I will open the door for (self) acceptance a little wider, when I fix my appearance. That is when I'll like myself – my facade because this is what I am – and others will notice this. I will also be able to accept their compliments, according to the principle that you can get only as far as the door is open."

When this person changes his or her appearance, he or she realizes that **he or she still carries the same patterns, habits, personality, etc., which he or she does not like, within**. The new outward appearance did not change the way he or she sees himself or herself. And so the individual is dissatisfied with the operation and makes excuses to convince himself or herself, and others, as well, that the problem does not lie in him or her, but elsewhere; in the surgeon's mistake, for instance.

This should also be the starting point for anyone thinking about plastic surgery. **Plastic surgery usually does not bring everlasting happiness until changes are successfully made on the inside.**

Well, sometimes surgery alone puts a person into a new vibration: He or she now sees himself or herself in a better light – and **accepts** this new self. However, this is not the rule, but rather an **exception** that the Law of Critical Mass allows. If we direct our consciousness into this new appearance and **allow it to enchant us**, it will be fine. But if our consciousness is stuck in non-acceptance of our selves – which is very common – **then not even plastic surgery will cause the consciousness to rise above self-criticism.**

So the most important question you have to deal with before plastic surgery is probably **not what you want to gain with it, but what it is that you want to run away – or escape – from**. When you address this question, the answer usually presents the **true reason for plastic surgery**, which perhaps you will even be able to resolve without surgery.

We can say this even another way: If we **already direct our life force energy into a particular goal** and one part of our body literally blocks this achievement – or stays between us and that goal – then plastic surgery (dealing with this defectiveness) will help. But **if we expect the surgery itself to direct our energy into some goal, the surgery will seldom help**.

Here is a perfect example. If we have a workplace where we try hard to establish a perfect relationship with customers, but our unusually big nose attracts more of their attention than the conversation that we try to establish, then plastic surgery correcting our nose will be **extremely helpful**. Namely, we had our goal, and the motivation, and desire to communicate with customers **before**, so after our nose job, **we can establish conversation**. That is to say, because our nose was the only problem on the path toward our goal, we are now happy: **nothing hinders us any more, and we are about to achieve this goal easily**.

In this way, surgery provides **miracles**.

On the other hand, if we **do not know what to do with our lives**, so we **do not focus and direct energy anywhere** – waiting for some opportunity to appear – and we blame, for example, our nose, then surgery probably will not help. This is because even after the operation **we still will not know what to do with our lives**... and nobody will approach us and offer us the deal of a lifetime simply because we now have a nicer nose.

In this case, the surgery failed.

6. The Reason Behind Every "Why...?"

Is there a reason for your current circumstances?

Nothing happens without meaning. Coincidences do not exist, even if it sometimes seems like they do. Sai Baba said that **whoever believes in coincidence, does not believe in God**.

Experiences always follow the initiative actions – either personal choices or karmic code – that caused them, so **they are not coincidences, but consequences**. "You reap what you sow," say the Sacred Scriptures.

If you do not like these consequences and you are not getting what you expected out of life, **ask yourself what it is you need to do differently, to achieve what you want**. Do you follow through on your promises? Are you honest? Do you show a true interest in people, especially those you are working with? Do you treat others, as you would like them to treat you? Have you secretly given up hope, simply because you failed once before? Are you afraid to begin your new assignment, doubtful of success? Do you focus on people's faults, telling them what bothers you about them, when in fact you are jealous and wish you were more like them?

Additionally, and most importantly, **are you honest with yourself**? Are you kind to yourself like you are to others? Do you feel you are worthy of everything you desire?

Life always gives you what you ask for – or trigger – either directly or energetically. In other words, **everything we get is an answer both to our vibration** and **the codes** that activate according to our karma (and consequently to our life's mission).

We know this is true because each of us has the **power to alter most consequences** by changing the previous action (vibration) that created the result. Namely, if coincidences existed, our very lives would be coincidental.

> *Whoever believes in coincidence, does not believe in God.*

A very interesting concept is derived from this: **The question comes from the same place as the answer**. Or said another way: **A question cannot just appear if at the same time – at the same level within us – there is no answer**.

Because the reason is in the vibration, **the answer must satisfy the vibration from which the question came**. So if we have a deep and heartfelt wish for something, the question, "How can I achieve this?" arose as a **consequence** or as result of the fact that **we have come to a situation where we are able to reach this state** (in thinking about that wish at all).

We have probably noticed this in ourselves. When we change our values, character, habits, our outlook on life also changes. And in this way, we get a **new vibration**, which brings with it **new questions**. We will look for (and find) the answer in the new vibration where our consciousness is now located and exploring. So we could even say that **the question is a sign that we have come to the point where we can find the answer within ourselves**.

The Reason Is Always Within You

Nature, God, the Universe, Boundless Intelligence, Primitive Force, Creative Force, or whatever you call It – that "something" is the only "thing" that is perfect and can therefore act and perform perfectly. The sun rises every day, birds fly south every fall, soil brings forth what you plant, cherish, and nourish each day… **and every day, you always get what your vibration asks for.** If you do not like what you are receiving, the problem is in what you are seeking (or what you are energetically expressing), not what you are getting.

If you do not have as much money as you would like, if you do not communicate with your spouse or enjoy his or her company as much as you used to, if you are ill or depressed – there is always a reason… within you.

And even if you are happy and successful today, this is not a coincidence: At sometime in the past, **you directed your energy in the right direction.** If you did not, but want to change your life for the better, today is another day and another chance to **open your heart and overcome fears by focusing on the right direction and following this path with dedication.**

So ask yourself what you want from your life. Is what you are doing today what you want to do forever? Is your family life everything you hoped it would be? Do you take enough time for you? Do you have time for the hobbies that add spice to your life?

All too often, people discover that **they are doing exactly the opposite of what they should be doing to get what they want.** For example, maybe you want to become a pilot but are studying to be a cook. Perhaps you want to spend the winter in Australia but are doing nothing to earn the funds required and to be able to take the month off from your current occupation.

Everything you need to know is in front of you. It is only by changing your initial action that you permanently alter the consequences. Every action is tied to its inevitable outcome, and for every cause there is a particular effect – a unique result!

Again, in these areas one must pay attention to the (Sub)Law of Life's Mission. If our actions are in harmony with it, we **can change almost everything imaginable… at least as long as the Law supports our actions.**

On the other hand, it is true that we will be **irrepressibly attracted** to things that support this Law, as we have already mentioned. And so it cannot happen, for example, that we would have a very strong desire to do something, which would later turn out to be a waste of time.

(This is always true when the desire **comes from the heart**; it is not true, however, if we have taken on someone else's wishes, which our own life's mission does not support.)

And so it happens that we are irresistibly driven into something, including things in which we are intended **to not succeed** so that we can **attain priceless experience**, which will either cause us to harmonize with these energies, or will benefit us in the further achievement of goals. For instance, if someone cheats us, we will be careful next time.

On the other hand, maybe we need the experience of being cheated for our karmic growth. Well, maybe not the experience itself (as punishment), but as **energy of the vibration** that will **help us learn to accept those kinds of energies. After this experience is concluded, wisdom and power** (that overcame the experience) **remain**, so we can use them in our lives in the future.

Every situation shows the Universe's mercy, which helps us on our path.

Here is a story about a situation that happened a few years ago. It summarizes the basic points regarding the cause and effect relationship.

At the last New Year's party, we sat around our table talking. A common looking man approached and addressed us pleasantly. Friends said he was the general manager in a company, a tourist agency, that organized meetings, including the one we were having, and that their meetings **always attracted more people than the competitor's**.

The success of his company was admirable, and I heard that it was not uncommon for them to have **2,500 people attend any one of their events**, while others try really hard to gather twenty or thirty people. I asked how he achieved such a high turnout.

What he told me was even more phenomenal. **This man was an economist by profession and had only been in tourism for just over a year.** His employees also lacked specific experience in the field and yet something was setting them apart from the rest.

He simply said, "We take care of our clients' customers and employees as if they were **our own children**... and **we also know how to show our** customers that we care for them." That was the crucial energy that led him to his incredible success.

It is not about an opportunity, starting capital, connections, or acquaintances. It is about people and it is about working with people. Once they discovered that this was what they needed to succeed, **they did whatever it took to give the very best to people – their customers** – and their achievements speak for themselves.

When observing all of this from the sidelines – without any background information – we often think that someone is **just intended to be happy**. In essence, it is the relationship between cause and effect. People that are satisfied (within) are those who **listen and follow their intuition and heart, greeting changes** rather than **resisting growth**.

Thomas Keller said, **"The areas in which you aren't successful, happy, or satisfied are areas where you do not listen to your intuition and heart."**

So we are – again – back at the beginning: **Open your heart and allow it to touch you**. By doing so you will recognize your true self, your true wishes, and your heart's desires; and you will also get a blueprint – or a roadmap – for achieving them.

If you have doubts, or you lack the motivation, here is another word of caution that might help. Your mission right now is to **absorb new information** as much as you can, and through it achieve an **understanding** of what is truly valid. **Everything you read must feel true and not like just some distant theory.** Later, you will see that belief is a necessary condition for success. All the people who have ever succeeded, in any area, have at least one thing in common – the energies of **faith, trust, and hope**.

Often like attracts like.

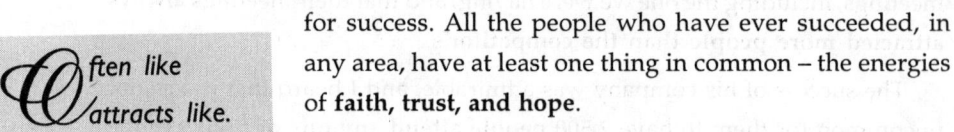

So if you do not feel these energies, you have to evoke them before undertaking any other activity.

7. Birds of the Same Feather Flock Together

Who called you when you were old enough to have your first phone? People like you called your friends. Now that you are older, it is still the same in life. **We love to associate with people who think like us because we understand them better. They also understand us better** and **seem**

more intelligent to us. If you do not like someone, you will not want to be around him or her.

Often like attracts like.

We can put it this way: **We are usually attracted to some thing(s), which we believe will make us happy,** or we are attracted to thing(s) that **we already have, but would like to have more of.**

So if we believe that something makes us happy and is good for us, we are attracted to people, things, and situations that **express this energy**.

On the other side, if we believe that we are **missing** something, we usually choose things, people, and situations that **fulfill this gap**. In this case, we oftentimes choose people who think **differently** than we do.

If this is so, we are searching for happiness **outside of ourselves** (the alternative is to awaken the energies we want to experience within us).

When we take that kind of approach to our lives – searching in others what we lack – we create a **codependent relationship** based on **attachment and the conditioning of happiness.** We need that person, activity, or thing that brings us happiness. This relationship cannot be based on Love – which is unconditional – because we will **use** this person, activity, or thing to **satisfy our need.** This is not Love.

This is the foundation of the concept of polarity (duality), which we have already mentioned. If we want to be happy in this relationship, this outside energy – a person – will have to **react to our actions exactly as we expect.** Or if we talk about things or activities, they will have to **satisfy our need** exactly the way we imagined.

That is the only way we will be happy. If this does not happen, we will be disappointed.

Energetic Attraction

On the other hand, if we look at the attraction between vibrations, we discover that we will **only attract people that our energy** – or vibration – **attracts**, and vice versa. This can also mean that in certain situations, opposites attract because **one extreme is on the same vibration as its opposite.** For instance, we have mentioned how the vibration of heroism is very close to the vibration of exaggerated carefulness.

The Millionaire Mindset

The purpose of all these attractions – as in all other important things – is in the **soul's growth**. And so people who are attracted to each other are divided into **three groups** depending on the intention or experience, which they are supposed to share with each other:

a) **Teachers** : You will **learn** from them.
b) **Students** : You will **teach** them.
c) **Mirrors** : People who will reflect you and **show you your true nature** and the hidden habits you either do not want to see or are not currently able to see.

How do you know if the person next to you is your student, teacher, or mirror? **If he or she can put you out of (energetic) balance, he or she is definitely a teacher or a mirror.** If you can stay calm – in the same vibration you were in before the interaction, no matter what this person does – you are a **teacher** or maybe a **mirror** (if he or she also stays in balance) to him or her.

Every person brings us a lesson we can learn from, which will expand our awareness and contribute more to our lives and also the lives of others… even if this person or lesson does not fit our expectations.

So there is always a purpose, a reason you attract someone or something to you. **If you can recognize the purpose and accept the whole situation, you will rise above the circumstances, graduate, and move on to another level.**

If we do not see and embrace this lesson, we will usually deny it or even fight against it.

The more we deny our involvement in an event, the further away we turn from the gift, which the lesson brings. The extreme step is to leave, leaving **unfinished energy** behind. In this way, we leave a lot of energy in the past and the more regularly our thoughts escape to where we feel we do not have closure. One of the consequences will also be the **drop in our energy level**, which will make us feel tired, uninspired, stuck in the present situation, and so on.

This vibration, carrying "unfinished business" within, will also **strive for closure**, which can happen only by **completing a situation similar to the one we left**, but with a **different response**.

So either with the same or similar people, a new situation or **similar event**, which will give us a new opportunity to finish the energy, is provided for us. This can either take time or happen very quickly.

And if we do not deal with this repeated lesson so that we lift energy into the heart, we will be **forced to repeat the situation again.**

We have already mentioned what will happen when we deal with situations in that way. If we respond to similar situations (lessons) the same way we did the first time around, this response **can become a habit**, and we will respond to the energy unconsciously or automatically... and it will therefore become even **harder for us to disconnect from it**.

How do we know when we have "passed the test" and can move forward?

We will explain this with an example that involves an experience with someone close to us, with whom we have been through hard times that later calmed down.

And now we want to know if we have harmonized energies with that person. Here is a simple, but effective mental procedure that will give us the answer in seconds.

First, remember **what kind of energy brought you together before you became involved.** Most often it was a very **uplifting energy**, full of **joyful expectations**; otherwise, you would not have continued to build the relationship.

We have finished the lesson with some person if, whenever we think about that person, we are overcome with the same (joyful) energy or high vibration – perhaps even higher – as at the beginning of the relationship.

People who can leave the past behind and move beyond the desire for revenge, come to such a state in themselves and get through experiences very quickly. On the other hand, people who **strive for revenge** leave a lot of energies in these unfinished situations and – because they do not live in the present moment – usually have all kinds of problems in life.

The Connection Between People Occurs on the Basis of Resonance

We have mentioned a couple of times that when we direct the consciousness into one particular vibration and successfully maintain it there, **we are**

proceeding from it and connecting to others on the basis of this vibration. This vibration, for example joy, is then noticed by others and connects to other people's joyful vibration, just as **anger that occurs in someone connects with someone else's vibration of anger.**

This is based on the Law of Resonance. Similar vibrations resonate with each other and so connect and **become stronger.** For instance, if two people in high spirits meet, they will both leave in **even better spirits.** Also, if two people who are generally disappointed with life meet, complain about life, and list all their problems, in the end both will be even more convinced that life is hard. **Resonance represents the method to come to (more similar) energy.**

That energy could be of a high vibration (happiness, peace...) or low vibration (anger, fear, desperation...). In both cases, **if we can awaken the energy and allow ourselves to be occupied with it, this energy will multiply.**

We have also explained how **you can never really feel another person.** All that we perceive in a relationship with someone else is **what we are feeling and expressing.** Keller stated this very nicely, "I experience what I express." So we do not experience what, for example, our partner expresses, but what we choose to put out. It is true that our partner, for example, **establishes the environment** for our expression and even **presses certain buttons in us,** but everything that follows is **our choice and decision.**

That means if someone else is angry with you, you can only feel this anger if you **allow yourself to lower your consciousness to this vibration** and therefore **make it possible to resonate with the energy (of anger) that comes to you.**

How can we be sure about that?

Consider the example of a neighbor, who always complains about how difficult life is. Over and over again, this wears you down.

Imagine now that one day you **win the grand prize in the lottery.** That means that you are financially stable for the rest of your life, and most of the problems that troubled you up until now simply disappear. This revelation makes you incredibly happy. At the very moment when you find out about your winnings, the same neighbor appears at your door with the same sad story. Would you – like yesterday – fall into a bad mood when he began to gripe?

Probably not... because you would have your **consciousness directed somewhere else**: toward the fulfillment of dreams. You would be thinking about the extended vacation you always wished you could afford, trips around the world, a new house, etc. You **would not allow your neighbor's energy to even reach you** and so drag you into resonance with his (lower vibration) energy.

In this way, you can be certain that **you never felt your neighbor, but only your own energy.** Your neighbor radiated a certain vibration and, through resonance, triggered the same energy in you – when you allowed it.

So even when we are angry with someone because they disappoint us, it is about us. **We allowed this person to influence our expectations.**

For instance, we expected something, which did not happen, from this person. The consequence is that we notice that outcome, compare it with our expectations, and figure that we were cheated. This is the trigger – or the **permission** we give ourselves – for **lowering our vibration**, which drops into anger, sadness, despair, and so on. Now we direct this energy towards this person... and if we cannot control ourselves, we may even express it towards **whoever meets us** or we suppress it (but we certainly feel it).

Here we can see that anger did not come to us from that person, but was awakened within us as a consequence or **reaction to expectations**: Because this person did not act according to our plans, we **chose to react with anger**.

This last sentence is very important. **We ourselves chose anger to be our reaction.** The reaction could have been something completely different, for example, **sympathy, understanding,** and so on. (But this reaction cannot just happen overnight. As long as we expect something, **our reaction to unfulfilled expectations will, most often be, an unpleasant emotion.**)

And so it follows that **everything we feel when we think about someone else is basically our energy, which arose as a reaction to a certain thought.**

It could also be a pattern that we unconsciously use. For example, whenever we think of a certain person, our hairs always stand on end... although this person has not done anything recently; we are just accustomed to reacting this way!

You will have taken a big step in life, when you know how to do two things:

- **Bring closure to every energy we put in motion**; that means not allowing things – especially in relationships with others – to remain unfinished in the sense: You help friends build a house and when they ask how much they owe you, you say, "We'll settle it eventually…"

- Choose one of the responses (either to resonate with a person or situation… or to remain in a state of integrity) **after considering intuition, the realization of your own life's mission, and the wishes of the heart and soul**. That means you will not allow yourself to be pulled in when this energy knocks you out of balance. Jesus described it in this way, **"Do not give what is holy to dogs, and do not throw your pearls before swine, or they will trample them under their feet and turn and tear you to pieces."** (Matthew 7: 6) Or as in Thomas' Gospel, **"'What is the evidence of your Father in you?' say to them, 'It is motion and rest.'"** (*The Gospel of Thomas*, saying 50)

How to Make People Like Us

So if **we want to make a friend, we must first also be friendly**. If we want love, we must be prepared to **give** it. If we want to be successful, we must act as though **we have already succeeded**. That means we have to **move our consciousness into that vibration and proceed from it**.

That will result – among other things – **in our socializing with people who are successful** because we will suddenly understand them and find them interesting. It might happen that we may have never noticed these people until now, although they had been there the whole time; before they may have seemed strange, preoccupied, withdrawn.

But now they think like we do, and we will soon find common interests. Therefore, it is necessary to proceed from that common vibration and look for resonance with these people.

If we want to truly resonate with them, we will find a way if we ask ourselves, **"If I were in his or her place, what would someone have to do to gain my attention or seem pleasant to me?"** Obviously, we cannot expect approval and friendship from people if we speak and think badly of them. Not only does what goes around comes around, but until we develop a genuine interest and compassion for our fellowman, our disinclination will be seen and felt in our tone, voice, and behavior, which is a **visible expression of the vibration we are in.**

If we follow these simple principles and look (and find) only the good in all things, people will want to be in our company and will consider us pleasant.

But we have to be careful. If we **don't everything from the heart** and for the right reasons, we will encounter **two problems**:

> *If we want to make a friend, we must first also be friendly.*

- We will not actually feel it, but will only **pretend to be in that high vibration** in order to make a good impression.
- Our energy of accepting people will change into **idolatry, worship, and adoration.**

We have already touched on the topic in regards to the first point: What we really feel within – our vibration – is more important than what we show outwardly. The energy we experience shapes into a clear form, which will, when there is enough of it, begin **shaping our character**. The irony in this is that when we are pretending in front of others, we believe that we are doing ourselves a big favor while the **exact opposite** is actually true.

The second point – adoration – also comes from **denying our true selves** and directing energy into others.

This strong emotion, which praises someone else, is often an **expression of a shortage of self-love and a lack of clear identity**. It is also **surrendering your own energy into someone else's hands** because you obviously **trust that person more than yourself.**

Idolatry comes from the **comparison of** your **talents, character, career, material wealth, etc.**, with someone else's, and the discovery that this person has something that you do not have, but which you respect and appreciate. This is fine as long as you can say **something similar about yourself** at the same time. But if you have these strong feelings only for others – your idols and people you respect – it is the **denial of yourself.** You are obviously at the first level (or at the first phase), and the next step forward has to be standing up for yourself.

It is necessary to realize that a successful person is someone who knows **how to honor and respect life and accept it as it is.** In this way, at every step and in every situation, he or she can find something beautiful, and in so doing, finds contentedness. It does not matter if it is a farmer who works the land, a successful businessperson, student, retiree, or ordinary worker. **What is important is the energy – the level of vibration – from which he or she experiences his or her world.**

Everyone could admire someone else, but no one has everything he or she wants. But as long as we compare ourselves to others, which is only a mind game, **we will never come to the solution**. It is necessary to rise above it into **acceptance**, into the heart.

Our State of Consciousness or Vibration is Visible (Noticeable)

So far we have talked a lot about consciousness and vibration. Let us examine this further.

We have found that our vibration is based on the energy of our **thoughts, emotions, perceptions, words, and expressions (activities)**. The way we think, what we hold in our minds, clearly shines through in our self-image and the resulting performance of actions based on the picture of the person **we think we are**. The part of our personality that manifests externally is, in fact, a mirror reflection of our inner feelings, thoughts, reactions, and common attitude towards life. These inner influences affect our nervous system, and ultimately command our physical system – our body – to work in concert with our inner state.

Sometimes we are aware of these internal triggers, which come out of our vibration, and sometimes we are not. For example, we are not usually aware of karmic codes that evolve from our life's mission.

Our vibration is never clearly seen with or through our own eyes, although we wear it like a coat and others notice it easily. **Our habits and other behaviors represent the physical realization of our individual self-image.** Others draw conclusions about who we are based on what they experience of us – our inner/outer self.

Take note that what bothers people about us, actually bothers them about themselves... because they proceed from their vibration and resonate with a similar vibration in us. And, like most of us, they **probably do not accept those personal characteristics as being true.**

Aristotle Onassis, one of the wealthiest and most influential people ever, shared his formula for how to get close to and contact wealthy and successful people. He asserted:

"Always **dress like a millionaire** – this gives you the confidence and advantage at first contact. Live in the **largest and most luxuriant area you can afford**, even if all you can afford is to rent a small apartment – the person you meet in the elevator or on the street could be your springboard to success. When you travel by plane, sit in first-class for the same reason. Even if you are only drinking one glass of wine in an evening, visit luxuriant places and restaurants. **You'll notice that wealth accompanies solitude.**"

PS: We have to keep in mind that this advice was given in the previous century and the vibration of this time is much, much higher than that.

8. What You Send Out Returns to You Like a Boomerang

Do you want to receive everything and give nothing in return? How would you like to be popular everywhere and yet feel hypocritical, malicious, and jealous inside? **It will not work.** (Well, it is possible – more in theory then in reality – if our life's mission so requires, but **do not count on it**.)

You are more familiar with this principle than you realize. Have you ever noticed that people who talk about others behind their backs are also spoken about behind theirs? Likewise, cheaters and thieves attract and surround themselves with others who cheat and steal.

One of my acquaintances from abroad lends money to some of his acquaintances for high interest rates. It is no surprise that he always has trouble collecting these debts – and not just the interest but the principal they owe him, as well!

When people want advice, they seek out a trustworthy person. You are familiar with the saying: "He who lives by the sword, dies by the sword." This plays out in all areas of life – business and personal. Have you noticed that **most wealthy people donate money and contribute in other charitable ways**? This is not just because of the tax write-off.

The reason they do so is because they know they cannot expect something without giving first – **what you give returns to you tenfold**. To earn interest, you must first invest. Said another way, we have to harmonize our relationship with money if we want it to flow freely – both to us and from us.

The Millionaire Mindset

> *Whatever you want to receive, you must first give.*

That way we also show no fear about losing it or not having enough of it.

You may know individuals who often "forget their wallets" on the day it is their turn to buy lunch, or excuse themselves to the restroom after a nice evening out, just before the waiter brings the check. People like this exhibit an astonishing truth – **they are without money all the time**. On the other hand, you may know someone else who does not have much money, but is always willing to pay when it is his or her turn... and probably has enough money to cover his or her expenses.

Do not think you will save money by being tightfisted and stingy; on the contrary, you are doing yourself the worst damage possible. All generosity is eventually rewarded; it is – again – about vibration: **people feel your open heart, and they assume this energy**. But they will not notice they fell into your vibration – they will feel that energy as theirs. The consequence is – if fear does not overcome their vibration – they will **want to give you something back**.

On the other hand, how you feel about that is most important. If you want to buy your boss lunch to impress him or her, for example, you are denying yourself, turning away from your power, and **investing your life energy into your boss**. By doing so, you put him in first place in your life – before yourself.

Do not be disappointed if he or she reacts to that vibration the way you have already taught him or her – by putting himself or herself **before you**. That means he or she will care about himself or herself, but not about you.

Whatever you want to receive, you must first give – whether it is affection, friendship, love, or money. Or, more clearly, **you have to first harmonize with that energy within yourself** if you want others to respond to it. Does this mean no one will ever cheat or take advantage of someone who is honest and generous?

No, there are always likely to be circumstances where someone gets rich by stepping on others or by cheating or using fraudulent methods.

Still, in all of these cases, it is necessary to keep in mind that even here the (Sub)Law of Life's Mission is above everything else. Someone is intended

– or has been chosen – to taste unlimited material wealth; someone else no longer needs this experience, while a third person may never come to the level (vibration), which carries this area within. So the first person may cheat or steal, but material wealth will follow. The second person can get wealthy, but if he or she listens to his or her heart, this will not be necessary for personal growth; this accumulation of money may even turn out to be a waste of time or a step backward.

The third person may also get wealthy – if he or she completely denies himself or herself, closes his or her heart, and solely focuses his or her energy on getting money. (But this life will be **full of pain and suffering**.)

Everything can happen because money is one of the biggest teachers we can have. For instance, someone gets rich and then went bankrupt, no matter how much he or she resists this experience. **If his or her soul will grow the most from this experience, everything needed for this to happen will be brought into his or her life.**

It is not about punishment or inferiority, even less so about inability. If this is the experience, which the soul chooses for this life to experience, it will happen… and the person cannot escape it. If it does not happen sooner, it will happen later. Well, this person can – theoretically – escape it, if he or she is able to harmonize with the energies that this experience brings without the experience itself.

On the other hand, someone else's soul may choose to only enjoy unlimited material wealth in this lifetime. And in this way, everything this person desires will be literally handed to him or her. Maybe this person will, at the end of his or her life, come to the realization that money is not everything; even if you have plenty of money, but nothing else, you are not content, much less joyful.

At any rate – **each and every experience brings us further in the growth of the soul**.

9. Who You Associate With Tells Who You Are

In one minute flat, you can discover just about everything you need to know about other people. From their own lips, they will tell you everything you need to know and will not even be aware they have told you anything important at all. How, you ask?

Ask them what they think is missing from most people they meet and what difficulties they encounter with other people.

They will not realize it, but they will describe their own vibration. (And their motivation for doing so is mostly **tension releasing**: They unburden themselves and feel great relief.)

Who you are – your vibration – is a direct result of and product of what you think, process, and express most of the time. If you feel capable, successful, and self-confident, these attributes give you a head start towards success, providing you with the perfect opportunity to succeed right from the start.

So as you know, **what you see in others always reflects the vibration you are in.**

If you happen to be an optimist, then you are likely in a good mood. You search for such qualities in others. And people who are happy, as well, surround you. If you are a pessimist and blame others for your failures, all of this will reveal itself in your character.

And **you will also see those kinds of "qualities" (that match your lower vibration) all around you** because **you connect with people only through your vibration,** as we have already discovered, or sometimes on special occasions through **higher vibration** – if you go **into your heart** and unconditionally and honestly ask for help.

Once, before I knew these principles to be true, I complained to a friend: "Look! Our business partner is acting strangely towards me – sometimes he's nice, but other times he hardly gives me the time of day. I don't behave that way to others, do I?" My friend thought for a minute and then answered, "Well, that's an interesting question. When you call me and my wife answers, how do you speak to her?"

I did not have to think too long to realize that he was right. Most of the time, **I just ask her to put her husband on the phone.** The behavior, which I found so irritating when I noticed it in someone else, was something that was present in me, as well.

This is how the Principles of the Universe work to show you what you need to work on in your own character.

> Every conversation you have can help you discover another truth about yourself, and everything around you can, in a way, show you your own qualities, illuminate your character, and point you towards discovering your true nature. Even more – if we look at life from an esoteric point of view, we can say that every word we speak is a **conversation with ourselves**: What we express is what we notice and experience.

If you envy someone, maybe you should ask yourself, "Why do I feel this way? What is happening here – do I perhaps want what they have? Why is their success bothering me?"

You will quickly discover that there is **always** a reason. Do you envy someone for having two legs? Of course not, if you yourself also have two legs. Do you envy people who are homeless? Probably not – their lifestyle is not the lifestyle you would want for you or your family.

10. You Are Never Alone... and You Are Loved All the Time

So be grateful for everything that happens in your life and try to find something supportive – or informative – in what has come to be. Napoleon Hill said, "Every adversity carries a seed of equal or greater value." Though it can be hard to find at first, it is there, **every** time.

This is the constructive way of thinking, and it will always lead you to greater awareness and achievement.

Let us explain it by example.

Imagine that your longtime friend decides to move away suddenly. You are overcome with the sadness of losing him or her. What now?

First, if your friend is really your friend, you are not losing him/her; you are just **losing his/her physical presence in your everyday life.**

It is important to begin the process with the correct assessment. Granted, his/her departure will create a physical and emotional hole in your life that was once filled with their presence. However, **what you choose to do with that space makes all the difference**; if you do not fill it with something else that fulfills you, it will consume you with the negativity of sadness and longing.

You could take up a new hobby or earmark that time to begin reading all the books you have been trying to get to for so long. You could start a business or even a new friendship with someone else. Besides, your friend will still be available for phone conversations and visits. Also, wherever he or she moved is a new place you can explore when you visit, maybe even a place where you could find and develop new business and personal connections.

The point is, **while initially filled with sadness, the event of your friend moving away is ultimately an opportunity and that means there is a seed of growth that can come of it.**

One of the greatest gifts that this opportunity brings is the **discovery of something new about yourself.** For example, what purpose did you "use" your friend for? What kind of void was he or she filling in you? What do you now lack without this friend – someone you can release your tension and frustrations on? Someone you can resonate with the way he or she unconditionally supported you, giving you the courage and strength to go on in life?

Here is another similar case. Almost all of us have lost or left a job before. As you have already read from my own experience, it became a great opportunity for me to finally ask myself what I wanted from life and whether I was conducting business as I wanted to.

Here is a secret: **If you lose your job, I am almost sure that the job you lost was not the one to make you happy.** And I am 100% certain that this job was not **the one your soul rejoices in.**

Even if losing your dream job turns out to be for circumstances beyond your control, like a bankruptcy or major downsizing where many good people lose their jobs, there is still a **cause for why this event is happening.** This cause is what you must focus on – **losing your job is just the catalyst to your next experience.**

It is natural to spend some time questioning, "Why did this happen? How will I pay my bills? What will others think of me?"

However, when you ask – while in high vibration – the question, "What shall I do now?" you will link with your heart and intuition and get the answer. **Listen closely to the answer your inner voice gives you.**

Remember, **you are never alone, much less forgotten**... and help and assistance are provided for you in every situation, all the time. You just have to **open your heart and trust.**

Also, make sure that the lens you are interpreting this answer through is a supportive one; that way you can be sure you are processing information with your heart. (If your inner voice does not support the true wishes your intuition brought, you are processing information with a judging mind.)

Another thing, **you have to choose your company very wisely.**

Pessimism steals your life energy, optimism, and joy to live. However, if you look around and find yourself surrounded by pessimists, then there is a reason, and an answer to why they are here… and more importantly, **why you are allowing them to stay. The answer can only come from inside you.** Since like attracts like, **your energy is attracting them** and vise versa.

As we have already said, **every conversation with anybody you have is a monologue with your self**; you just need to learn how to find out what the conversation means and what it is trying to tell you.

At the end, you will find out that at any given moment, **there are really only two of you – God and yourself.** Everything else just **serves you to know yourself** better.

Find Your Own Way

If you could record your daily conversations, you would soon discover what bothers you about yourself and the issues you need to work on. Through the recording, you would immediately notice every time you exaggerated or glorified things to make yourself look superior, for example.

All of us do this to varying degrees. However, by becoming **aware** of it, those moments will show you **what you need to work on to overcome that particular problem.**

Once you overcome your challenge by making a positive change, **a small miracle will happen.** The people in your life, who previously disturbed you with their negativity, will either disappear or they too will transform into supportive and pleasant people and thus, harmonize with you. A situation can change incredibly in just one short moment!

There is an interesting story about a man named Peter. On the outside, he was a man every woman would love to have for a husband – charming, well mannered, loyal, patient, helpful, and devoted. He had a good business, owned a large house and an expensive car. He took skiing vacations and visited the coast every year. He often spent weekends in his mountain cottage or went on short trips.

The Millionaire Mindset

However, Peter had a problem – **no woman would stay with him for long**. More than anything, he longed to have a real family, but his failed relationships stood in his way. He discussed this problem with many people and their response was always, "It wasn't a good match. That woman isn't right for you."

One Saturday evening, he and I were the last to leave at the end of a nightclub party and he took the opportunity to tell me about his problem. Although I listened carefully, I was not able to identify the problem that he was experiencing with his current girlfriend. I proposed that he allow me to spend some time with them and maybe, if I were present when things got tense, I could help him figure out what the trouble was.

I did not have to wait long. Two days later, we were sitting in a restaurant having dinner. His girlfriend had no sooner excused herself to the restroom than he started complaining. "Do you think she is the right person for me? Do we make a good match? Do you think she is just with me for my money? Look, **she ordered the most expensive dish on the menu and she is drinking cocktails she has never tried before**. Does she think I won the lottery, or what?" I did not comment on his remarks, but suggested that I speak with her. I got the opportunity a week later.

She told me that she had never looked at Peter as just a person with money; she just liked him as a man. However, she also said she had never had a wealthy friend before. She admitted she took advantage of the opportunity to experience some new things she could not otherwise afford, but **Peter offered this to her simply because he loved to please her**. I then asked her about earlier disagreements. She said there had not been any and everything had been going great with them until then.

After that, I met with a former girlfriend of Peter. She was uncomfortable with the idea, but when I explained why I wanted to see her, she agreed to meet me and have a brief discussion over coffee.

She revealed that they had not had any big disagreements. A problem occurred when **he said she did not love him and accused her of just using him to please herself**. To him, his proof was noticing how much nicer her behavior was **when he gave her a present or invited her somewhere special**. The conversation proved what I suspected. I waited for Peter to return from a trip and then asked to meet with him.

After ten minutes, the situation was very clear. **Peter was a person who had a difficult time sharing his wealth and giving his money away.** He had worked hard to earn what he had and had achieved it all on his own. He appreciated and respected that about himself. Paying for someone else to enjoy a lifestyle he had worked so hard to achieve made him uneasy. It bothered him that people did not return his favors. **He cited every acquaintance and business partner who had allowed him to buy drinks, but had never reciprocated.** He also remembered every penny he had loaned to friends because they did not have change at the time and said they would pay him later. In short, Peter was keeping score.

I explained to him how only giving can turn on the green light for receiving. Or, until you give, you cannot expect to receive.

The girlfriends he was also complaining about were not with him to steal his hard-earned money; rather, they enabled him to **open himself to receiving by providing him with an opportunity to be so giving.** He should be grateful for the opportunity to give a small percentage of his wealth so elegantly.

We made a deal; he would write the following sentence on a card and carry it with him always, **"Thank you for the opportunity to give money which enables me to earn even more of it."** He was to read this affirmation several times each day.

This happened a few years ago. Peter did not stay with the woman he was with when we had our chat, but they parted company for different reasons. He has been with the woman he met next. Whenever we meet, he invites me to lunch and thanks me again. He told me the message he keeps in his wallet enabled him to truly, and without burden, begin to enjoy his life. Oh, and something else – he almost doubled his monthly earnings.

Only by solving the root of the problems, which are the reasons for all the events in your life, can you live happily. However, **you have to realize this yourself.** That does not mean you have to realize it by yourself, but the change has to begin within you.

Everyone has to find his or her own way. Others can provide signals, like the beacon on a lighthouse that guides ships home from sea – but it is you who must recognize the signs and admit to yourself some uncomfortable truths about you. Your decisions always have to be the outcome of self-discovery.

For the same reason, if someone you know does not recognize the obvious, which you clearly see, your persuasion will not help.

As long as you try to follow the path of another person, you cannot fulfill your own happiness. You must be true to yourself to fulfill your own personal legend as Paulo Coelho reminds us in his book *The Alchemist*. Once you identify your goals and choose to find your happiness, all the Universe conspires in helping you achieve it.

The following sentence will aid you in outlining your goals in life or in discovering your greatest desires:

"Achieve what you want... by being who you really are... and by having what you already have."

To finish this chapter, let us look at how to end your day today and how you should end every day for the rest of your life.

Ending Your Day

Every evening, before falling asleep, **look back on the events of the day**.

First, begin with two questions:

"What did I experience that was beautiful?"

"What did I learn that was new?"

Memorize experiences that could help you in the future, even keep a **"Diary of Experiences"** to use as a reference for situations in the future.

Second, think of your plans for tomorrow. **What will you do to make the best use of your time and energy so that you will spend a day with yourself and others in the highest vibration possible?**

Finally, **give thanks for everything given to you.** Fall asleep in contentedness, not only for the beautiful gift you experienced that day, but also in the joy of anticipation for the new tomorrow that awaits you – wonderful and unforgettable.

These are the principles that mark all of our lives, yours and mine. It is not enough to know them; **you have to make them work for you**. To succeed in this task, you need to know a few more details. Gradually, you will learn them all and at the same time you will learn to creatively use the powers you have hidden inside and may not even be aware of.

For starters, we will a look at how your mind reacts when you include it in each thought or task. This recognition is important if you want to discover and live your dream.

But before that, follow-up with the workshop below and bring these ideas into your life!

The Plan for Achieving Wealth, Success and Happiness

1. Consciously **follow your thoughts for one day**. Discover and write down the questions you pose to yourself: those that **give you power** and those that **take it away**; those that fill you with energy and joy or reinforce fear and doubts (mistrust) in yourself.

2. Begin writing a "Diary of Experiences." It should contain the following:
   - **The good events that happened today.**
   - **At least five things that happened today for which you are grateful and why you are grateful for them.**
   - **At least one event that happened today that you wished you had reacted differently to and how you would like to react to that situation in the future.** Be specific because it is likely to occur again in some form. Ask yourself, "What message does this experience bring me?" Write down the answer that comes to you.

   Attention: Do not ask yourself **why something happened.** Sometimes the answer to that question is not obvious or ready to reveal itself to you. Still caught up in moving through it, you are not looking at the event from the soul, but rather still viewing it from the personality. **Just believe – everything that is happening is for your own good.** Thomas Keller says that there is always only one answer to the question "Why?" **"Because God understands... and because God is love."** Therefore, if you simply believe, you do not need an explanation why.

3. The solution for the occurring events and circumstances that drain your power, life energy, and motivation is to ask yourself the question, **"What is the fastest way to get beyond this?"** Then consider the answer that comes from the heart – you will recognize it because it will be supportive, gentle, and compassionate – and move forward.

The Millionaire Mindset

4. When you feel the urge to help someone, ask yourself, **"Did he or she ask me for help?"** If the answer is "No," then you will help him or her best by trusting that he or she can solve the problem on his or her own. However, when someone specifically asks for your help and you notice a positive response in your heart, **respond immediately**.

   Sometimes helping someone or accepting help from someone is a learning experience for both. Maybe this experience is just what you both need to set you free of certain patterns and mindsets that have slowed your personal growth and prevented you from moving forward. **Trust!** By the way – this also goes for helping older people and children. Of course, you take care of children until they can stand on their own feet, but then they must find their own way and **live their own life**. Ask yourself, **"Am I worried about my children** (or parents, or spouse), **or am I caring for them and trusting in their success?"** There is a **difference between worry and care**; it is in the vibration and thus the energy you radiate, and it is **essential**.

5. Here is a technique for raising your self-confidence. Do the following exercise and answer all questions honestly:
   a. Call to mind **all the successful events you have experienced in your life**. Surely there are many things (personal, educational, business), which you are proud of from your birth up to today. Take a moment to relive them now. (Here you can see the power of posing the right question.)
   b. Think about the people you have met in your life since you were a child through school, vacations, business trips, social events, hobbies, intimate life, etc.
   c. Now answer this: Of all the people you remembered in the previous question, **who among them could realize everything you have realized in life – as successfully or more successfully than you have**? Be honest! This is not about self-praising (which is another pattern given to us: You should not think of yourself as bragging), it is about recognition.
   d. Did your answers surprise you? **Write them all down so** you can go back and read them for encouragement whenever necessary.

3. Your Conscious and Subconscious Minds

The human mind is divided into two parts, the **conscious** (objective) mind and the **subconscious** – or unconscious – (subjective) mind.

(Some people divide it into **three parts: conscious mind, subconscious [mind], and super-conscious**. We will unite the subconscious and super-conscious parts into one because people are most familiar with this explanation.)

Conscious Mind: The Objective Part of Your Mind

The conscious mind, better known to you as intelligence or your brain, is the part of your mind that interprets signs from the **five basic senses** (sight, hearing, touch, taste, and smell) and makes decisions based on these interpretations. For instance, when you go to work, it is the conscious mind that tells you what to wear – possibly based on the weather – when to leave, which route, and so on.

You can monitor your conscious mind, if you want to, because if you pay attention, you can notice what you are seeing, thinking, smelling, tasting, and hearing. Because of this, it is important to know that **it is possible to influence the conscious mind** and control it in this way. (You can even change the general direction that your mind is moving in: from **turning outward to inward**. This is – like all choices you make – based on your **decision** and **motivation**.)

Here is an example how quickly we change the decisions of our conscious mind.

You are in a store trying on a new hat and it suits you well, but then your friend comments, "You're not getting that hat, are you? It looks like a bird's nest. What will people think when they see you?" After hearing such a statement, you look in the mirror a few more times and finally decide the hat is a bit too loud for you – and **you decide not to buy it**. Even more – you are grateful to your friend for warning you and saving you from the embarrassing stares and comments from your neighbors, colleagues, and other acquaintances.

As we can see, you changed your decision **instantaneously**.

Whenever you are thinking logically, you are thinking with and connected to your conscious mind. It is about **connecting one thought to another thought**. In this way, you build opinions, beliefs, and personal truths.

The main tasks of the conscious mind then are: perceiving, processing, and saving (the most important) information, which we can recall instantly. Besides this, the mind's job is also to **protect us**. This is good and "not so good" news: Among all valid protections that serve us – like "Watch out for a fast moving car heading toward you" – the mind also **protects us from everything that may not be most suitable for us** (read: from **everything that the mind is not familiar with** – like new experiences).

Desiring to prevent anything unforeseen from happening to us, the mind offers as a solution something **old and verified**, which it **knows from previous experiences**.

The problem arises when we realize that **we do not want to do things in the same way that we have up until now** or when we **want to take a risk**; not to put our lives on the line, but to try a new idea, approach, and so on. This the mind does not like.

Anyway, most people are certain the **conscious mind plays a major role in our lives,** simply because it is the noticeable part of our mind that perceives, makes objective decisions, and holds our tangible memories – what could be more significant than that? (That is also the reason why they trust it so much.)

In reality, the conscious mind takes a backseat to the subconscious mind and thus only plays a surface and far less significant role, despite how it may seem on the outside (as we will soon find out). But if we decide to put our lives into the hands of the conscious mind, it may seem to rule our world.

Relying on Your Intellect Hinders Development

Do you remember the last time you were thinking about a specific problem or about implementing a new idea?

Maybe you were trying to come up with a creative solution to a challenge or had even stopped consciously thinking about the problem... when **suddenly a fantastic solution pops into your mind**. Your first thoughts are: "Great! Unique! I can't wait to get started!" However, after a while, your conscious mind is called on and your intellect kicks into high gear, saying things like, "Hey, hey, take it easy. How will you do this and that? Who will help you implement such a utopian idea? You have never tried anything like this before – **what makes you think you can pull it off**? Besides, do you think you are the first person in the world to come up with this idea? Surely many people have thought the same thing and dropped the idea because it was impossible to make it work. You are really going to look silly trying to do this. No, this isn't for you. Think about the cost, energy, and time involved."

And the great idea fades into the distance.

You abandon a fantastic idea because your intellect convinced you to believe more in the rational solution of the problem than the seeming craziness of the subconscious mind's great idea. Why? Because you believe that **your rational mind is smarter**, of course, and **it could not be wrong**.

If you think this is true, in the next chapters you will find some amazing fact that might surprise you.

Giving Power to Your Intellect Often Means Taking Power Away From Your Creativity

Think about the very first car you bought. Was it not something? It was... **until you tried a different, better one**.

If you brought a scooter to a tribe living far away from civilization, it would seem like the **greatest miracle to them** – until a car pulled into their village. And they would be awestruck by the car until they saw a plane landing in a field nearby.

What is this all about? Often, **you cannot see the facts around you until you disconnect from your current reality, take a step forward, and move on**.

If you do not try new things, then you have nothing with which to compare your current version. Therefore, you cannot see the truth about it. Something is only the best until something better comes along.

You will never know just how great your ideas are until you try to bring them into reality. Who says you cannot realize them? **Do not always believe what your intellect tells you!**

When police officers gather information about the perpetrator of an attack at a crime scene, they ask every eyewitness for their description of the attacker. **The answers are surprisingly different – even opposed – from one person to another.** To make matters worse, a lot of eyewitnesses will claim to be 100% sure that their descriptions are accurate and that they could positively identify the perpetrator if they saw him or her again. They cannot all be right if their descriptions are all different – someone is wrong in this, case and it is because of the way his or her conscious mind records the details of the attacker.

Your intellect is a tool which, used incorrectly, can **hinder your development** because your mind arrives at its conclusions based on what you have succeeded or failed in up to that point and **not based on your potential or future possibilities.**

Fortunately, the sum total of a person and his or her ability to succeed is not limited to just what he or she has done up to that point. It must necessarily include what he or she can achieve, which is where future possibilities and his or her potential enter the picture. I never cease to be amazed by the sheer power of human potential – of a person overcoming all obstacles and surpassing all expectations.

Examples of the Intellect's Errors

You are probably familiar with the story about a baby elephant tied to a pillar with a thin chain. The elephant wants to be free and tries to escape. After enduring much torture, the elephant discovers the **chain is too strong and it cannot break free.**

In a few years, the baby elephant grows up to be a big strong animal, four times its original size. The adult elephant, still chained to the same pillar with the same thin chain, which it could easily break now, does not try to escape because its intellect says, **"The chain is too strong. You cannot break free. Remember the pain you endured trying to escape before."**

The same thing happens to all of us once we have experienced failure – **our intellect reminds us of what happened before and then convinces us that circumstances have not changed and that we will fail again**. The result is either we do not bother trying, like the elephant above, or we try without believing you can succeed. Both results are likely end in failure and once again **the experience of failure is reinforced**, making future attempts to succeed even more difficult.

The whole premise of the mind's argument that we will fail rests on the mistaken belief that **circumstances have not changed, so the result will be the same as before – failure**.

Nothing could be further from the truth. Everything could have changed and while that does not guarantee success, it does not guarantee failure either. If nothing else, you may wind up with another unique experience to learn and grow from.

It is even worse if such thinking is implanted and reinforced by your **surroundings**. People who believe in themselves and do not allow others to place the limits of their beliefs on them, almost always succeed in life. Did you know the bumblebee's ability to fly defies all the laws of aerodynamics? Experts in physics can **prove that a bumblebee cannot fly**. It is a good thing the bumblebee does not know that. Has this discovery stopped the bee from flying? **No, it simply flies.**

If you read the biographies of highly successful people, you discover that **they all began by believing in their own ideas – right from the beginning**. Their friends and family usually thought they were crazy; almost everyone thought they would go bankrupt, but instead, they made a fortune and an unbelievable profit. They believed in themselves and not in the valid "facts" stacked against them.

Henry Ford liked to stress that it is your thoughts that control your success: **"If you believe you are capable or incapable of doing something, you are right in both cases!"**

Everything Begins With a New or Different Way of Thinking

Do you think differently from most people around you?

Good!

Maybe this creates (short-term) problems for you, you have a smaller group of friends, perhaps you associate with different people whose goals and values are similar to your own. **As long as you trust in your heart's desires and do not allow other people's opinions to bother you, everything will be just fine.**

Unfortunately, most people thrive on the failures of others. Instead of acting supportive toward themselves, they spend their time hindering the efforts of others. They do not like others to be better or do better than they do.

They do nothing to encourage or support them and everything to divert and discourage them.

They are the people who **fill the bars at night and blame everyone else for their failures and lot in life.** Afterwards, they go home in a bad mood where their annoyed and unsympathetic wives and families are waiting for them. In the evening, they watch television, which makes them even more depressed with all the bad news and unpleasant coverage, and then the day is over.

Day after day, year after year, it is the same routine... and **life passes them by.**

There are many of these unhappy and always in a bad mood people. Pay attention to the expressions you see on people's faces; **the happy faces are rare.**

These same people are surprised at their solitude. Who do you prefer to spend time with, a fun and contended person or a grumbling, unpleasant, and unsupportive one? Everyone prefers associating with happy people. **Do not allow yourself to fall into a monotonous life enclosed in a circle of common mediocrity.** Adjusting to others around you, instead of following your own mind and heart, harms everybody.

Here is an example. A friend tries to convince you to start a business selling cosmetics door-to-door, like he or she does. You do not have any desire to sell cosmetics, but **you do not tell your friend that because you do not want to offend or reject him or her.** Instead of telling him or her you are not interested, you tell your friend you'll think it over or come up with some other non-definitive excuse like you do not have time, you need more information, you may join later, etc.

Your friend is now in limbo, **living with the hope that you will join him or her in selling cosmetics**. The situation is now awkward for both of you. **Someday, you will have to tell the truth** or suffer to please him or her. Would it not be better to tell him or her what you really feel **at the beginning itself**, when your friend is not yet emotionally attached to the thought of sharing the same kind of business?

What happens when you tell your friend the truth? (Or will you rather choose to say "Yes," walk door-to-door, and **totally deny your true feelings and power?**)

Do Not Be Afraid to Be Different

You chose a different path. You are not satisfied with an average life; you want to create and experience more. You study, read, and attend seminars.

Because you have different ideas, goals, and dreams, you may seem **weird in the eyes of others**. Nevertheless, you would do well to remember: **Everyone, and I mean everyone, who has succeeded in life, began as just such a person to his or her friends and maybe even family.**

So be "weird" and stick to your own ideas, heart, and intuition.

Just think, all great ideas are not obvious and it takes being able to think outside the box to bring them to fruition. If this were not the case, success would be easy and everyone would be wealthy.

Dr. Walter Doyle Staples says that **as long as everyone thinks in the same way, nobody thinks at all**.

Anthony De Mello expresses this thought a little differently. He says that **when we all share the same opinion, something must be very wrong**.

Those who manage to break free of the chains of an average person's daily routine, look at matters from a different perspective, and follow their hearts without fears, will have **tremendous power and success**. Distinction of thought is the motion of development.

There are some people who give them a hard time, trying to push their advice and ideas on these people. These are people who direct their life force energy into others, so they are not occupied with their own lives, but other-people's lives.

Their favorite saying is: "I know this is good for you, which is why I've pushed you so hard."

De Mello has advice for these people: **"Don't try to teach a pig to sing; it wastes your time and it irritates the pig."**

Relying on Others

A biologist shared this story. A group of caterpillars were placed end-to-end, each caterpillar holding the tail of the one before it, forming a great circle. Then biologists placed a pile of food in the center of the circle.

The caterpillars were very hungry, but **none saw the pile of food in the center of the circle**. Instead, each blindly followed the tail before it, looking neither to the left nor to the right. They eventually died of starvation.

A similar situation happens with people. It is called **group mentality**. People follow the crowd because they are fooled into thinking, "This must be right or there wouldn't be so many people doing it."

Step outside the group and you will find others that think in a different way or have access to better information than the group. Group mentality relies on the speculation, "What's right is what most people are doing because they can't all be so stupid." Therefore, they rely on one another and **trust the group more than they trust themselves and their own ideas**.

I am sure you can think of many examples. Here is a common one: If you live in a big city, or have driven through one lately, you are familiar with the tollbooth lines. Driving up, you see three booths with green lights above them. Two of them have at least twenty cars lined up in front of them; the third has only one.

Be honest here – what goes through your mind as you analyze which booth to go to? Most people would think: "The booth with only one car must be a special booth for those who have passes. Surely the rest of these people would not be stupid enough to wait in a long line if another booth were immediately available. I'll wait." You will never find out whether or not this booth was an **ordinary one** because you have decided to **follow the masses and wait**.

The danger lies in the assumption that **someone else has already done the thinking, weighed all available alternatives, and arrived at the best decision for you**. Although this may be true… it is **rarely** the case.

Here is another example demonstrating this point.

A special aquarium with a removable glass partition was designed. Hungry fish were placed on one side of the barrier with their food on the other. Repeated attempts to reach the food resulted in the now starving fish slamming into the glass. Once they stopped trying to get to the food, the glass barrier was removed.

Not one fish tried to reach the food. They would die of starvation while literally swimming in food.

What caused them to act this way? Repeated attempts to reach the food were unsuccessful. Their brain recorded it was impossible and convinced them of this. Their **incapacity to sense a new situation**, and therefore **act differently**, dragged them to passivity and closer to death.

Test Your Mind

In his book, *Think Like a Winner!*, Dr. Staples suggests an interesting test for your conscious mind.

This test assumes you wear a wristwatch, but even if you rely on other timepieces, the clock in your office, or a pocket watch, the end-result will be the same. This test also assumes the timepiece you use has a minute and second hand, but again, you can alter the test to fit any timepiece by adjusting the questions and the results will be similar. So **do not look at your watch now** and let us begin.

Without looking at your watch, answer the following three questions:

- What color is the second hand?
- Are full hours marked with numbers, dots, or Roman numerals?
- Are all hours marked the same or are the hours 3, 6, 9, and 12 marked differently?

These are my findings: Very few people can answer these questions correctly. **Where is your intellect now?** Is it not logical to know your wristwatch... after all, you have looked at it probably ten thousand times or more.

Namely, scientists have proven that people who wear a wristwatch check the time, on average, a **hundred times each day**. Therefore, over the course of the past year, **you have looked at your watch roughly 36,500 times.**

As you can see, **your intellect can fool you, and your mind is fallible.** If you cannot trust your mind to tell you what your watch looks like, **why** would you believe it when it tells you that you cannot succeed in something?

Let us do some more examination.

Two things are important. First, **your mind conducts its evaluations based on the sum total of your experiences and not based on your abilities or your potential,** as we stressed earlier.

Second, the physical Principle of Inertia – closely connected to the Law of Critical Mass – works everywhere. Newton's first law states: An object in motion continues in motion with the same speed and in the same direction unless acted on by an unbalanced force.

Therefore, it is the natural tendency of objects to **keep on doing what they are doing.** Objects resist changes in their state of motion and, in the absence of an unbalanced force, **will maintain this state of motion.** This is the principle of inertia.

There are many examples of it. For instance, when a ship turns its engines off, it continues to move through the water at the same speed and in the same direction – until resistance (in this case the resistance of the water) slows it down and eventually stops it. This is inertia.

Another example: When you run (in a short distance race, for example), you do not stop at the finish line – like you freeze the frame of a movie – because inertia drives you farther until you resist enough to overcome inertia and stop.

We are all subject to inertia. In our lives and in our minds, inertia makes sure the status quo is upheld, that our thoughts and life preserve the current state, whatever that is. When we begin to think in a new and different way, it is difficult at first because **we have to overcome inertia.**

It always takes great power and a great effort to overcome inertia and move in a new and different direction. The good news is, **once you begin to move in a new and better direction, inertia will work in your favor and keep you moving down the path of success** instead of the path of failure!

Now that you know how your intellect can fail you, ask yourself how many times it stopped you from realizing your dreams.

   a. **Which ideas, presented by your intellect, distract and hinder you?**

b. How do you see yourself, thanks to your dubious conscious mind?

c. Are you, like the little elephant, chained with a chain and afraid to start over because of painful experiences from your past?

d. Is it possible that you have the answers right in front of your nose, but you cannot see them because of inaccurate perceptions and complete trust in your intellect?

Subconscious: The Subjective Part of Your Mind

The **subconscious mind** takes up most of your collective mind. Yes, you think with the conscious part, but everything you have ever encountered – every experience, every event, every emotion – is recorded in your subconscious mind; whether you know it, remember it, or not. This part of your mind has four important roles:

1. To **preserve** all thoughts and events.

2. To be **the treasury** of all your ideas, instincts, and flashes of wit, which you cannot access directly through your intellect (thinking).

3. **To care for the processes occurring in the body** that we do not usually control with the mind; for instance, the proper functioning of all organs.

4. To **execute orders**, based on the first two roles, received from the conscious mind. For example, if the conscious mind says, and sincerely believes, "I'm the best," or "Everybody hates me," the subconscious mind makes all efforts to make it happen.

We can think of part of the subjective mind as a **large data bank** (similar to the memory bank of a computer), where all our thoughts, words, and actions are recorded. Our subconscious stores all of our previous experiences, feelings, desires, fears, events.

This information is later used when we **subconsciously make decisions**. A lot of the subconscious' processes occur **without our awareness**; we usually refer to them as routine, practice, or (learned) experiences.

When something happens subconsciously, we have the feeling that it is **independent of us** or that it **occurs by itself**. It often happens that we suddenly remember things we have long since forgotten. This means that the information **has come from our subconscious**, which never forgets information, but has only stored it deep within.

Specifically defined conditions must be fulfilled for this information to come to the surface. The visible working of the subconscious is only shown **when the conscious mind allows the subconscious to express itself**. Oftentimes, this is when the conscious mind is less active and not giving the subconscious any orders; that is, when the conscious mind is at rest.

Your Subconscious Orchestrates Your Life-Support Automatically

Your subconscious mind supervises everything that you do without having to think about it. It detects your desire to live, breathe, and move, and is in a sense hardwired by habit to do the work of keeping you alive without the supervision of your conscious mind.

> *Your subconscious mind supervises everything that you do without having to think about it.*

For instance, when you are walking, you do not have to tell yourself to lift your right leg, move it forward, set it down... then lift your left leg, move it forward, set it down, etc. Walking is such a complicated activity, requiring the perfect orchestration of your entire body. It has taken decades for robotics engineers to design a robot that can smoothly mimic the gait of a human.

Walking also has to be harmonized with breathing, the flow of blood, circulation, muscle control, balance, and hand movements – all **in perfect synchronization**. And it does not stop there; the subconscious also makes sure all your organs and the systems they are part of, digestion, oxygen maintenance, etc., are working smoothly and continuously. This is where **the higher intelligence of the subconscious over the objective truly shines**.

The Conscious and Subconscious Minds Interact

The subconscious mind is not subject to influence like the conscious mind. In other words, the **subconscious mind does not play a decision-making role**; it only carries out orders received from the conscious mind.

The subconscious **seeks to satisfy** whatever task the conscious mind puts to it. It does not distinguish between right and wrong, good and bad. Like a computer, it does what it is told to do, **bringing about whatever the conscious mind wants**.

It is important to understand how this connection works because everything you do in your life follows this principle.

Here is the explanation.

Your conscious mind sends a signal (order) to the subconscious mind, which, based on all experiences up to that point and any other information it has, carries out the order received. If the subconscious receives opposing signals (orders), it selects and carries out the **most powerful**, deepest one – usually present the longest and repeated the most – which is **accompanied by the strongest feelings or emotions**.

This process can happen immediately or after a few hours, days, or even months.

Let us look at a common example.

Think back about your school days or even the last time you had to learn a new job. After a hard day of learning, training, and feeling good about your accomplishments, your boss or instructor asks you a question and suddenly everything you just learned **vanishes into thin air**.

What is going on when this happens?

The fears and doubts of your conscious mind translate into orders for your subconscious, which produces exactly what your fears and doubts tell it to do.

In that instance right before you heard the question, your conscious mind thought, "What if I don't know the answer? Maybe I won't be able to remember it... Did I study enough? How horrible!"

The subconscious **detects all energies** – what we have learned, but also fear, stress, and panic – and because it does not assign any judgment to the thought, **the strongest one becomes the order that your subconscious mind carries out**. And because momentary fear, stress, or panic is not just a thought, but also an emotionally, strongly-charged thought, it **ranks highly in the subconscious directive**.

Therefore, the moment of your fear or panic, and lack of concentration, is heightened and emotionally charged, and becomes the order the subconscious acts on and expresses. The subconscious interprets this event as, "My boss (conscious mind) says it is afraid and doesn't know, so **I'll make it happen**." And it does.

How do we know this principle works this way? Because **after you sit down for a minute and the pressure to produce the right answer is off, you remember everything you knew**. Therefore, you cannot say the information escaped your memory and mysteriously reappeared after a while: It was there all along, but **only the strongest (momentary) thought wins**.

Said differently, when the pressure of the strong emotion of fear and panic vanishes, **the next strongest information – what you learned – takes its place**... and you suddenly remember.

Behind the Fear and Panic

Oftentimes, this process of stage fright is also related to the **transfer of energy**. If we were in a state of integrity, completely confident and sure of ourselves, **we would not take in outside circumstances any differently than when we, for instance, were in our room studying a day earlier;** we did not feel any pressure then and neither would we now.

It is important that we know that **we ourselves decided and realized this transfer of energy;** no one forced us into it! And we can notice that something interesting is happening in our lives: **As long as we are certain that others appreciate, respect, and unconditionally desire our company, we are confident and talkative**. When we begin to have self-doubts, this energy vanishes and fear appears.

The first step into this trap is to not hold the uplifting energy that serves us inside ourselves (integrity), but to **direct it outwards and look for allies or people who think alike**.

If we find friends who support us, our self-confidence is boosted and we are right. If we do not get the reaction expected from the other side, we remain in fear, which can become even stronger.

Again, it is a process, which is completely dependent on us. **As long as we search for energy outside of ourselves, we may or may not get it; so too, our internal state will be dependent on the support of others.**

If we always proceed from within, **we do not need anyone outside to support us**. In this case, we will **always be strong**.

One of our biggest goals is to **pass into the state of integrity in as many situations as possible**. That way, we will control our energy in perfection and will no longer be dependent on anyone.

This does not mean that we will be rude, reserved, or ignore others, but quite the contrary. **Integrity brings trust within.** A rude or ignorant individual always shows a **lack of trust** in himself, life, and God, which comes from fear.

The less we look for things outside of ourselves (in others), the more we control our own lives.

The Subconscious Confirms What the Conscious Mind Accepts

We know that self-confidence and trust in yourself and your abilities play a crucial role in success, no matter what you are trying to achieve. Now you know why. **The subconscious will make happen whatever you seek (deep inside).** If you are truly committed to achieving something good, your subconscious will deliver it. Likewise, when you doubt, your subconscious acts to stop you from achieving your goals.

Well, there is only one exception to this: **your life's mission. If you come to a point in life when you trigger the karmic code, anything can happen**... regardless of what you believe in that moment. But even here your subconscious, which guided you to this experience, is at work; so we cannot say that what you believed most happened in that particular situation, but we can say that our subconscious brought us to this realization.

But this is a rare situation that seldom happens. More likely, **our conscious decisions and choices lead us to new experiences**. Let us take a look.

You may not be a basketball fan, but you can substitute any activity or project into the following example.

You are playing basketball (or putting together a presentation for a project at work, or anything else; substitute any activity you want). Your friends and colleagues **praise you and tell you how well you play**. You accept their praise **and your subconscious sees this acceptance as the order**: "My boss (conscious mind) says I play basketball well – so be it!" Thus, your thoughts are clear and your moves are determined; your fear, stage fright, and doubts about your ability disappear. The result is an excellent game (or successful presentation, etc.).

What if your subconscious receives different information? Friends tell you, for instance: "What's wrong with you today? Are you ill or having some personal problems that are affecting your game? **Your game is off and you aren't playing well today."**

Your conscious mind now has two possibilities open to it:

1. **Accept the assessment,** doubt your ability to perform well, and thus believe you are not playing (or presenting) well. The subconscious then reacts to this, and you will **experience the inability to perform well.** You now make unreasonable moves and errors, display fear in throwing the ball or delivering a speech, experience stage fright, etc. In short, you have created the expectation of something bad happening; the outcome is a poor performance.

2. **Decline the assessment and fight back with opposite thoughts** like, "What? I'm not at the top of my game today? No way, I am ready to play and win, like always!" In this case, your subconscious does not receive any new or conflicting information. Instead, it reinforces the truth it already held, **that you are a good player,** which makes this fact even stronger and the result is an excellent game (or successful presentation).

This example shows that you – your conscious mind – by virtue of your opportunity to accept or reject incoming information, is usually **the one in control of making the choice.** It is usually up to you whether to consciously confirm or deny what comes through your conscious mind and thus what ultimately affects your future life. (It is a little more complicated when it comes to automatic responses, addictions, and habits, but we will handle these kinds of experiences later on.)

Your Conscious Mind Is the Doorway to the Subconscious

As we see, your conscious mind operates like a **doorkeeper** selecting which thoughts and what information it allows to reside within you to be realized at some point in your life. You hear and read hundreds or thousands of sentences and statements throughout the day, accepting and approving some, while denying and rejecting others: What you perceive as important stays in your conscious mind (read: you remember it), while others, which you decide are unimportant at that particular time, pass by.

Your conscious mind now acts like a **police officer directing your thoughts,** and will likely store that news in your useful information bin, turning on a green light and allowing it to enter the subconscious.

Once thoughts are gathered and allowed to pass, they cannot be wiped out easily.

The Subconscious Mind Is a Garden Where You Reap What You Sow

There is another way to explain the mutual and symbiotic connection between your conscious and subconscious minds.

What grows in the latter (subconscious) comes from the seed the former (conscious mind) plants. **If you plant weeds, you cannot expect beautiful flowers to grow.** What you sow is what you harvest. The fertile soil of your subconscious does not decide if what you are planting is right or wrong, good or bad – it just makes sure the seeds you plant bear fruit. Thoughts fall like rain onto the fertile soil of your subconscious garden.

Like a real garden, if you want it to be beautiful, you have to pull out the weeds and remove the thorns that are likely to grow. Also remember, if you do not pull up the whole root, the weed will grow back.

The Subconscious Records Everything

So it is wise to pay attention to **each thought and feeling**, no matter how innocent it seems at the time because your subconscious records everything. This probably seems like a daunting and overwhelming task, and in the beginning – like everything new – it will feel uncomfortable. Nevertheless, like everything else you learn, diligent attention and practice will quickly create **the habit of supportive thinking** that will serve you the rest of your life.

You should know that when your conscious mind registers a thought, for example, "This is too expensive," it is just like giving the subconscious **an order**. So the subconscious reacts to the information provided: "My boss (conscious mind) says that this is too expensive, which means he is rejecting it – I will make it so he will not get it."

Do not be surprised if this really happens, if you persist in this energy and reach critical mass.

The Subconscious Is Often a Few Steps Ahead

We see how the subconscious stores and, if you give it the opportunity, presents your treasury of ideas. **It is from there that all your dreams, desires,**

and intuitions arise. How many times have you felt like an idea just fell from the sky into your lap? The subconscious, as the seat of your intuition and creativity, produces ideas that present themselves as flashes of wit, are unordered, and **seem coincidental or accidental and not necessarily tied to anything specific.** You know the idea did not come to you consciously – as a consequence of building one thought onto another, so you can be sure your subconscious acted to produce and deliver it.

Unlike the conscious mind, the subconscious does not work based on what you already know, or what you have in your mind right now. Rather, it is a **few steps ahead:** If you analyze subconscious ideas in detail, you will see that there is nothing coincidental or accidental about them – you are simply **receiving answers for questions once put to it.**

The most important difference between the conscious mind and the subconscious is that **the former proceeds from comparison, judgments, and positions,** whereas intuition, for example (as a part of subconscious), functions **unconditionally.** That is why we sometimes say that ideas **from the subconscious come from the heart** because the heart is the most well-known representative of unconditional energies.

How to Maintain High Vibration

If you want only supportive and uplifting events to happen, then **you must not allow unsupportive thoughts that contain hypocrisy, envy, malice, fear, and doubt to slip through the door** of your conscious mind and settle in the recesses of your subconscious.

How you can do that? By **living in a high vibration** that is supportive, and **resonating only with these kinds of surroundings.** Also, look at everything else that does not support your path with **detachment.** Unlike criticism, detachment **does not allow you to be dragged into a lower vibration.**

That way, **you will create a world of happiness inside and spread it outwards.** You will not be affected by energies of lower vibrations.

To maintain this task, you have to be **prepared, determined, and persistent.**

Information from the outside physical world enters the door of your conscious mind via the **five senses and the mind (thoughts).** Since your door is virtually open all the time, you should endeavor to censor all incoming information as much as possible, making sure that what you allow through seats itself in a supportive way. Of course, you cannot always control what presents itself to you, but you can control how you comprehend and record it.

As we have already stressed, you choose what you say, what you read, and what you think about – **so you, yourself, influence what your subconscious records on its tape.** Moreover, **you choose how you explain events to yourself.** Thus, you can see yourself as a victim or as a treasure hunter who lives a life full of adventures and experiences something new every day. You can see an opportunity and challenge in every situation – or a chance to be defeated and burned.

You decide...

Here is a word of caution. You should perform the tasks the way we have already described – being careful about what you resonate with and allow to pass by your conscious mind and into your subconscious – **until you reach a permanent state of integrity** (or the fifth level). Once you are there, **you will affect the outside world,** and not vice versa.

Our Selection of Information Is Based on Resonance

If we go a step further, we can say that essentially the gathering of information is a process of resonance. When we read, hear, or think about something, which is located on our wavelength, resonance is immediately achieved – like with the tuning forks: If we place them next to each other and activate the first, the second will soon begin to resonate with the first and give off a sound.

This is how **many life lessons reach us.** When we vibrate at a specific vibration, only that which **coincides with this vibration** resonates with us and vice versa. So for instance, out of a hundred people we can pick someone who is "the one" in a matter of seconds; in this way, we can feel that **we are on the same wavelength** before we even speak a word to them.

When our vibration, for instance, drops, someone else who is on our new (lower) vibration will seem close.

Programming the Blocks That Affect Your Life

Another way of getting new information into the subconscious is by **creating it on our own** – with the help of our **imagination.** Let us take a look.

The Millionaire Mindset

Here is an example of how parents – with good intentions – unknowingly influence their children's lives in an unsupportive way.

The energy children exhibit as they run around all day long can really try the patience of a parent begging for a moment's peace. Such a parent will often tell his or her child to **quit bothering him or her and find something better to do** or simply tell them to go play somewhere else.

Unfortunately, the message received by the child is quite different from what the parent intended. What the child understands from this kind of repetitive interaction is, **"Whenever I try to show and receive love and affection by getting close to someone I love, I am rejected and told to go away."** Such a child, incapable of expressing or dealing with emotions properly, has little or no self-confidence, diminished self-esteem and, feeling unloved and rejected by others, shows very little – if any – love for himself or herself.

If this occurs often enough and for long enough, it can become **the source of many socialization and relationship obstacles** the child will need to address at some point later in his or her life.

The challenges that stem from such a source are many and varied, ranging from low self-esteem and issues with trusting others, to deep emotional distress and antisocial behavior. You can recognize such a person easily by their **apologetic, guarded, or emotionally absent behavior**.

Cases from the business world are also very interesting: People who do not appreciate themselves, do not succeed in selling their **time or services**. They may have no problem charging for a product, **but it does not seem right to them to charge for their energy**. (You can read more about this and similar problems as well as "enlightened solutions" in the book, *The Enlightened Salesperson*.)

What began as an innocent comment, made repeatedly by a parent in moments of frustration over the course of a childhood, often causes development of the most unpleasant behavior and emotions.

Some parents also implant, unknowingly, something else in their children: the thought that there is a **connection between giving something (up) and getting something in return**. How often did you hear these words growing up: "Behave yourself and you can have some candy," "If you help your mother all weekend, I'll buy you the bike you've been wanting."

Consequently, this instills in us the obligation that **we must give something when we receive something**. In time, we **do not approve of anything we do not have to pay for** or sacrifice something for. An example would be not allowing yourself to ask for a raise in pay, or a bonus at work, without also raising the number of hours you work in a week or adding extra projects to your workload.

It is most unfortunate, but usually those who think they are wishing us well with their warnings, do the **most damage** to our subconscious mind and subsequent lives. Well, their intentions may be good, believing that they are encouraging and motivating us. But in truth, something completely different, of which they are usually totally unaware, is really happening: **They project their worries onto us.**

This is not love, but **fear** because **care always comes from love**, and **worry comes from fear**.

The Strongest Thoughts Are Always Expressed... and This Can Be a Disaster

Quite often, we discover that unpleasant thoughts inhabit our mind regarding experiences that we cannot recall ever happening to us. Consider the following statements:

"You're worthless."

"You won't pass the exam with so little studying."

"If you don't finish school, you'll be pumping gas forever."

"You'll never be rich, so stop dreaming about it."

"Your business will never be successful; when are you going to get a real job?"

"If you don't behave, you won't get what you want."

"Good guys always finish last."

Where did these statements originate?

Probably **someone said them to you or you heard them said to someone else. Because you resonated with them, your subconscious stored them**... and then you let them grow and develop; not necessarily consciously, but **your vibration probably supported them.**

Now they are part of your self-talk and the first thoughts that spring to your mind whenever a similar situation presents itself. (We will deal with these problems in the chapters ahead.)

The Millionaire Mindset

Let us look from a different perspective at how a bad experience stored in your subconscious reflects in your daily life.

When a situation similar to the one stored in your mind occurs, your subconscious **offers the solution it has been programmed by your stored thoughts to give**. Because your subconscious does not differentiate between right and wrong, or supportive and unsupportive, if what you have stored is unpleasant for you, then that solution will manifest itself.

Your subconscious does this by unifying itself with the present state (situation), searching its "files" for all the stored information that it can fit into the current situation, and then applying that information in the form of necessary feelings and mindset to the situation on hand. The result is, unless it has received new information, **your subconscious solves the problem the same way as before.**

This is very efficient and supportive when the situation being presented is walking, playing an instrument, singing a song, etc. Practice certainly does make perfect, and that is exactly what practicing is all about – writing and rewriting the information stored in your mind until it **becomes automatic.**

But there are cases when this does not work in our favor.

How the Subconscious Creates Automatic Programs

Think of a song you like. When hearing it for the first time, you had no idea what the lyrics was, but **you liked the song and wanted to learn it**. This desire was transformed into an order to your subconscious to remember it. Subconscious replied, "No problem, I've learned lyrics several times, I can do it again." With those words, your subconscious received a green light to remember the lyrics of the song. Learning the song, reciting the lyrics was the only incoming and thus prevailing thought.

In the absence of any stronger, competing thought, your subconscious did not oppose and stored the lyrics. Each time you sang the song, you strengthened the information in your mind. After a while, you probably were not even aware of when you could sing the song without thinking. **Now upon hearing only a few notes of the song, your subconscious delivers the lyrics to your conscious mind and you happily sing along with the music.**

Such a chain reaction always happens the same way every time... regardless of whether this experience was pleasant and supportive to us or not.

For example, what if the recorded experience is one of **being bitten by a dog**, maybe even as a child? This painful memory would be stored in the subconscious. How would this person feel and behave when he or she saw a dog the next time?

Most assuredly, they would be fearful and maybe even cross the street and walk on the opposite side. Well, this also depends on how bad their experience of being bitten was – they might not even be able to tell the difference between an over-excited puppy and a dog that might be dangerous, especially if they have no pleasant experiences with dogs recorded.

If the biting experience happened in his or her youth and if it was dramatic, it is probably well ingrained in the subconscious and **strongly associated with a fear of dogs in general**. However, the experience would not even have had to happen to him or her directly to be recorded in the mind; maybe a close friend was attacked and bitten by a dog or they watched the experience on television. It is even possible that someone told them about it, and they have no firsthand experience of the attack at all.

"Those being bitten by a snake are afraid of a twisted rope," says an anonymous quote. And the truth is, **the more you repeat this process of being afraid of the dog** (in your mind or in reality), **the stronger and stronger this pattern becomes in your subconscious and the more energy will be required to break or replace it.**

Here is my personal example of how a similar chain of events can occur when presented with a particular challenge for which you have no similar direct experiences recorded.

I remember taking my driver's exam as an adult. I was a real novice, an absolute beginner to the world of moving vehicles. At the end of one of my early lessons, the instructor told me: "Do you see that boy driving? Well, **you will never be as good as he is behind the wheel.**" Thank goodness I was not a novice to the ways of subconscious programming. I knew right away that allowing a thought as powerful as that into my subconscious would influence my driving capabilities for the rest of my life.

What did I do? In my mind, I edited the instructor's words immediately so they would not be the prevailing thought regarding my driving abilities. Then, of course, **I found a new instructor**.

There is a real danger in believing the "experts" when it comes to assessing your abilities. **Just because a person is good at something does not mean he or she has an objective idea of your capabilities or potential to achieve something.**

Deeply Rooted Mind Programs

Let us take one smaller test that shows how difficult it is to overcome a certain belief once it has taken root in your mind.

Remember the Pink Panther cartoon character? Sure you do! Picture him very vividly; the way he walks with a confident and sophisticated swagger, almost strutting with his tail trailing disobediently behind him – stopping to scratch his head and tap his right foot. He played a saxophone and typically wore some crazy pair of mod sunglasses. Can you hum or whistle the theme song? They played it with a flute and it went something like - Da dum, da dum – da dum, da dum, da dum – dah da da daaaaaaa – da dah da da dum.

Now **stop thinking about him. Forget everything** you just remembered and do not allow yourself to think about him at all – **think of anything and everything except the Pink Panther.**

Do it now.

Were you successful?

At best, you have had a hard time trying, and **the more you consciously focused on not thinking about it, the harder it was to succeed in doing so.**

It always works this way. For example, when you say to yourself, **"I won't think about failure,"** (I can think about everything else but failure) images of defeat flash, even if only for fleeting moments, in your mind. As they do, you become more and more anxious about not being able to stop them from flashing in your mind. Now you are more involved with the act of blocking these images than in finding a real solution.

Why is that? Because you subconsciously know that with **every rebirth of this vibration and these emotions** – by letting them pop into your mind

– and by **repetition of these feelings of failure,** you just **revive them and make them stronger.**

What is the successful solution for the Pink Panther test? **Focus on something else,** for instance Mickey Mouse! If you can hold his picture in your mind for ten minutes, you will not "see" the Pink Panther at all.

You can **overcome worries this way, as well.** Your mind can only hold one thought at a time – or your consciousness can be only on one vibration at a time – so **focus on what you want rather than on what you do not want.**

How the Subconscious Helps to Sell

Are you beginning to see how your subconscious retains the thoughts and ideas you believe in most, no matter where they originated… without regard to whether or not they are true… or even whether or not they are supportive to us?

This is also the essence of successful advertising. The media repeatedly bombards the public with messages like, "If you want to be a good housewife and appear perfect in other people's eyes, use washing powder X!" If your conscious mind turns on a green light for your subconscious to record an experience (or at last does not reject it), the process for turning that experience into a belief begins. Once ingrained, the subconscious responds the only possible way – the next time you are in a store shopping for detergent and see product X, you subconsciously choose it.

This happens because upon seeing X, your subconscious brings forth all the feelings and emotions it has recorded about X. The bombardment of information from the media, along with the emotions of joy, wish, desire, etc. that it evokes, brings about the information that results in your purchasing product X.

After the purchase has been made, how does the conscious mind react? **It justifies the purchase.** For instance, maybe the first thought is, "I don't have any money, and I really shouldn't have purchased X," but because the desire to have X is stronger, the conscious mind is forced to confirm it as a good purchase.

"It has to be good. It was only a few dollars more – I can save elsewhere." Or "Using X detergent means I don't have to buy additional stain-removing products; that in itself will save energy, time, and money, and that compensates for the extra dollars spent."

You (Mostly) Make Your Own Decisions

"Don't judge destiny, judge **yourself**," says Emile Coue, a pioneer in the science of using the power of the subconscious.

But let us not forget that **we are talking about things for which we have the clear chance to decide** or choose. Oftentimes, it seems that **we carry some things within and that we cannot just change them**. These are:

- Our **automatic programs**, which change into patterns with time.
- The **code** we carry within, which expresses our life's mission.

In both cases, we feel an **unstoppable desire** for some specific activity, although we do not know where it comes from or where that action will lead us.

The Tremendous Power of the Subconscious Mind

In the next few chapters, we will see numerous examples that will explain how the subconscious dominates over the conscious mind – if we let it.

The Conflict Between Intellect and Imagination

If you had to **choose between intellect and imagination**, which would you say is more important in influencing how you act? If you had to give one of them up, which would you keep? Without careful thought, most people would choose their intellect. Surely, that must be more important, right? Well...

Your imagination is the strongest creative force you have. It is always working for you in both supportive and unsupportive senses.

Imagination is also the real expression of the Creator, as the Creator also spends **all time creating and expressing**. Children spend a vast amount of time in their imaginary worlds. Sometimes these seem more real to them than the "real" (material) world. As long as they live in this world of imagination, which they shape by their own rules, they are usually **happy and healthy**.

Your imagination is the strongest creative force you have.

We have already talked a lot about vibration and how the stronger emotions affect it. **When we live in the imaginary world, we can create very strong feelings and emotions,** which then influence our vibration. **Imagination is a miracle worker, which is always available to us.** We can always imagine a miracle, pretend that we are king of the world, and so on. And every one of these feelings will be noted in our consciousness and expressed – if they appear often and are strong enough – through **our vibration.**

And so the imagination can become the "intensive care unit" to which we turn when we want **to create a certain vibration.** Because the subconscious works so that it does not judge or **differentiate between the truth and imagination,** but only adopts the strongest feelings, regardless of where they come from, this will work for us **as long as we truly believe in it.**

We can use the imagination to our benefit in **meditation and visualization** (you "see" in full detail the successful resolution of a present challenge, problem, or situation), as we will discover later. Actually, we all know how to use our imaginations, but often in an unsupportive sense – **when we are worried.** That is when **we imagine everything bad that could happen.** Just as this energy influences our vibration, it influences also in the opposite way – supportively.

Imagination is very strong energy… probably much stronger than we realize and thus has a **tremendous influence over us.** The following examples will clearly show this.

How the Subconscious Creates Our Physical Reality

Dr. Walter Doyle Staples, in his book, *Think Like a Winner!*, describes an interesting experiment about mind over matter (or influencing the material world with thoughts).

A group of high school students is divided into three teams for a test that would run over a twenty-day period.

With approximately the same knowledge and experience-base in basketball, all students are asked to make as many baskets as possible from the penalty line.

The first day, the number of successful free shots recorded measures a group's success. Afterwards, each group is given the following instructions:

The first group is to **practice free shots for twenty-minute intervals** for the next twenty days.

The second group **cannot practice at all**.

The third group is instructed to spend **twenty minutes every day imagining taking shots and visualizing in their mind scoring baskets every time**.

At the end of the twentieth day, the evaluation is repeated.

The first group **improves their results by 24%**.

The second group **does not show any improvement** and finishes the evaluation with an average score.

The third group improves their results by 23%.

So this is additional proof that **it does not matter if something really happens or if you only imagine it – your subconscious will listen to you and record it as an event, as though it had actually happened.**

So whatever the subconscious believes will influence your way of thinking, processing, and performing. The only reason a physical event may impact the subconscious harder is simply because it is recorded in "3-D," meaning you see, hear, taste, smell, see, and feel the physical event. However, with practice, **your thought events can have just as much impact on your subconscious as an actual event does**.

We have also already discovered that this is sometimes supportive for us and sometimes not. You can use this process to **build an image of success in your mind, even if you have not actually experienced it yet**. Then, when your subconscious perceives a similar situation in your life, it will draw on this imagined experience – just as if it were real – and manifest a successful solution that coincides with what it has been ordered to bring about. Here **visualization** is extremely effective when you have to implant new thoughts.

Using a sales model, here is how it works. Keep in mind that **the more detailed your visualization is, the stronger it is embedded in your subconscious**. If you have a specific situation, visualize a specific image that fits that situation. For example, if you simply want to be a better salesperson, then your visualization should be general in terms of context, but specific regarding technique and content.

For example, you are a real estate agent and you want to sell more houses.

Imagine your prospect admiring the house and saying, "This is exactly what I was looking for, and I am so happy you've found this for my family. The payment arrangements you've laid out fit my budget and are even better than I expected."

Now **you have to feel the elation of making the sale** and the satisfaction of a job well done. You have to **see the joy in your clients' eyes** as they begin to imagine the start of their new life in the house you found for them. You **hear yourself sharing your sales success with others** at the agency and instruct your secretary to schedule the closing appointment and so on.

Visualize the whole process right down to the closing meeting, the signing of the papers, the removal of the "For Sale" sign from the front yard, and especially the feeling you have when you put up the "Sold by (Your Name)" sign in the front lawn for all to see. **As often as you can, allow yourself to experience the complete and successful process of selling a home using this visualization technique.**

Needless to say, the energies of **trust, faith, and hope have to accompany the whole imaginary process**; if you want to influence your subconscious, you (still) have to believe in it.

Imagination is powerful energy. Here are some more real life examples.

Testing the Reality of the Principle That Governs the Conscious and Subconscious Minds

Your friend invites you to lunch. You know she always uses tofu instead of meat, so you choose not to again remind her that you are a vegetarian because **meat and poultry make you sick**. After enjoying yet another of your friend's fabulous dishes, the afternoon passes while you chat and sip coffee in the garden. Just as you are getting ready to leave, you ask your friend for the recipe and when she tells you it called for chicken and she forgot to substitute tofu (Oooops!), **instantly, you become sick.**

What caused the sickness? The meat you ate or the thought, "Chicken makes me sick," which immediately went into your subconscious when you heard what you had just eaten?

Let us see what happened. In the beginning, after dinner your conscious mind said: "My friend is a great cook and I enjoyed the meal very much."

And you felt well. After hearing the news that there was chicken in the dish, your subconscious received the signal, "I just ate chicken, and chicken makes me sick." A dialogue occurred between your conscious and subconscious minds: "When I eat chicken, I always feel sick... so I have no choice – **I have to be sick, because this is my personal truth!"**

The subconscious reacts: "Oh, my boss says he is sick. The boss has to be pleased, so hurry up, make the boss sick!" Moreover, it happened; not because of the chicken, but because of your personal truth. It is obvious: **If chicken were the reason, you would feel sick right after taking a bite**, not later when your friend tells you what you ate... maybe hours after the meal.

Such a flow of conversation is typical for your conscious and subconscious minds' connection.

Here is another case. It comes from Joseph Murphy, an American author famous for his various books especially *The Power of Your Subconscious Mind*. He describes an interesting event that took place on a passenger ship.

Turning randomly to a passenger who looked of average health, the ship's captain said, "Ma'am, you're looking quite pale today. Several of our passengers have been stricken with seasickness, and you look like you're coming down with it, as well. **Perhaps you should return to your cabin and rest because you look a little green to me."**

What followed? Obviously, **seasickness**.

The passenger, new to the sea, believes the expert and allows the signal (order) "I am seasick" to pass by her conscious mind and into her subconscious, which responds – seeks to satisfy what the conscious mind has already told is true – in the only possible way: **It manifests seasickness symptoms, and the passenger becomes ill.**

Similarly, the ship's captain tells an experienced sailor the same thing he told the woman passenger: "You're looking pale today, Sailor. Sure looks like you're getting seasick." The sailor laughs at him and says, "Captain, I've sailed around the world several times and have never been seasick. Thank you for your concern, but **you are mistaken.**" The sailor thinks, "Seasickness? Come on! I'd sooner get frostbite in July!"

What really happened in the last example? **The sailor simply did not allow his mind to accept the assessment that he was seasick.** His doorkeeper did not let the thought of seasickness pass through his conscious mind and into his subconscious where it would compete with and try to replace the previous knowledge and belief stored there that said, "I don't get seasick."

Because he censored this information, even turned it around and reinforced his belief that he did not get seasick, **his subconscious did not receive any new information**. Therefore, it acted on the only information it had, "You have never gotten seasick before, and you are not seasick now, nor are you likely to ever get seasick in the future." Unfortunately, the woman had no such previous knowledge or belief stored – her subconscious did receive new information and acted immediately to bring it about.

How Your Thoughts Control Your Life

This next example is taken from Martin Kojc's book, *The Manual of Life*.

Marden, a psychologist, shares an interesting experience. A man writhing in pain from **swallowing his dental prosthesis** was brought into the hospital. It is probably hard to imagine all the pieces, plates, teeth, and gums of this prosthetic device entering his stomach. The patient had to be in unimaginable pain.

While the doctor was setting the patient up for x-rays, etc., he received a call from a family member at the patient's home – **the dentures were found under the man's bed**.

What happened?

Upon hearing the news, **the man who was in horrible pain just moments before stood up as though nothing were wrong, dressed, and left the hospital, instantly pain free**.

Here is another true story from the same book.

A wealthy young man found out he had an incurable form of tuberculosis that was beyond the scope and reach of medicine. He did not want to spend his final days in sadness and depression, so he decided to **find death by himself**. He began eating forbidden and dangerous food, and took up a few daring sports, among them speed car racing and acrobatic flying. With his heroic way of living, without being scared of losing his life, he set a number of records.

But the death he craved just would not come. After many years of living like this, he discovered that **living is beautiful** and decided he would **no**

The Millionaire Mindset

longer challenge fate. Soon after his decision, he died in a plane crash. The real shock, however, came to his doctor when an autopsy revealed **there was no sign of the illness anymore.**

How the Power of Your Imagination Highly Influences Your Life

This next case is really unbelievable... but only if we are not familiar with the miracle called the unconscious mind.

A worker accidentally trapped himself in the freezer of a truck. The temperature inside a truck freezer is so low that a person trapped inside for any length of time would have no real chance for survival. When they found the worker, it was too late – the victim's core body temperature was affected, and he showed all the symptoms of hypothermia.

A sad story, to be sure, made even sadder by the realization that **the freezer was not turned on.** The temperature inside was actually between 10 and 15 degrees Celsius (50 to 60 degrees Fahrenheit) – certainly **not a temperature that would cause hypothermia and death**! It was the worker's imagination – his conscious mind telling his subconscious what to bring about – that was lethal, not the temperature inside the freezer.

Here is yet another case that Kojc describes in *The Manual of Life*. At a death penalty execution in Cleveland, they were testing the strength of the imagination in comparison to the strength of will and intellect. They told the accused that they would sever a vein in his neck and he would die painlessly as the blood flowed from the wound. They covered his eyes, and made a tiny cut in his neck, which amounted to not more than a scratch. Below him, a container was set and water flowed into it with a steady sound. After a while, the man died.

What caused his death... blood loss or imagination?

This is just one of many such examples showing that **you mostly control what influences you** – via your conscious doorkeeper.

What you think of yourself – your own personal truth – is what matters. Do you trust yourself? Do you follow your feelings or do you allow others to mislead you? What areas are you vulnerable to being misled in?

Your Conscious and Subconscious Minds

Testing the Strength of Your Intellect

The test that follows is perhaps the most convincing evidence of the power of the imagination because you will take part in it. It shows explicitly what really happens in the thought process, and thus demonstrates how imagination is favored over intellect.

Imagine these instructions are being given to you right along with the example and pay attention to your thought process as you follow along.

Place a one-foot wide plank on the floor and walk the length of it.

Is everything OK? How do you feel? Did you fall down? No.

Now lift the plank two feet above the floor and walk the length of it again. Now is everything OK? You did not lose your balance or feel light-headed?

Walk back and forth a few times. Still OK? Excellent.

Now **lift the same plank thirty feet above the floor and walk the length of it again**. I can hear you saying, "No way, I'm not crazy enough to do that!"

So what is going on in your mind right now? Based on your immediate experience, you should be saying: "Piece of cake. I walked the length of it several times when it was two feet off the ground and had no trouble keeping my balance; it's still the same plank, so I can walk the length of it now."

However, is that what is happening in your mind? No...

Your **fear of falling off** is in full swing and your imagination is saying, "Walk the length of this plank thirty feet up in the air? I wouldn't do it if the plank were two feet wider. **What if I fall off?**" By now, your imagination is, through your mind, flashing pictures of you falling off the plank... and because these pictures are the strongest ones, they prevail.

Every day you have to make decisions; you react to them either **intellectually** ("wisely") or **emotionally** – through your imagination. **Your intellect will rarely, if ever, win without the emotional approval of your imagination.**

In other words, your wise intellect often tells you what you should do, while your imagination tells you what you want or do not want to do.

Here is an example that will confirm this theory.

The Millionaire Mindset

> *Doubt destroys hope. So do not doubt...rather believe in yourself.*

If you are shopping for a dress or a new suit, the intellect says, "This one is a good buy; it looks nice, but it isn't too expensive or extravagant. It is made well and will last five years; it is the smartest choice." However, the imagination responds with, "Five years – no way! It won't last half that long. If I want to dress in the latest style, it won't even last two years! It doesn't even look like the one I saw in the last fashion catalog. No, I don't want this one. I don't like it." The chances are good that you will not be buying the suit or dress the intellect tells you to buy; rather, your **imagination will sell the one it wants to your intellect**. Imagination wins again.

The same thing happens in the process of solving problems: **You think about failure and are afraid to take the first step.**

The good thing is that supportive emotions work in the same manner; once you believe you will succeed at something, you **start doing it**, or working towards it with faith, trust, and hope.

So if you can manage to **keep your mind occupied** with thoughts of a higher vibration until you move beyond the doubting stage (critical mass, remember?), your subconscious will bring you closer to the goal. Once you begin to doubt your ability, images of defeat will appear in your mind and affect your concentration, enthusiasm, and energy – the very things you need to succeed – and the result will be a negative realization: You will fail.

Take action instead. Get busy making it happen and engage your energy in bringing about success.

Shakespeare said that **doubt destroys hope. So do not doubt... rather believe in yourself.**

Are you ready now to take action and **try an experiment on yourself**?

Make a pendulum by tying a weighted object to a string or dangling a pendant suspended from a necklace. Holding the string/necklace between your fingers, lean on the table with your elbow, allowing the pendulum to hang with enough room to swing freely. Calm your arm. You will find that the pendant or weighted object is standing still, possibly inclined slightly by your heartbeat. Once you have achieved calmness, "tell" the pendant, with your mind, to swing in whatever direction you have chosen, back and forth, side to side, around in a circle, etc.

It will start to move in exactly the route you have choosen.

Yes, **just like you imagined**. If you clear your mind and really concentrate on telling the pendant to stand still, it will stop moving. What causes the pendulum to swing and stand still? You are holding your arm in the same calm position throughout the experiment, so how can the pendulum move independently of your arm?

The experiment is very important because until now we have only spoken of the mind controlling internal events of the body, like organ function, etc. Here, the mind has transcended the confines of the body – **your thoughts can influence inanimate objects and events outside yourself**.

Thought: The Energy in Its Purest Form

More we discover that **our thoughts are very important – they can directly influence our results**. Besides that, they represent the connection to the surroundings, to both the living and non-living worlds around us.

If we take a closer look at the micro-world of molecules that are the building blocks of all matter, we will find out that **nothing that exists is static**. On the contrary – everything changes and moves from one form of energy to another in a never-ending cycle of birth-growth-death-decay-rebirth. What we see as solid material is mostly empty space where billions of molecules are in constant motion!

Thought is one form of energy, a very sensitive one. How can we prove this is true?

As we stressed before, have you ever noticed how quickly you can dislike someone you have met just seconds ago? Or how fast someone else grows close to your heart and only a few minutes after you have met him or her, you would do everything for that person?

People emit certain energy, like waves, in surroundings where others notice it and resonate – or not – with that energy and therefore respond (or not) to it. That way, people always find someone similar to themselves; we say they are **on the same wavelength** or **on the same vibration**. It is often said, "They're perfect for each other."

Your daily thoughts attract similar things by the same principle. Apart from that, our thoughts change form – from something imagined to something real. Energy as unstable as thoughts are, is influenced relatively easily and because of that, thoughts change rapidly. However, **thoughts have a strength that few, if any, things in the Universe can surpass.**

Thought Is the Only Creative Force

Everything that is important and perceivable on this planet began as a thought – idea, vision, wish, goal, etc. – in someone's mind. Every object you see was once imagined by someone who believed in it enough to bring it into existence exactly as he or she saw it in his or her mind.

Thought is the only force that creates objects and events.

How do we know that?

Look at a rock. Can one rock beget another? No. Can a car create a new car? No. People, through the development process – which is nothing more than a process to actualize what a person sees in his or her head – create cars. The character of creative people influences the creative process and their habits influence their character. Actions influence their habits, while conscious and unconscious impulses (with motivation, determination, and persistence in the background) influence their actions.

Where do impulses come from? **Somewhere within you and me.** You receive an impulse that says, "This could work," and the subconscious accepts the accompanying thought and offers its solution to how this can be realized in your life.

When we are in harmony with our souls, we express the soul's desires, and we easily notice impulses that come directly from our souls. If we do not get overwhelmed with fears (and thus lose motivation and desire), but instead follow our desires precisely, we real-I-ze them and bring them to life. This kind of manifesting internal impulses represents the **fastest personal growth possible.**

Cherish Your Thoughts

So cherish the strong and supportive thoughts you believe in. This is literally **God speaking to you.** You have to take care of them every day and all the time, **protecting them** – like a mother protects her young – from being attacked by lower vibration thoughts.

If you place a seed in the Earth's soil and remove it after only an hour, then replant it a few hours later, uproot it the next day and so on, nothing

will grow. Similarly, if you replace the seed with another, the new seed will grow in its place.

Be careful what you place in the soil of your conscious and subconscious minds.

> If you find yourself wavering between supportive thoughts in one moment and doubts, which bring fear and panic, in the next moment, you will never achieve your desired result – even if you force yourself at the very next moment to think of a successful solution or outcome.

Perhaps the time has come for you to admit to yourself exactly what it is you want and feel deep inside. **Do you know what that is?**

Your Thoughts Create Your Self-Image

I have often read the statement, "You are what you think you are." There are two sides to this statement. **All people sometimes think they are unique and special,** if asked and answer sincerely. Perhaps you think you are wiser than others in certain situations, know more about a specific topic than others, or have a unique perspective that makes you special. Yet, when you look at your individual circumstances, your life does not reflect what you think you are.

Be careful what you place in the soil of your conscious and subconscious minds.

Therefore, you are not what you think you are – **you are what you think (about) most of the time.** Your thoughts express your vibration, which forms your reality.

So it does not matter what you think or tell others about yourself – good, bad, unique, etc., when asked. What matters are **the thoughts about yourself that are ever-present in your mind.** This is our self-fulfilling prophecy. Like the ancient Greeks said, "There is no problem… **we created it in our heads."**

Now let us use all this knowledge for creating what we want. In the next chapters, we will discuss **fulfilling our dreams and desires.**

Searching for a Solution

Let us analyze a typical situation where you obviously want a favorable solution (for example, to become wealthy), but your experiences and present circumstances make you believe it is going to be difficult to achieve.

> **The strongest and clearest energy always wins.**

The common question is: "Why don't I become wealthy, even when I consciously desire it and hold it in my thoughts?"

As we know, **the strongest and clearest energy always wins**. You want to be wealthy and your subconscious is receiving the signal to get rich, but on the other hand, you can **see and feel your failures, obstacles you cannot remove, fear, weakness, anger, maybe even envy or malice are present**. Unintentionally, you are sending two opposing orders to your subconscious, which is aware of the first, but is paying attention to the stronger and clearer of the two. It is almost as if you were giving your subconscious the order to want to be wealthy, which produces a want to be wealthy, instead of the manifestation of being wealthy, which would arise **if your belief was sufficiently strong**.

As we said, **the image that is clearest and strongest is accompanied by stronger emotions, has greater meaning for you, and is present in your mind longer**. That is the image that manifests, and unfortunately it is most likely the want to be wealthy instead of the deep and sincere belief **you are getting wealthy**.

In fact, most people spend an incredible amount of time thinking about failure instead of searching for solutions or trusting they will succeed.

Wishing for Something That Does Not Come True

Does that mean that if you consciously truly believe you can become wealthy – or even better, that you are on your way to riches – your subconscious will bring it about? Yes, if your **life's mission is not opposed to it** and if you **persist and complete the process**. Namely, **you can have as much money – and other goods – as you need to fulfill your life's purpose**.

The problem is elsewhere. **Your conscious thoughts and their resultant orders to your subconscious are rarely clear.** Almost the moment the thought, "I will become wealthy" enters your mind, a worm of doubt crawls into your head saying, "It's impossible. I can't become wealthy just like that."

That way, your subconscious receives **conflicting information**. You experience this happening when you desperately want something, but at the same time are afraid your desires will not be fulfilled, as is usually the case when the desire is to be wealthy. **Fear is one of the strongest emotions we experience, far stronger than any desire, which is why what we fear the most is what, in the end, is often brought into being.**

Now you know why perhaps you cannot forget an old love, why you are bothered by your neighbor having a better car, why you never have enough money, and so on. Everything that receives more of your attention takes a leading role in your daily life and ultimately becomes drilled into your subconscious mind.

The more you think about it, the stronger your conviction grows, but if the unsupportive thoughts of weakness, envy, despair, and fear are present when you think about it, you are heading towards misery and sadness. Each repetitive thought **confirms old resolutions while deepening and amplifying them – making them stronger.** In the end, you realize what a terrible state you are in and become even more miserable.

Caught in a bewitching circle, you have looped a rope around yourself and are now tightening the knot. The more desperately you struggle, the tighter the knot becomes.

For the same reasons as above, various psychotherapeutic techniques for relieving traumatic experiences fail to have a positive effect – **because you are concentrating on what you do not want instead of what you do want.**

The Truth is that **you cannot get what you want if you are focusing on its opposite.**

How to Solve Problems Quickly and Easily

You have probably experienced the next situation. At some point in your life, you have struggled with a problem that you could not solve. The natural inclination is to become instantly occupied with hyper-focusing on the problem; the more you think about it, the more unsolvable it becomes. After a while, it feels like the worst thing that has ever happened to you.

What is the solution?

Stop the thinking pattern and start to think about a successful solution rather than the problem.

> *You cannot get what you want if you are focusing on its opposite.*

For example, most people struggle with their **finances**. You have probably experienced a time in your life when the month is not even half over before you are in a financial mess, worrying about how you are going to pay the bills that are becoming due. Your bank account is as dry as the Sahara Desert, you do not have any savings, and your troubles just get bigger. Your heart begins to beat harder, you start breathing faster, and the more worried you become, the more terrible you feel. Every time you start thinking about your financial problems, you feel this way.

Stuck in this lousy financial state, it is easy for unpleasant thoughts to overwhelm you, "How am I going to get through this month? How am I going to pay my bills? I won't be able to join my friends for an evening out – what will they think?" and so on.

When we are in this or a similar situation, it is first necessary to **break the pattern**. Oftentimes, it is the subconscious reaction to the above mentioned financial state and not the conscious direction of energy.

It also happens that this pattern of (unconscious) worrying – which can perhaps **even become a habit** – is so strong that we cannot influence it by repeating pleasant and supportive thoughts. As we said, we have to deal with it through some **unexpected effect** – like a shock – which the pattern will not recognize and, for that reason, **will not automatically react to**. This is often the only way to break out of the cycle in which we are so profoundly stuck. (Like a car that is stuck in mud. Even, gentle pulling often does not help. If you want to pull the car out, you need a sudden "jerk" or special, lasting strength.)

After we break the pattern, **we begin to focus our energy in another direction**, and no longer ponder questions like, "Why does this keep happening to me?" Thoughts of helplessness, failure, an unhappy fate, and victim-like feelings **drain us of our will and energy and deter us from acting, which is the only cure.**

Sometimes it is very useful at the beginning to ask: **"What can be done now to improve the situation or at least keep it from getting worse?"** Put your problem into perspective and do some creative troubleshooting. You can also ask yourself, "What is the worst that can happen here?" By answering these two questions, you will discover two things.

First, you will realize that the situation **probably is not as bad as you have imagined** because there is a way to influence it and thus improve it.

Second, when you mentally engage in a controlled thought experiment – one that takes your problem to its logical consequence in a worst-case scenario – and mentally accept it, you **remove the fear factor** (because fear is fed by the unknown).

That way, you have just taken the first step in solving your challenge because now you have **fully identified the problem, so there is no mystery in it anymore and you are free to focus on solutions.**

Do not worry, there **is always a solution**, and once you start thinking clearly about the situation, you will probably find many.

Next, get creative. Get some help from others and **write a list of possible solutions.** Then **choose the solution that best fits your needs**. No one else can do this for you. Others can offer their advice or provide options, but you must do the choosing. Once you have decided, do whatever is needed to **take matters into your own hands – lay out the steps necessary to correct the situation and act on them**!

It is hard to be afraid when you envision a successful outcome, are motivated, and when your mind is occupied with solving the problem. Once you decide on your course of action, there are many techniques available – like affirmations or visualization – that may help.

If you take a closer look at a situation where you have solved the problem and moved beyond it, you will likely find two things: firstly, that **accepting the situation** (and not running away from it) brought you to the solution. And secondly, you **gained wisdom and power** from that process… and they are yours to use later on (as we have already stressed).

Realizing Your Dreams

There are many miserable people in the world, and some of these people already know how the mind works and the subconscious acts, and their important role in achieving goals. Yet, somehow they **just cannot make it work for them**. Why is this so?

First, **they put too much mental effort into calculating solutions**. They say something like, "From now on, I'll tell myself that I'll earn $100,000 by the end of the year. If I tell myself that every day, and put all my energy into it, I will surely reach my goal." And at the end of every day they say, "Oh, I haven't worked on my goal enough today. If I'm not consistent, things

The Millionaire Mindset

> *The solution is in feeling your goals as if you have already achieved them.*

won't happen right. Let's go, I have to repeat affirmations some more: I'll get rich. I'll get rich. I'll get rich."

Will this person ever realize his dream of making $100,000 by the end of the year? **Never.** Clearly, he or she does not truly believe he or she can achieve the goal. The subconscious does not work on the principle of, "If you behave, you'll get candy," but rather, "Think and act as if you already have candy and I'll make sure you get it." As we have already said, when you fully act **as if you have already achieved a certain vibration** – and therefore harmonize with it completely – the subconscious can accept this state as a real one (and consequently get you there).

We cannot consciously decide to believe and trust something because this process is within the domain of your objective – logical and thinking – mind. This is why **conscious effort and discipline alone never really help in successfully reprogramming your subconscious.**

The solution is in feeling your goals as if you have already achieved them. Engage your senses and allow yourself to be overcome with feelings of joy, victory, happiness, satisfaction, and relief, and expel the feelings of fear, need, and longing.

When you reach such a state, you are moving your subconscious in the right direction and are laying down a wealth of information from which your subconscious will draw on later. Then when similar circumstances occur in your life, **your subconscious will recognize them and provide the solution that is already reflected in your thoughts.**

One of the characteristics of such a state is **unconditional trust**. It is demonstrated when **we do not try to force or even influence anything anymore.**

The following example (watching a sports event on TV) illustrates the thinking states that accompany you when you trust, and when you do not. **If you know the final score beforehand, you do not worry about all the minor victories and defeats along the way.** Your attention will even wander to other things surrounding the game, the commercials or team composition and statistics, which might otherwise go unnoticed.

If you do not know who the winner will be, you will be on the edge of your seat the whole game, nervous whenever the opposing team has the ball. Nothing else will matter or gain your attention until you see the final, winning score.

It is the same with other situations you face each day. **Whenever you are not certain of a positive outcome, you always try to force one**... by doing what your intellect tells you to do; **because you are afraid of an outcome that you will not like, you do everything to avoid or prevent it.**

However, this behavior is telling your subconscious **you have little faith, and what you are feeling is fear.** Because **your fear is stronger than your belief** in a positive outcome, the result is exactly what you were afraid of.

Fulfilling Wishes and Desires – The Correct Procedure

The simplest way to open the door to dreams and desires is to be 100% certain they will come true. By maintaining that kind of thinking in your consciousness, you easily resonate with the vibration of dreams and desires, and therefore let the solution in.

When this happens, fear, doubt, longing, and all the other unpleasant emotions are gone. You are certain that the situation can and will be resolved favorably, and you do not even have to try to prevent the unwanted from happening. There is no doubt in your mind whatsoever.

You can achieve this state of maintaining the proper vibration in two ways:

- Forget everything and firmly **plant a picture of what you want in your subconscious** (through meditation, visualization, positive affirmations, etc.). Then **do not think about it anymore.** Simply leave it alone and **turn your attention elsewhere** – when the time is right, the subconscious will bring it about. Why? You filled your subconscious with a clear and concrete task. The response may come immediately, or it may take months or even years. When the subconscious finds a solution, you will receive a signal, and you will intuitively perceive that hint, idea, or flash as the solution to getting what you want.

- Alternatively, you could **hold that image in your mind always, engaged in constant movement towards a favorable conclusion.** Hold the vision or goal in your mind and align your actions in harmony with your desire. This may mean you will have to give up other thoughts for this, but it will not matter; nothing will deter you from your path.

Well, there is another (special) way to achieve a goal, without following either of the two suggestions above, **when a karmic code is activated**. As we know, this activation can happen even when we do not direct our energy in any particular direction at all. But as said before, **do not count on it**, but rather **do whatever it takes**.

Here is a common story of success achieved by **(constantly) directing energy** into one direction. Let us look at the path of an average young man on his way to becoming a successful businessperson:

The young man **feels a desire** and can easily see himself in the role. He sees the cars he will drive when he succeeds, the clothes he will wear, and the house he will own. Each time he sees something he likes, the thought occurs, **"This is for me. I want the same thing."** Of course, he gets the proper education, but this is more like a game – **instead of feeling an obligation, he is having fun**. If someone tells him he will never achieve such a success, he laughs inside. "Just wait and see what you'll say when I'm driving a new Mercedes."

He does not allow anyone to shake his confidence or deter him from his goal. With each new day, his awareness of being on the right path increases, and it is now only a matter of time before he achieves his goal and the resultant success he seeks. Knowing this, he is not afraid, and he falls asleep each night with a smile, knowing he is one day closer to his goal. Soon, he will no longer be the young man with a dream – rather, he will have become the successful businessperson he has seen in his mind for years.

There is no fear of defeat, and he has the feeling that he holds his destiny in his hands. He focused his energy in one direction, and he holds that vision.

We have already stressed that when you truly desire something, and that desire is accompanied by a deep belief in its realization, **all the forces of the Universe are directed towards fulfillment of that desire.**

You only have to trust them and give yourself to them when the signs show you how to take the next step.

The Truth Behind Fulfilling Wishes

The fulfillment of wishes always accompanies the (Sub)Law of Life's Mission. **There is a reason for each of the wishes we have.** Oftentimes, **the wish itself suggests, if not directly expresses, this Law**. If we perceive life in this way, we can really say that we are **capable of fulfilling every wish that appears within us**; or better said, every wish, which turns up in the heart and not in the mind.

The problem arises only when the wish comes from the mind (without the support of the heart) and when it is not ours; that is, when it does not come from inside, but is the result of **falling into someone else's energy** and **connecting ourselves to his or her wishes**. Such wishes are often not only **more difficult to fulfill**, but also **fail to benefit our development and growth**.

That is why it is best for us to **take into consideration only wishes that come from the intuition and a state of unconditionality** – when we are calm, relaxed, or in a supportive, loving energy. Namely, if our consciousness is on a very high vibration, every thought that reaches us will come from there and will surely carry within it the seeds of growth. This thought will also be very uplifting, encouraging, and motivational **because the heart never judges, but only expresses loving and supporting energy**.

This is yet another reason why we should spend as much time as possible **in contact with this loving energy**; not just in meditation, or the performance of other relaxation or spiritual techniques, but also **while going through an ordinary working day**.

Be Careful What You Wish For... You Might Just Get It!

It is also very important that **we carefully define what we want**. The old proverb is well known, "Be careful what you wish for, **you just might get it!**" This often works in our favor, but can sometimes become very tricky.

As we know, the subconscious fulfills only the **result without selectively choosing the path**. And so it can happen that an overburdened worker **who wants peace and quiet loses his job** (and he or she feels that everything is wrong again).

Something similar happened to a friend of mine. She once clearly expressed the wish that she **wanted 4,000 Euros** (Slovenian national currency) – that is approximately $5,500 – in savings. Well, today she has

The Millionaire Mindset

4,000 Euros in various accounts, but one of the ways she came to have this savings is particularly interesting.

She went about her usual shopping in an electronics store when **a big pipe fell on her head**. It happened because of employee negligence and my friend just "happened to be" standing at that very spot at the very moment the pipe fell from the upper floor.

She inquired as to what to do, and it was suggested that the company pay her compensation, which ended up amounting to a little **4,000 Euros**.

Sometimes something even more drastic can happen to us if we do not express our wishes precisely. The following example is taken from Boris Vene's book, *Becoming Rich and Wealthy Through Divine Touch*.

Sai Baba, the Indian wise man to whom millions of people turn for advice, is known for receiving people and then realizing their various wishes. Friends told me an interesting story about a materially-oriented man who **wanted a million dollars**. Baba repeatedly asked him if that was really what he wanted and he replied, "Yes, that's all I want. Give me a million, and I'll be the happiest man!"

"OK," said Baba, "when you reach home, you will have a million."

When the man was driving home in his car, he had a serious accident and **remained paralyzed from the neck down**. The insurance company gave him compensation, which amounted to exactly one million dollars.

Of course, the subconscious can work **in our favor** in the same way. For example, if we want a cottage at a seaside resort, we first think about buying or renting one. When we allow our subconscious to have free hands to fulfill our wish, it may happen that **a friend asks us to maintain or occasionally check up on his cottage**.

That is why, with every wish we set, we also define the energies, which accompany us on our path. For instance, "I want to increase my earnings by enjoying my work and also enjoying myself in other areas at the same time." Then, as said, **we trust and surrender to life until we have a "lightning bolt"** or clear sign as to what we should do.

In this way the wish is **extensive enough to be realized in a variety of ways** – we are not forcing it – and we have also clearly expressed the feelings we want to experience at the same time.

Reverse Psychology Technique – A Magic Wand for Everyone Who Seems Plagued With Failure

Here is another method for getting what you want, which might work for you.

Vera Pfeiffer, in her book, *Positive Thinking*, says that **the more you try, the less you can do.**

Actually, it is not quite that simple (or that hard). All successful people, whether they are businesspeople, artists, scientists, etc., achieve their success through acting to get results.

On the other hand, that thought is valid when we want to **force** something, and not listen to our inner voice, intuition, and signs, but instead **do what our rational mind offers** or **act out of fear**.

So let us take a closer look at Pfeiffer's thought.

Martin Kojc, in his book, *The Manual of Life,* describes how a Professor Chodoansky was experimenting with how to cure the common cold.

The Professor decided that he could conduct his research better if he had a cold. He then consciously decided to get a cold, but that was not successful, so he tried to speed up the process and make himself sick. After taking a cold shower, he stood naked in front of an open window thinking that he would catch a cold. Then he lay down in an ice bath, so cold that he shook from head to toe. **No matter what he tried, he could not make himself catch a cold.**

Has something like this ever happened to you? Of course, it has. You can probably remember a sleepless night when you tried hard to fall asleep. Finally, when all else failed, you perhaps even tried to use the popular technique of counting sheep. You said to yourself, "If I can't sleep, I'll count sheep, because I heard it might help." **Did that solve your problem?** Probably not, but depending on how strong your belief in that method was, coupled with your experience in using it, you may have had some measure of success. Most people say it has the opposite effect. Why?

Because wishing and hoping something will work or happen does not make it so. If you are not convinced, deep inside, that it will really make a difference, while you are wishing and hoping strongly that it will work – the stronger thought wins. Wishing and hoping, without the essential belief

The Millionaire Mindset

to bring it about, may even be sabotaging the possibility of realizing what you want.

How can you use this discovery to your advantage in real life?

The next time you cannot fall asleep, say: "**I have to stay awake today.** No matter what happens, I must not close my eyes even for a second. I'll take some books and read them until morning, or meditate, or listen to good music. I will have great fun tonight! Then I'll take a shower and go to work."

What is the result? **You usually fall asleep within a few minutes.**

Let us analyze what happened.

Deep inside, your inner voice said, "Really? You think it can be so simple? **What if you fall asleep?**"

While you were consciously telling yourself to stay awake, you **unintentionally saw yourself sleeping with the light switched on and the book in your lap** instead. At the same time, your **intellect doubted your goal**; as is always the case when you are not certain about its successful realization.

So the **background image** of falling asleep – along with strong beliefs and emotions, which were active the whole time – was so strong that it hampered all your efforts to stay awake, because that is what the subconscious saw and brought into reality.

Can we use that knowledge in real life situations? Yes. Here is how you can test it.

First, engage in a thought experiment. **Think about an unsuccessful solution to your problem; think about the worst-case scenario of this problem happening to you.** Bear in mind that if you do not yet believe in yourself, you are preprogrammed to basically doubt everything you put to yourself. The same is happening now – **you do not believe that what you see is a solution to your problem**, even if what you are seeing is an unsupportive (unpleasant) solution. Your mind now tells you, "What(ever) you're planning won't work. Reality is always different from what you think will happen, and you will not be successful in bringing about the resolution you imagine."

Because you imagined an unsuccessful outcome, but doubt it, your mind will show you how to achieve the opposite and in the end – success.

You just have to be careful enough to **avoid resonance with that unsuccessful outcome** because if your consciousness slips into this vibration, you will **start to believe** in an unsuccessful outcome. That way, **everything you express would confirm that energy;** and subconscious would have nothing to choose between... and therefore no other option but to give you what you (energetically) ask for.

Magic in Practice

Most of us can probably relate to the next example of **trying to get attention and affection from a certain person.** After paying compliments, doing little favors, trying to show them how much you respect their opinions, making obvious efforts to be understanding, and showing support for their ideas in front of others, you do not get back the affection you want. Feelings of weakness, anger, and disappointment are born.

After a while, you have had enough and stop doing all the little extras to win their attention and affection. You **stop bragging about them and give them no special attention** thinking, "If they're not interested in me, then life should simply return to what it was like before we met." So you redirect your thoughts to other matters.

Now you only pay that person **as much attention as you do with everyone else** (it is wrong to ignore the person – and that happens often as a reaction of ego, pride, etc.). So you continue to be kind and good, behaving as though nothing ever happened between the two of you. Even if that person's reaction to your attention is an unpleasant one, you are not adversely affected; just carry on this average relationship with him or her. (Can you see how easy it is to forget your greatest love once you unplug and distance yourself from it? You can read much more about this in *Charisma, Self-Confidence and Personal Power.*)

What happens?

It is likely that **the same person who did not pay you any attention before now begins to take an interest in you.**

It is a game of energy. If you want something from someone, or try to **impose** your needs on him or her, a similar situation arises because **it is not what that person wants.**

Returning to the example where the situation is completely reversed, **suddenly your opinion matters and he or she now perhaps even finds**

you trustworthy or someone he or she wants to confide in. In the first case you were giving your energy to the other person – in the form of affection and approval – while in the second case, you **withdrew your overwhelming energy.**

We saw in that case that the way to fulfill the desire was based on **disconnection from the situation, redirection of your energy,** and **giving up your desire** (regarding the other person who did not agree with you); then it came true.

Whenever you feel the compulsion to force a situation, you are in danger of any disbelief you may harbor for a successful outcome overtaking you and extinguishing any tiny spark of faith and hope you have.

This happens with everything in your life that is going well for you – **the bulk of your current efforts, coupled with the positive direction you are headed in, is overshadowed by a general background image of doubt and disbelief.** This is where you find the answers to your specific challenges.

This could also be the root cause of many unpleasant situations in your life; for example, why you have been unable to climb out of financial hardship, the reason you cannot harmonize with your spouse or significant other, why you have been unsuccessful at realizing your dreams, and so on.

A Step Ahead: A Shortcut to Success

As you were going through these examples, you probably became aware of the **importance of implanting a correct thought – and also in the correct way – into the subconscious.**

So a common question might arise in your head. "Is it possible to **directly influence the subconscious,** and so, also the results? To somehow skip or evade the gatekeeper – the conscious mind?"

Well, it is. But one must be able to establish direct communication with the subconscious in such a way that it will bypass – or firstly **change** – all implanted mind programs. (In the next chapter, we will look at how to do this in practice.)

You can see how this happens if you observe a (good) hypnotist at work.

In a **hypnotic state,** the hypnotist gives a person senseless orders, which they carry out. You are probably familiar with such examples, and they perfectly illustrate our point of imagination over intellect and how the subconscious works in the absence of the conscious gatekeeper. In one such example, the hypnotist puts the client in an altered state of mind and hands her a **glass of water, telling her it is full of pepper.** When she brings the glass close to her nose, **she begins to sneeze.**

We know that **her imagination caused the sneezing, not the water.**

Why is it so simple to accomplish this under hypnosis, but so difficult to achieve similar results when we are awake, despite the best attempts of a wild imagination? The answer is clear – **because you and I have a conscious mind** that judges the information and therefore dictates our lives.

When you hear, "This glass (of water) is full of pepper," your conscious mind sends the signal, "No, that's not true; this is a glass of water, and water doesn't make me sneeze." The subconscious gives way to the strongest thought, in this case, the gatekeeper's answer. **In a state of hypnosis, however, the hypnotist puts the gatekeeper to sleep, shutting off the conscious and logical part of your mind, and connects directly with the subconscious, the executer of action.**

We said the subconscious does not decide – it simply acts on the strongest order and brings it into being. In a hypnotic state, there are **no competing orders**, and thus, the subconscious simply brings about what it is told to do by the hypnotist, making it true and recording it as an event.

Just think for a minute: How could you use this in your life? **If you could achieve a state similar to hypnosis, that would mean you would have a direct connection to your subconscious and the resultant opportunity to instruct it how to unfold your life.** But can this be done?

How to Directly Communicate With the Subconscious

Fortunately, we are not the first to think about this; verified methods exist for connecting to the subconscious, or to our virgin nature, as we sometimes call the heart and intuition. These are states in which we can **turn off the intellect and investigate our inside** and (oftentimes) the unknown world of unconditional energies. These are various meditations, autogenous training, visualizations, yoga, tai chi, and so on.

Which of these techniques is better than another? None. What is important is that the **technique brings us into contact with calmness,** and the one that does this best is the best technique for us. There are no limits, restrictions, and no general rules in choosing the method best suited to us. **Individuals choose whatever they feel is right for them; that is, the one that brings them to their goal faster, better, easier.**

There is, however, one rule that needs to be considered: When we choose a method of action (technique), we have to **stay with it and perform it regularly and lovingly.** A change in the technique, and/or searching for a new method, indicates our **mistrust in the technique** that we have interrupted.

The fact is that all techniques work, if we perform them regularly and lovingly. Or in other words, **all techniques work... if we are willing to work the techniques.**

Meditation, Relaxation, and Breathing

Several decades ago, only a small percentage of people in the developed areas of the world knew and practiced meditation and other techniques mentioned above. Today, as individuals worldwide experience increasing levels of daily stress – and also discover the **power of conscious awareness** and the **possibility of self-influence over their lives** – more and more people are discovering the **practical use of relaxation through meditation** and welcoming the relief this ancient practice brings to the challenges of modern living.

There are several forms of meditation, which makes it difficult to address them all in a single text. However, there are characteristics of meditation that are **common across all forms.** We have already found out that the form of meditation that is right for you is the one that, through persistence, you can regularly and lovingly devote yourself to; that way **you stay in a very high vibration** while doing it.

> *When we choose a method of action (technique), we have to stay with it and perform it regularly and lovingly.*

Before we discuss some of the essentials of meditation, it is important for you to realize that the mindset and techniques outlined will be **difficult to engage in at first, but like everything, practice will make it easier.**

Here are some guidelines.

During meditation, it is essential to divorce yourself from your train of daily thoughts, to calm your body, clear your mind, and finally surrender yourself. Breathing is also very important, primarily for two reasons:

- Breathing correctly **increases the flow of oxygen** to the vital organs in your body, which means they can work better.
- Concentrating on breathing in a predetermined way **enables you to clear your mind** of other, intrusive thoughts.

Most people are aware of the first point, but it is the second point that is interesting. We know that your mind can only hold one thought at a time. Thus, the most elegant solution to temporarily clearing your mind of intrusive thoughts is to focus on a breath – by simply **observing it**.

Also, we can clear our mind by focusing on a specific image, or a special word, or a series of words.

This is called **mantra**. It is a word that has a deep and specific meaning to the bearer and serves as a guide into a pure state, absent of thoughts. The word itself comes from the Sanskrit language and means, "to liberate." Actually, the word mantra has a lot of meanings and explanations.

In Hinduism, for instance, a mantra is a mystical formula of invocation or incantation and thus serves as a sacred counsel or guide in the meditative process.

What about breathing? You probably do not remember anyone **teaching** you to breathe, and like most people, unless you have had some specific training, you probably breathe with the upper part of your lungs/chest area. This is – in the words of some Masters – **not the best way**. For centuries, Eastern cultures have taught breathing as a process that first fills the lower lungs (stomach area) with air and then the upper lung area. In this way, you achieve the maximum benefit from every breath. It could take practice to perfect it, and in the end, you must find the way that helps you relax the most.

Breathing is life itself and connects us to God in the most direct way. If your breathing is calm and deep, allowing you to observe the process, you will notice that after a while, your mind is clear of all thoughts. Unfortunately, only up to the moment you notice it; when you start thinking of how good you are at doing it, you activate your conscious mind with that very thought.

But you can return to your calmness in a moment: just **refocus on your breathing again**. That way you will stop the thinking process, clear your mind, and return to the relaxing bliss that only an uncluttered mind can bring.

When focused in meditation, you are calm and fall into a state similar to **half-sleep**. The most important part is achieving this state, which will take some practice. The state of half-sleep is a state free of the constraints of consciousness (instead of thinking, you flow... like swimming, or flying).

Having achieved this state, **the door to the subconscious opens**, and this is the most effective time for repeating an affirmation, suggestion, or visualization.

Therefore, before you begin a visualization session or some other technique, it is effective to **meditate first**, and once you achieve the half-sleep state, then enter the visualization (or other technique).

When Your Mind Sleeps

A calm mind is the doorway to the subconscious. When a challenge presents itself, be calm because that is when your subconscious will deliver the fitting solution, and the time when you can most recognize it for what it is.

A sign or a solution can come to you at any time – while you are walking, admiring the beauty and wonder of nature, engaging in sports or hobbies, eating, etc. Why?

Because **your mind is "switched off" (rests), or is totally focused on something else**, and this is when the subconscious does its best detective work. Actually, the result is the same when **we are absorbed in certain work, which requires concentrating on that moment and space, driving away thoughts about the problem**. In this way, our subconscious has the opportunity to offer the solution. That is why we often say that it happened at a moment when we least expected it. This "eureka effect" can also happen in our **sleep**.

We are all in that natural state of calmness just before we fall asleep or right when we wake up (before you start to think), which makes these two times **the best for suggestions and affirmations**.

Our subconscious never sleeps, so we might as well give it something constructive to work on while we are resting.

When Athletes and Artists Achieve Their Top Results

Top athletes and artists know the state that helps them achieve top results. Psychologists call it a state of great enthusiasm or a state of altered consciousness. Athletes call it "the zone."

It happens during moments of **greatest pleasure**; when you forget everything around you and allow yourself to go with the flow, get into the zone, contact your higher self, etc. Your conscious mind rests in the background and **does not give any instructions**. Champions have defined this state of ecstasy as a reward greater than glory, prestige, or medals.

Looking at when such perfect performances happen, you will discover that they only happen when **you are not burdened with how you will perform**. The routine of your experience carries you through. This heightened state will remain as long as you **do not think about the results**.

For example, the football player standing in front of the opposite goal experiences exactly this. He quiets his self-talk; he does not say, "Watch what you're doing. Aim, look at where you'll shoot." He trusts his experience and mentally **leaves himself to his performance**.

Just moments before scoring, he "sees" in his mind how the event will end, and the subconscious takes care of a **myriad of tiny details and corrections** that enable him to kick the ball the way he envisioned. If amid this complex process he consciously starts thinking about it, **the automatic flow of the process stops**. Having to now think about the myriad of details and body adjustments that go into kicking a field goal himself, he will probably fail.

Have you ever been walking and suddenly become aware of the process? **It is hard to walk when you are actually thinking about it.**

Shamans of the ancient tribes said, "Everything is possible after disconnecting from the internal dialog in your head" – the "discussion" between the subconscious ("I'll win") and conscious mind ("You? No way! Don't you see others are better!").

Probably the most well-known example is a historic anecdote that shows how the subconscious offers a solution at the most inappropriate moments. Archimedes, the Sicilian physicist, was taking a bath when his subconscious delivered the solution to a long-puzzling mathematical problem. He was so excited that he ran naked through the streets yelling, "Eureka! Eureka!" (I have found it.)

Successful businesspeople know this secret and therefore plan their holidays with the same care they take in their work. An aphorism is born, **"The result is a consequence of (also) rest, not just work."**

What prevents so many others from acting this way?

They do not yet believe that their subconscious will help them detect problems and offer them solutions. Instead, they let their intellect decide. (We have already stressed this: **We trust our mind more than God**.) You know, however, that often the best solutions are those that first seemed impossible.

We can even say that many times you **find the solution once you forget about the problem.** When you are not burdened with the outcome, you do not pay much attention to the problem, and it is then the subconscious mind does its best work. Working tirelessly for you, your subconscious brings about all the necessary conditions for the successful realization of the solution to your problem.

The next time you are searching your mind for an answer that you know is right on the tip of your tongue, instead of repeating over and over, "I can't think of it. It's right on the tip of my tongue, but I can't remember." Just say, "It will come to me in a minute" and consciously think about something else... anything. Most of the time, **your subconscious will deliver the answer eventually, and will prove to you how priceless this system of yours is as it works to fulfill your every expectation.**

This explains the anecdote: "Lucky in cards but unlucky in love." Those who fall into this category are so preoccupied with thinking about how to solve personal problems that they do not think about the card game in front of them – and just let the game happen. Not forcing the victory consciously allows them to win naturally.

Influencing the Subconscious Mind: Affirmations and Mental Suggestions

Until now, we have looked at how to free ourselves from the mind's stream of thoughts and directly connect with the subconscious. The next phase is to implant some new, more uplifting and supportive thoughts into the subconscious.

How do we then form the kind of thoughts that the subconscious will **accept**? In what way should we communicate them to the subconscious? What happens when we return to a waking state and our old (or normal – less supportive) thoughts surface again?

If we want to exceed existing programs and habits, which are going on in our subconscious, it is necessary to **write them anew** so that we overwrite the old ones, which then vanish. We cannot just **remove** things – we must replace them. This is because the Universe does not allow vacuums; if we do not replace a pattern, the **original pattern will return.**

The easiest way to program your subconscious is to **repeat various suggestions over a given time period**, allowing your mind to store them. It is most important to **truly believe in what you are saying**, as we stressed before.

In the next chapters, we will take an even closer look at affirmations, and you will get all you need to perform them well.

Difficulties With Suggestions

Challenges with reprogramming mostly occur when you try to implant a thought that is contrary to an existing – or old and less supportive – one. **Your mind will resist the new information in its first attempt to correlate what it is now receiving with its existing archetype.**

For example, speak this thought and follow how your mind initially responds: "Luck accompanies me at every step." If your mind responds with banter similar to: "What? Who are you kidding? Your car broke down yesterday, and you just received another bill you won't make enough this week to pay. You hate your job, your kids just came down with the measles, and you can't afford to take your spouse out to dinner! Luck accompanies you? Dream on!"

Such responses from your mind can be a difficult barrier to breach. In fact, it is the primary reason that many people never get beyond this point and choose to give up.

Contradictory Thoughts Are Self-Defeating

Here is another situation to consider: It is crucial that your affirmations are **not in conflict with your (other) desires** – in any other area either.

For instance, you **cannot realize a desire to be independent in your job if your accompanying thoughts express a dislike of the burdens of responsibility**. It is like giving a cabdriver two different addresses that are in different parts of the city – he cannot take you to both places at the same time.

It is crucial that **you are willing to walk the path that will lead you to the realization of your goal**. So many people want to achieve something, but do not want to do whatever that achievement requires. "God, help me lose weight, but I don't want to change my diet or have to exercise." Well, conquering that thought could be dangerous even for the subconscious… because it may react in a way that makes you lose weight some other way – like by **becoming ill**. (Remember the story about the man who wanted a million dollars.)

If you want to achieve what you want, you have to give up whatever takes you in the opposite direction. That is why motivation and the right direction – so that we do not perceive goal achievement as suffering or denial – are so important. In this case, it is good to **double-check that we really want this particular thing**. And then check again.

Affirmations Can Be Your Way to Success

So if we go back to affirmations, you do not say, "I'm getting rich," when all you see in your mind's eye is poverty, defeat, and bad luck. The right affirmation, in this instance, is one that **fills you with the feeling of wealth**. Also, your thoughts must be completely uplifting and expressed using only words in the present tense. So when you feel the wealth you want to realize, you do not say, "I'm not poor." Rather, the proper affirmation would be something like,

It is crucial that you are willing to walk the path that will lead you to the realization of your goal.

"**At this moment, I have enough of everything**… and I can feel that it's getting even better."

Phrasing your affirmation in the present tense is a little awkward at first. However, it is imperative that your affirmations are not pushed way into the future with phrases that contain future-tense words like, "will have," or "will be," etc.

Also, as we have already stressed, use **affirmation as a reminder**, not a thought builder.

Your Conscious and Subconscious Minds

If you want to build a new energy with an affirmation you do not believe yet and so attempt to affirm something to your subconscious that you do not totally believe in, your intellect will immediately fight against it. What you store then is **your doubt and fear regarding the statement you are affirming**.

Well, it is (theoretically) possible to implant a completely new energy – solely by repeating an affirmation you do not believe in yet – but that way you **have to clear your mind and not allow any opposing thought to overwhelm you** with its (unsupportive) energy.

The other way – even less believable, but possible – to change your vibration without supporting it at all is connected to your life's mission. If you have chosen for this life to experience such energy, it can be yours with **literally no effort**. You just have to wait for the code to trigger and then let it take over.

But these are just **possibilities**; as said before, if you want it to happen for certain, work on it.

Here is some more valuable information to consider regarding affirmations.

How do you know that you are on the right path while using this method? The clear emotions of **relief and pleasure**, which are by-products of belief, should accompany all thoughts. **If a concern arises instead, then you are not yet at the phase when you can successfully implant new energy.**

At this moment, I have enough of everything... and I can feel that it's getting even better.

Concern, a by-product of fear and doubt, means **you are not sure you are capable of achieving that state in reality**. This kind of unpleasant emotion is so strong that it **nullifies any opposite emotion** of joy, happiness, peace etc., you might express. And once that has happened, you cannot expect to achieve a supportive solution or any measurable success.

Develop affirmations tailored to you, your dreams, and desires, and make them part of your daily thoughts and self-talk. Repeat them as often as possible and **feel them with strong emotions**. It is good to repeat them as often as possible, and that they are accompanied by deep joyful feelings. At the same time, do not allow some other thought to undermine or replace your affirmations.

Once again, bear in mind: Affirmations will work in your favor if you **believe in them with all your heart, and not only with your mind**. That way, you will get **from that energy** the **strength, motivation,** and **inspiration** needed to fulfill the goal.

If you notice that affirmations cause you unpleasant emotions, or if you find yourself questioning or doubting your affirmation, immediately **alter the affirmation to something you can truly believe in**. Here is an example.

Thomas Keller told his own story regarding this. In primary school, he did not exactly shine with success, which is why he was sent to the school psychologist. She advised him to repeat the sentence, "I'm smart!" He said that this technique helped him for a day or two, but then he discovered that it did not help him – because **he did not believe in the words he spoke**.

He continued to search and found a sentence, which expressed a truth in which he believed, and with which he had already often prevailed. Furthermore, the thought was very pleasant and supportive and indirectly carried the same message as the statement "I'm smart!" The sentence was, **"Whenever I decide to learn anything new, I succeed."**

Success will come when all your decisions arise from that affirmation; or when that affirmation **becomes the filter through which you make all your decisions**. When this happens, your subconscious will have accepted the thought as a truth and will return the necessary information (what to say, what to do, etc.) that will transform the energy of affirmation into reality.

It is possible to **combine several methods of subconscious programming successfully**. For example, along with repeating supportive statements and affirmations, visualization can be used, as well.

A well-known millionaire in the oil industry said the secret to his success was in "seeing" the end of a successful deal – oil in the tankers, the satisfied customer signing the contract, handing him a check, and shaking his hand. He could even smell the oil! It is all in the details.

While affirmations and suggestions can be spoken aloud or said in your mind, the former is much more effective, if circumstances allow. You can also **write them down** first and then read them, instead of just saying them. Engage as many of your senses as possible in this process.

In the next few chapters, you will get some of the most effective ways to present your thoughts to your subconscious, creating the best-possible environment for them to be accepted, absorbed, and acted on.

Here is a collection of suggestions for affirmations:

- Always find a **short, substantial, doubt-free thought.**
- Set it in the **present tense,** so you can immediately sense the feelings that come with its realization now and do not delay that realization beyond the first opportunity to bring it about.
- Always use the **supportive and uplifting form** of a thought because an image of "I'm not poor" could create a picture of poverty in your mind, and thus you would be striving for and achieving the opposite of what you want.
- More important than the meaning (of the words) itself are the **emotions that accompany it;** you have to feel relieved/uplifted and (or) at peace.
- The success of achieving new and positive mental states depends on the **intensity and continuity of your actions.** The stronger you believe, and the more often you act on the solutions your subconscious delivers to you, the sooner success will come.
- You can conclude every programming session with the following affirmation: **"I have already begun to realize all of this in my life and I have, through connection with the limitless intelligence (God in me), everything I need to realize my dreams and goals."**

Learning From the Master

Here is a word of caution regarding the last sentence in the last chapter. We must be careful not to fall into the energy **may whatever is best for me happens** because **we then use this as an excuse or apology to do things we are not proud of.**

This approach of, "Let either whatever I ask or something even better happens," is often an abetment and a way we elegantly **avoid responsibility for our decisions.** For instance, we ask for something, but something completely different happens; and we argue, "Gee, something better happened. Time will tell why this was better than what I had planned."

The aforementioned method ("May whatever is best for me happen") is effective and welcome in cases **when we are not certain that we have decided based on intuition;** meaning, when we suspect that it is the influence of the intellect – our conscious mind – on our decision and we do not know that what we are expressing is the right decision (in our best interest), or what we are striving for.

If we release an energy, which inside we feel **must without a doubt be realized**, such a thought can be a **last escape in case we do not succeed**. For instance, if we succeed, we say that our wishes have been fulfilled; if we do not succeed, we defend and protect the result as something better happened. While all of us do not do this, many people use such apologizing **unconsciously**, deeply believing that they are doing everything to the best of their abilities. That is why this is so much more dangerous.

As long as we are aware that our mind wants to choose shortcuts or easier paths, it is acceptable because we are conscious of this; we just need the **courage to admit this to ourselves and move forward**. Trouble arises when we are **not aware** that we are doing it.

That is why we must take a **very strong position and persevere with it** once we have decided on an exactly-defined goal; that is when we will not long for "something better," but will stick to our **original energies and intentions** that intuition brought to us.

Anyway, you can always follow Jesus' example (when you do not know if your rational mind or the heart dictates your activities). He said, **"...not My will, but Yours be done."** (Luke 22:42)

That is how, in situations when it was difficult to accept a decision, He **surrendered his life into the hands of the Creator**. For instance, when He was waiting in the Garden of Gethsemane to be led away and imprisoned, He said, "My Father, if this cannot pass away unless I drink it, Your will be done." (Matthew 26:42)

That is enough for now about affirmations. We will refer to them several times throughout the book and reveal some more of their **practical applications**. Here is the first.

Exercise: Defining Your Desires by Naming What You Want

Let us try in practice some things we have learned so far. In this exercise, you will find out **what you really want and how much you want to achieve your goal**.

Imagine one of your goals. Think again about the reasons **for** and **against** the goal you have set for yourself.

Divide a piece of paper into two columns and label one side "For" and the other "Against." Now write down every reason you can think of that **supports your desire to achieve the stated goal** in the "For" column. And write down everything you can think of that **supports your fears and doubts** about why you should not pursue your stated goal in the "Against" column.

It is important to be frank. Once you have your lists completed, **evaluate their importance** and assign each a number according to its priority, using, for example, the numbers 1 to 10. Assign the value of 10 to **all the most important reasons**, the value of 9 to all a bit less important reasons, and so continue the process until you have assigned each reason a value – both the pros and cons.

You do not need to use all the numbers (1 to 10), as long as you value each item according to its true importance. For example, you may even finish with only tens, nines, sevens, and threes.

For instance, if your stated goal is: "I want to lose fifty pounds by next Christmas." (It is also important you state your goal as specifically as possible – it is not enough to say, "I want to lose weight." **That is not a goal; it is just a desire.**)

Under the "For" column, you write: "Improved self-confidence – I will be able to accomplish what I set out to do with a greater belief in my ability to achieve other goals in my life," and you give this a 10-point rating. Then under the "Against" column, you write: "I'll give up sweets and snacks while I watch TV," assigning it 3 points (and so on).

When you total your points on both sides, **the side with the most points is a reflection of your current attitude towards your stated goal** and represents what you currently believe you can or should do.

Can you check if it is true? Of course, you can.

If you (unconsciously or consciously) do not agree with the outcome of that test, you will **not feel complete satisfaction**, but will be haunted by suspicion, doubt, and worry. You may even want a reexamination of the test and will look for an opportunity to **change the final decision** of the test.

It is like you support the opposite of that which the test decided. These are your powerful wishes and desires – or fears and doubts – that want to be realized.

There is a much faster way to discover whether your desires are in harmony with the image you hold of your future.

When trying to decide whether to embark on a new goal, **toss a coin.** Heads, you will do it; tails, you will not. Now **what do you feel when your coin confirms or denies your decision**? Sometimes you feel relieved – that way we know that our decision was the right one and that it supports our vision.

But sometimes you find yourself **wanting to toss the coin again,** or trying to **justify or excuse the decision that the coin selected**. In this case, you do not need to check your desires on a point list; it is clear what you want – the opposite of what the coin selected. All that remains is to admit it to yourself and move into action.

Go With the Flow

Once you firmly believe that everything happens for your greater good, then and only then, can you **surrender yourself to the creative force that is constantly working on your behalf.**

The creative force always delivers what you need. Trusting a higher force means paying attention to what it has to say to you and not allowing its message to be silenced by the opinions of others or even your own intellect (objective mind).

Believe in the force that created you, for it keeps you alive and fulfills what you desire; **why would this time be different?**

Some Religions Teach That Giving Up Is the Solution

Have you ever wondered how a person who is completely happy would look?

There would be **no desire** because the person would already have everything he or she dreamed of for a good life. Also, he or she would be on the "fifth level" (remember levels and phases?) when **working on fulfilling their life's purpose**. That means that he or she would not have any problem with identity or tension releasing, but would only want to serve.

While it is true that it is necessary to let go of a desire to allow it the opportunity to be fulfilled, that does not mean that it is necessary to **give up everything you have**. The whole point of life is to **satisfy your desires in some way and not suppress them** because a suppressed desire is an obstacle for further freedom.

You stop being a slave to desires through either of these two ways:

1. **Fulfilling them.**
2. **Moving through them,** by **harmonizing with that energy** (without the need for the physical experience).

If people feel they want to live freely, without any material possessions, and thus give up their possessions or fortune to the church or the poor, they do as everyone else: They are **fulfilling their desire**. In giving up their worldly possessions, according to their desire to do so, they free themselves from the desire itself, **by fulfilling it**.

When Self-Improvement Becomes a Fashion

Daily, we meet more and more people who research the **higher human values you and I carry within ourselves**. Self-help and self-improvement have become quite the fashion. Unfortunately, too many people – such as disappointed people, who have not been able to succeed in a "cruel, materialistic world" – use much of it as just **another excuse or crutch**. They say, "If I don't become rich, at least I will grow spiritually."

How do you recognize these people? Ask them about their job or their worldly possessions, and they will answer, "That doesn't concern me; I'm not materialistic. I work to build character and become a good person."

Real self-improvement, which overwhelms us as a deep desire because of its final goal (higher vibration) – not comparison with others, proving to be good, and so on – is a worthwhile cause. However, the moment of truth has arrived, and it is time to discover the **real cause behind your activities regarding spiritual growth**.

Answer these questions and actually see how spiritually evolved you were at the end of last month.

- How much time, money, and energy did you give to charities or others in need... and **feel great and fulfilled while doing so**?

- How did you treat yourself? With Love or with fear? Did you put yourself last, available for those in need, but not taking time for yourself?
- Have you overcome any cherished desire for great material wealth and resolved yourself to being happy if you do not ever fulfill it? What do you feel when you imagine yourself in your current state (physical and financial) twenty years from now?
- **Were you able to restrict unpleasant and unsupportive thoughts (longing, greed, anger, envy) anyway?**
- Did you exhibit true, unselfish Love to all people through a kind word, greeting, or gesture?
- **What did you generally do to make the world – inside and outside of you – a better place?**

If you assess your personal growth differently, then adjust the questions above to match your model, but be sincere in both your questions and your answers.

Your answers will help you establish what your **basic purpose** is – are you seeking a higher meaning in your life or are you running away from reality?

It could even happen that we do not know what is going on. For example, we could meditate, not to reach the critical mass of Love, but for meditation itself. That way, the **performance of meditation becomes** the **goal itself**, instead of the goal that this technique brings (i.e. peace, serenity, freedom). Thus, we do not strive to reach the higher vibration – it is more important that we **regularly perform the technique**.

It is important that we admit things to ourselves.

For example, if you want material wealth, admit it and finish with the experience! If you stifle it, **your development will stop on this vibration (unbalanced relationship with materiality)** because your energy will be stuck here.

Now think further about your actions and activities. If you discover that you are not on the right path, this might be just the time to return to it.

Life Is Now

Only when we are truthful to ourselves and others... and recognize our desires and deal with them, can we live here and now.

This is the point – to **live in the present**.

Life is nothing more than a series of moments strung together. **If you are constantly waiting to have a better life and striving for a better time, you nullify the meaning of the present.** There are many distractions and substances available today that can distance you from reality and fill you with only illusions – alcohol, drugs, cigarettes, etc. All of these suppress your present emotions and replace them with a false feeling of relaxation and freedom.

The first step to disconnect yourself from such behavior and patterns is to acknowledge that they exist, to accept them, and to be able to recognize them when they appear.

Let us see how it works with relaxation. If you want to relax, you must first realize that your muscles are tense. You can do that by tensing them even more to discover precisely what causes momentary pain or increased tension. This is how we can – through **awareness** – bring relaxation to our muscles.

Sometimes we **try to avoid the recognition**... to avoid the pain.

The same thing happens in other areas of your life that you are not satisfied with; **if you want to change them, you need to confront them.** Confrontation brings unpleasant emotions to the surface so you can deal with and overcome them – by **accepting and loving**. Avoiding the unpleasant emotions deprives you of the confrontation necessary to deal with them.

Avoidance does not solve problems and will only postpone and push them further into your subconscious where they will cause experiences that are even more unpleasant. If your desire is to be released from the chains of such energies, you must first recognize that you are bound in chains and deal with that situation.

Do not run away from you! Sometimes, when you have the feeling that you should **run faster** (or the opportunity will slip away), **you have to stop**.

193

Recognize the Beauty in Every Moment

It is sad, but **many people do not live in the present... and even less so in their hearts.**

How can you recognize that?

Because **they forget things easily, do not remember where they left something, eat without tasting the food,** and do not hear the sounds of nature around them, or see the scenery outside their window when traveling. Their thoughts are always occupied with some more important things.

> *It is sad, but many people do not live in the present... and even less so in their hearts.*

Many people are **hindered by the chains of the past**, which weigh them down and follow them like a dark shadow; thoughts of an **insecure future** burden them, as well. They spend most of their time drowning in past events and worrying about what tomorrow will bring. Or they direct energy into the present – but outside of themselves – comparing, proving, and affirming.

Here is an idea of what most people think about their present circumstances and how they escape to the past and future. When they were of school age, they said, "I can't wait to get into the sixth grade where I will be happy." They get there and realize **it was nicer in the third grade**. Because there is no way back, they then say, "It's not so great here. I can hardly wait to get into high school."

Facing the challenges of high school causes them to remember easier times in earlier grades. Now they look ahead and cannot wait to complete high school and find a job so they can finally be free and away from the control of their parents and teachers. Once they secure a job, they wait for the next promotion, the coming holidays, or even a new job that pays more.

They have spent their entire lives waiting for the next thing that will change their lives for the better.

We constantly forget that **the present moment is all that any of us have**. If you wait day after day for better times, you will spend most of your life just waiting... and no one can assure you those days will ever come. In fact, the more you burden yourself with problems, worry about the disapproval of others, or lament your current surroundings or circumstances, the less likely it is that you will attract the opportunities necessary to improve your situation now.

What is more important than the present moment... if **it is everything you have, and the only time you can control and influence**?

Here is one more fact to consider: **When you meet God... it will happen now**, in the present moment of your beingness. So if you are in constant anticipation of what tomorrow brings, you will pass Him by.

Do not waste time blaming yourself for mistakes you made in the past, you just did not know any better. **Now you do know better and that is your reward, so it was not a failure.** You cannot change the past; you can only take what you learned and **apply it to do better now**.

Here is another story about a situation that happened to me a few years back.

I found some of my longtime business partners in a bad mood. Because of a change in local laws, we had to alter the business project we had been working on with such high hopes. **They all looked as though someone doused them with water.**

Although I knew the problem, I asked them about the cause of their long, sorrowful faces. They told me how disappointed they were because they would not be able to complete the project as planned. **"If this is your only problem in life, then you should be happy,"** I told them.

As they looked at me with surprise, I continued: "You are sitting at a table in a warm room, with food in the middle of a winter storm, surrounded by friends. Your luxury cars are waiting for you outside the door and your wives and children, who love you, are waiting for you at home. **What are you missing in this moment that is making you so sad?**" Their reply was that they were uncertain of the future surrounding this project.

I took the situation and presented it to them this way: "**What if this is the happiest day of your lives?** What if not doing the project will open your eyes to new possibilities and projects that you have neglected because of this project? What if you were horses with blinders on up to this moment, and you will now be able to look around and see a better project that you didn't see before simply because you were so focused on this one?"

"Think about people that are hungry, those who are invalids or handicapped, or those who have no paying job today – do you really have a cause for such sorrow? On the contrary! Many people who have become paralyzed or blind later say it was the best thing that could have happened because it opened them up to more important things they had never sensed before."

Their foul moods soon passed, and we spent the rest of the evening in a much more pleasant atmosphere.

So let us bear Jesus' advice in mind, "So do not worry about tomorrow; for tomorrow will care for itself. Each day has enough trouble of its own." (Matthew 6:34)

That is to say, let **each day carry its own care**.

How We Do Not Allow Ourselves to Live Here and Now

Here is a story originally written by Anthony DeMello.

Two monks, sworn to their obligation of chastity, set off on a journey. They came to a river where there was no bridge and had to wade across the river.

A well-dressed young woman who wanted to cross the water but did not want to get wet, waited on the bank. She asked the monks if they could help her somehow.

The first monk immediately refused to help her, "I'd be glad to assist, but **I can't**; you see, I swore that I would never touch a woman. I wouldn't break this promise for anything in the world!"

The other monk did not say anything. He clutched the woman around the waist, hoisted her up on his shoulder and **carried her across the water**. He set her down on the other side, said goodbye, and continued on his way with the first monk.

Soon afterwards, the first monk began talking about sin and how the second monk violated his oath. Then he was silent for a while and after a few minutes again started on the same subject – that they are not allowed to touch women, even those who find themselves in trouble.

This went on for a while. Even though more than an hour had passed since the event, **the first monk was still explaining to the second monk** how imprudently he had behaved by carrying the woman across the water.

The second monk stopped, looked him in the eyes and said, "My brother, I put her down long ago… but **you are still carrying her!**"

Are we not doing the same thing in life? We carry things we should have put down long ago, like the first monk. Although we may have avoided physical contact with something, we are still strongly connected to the matter **energetically**.

What is more important?

Considering that our goal is to direct the consciousness into very high vibration, our **feelings and emotions, which create this energy state, are especially important**. The physical contact is only important in so far as it **triggers these feelings**. However, if there is no physical contact, but we are still very closely connected to something energetically, the result is the same – perhaps even more intense.

DeMello said in his book, *Awareness*, "Every time a prostitute comes to me, she's talking about nothing but God. She says I'm sick of this life that I'm living. I want God. But every time a priest comes to me he's talking about nothing but sex."

The fact is that **things that are not in balance will be constantly coming to mind**. We can avoid them, deny them, or refuse to admit them, but this **does not mean that they are not there**. Tony Robbins said that **if your garden is full of weeds, it will not help to say, "My garden is beautiful…"** Well, it will not even help if you convince yourself of it.

Should we not rather admit and accept these facts… and release ourselves from them energetically… and thus disconnect from them **permanently**?

That is why it is appropriate to ask, for instance, **to whom does meat do more damage**: to the person, who consumes it in moderation, lovingly, and with gratitude… or to the vegetarian, who always thinks and talks about it with fear, avoids it at all costs, and tries to convince others how harmful it is?

This is no true vegetarian; this person just uses meat to prove to others how right he or she is. (A true vegetarian **does not talk about meat at all**, but only about the delicious fruit and vegetables he or she just ate. So **they are not focused on the rejection of meat, but on loving other food**.)

Long ago Jesus said that "poison doesn't come from outside, but from within." (Mark 7:15) So it is not just how it looks on the outside, but **what we feel during the behavior** that is important.

The Greatest Value in Life

Here is an interesting thought about your greatest value.

You pay for everything in life with – time… **your time invested**. Time is your life, and it is **irreplaceable**. How you spend your time is how you spend your life. For example, you pay for a new car with X number of hours or years of work. While all of us have the same number of hours in our days, the time in your life is limited, and everything depends on how you spend it.

There is no such a thing as not enough time. There is, however, **wasting of time**. If you **plan** your actions and **stick** to the schedule so that you do **what is most important first**, you will never get into a situation where you run out of time.

Also, make sure you pay for your next car (or condo, or whatever) **while building a high vibration**. That is most important: We all spend our time, but along with it we gain – among other things, i.e. money – a **certain vibration**, which depends on the thoughts, feelings, and emotions that accompanied our activities. It comes in the package as a "side product," and we cannot do anything about it.

Nothing is more important than the state of your consciousness.

Ask people with assets. **Most of them are still searching for happiness.** Ask happy people who are in a very high vibration. They do not search for anything, but are **enjoying – or reverencing – life here and now**.

So **fill your time with the highest vibration possible**, and you will make the greatest investment of your life.

"Don't waste time… because **time is God**," says Sai Baba.

Remember Something Good About Every Day

Fully exploit every moment you have because, once you spend it, you can **never get it back**. When you put this book down for the day, take a walk or a bubble bath, spend an hour of pure joy engaged in your favorite hobby, or go buy something for yourself or someone else. **Do not waste one minute of any day.** If you ask people near the end of their lives how they would live their lives if they could be young again, most of them will tell you that they **would live a more accomplished life.**

According to statistics gathered in sixty countries from people on their deathbeds, most people facing death said that, given the chance at a new life, they would spend more time selecting the right profession and/or bettering their education. Next to selecting the right profession, all said they would **spend more time with their families and have more fun.**

It is often true that we **sometimes take life too seriously.**

Consciously use all your senses. We do not just have five, but many more. If you want to explore all of your senses, you do not even need to know them all (by name); **if you live fully in the present moment, you will automatically engage them all.**

The Plan for Achieving Wealth, Success, and Happiness

1. Answer the questions from page 136 (A,B,C, and D) if you have not already.

2. **Play the game "hot seat"** with your closest friends. One person sits in front of the others while the audience of friends tells the person **things about him or her,** everything they feel when they are in contact with him or her, but were either afraid or felt badly about telling him or her. However, be careful. Do this only when you are all in the highest vibration possible. **Do not use this person (on the hot seat) for releasing your tension. The person in the hot seat is told about his or her patterns and positions he or she has taken.** Here is an example of how this conversation should go: "If I were you, I would take a completely different approach to that challenge," or "If I had that challenge, I would not bother with it so much – everybody sees this as beating a dead horse."

With the deepest sincerity, the person is told things that might be especially uncomfortable for the friend to express, and probably difficult for the person on the hot seat to hear. **However, they are things that need to be said and things that will aid in their personal and spiritual growth.** If this process is really carried out in a very high vibration (everyone is in his or her heart), this experience literally connects people. If not, it can separate even long time friends, so **be very careful**.

The one in the hot seat must limit his or her defense to comments such as, "Tell me more," or "Thank you." Not: "I didn't mean that the way it happened," or "Let me explain to you later why I did that," etc. **This process is not meant to be a session where you** (if you are on the hot seat) **heartily defend yourself or spend the whole time apologizing**. That would be a sad waste of the gift your friends are giving you – allowing you to see yourself through the eyes, ears, and experiences of those you affect in your life.

It is often difficult to see the patterns that we ourselves are stuck in, but others notice them. Allowing your friends to tell you about them gives you an opportunity to recognize them and apparently disconnect from some or all of them. You also learn something else in the process – **where you are spending your creative energy**.

Once you have this information before you, embrace it and accept it. Through this experience, realize that you spend your energy on the things you like, just as you do on the things you try to avoid. For instance, **the process of hating someone gives the object of your emotion a lot of your power** because you have to have resonance with it and therefore **be on the same vibration**. Obsessing about someone you hate takes an extreme amount of energy; just becoming familiar with whatever this person has done, or even just thinking about whatever way this person wronged you, drains your creativity. The more you think about something, the more energy you give it, and the more your personal power is drained and given to the object of your hatred. The same is true of unpleasant experiences – the more often and lively you remember them, the more the experience will become engrained in you and the more important it will become to you.

3. You could call the following exercise **"This means that..."** Your mind has plenty of answers ready and waiting to explain everything that happens in your life. Gathering from all the mental files it has stored, your mind gives you reasons and rationalizes everything you encounter, whether the event has any connection

to your present situation or not. An insightful exercise is **to take note, for a day, of the meaning your mind ascribes to each of the day's events**. For instance, when your neighbor does not greet you in his usual style, your mind may tell you (in the form of self-talk): "Mike didn't say anything to me on his way to work this morning – **this means that** he doesn't like me any more." But often, the explanation your mind gives you for an event is completely wrong. However, this news does not stop your mind from providing its explanation anyway, and unfortunately, **your behavior, and ultimately your future, depends more on these explanations than the actual event.**

4. Remember the story about Peter and his difficulty with giving money away? **Find the attributes within you that you would like to explore.** If possible, find the **roots** (not the cause or triggers of emotions outside of you) of the attribute in yourself, and then find a suitable affirmation that you believe in, which, when repeated, will help you in conquering the attribute you want to change. Write out the affirmation and place it in as many spots as possible in your field of vision. Repeat the affirmation every time you see one of your reminders and as often as possible between these times. Then **pay attention to the changes that occur and watch how it affects your life**. Once you have conquered this attribute, **repeat the process with the next feature you want to change**. You can use visualization and other techniques that work for you, as well.

4. The Next Step: Self-Acknowledgement

Testing Your Concentration

The following test is very important. Please take a minute of your time to complete it before moving on. All you will need is a pen or a pencil. Below is a circle with a point in the middle. Place the tip of your pen or pencil on the point in the center of the circle. Close your eyes. With your eyes closed, **lift the pencil** an inch or two **and draw ten circles in the air as close as you can to the size of the circle below.**

Now focus your concentration and try to **place the tip of your pen or pencil back on the point in the center of the circle below**.

Do this exercise five times and record your scores.

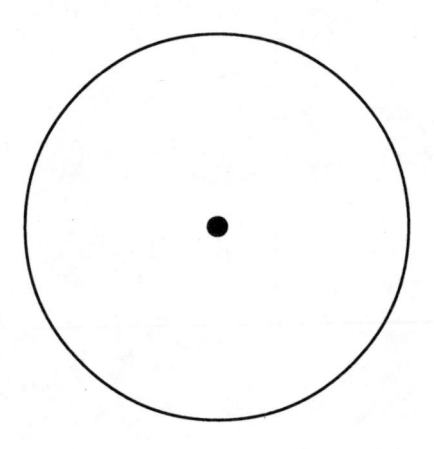

The Next Step: Self-Acknowledgement

It is important to really concentrate while completing this exercise – **the result is important and sincere effort is needed to show this effectively.**

The Result

Did you complete the exercise? Seriously?

It has often been said that a **readiness and willingness to play a game is directly connected to a readiness and willingness to play life.** In other words, if you think these kinds of games are silly and just a waste of time, then you are likely to have **the same assessment about anything new and unconventional that enters your life.**

In fact, there is only one thing we want to find out – did you succeed in hitting the center point **three or more times out of the five trials**? If you did not, that is fine. If you did, let me ask you again. Please answer honestly. Did you hit the center point of the circle, with the tip of your pen or pencil, three or more times?

If you still insist you did, then write, "Yes" on this line! _____.

Maybe you are wondering why I am not congratulating you on your concentration. Well, if you answered "Yes," there is a major problem. Because…

…**hitting the center three or more times out of five trials, if you completed the exercise following the rules provided, is impossible.**

The reason for writing down your answer is that you will be able to defend your answer confidently and not be in the awkward position of not being sure of your answer. So if you answered "Yes" above, then having you write it down prevents you from now saying, "OK, I guess I didn't hit the center, but I was close." The same thing happens in your life whenever you are afraid to take responsibility for something. **When you wrote it down, you took a stand – now it is crystal clear.**

Because of this, it is recommended that all your verbal agreements be confirmed in writing. For example, if you have just made a business agreement with someone, you can do this by sending a "Thank you for your time" letter after the meeting. You can also include a summary of the meeting. Or a simple "Please correct me if I'm wrong" letter that unobtrusively asks for a confirmation of your discussion.

Before we return to the exercise, if you wrote "Yes" above and you really did successfully hit the center point three or more times out of five, please **accept my apology**. Achieving such a result is not only above average, but also extremely rare and if you did so, you have my congratulations. Unfortunately, the results of the exercise have no connection to your ability to concentrate, although it may be a test of your steadiness and orientation skills. The real point of the exercise was something else.

The exercise was meant to show you exactly where you sit regarding your attitude.

It is time to be brutally honest. If you answered "Yes" to the exercise, but did not really achieve what your answer implied, then you need to think seriously about whether you want to go further with us on the path to success. Read the next pages carefully because they are dedicated to you in particular.

This is important... because **the path to success is paved only with Truth.**

Truth-Telling Is Crucial

Telling the truth, to yourself and others, is most important. It is especially important not to lie to yourself.

What do you gain by altering the facts? **Nothing...** At least – you gain nothing regarding your **vibration** (but you can get some illusionary benefits, if you direct your energy into external destiny).

In situations where we feel the need to tell things differently than they are in reality, there is always an **identity crisis** that expresses a **desire for recognition.**

That way, we take every situation as an opportunity to – through comparison – **prove that we know something (better)** or to show ourselves in a light different from that in which we think others see us.

For instance, you are scheduled to meet with a friend at a certain time. When you get there, you are ten minutes late, but your friend still has not come. Just as you get comfortable, he or she arrives and apologizes, "Oh, I'm sorry, I know that you've been waiting a long time... I owe you one, and I'll make it up to you right now – lunch is on me today. I hope you're not in a bad mood now."

How do you react in such a situation? Do you tell him or her that he or she does not have to apologize because you were late yourself, or are you become wisely silent and **take advantage of the opportunity to "earn bonus points" with him or her**?

Until we build a very clear identity **based on the talents and gifts** we possess and our **values and spiritual visions** (internal destiny), we will **continue comparing, proving, and affirming ourselves externally**.

When we see ourselves through the prism of positive traits and values and are very clearly aware that each one of us knows and does something better than others, we will no longer feel the need to prove ourselves in all areas.

That way we will confirm **our identity** in **one** – or maybe a few – **particular area(s)**; the one(s) that is(are) **connected to our life's vision**. And that will make us fully happy, so we will have neither the motivation nor inspiration to invest our energy into the other areas where other people are better than us.

The secret is also in developing our own identity on the basis of that **which we enjoy and are proud of**. If we can achieve this state, our consciousness will derive from this energy on the outside. And so others – according to the principle of resonance – **will perceive our (loving) energy and treat us on this basis**.

For instance, no one is interested in how many languages Mother Theresa or Gandhi spoke. All nations knew them based on some **other identity** – their **dedication, service to higher potentials, and unlimited Truth and Love** – which is all that is important when it comes to their lives. Who cares how many languages they spoke?

Until we have a clearly built identity, which satisfies us, we **search for opportunities** (remember the "five levels" and "three stages;" this is level – or stage – two). When we release tensions and begin to build our life based on the heart and our **own potentials**, which proceed from us and not the surroundings, this desire slowly fades, and **the more absorbed we are in ourselves, the more the sense for Truth and feelings of fulfillment come to the forefront**.

Is Telling the Truth Cruel?

Telling the Truth does not mean you have to be cruel. For example, if you do not like something about your friend, you do not tell him or her that he or she is worthless. (We know that **everything we think, say, or do, is just a reflection of our vibration**... not the other person.)

The Truth always comes from the heart. So if you feel anything other than supportive energy while standing in front of the other person, it is **your personal view on the situation** (and your energy, of course). As said once before, if you want to be truthful in such situations, you should begin your opinion about the other person with "I," and not "you." For example, you will not say, "You are not worthy," but rather, **"I can't resonate with your heart right now because some other thoughts and emotions have overwhelmed me."**

This is the Truth.

Namely, **if you were in very high vibration, you would see nothing but God in this person**. Mother Theresa said numerous times that **she saw Jesus in everyone she dealt with.**

There is one incredible story about a priest who teaches "bad" children, who were expelled from other schools because of their learning disabilities and their bad (violent) behavior. Unlike the other teachers, this priest was able to alter the children's habits and values to such an extent that the children not only made progress, but also became **exceptional pupils** and members of society.

When he was asked **how he dealt with the bad children,** making such progress in their minds, he answered, "What bad children?"

So we have to **distinguish the Truth from our personal view** on situations.

There is also another question we have to deal with: **When is it appropriate to tell the other person everything we feel or see in him or her... or to tell anything at all?** The answer is **when – or if – we are asked to.** And even then, we have to be very careful to choose a time when both of us are in a **state of higher vibration** (with open hearts). If not, this can lead into tension releasing and blaming others.

So **if no one asks us to tell him or her what we want to, why bother?** Obviously, if we feel an urge to say it aloud, **we have the problem with it,** not the other person. When we solve it within ourselves, it often miraculously disappears when we think about the person involved.

But if we do want to talk about something with this person, the best way is **to open our hearts and admit that we have a problem and ask the person for help.** This is proper communication, which can be a big problem if we are not ready to admit what is going on.

Losing Self-Appreciation

We have mentioned several times that taking responsibility for ourselves and our actions is most important – a lie deceptively offers comfort or **delegates our responsibilities to others.**

People who shrink from responsibility or openly lie **lose themselves in a destructive, repetitive cycle.** They crave to be acknowledged by others and to be seen in a different light. However, by shifting their responsibilities to others, they **lose their self-confidence** and self-appreciation, and they find that they must then embellish the truth to gain the acknowledgment, respect, and attention they seek.

What is it that a person is seeking to achieve by lying to him or herself? Who are they fooling?

Again, it is time for the Truth. So let us take a deeper look and see what is going on.

First, let us take a **personal inventory**. Do you know who you really are?

On the other hand, do you know **what you think you are**? You would be amazed at how many people really do not know themselves well enough to answer these questions. A lot of them simply sleepwalk through life; they have become **slaves to their habits** to such an extent that they believe **they have no choice.**

The next chapters contain exercises that will help you uncover more about yourself.

Exercise: Who You Think You Are?

Take a piece of paper and draw a line down the center so that you have two parts. Write down all the characteristics that describe you (positively) on the left side. Do not be modest; it is important to know your strengths. You should take several days, if necessary, to complete the list. Now write down everything that bothers you about yourself on the right side. Ask your friends, family, and colleagues to help with either list, if you so desire.

The Millionaire Mindset

You will soon notice two things:
1. That you are harder on yourself and more critical towards yourself.
2. That others see you differently than you see yourself.

You will probably find out that you have many more pleasant (positive) attributes than unpleasant ones. So you aren't so bad? If you are not sure of your answer here, or if your unpleasant attributes dominate the pleasant ones, **choose the one that bothers you the most, assemble an affirmation, and adopt it into your daily routine.**

For example: You note that you lack social skills and you feel this is the primary cause for your poor communication skills and the root of many of your problems; now you want to change it. Great! Now compose an affirmation such as this one: "People seek and enjoy my company, and every day I make new friends."

You thought about it and discovered that this is **actually completely true** – if you allow yourself to be yourself and socialize. Now when you are 100% certain of this thought, it is necessary to **repeat it as many times as possible and think about yourself in this way rather than the old way ("I'm unsocial")**. You can also use visualization or anything else that can help you start to accept this new image as soon as possible.

As we said many times, **when you repeat this affirmation, you have to feel it to be true**; if not, a "little voice" in your head argues with it, and thus you cannot truly believe it.

You have to think of yourself in this new way **from this day onwards**, using the power of the affirmation and other techniques to recall it to mind and reinforce it many times each day. This is, once again, the power of critical mass, a mass that will build to a level (through positive affirmations, etc.) where it can **overwrite your present thoughts and emotions about yourself**. Once this happens, you can easily **expand your boundaries** (this is what life is all about).

The best way is to set aside ten minutes each morning on rising and ten minutes each night before sleeping to do this and, as often as you can, remind yourself or think about it during the day. **Schedule this time with yourself**, just like you would with any other appointment, and then write the affirmation on several sticky notes and place them in key spots, like your briefcase, computer monitor, bathroom mirror, refrigerator door, telephone, etc.

The Next Step: Self-Acknowledgement

Now you are ready to receive a better tomorrow, and it will come.

Do not discard the paper on which you noted your pleasant and unpleasant characteristics; keep it in someplace where it will receive your attention regularly. And every time you overcome an unpleasant characteristic, **remove it from the right side and write it in red on the leftside.**

This is now your success list, and you need to consistently remind yourself of every success.

The Easiest Way to Discover What Is Hidden Inside of You

Here is yet an easier way to find out **how you really feel about yourself** (or what vibration you are in); even if your mind assures you that you are the best or that you are worthless.

If you are unsure of how you feel about yourself, you can find the answer by **asking yourself what you feel towards others**.

This is, in most cases, a **pattern of behavior** that forms on the basis of energies, which you do not separate into internal (yours) and external (someone else's) within yourself, but you **react in the same way to all of them**. For instance, if you are of the opinion that someone is unfriendly, if he or she does not greet you, you will take a special stance toward this person when you notice that he or she did not greet you.

But you also treat yourself in the same way when you encounter the same energy. If, for instance, you discover that you were passing by a friend and did not notice or greet him or her, you will have a **feeling similar to that as if you had done something wrong.**

That is why we must be careful about how we understand other people's bad habits because in so doing, we are at the same time, and in the same way, limiting ourselves: **everything we approve of in others, we will approve of in ourselves.** The same is true of the things we disapprove of.

So what is the solution? What it has always been up to this point – **to turn inwards and learn to accept life as it is; allow a person** to express himself or herself in the way that seems fit to him or her at that moment.

That is why **forgiveness** is necessary, **firstly to you** – because you took a certain position (viewpoint) towards others and categorized them on

The Millionaire Mindset

the basis of their **activities** (how they behaved towards you) and **on the basis of resonance with them**. That means if you were not in a certain vibration, you would not feel it when you think of – or get in contact with – others.

Once you become aware of your shortcomings, decide where you want to begin to change them, and then work on them one by one. As said, **working on one's self always means including the energy of the heart and reinforcing one's capacity for unconditional acceptance**.

Observe your new reactions. Have they changed? Ask your friends and family to warn you when (if) old habits come to the surface again.

Be Your Best Friend

A high-level of self-confidence and belief in their own abilities and self-worth are common characteristics of highly successful people. So **learn to be your best friend**.

It is time to confront the emotions that hinder our progress. Write down the following affirmations, written by Leonard Orr, a writer and spiritual teacher. **If you truly believe them**, they will empower you and raise your performance level. (If you do not feel you trust them completely, adapt the affirmations so that they will fit your vibration.)

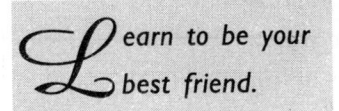

Learn to be your best friend.

- "I, [insert your full name here], love myself. I'm full of love."
- "I'm a friend to me."
- "Through loving myself, I love others."
- "Through loving others, I love myself."
- "When I give to others, I give to me… and when I give to me, I give to others."

Use the following visualization technique, as well. Think of a person you respect for his or her self-confidence. Picture others telling you how **alike you are**. You can even imagine meeting people you think highly of and receiving their positive reaction to you, as you look at them in their eyes, stand straight, and talk with them confidently. Everyone congratulates you for your success.

Phil Laut, best-selling author of the book, *Money is My Friend*, proposes some other methods for raising self-confidence:

1. Write down all the things you **really want to do**.
2. Write down all thoughts that express an **urge or fear** (they begin with, "I have to," "It's urgent that I," "It would be better if I," "It is necessary that I"). Replace the beginning of the sentence with, "I want." Now ask yourself if **the new sentence is true**.
3. **Allow yourself tiny delights** – take a bubblebath, get a massage, rest, spend time doing the things you enjoy, travel first-class, go to a restaurant and order a special dish without first looking at the price, etc.
4. **Speak respectfully and supportively about yourself and others and expect the same in return.** Find something you like in each person you meet and then view them through this favorable attribute.
5. **Reserve a set time for self-reflection.** This is a time to write affirmations and engage in other forms of self-approval. This will give you confidence and help you become your own best friend.

Self-Analysis and Self-Recognition

Sometimes you do not even need to know exactly where you are and why you are in a particular situation, but other times you do. Self-analysis, as we look at it, means **being open to explore your true self**, not simply researching how bad you are. It is a process of evaluating the filters that you view your life through, accepting and supporting some of them, discarding others, and changing those that remain.

In this chapter, we will expand on an exercise with affirmations from one of the previous chapters. What we will be doing, ultimately, is **comparing your personal truth about life with the Truth**.

With self-analysis, **sincerity is everything** – doing the opposite means, you are cheating yourself. So let us start.

Take the time to write down all the areas of your life that are important to you: family, friends, business, etc.

Select one of the areas you noted as important. On a new piece of paper, write it down several times. While doing so, whisper what you write, like "My family life is important to me." Allow your rational mind and subconscious to give you their suggestions regarding that area.

The Millionaire Mindset

Various thoughts will begin to take shape in your mind. **Write down everything that comes to you!**

Do not select or edit your thoughts, just write them down; you will select them later. Even if a thought does not appear to be connected with the chosen area, write it down.

When your thoughts begin to just repeat themselves, stop writing.

Now it is time to analyze what you wrote:

- Select all the unpleasant ("negative") thoughts. These would include bad hunches, fear, weakness, envy, anger indignation, despair, and so on. Do not worry about what percentage this unsupportive group represents of the total thoughts you wrote down.

- Focus on the biggest problems that most thoughts or emotions are connected with. Often, you will discover that the **central theme** of all, or most of your unpleasant thoughts or emotions, falls under the same umbrella. Therefore, even though you have many different unpleasant thoughts, one unpleasant emotion overrides, and vice versa.

- Ask yourself what can you do right now to solve the challenge consciously or at least make a plan of action that gets you heading in that direction. **The best time to start is now, this moment, not the first of the month, Monday, or tomorrow morning.** Taking the first step is difficult, but after a while, when you discover how much your life has changed, you will be grateful for every moment you gained by starting now!

- **Identify the most unpleasant or the "key negative thought" and turn it into a pleasant and supportive affirmation that best fits you and your circumstances.** It does not need to be the kind of affirmation discussed before; it could also be a picture, maybe even a smell, an emotion… or a combination. For instance, if the cause of your misfortune is a lack of money, then the affirmation, "I always have enough money" is one your conscious mind will **immediately reject**. You can get around this, as shown in the chapter, "Your Conscious and Subconscious Minds," but your results will be faster and better if you alter the affirmation to something like, "I have **all I need right now** – so I am wealthy. Today and every day onwards, everything works for me. Today is the beginning of my new life and I become richer in thought and wealthier every day."

Repeat the affirmations or other reminders over the course of the day – morning, noon, and night. Your subconscious will accept them and begin to work on them faster when you are in direct connection with it. It is always best to **write them down**, as well. If your schedule does not allow a planned programming session for your subconscious, then you can tape your thoughts and play the tape while you drive, ride the train, etc.

Thinking About Yourself

Scientists have revealed that we spend 90% of our thinking time **thinking about ourselves**; so make sure you do it in your favor.

It is highly recommended that you perform all affirmations used to increase your self-confidence **in front of a mirror, looking at yourself directly in the eyes**.

Since we are discussing how thoughts shape the world we live in, positive thought becomes critical and something that cannot be accomplished with low self-confidence or low self-esteem.

Always bear in mind that **you are not fixing things or making them look nicer; you are in the process of loving them**.

The difference is crucial. If you fix something, it means that you perceive that thing as bad – so you will probably want to **hide or suppress it**. The more you perceive something as bad, the more inclined you are to **generate emotions of shame or guilt**. And the more you try to fix that bad thing, the more shame or guilt you generate.

So **the whole process is based on the energy of Love**, which means you have to do it from Love – you have to hit critical mass so that your **consciousness will stay there no matter what** – and with Love.

We also know that if the critical mass of your energy of Love is not high (or strong) enough, you will actually generate more and more shame and guilt while repeating the affirmations because the strongest emotion will overwrite all others.

Accept Your Emotions

Earlier we discussed how actions are influenced by your thought patterns. **How you react to a certain situation is more crucial than the situation itself.** The analysis of your emotions is the foundation you can use to build the strengths of your personality.

It is natural for people to experience emotions they are not always proud of, especially since they feel that the emotions have been forced on them since birth.

For instance, most people experience at least a tinge of jealousy – some even anger – when they discover someone they know earns a far better salary than they do. If the person is especially angry, his or her self-talk might be, "He got this salary simply because he has the right connections." Some people cope with the emotions in these circumstances by denying the situation: "She doesn't really make that much, she's only bragging." Such denial brings about a sense of relief because it is no longer accompanied by the further assault that someone else succeeded where this person failed.

Whatever temporary relief the above scenario may bring, you will not get far thinking like this. **If you want to change, you must get to the root of why you react the way you do to such news.**

We said this before, but let us stress this again because it could be crucial: You do not have to know the reason why and how this happens, but it is important to **get to the root** so you can embrace the cause, not just the consequences, lovingly.

Let us return to our example of falling into a lower energy state when we find out that someone else makes more money.

If the energy of this situation bothers you, then obviously it has something to do with you. The other person is only the trigger that **boosted a specific energy in you**. That is why you reacted the way you did.

If you earned a lot of money – a great deal more than that other person – and were happy with it, **you probably would not perceive that energy as an interrupting one.** Imagine that you won the lottery in a big way – a million or more. Would you still bother about the salary of that other person? Probably not. Therefore, it has something to do with you… and your salary. Maybe you feel you deserve better; maybe you know that you are very important at your workplace; perhaps you know you do a lot more or better work than someone who earns the same or even more; etc.

Maybe you uncover many instances where you tried hard to command a higher salary, but failed and someone else always got the money you felt you deserved. Maybe it even felt like that person received credit for your work.

Whatever happened, you might have even developed an internal opinion that raises are nothing more than being in the right place at the right time and have nothing to do with whether or not the person deserves a raise. If this happened to you, hearing of someone else's raise would trigger you to infer, "He didn't get the raise because he deserved it – he was only in the right place at the right time. **I am the one who deserves it because I'm the one who works, but someone else is getting the reward.**"

Now you are faced with redesigning your emotionally charged reaction and that means you must change your thoughts, so that future news does not elicit the same unpleasant and unsupportive reaction. How?

As we said many times, first **consciously disconnect your life energy from that area** and then **focus it somewhere else**; wherever you like, but that new area **has to fill you with trust, joy,** and/or **peace**. When you feel uplifted and full of energy, look at this original area, and you will see it in a more pleasant light; of course, if you can remain in that higher vibration.

Once again, this is about accepting everything that happens. This does not mean that you should try to hide what bothers you. If you feel badly about something – **love that emotion**, like you love your child, even if he or she does something that is not nice.

You are what you express deep inside. Remember what we said: **We never experience other people, only ourselves.** (We **resonate** with the energies of others, then **awaken** those energies in ourselves and maybe even feel fear – as a reaction to these energies. And **that is what we feel** and what is really going on when we say, "You are behaving badly towards me.")

Then you can decide whether you want to apply a **different mental structure** – or meaning – to this situation. Maybe like this one: "When others have more, I have more because we come from One. I wish him all the best, because in doing so, I wish it for me. I am happy for his success because I am happy for my own, as well. His example can show me how I can make more money, as well. If he can do it, so can I. Thank you for confirming that it is possible to do better and earn more."

Needless to say, you have to feel it in your heart, which is only possible if your consciousness is (momentarily located) in high vibration.

Once this takes hold in your subconscious, you will always be joyful when you hear something good happened to someone else. The consequence will be that you will truly wish people luck – and they will wish you luck – and gain a stronger will as well as the motivation to do better.

This is who you really are. Did you know that **your natural state is one of peace, love, happiness, and relaxation**? Unpleasant thoughts and explosive reactions weaken that state to something far less favorable, a state characterized by a lack of love. When reduced to this unfortunate state, the mind is filled with **despair and the overwhelming emotion of the inability to change**.

This Might Poison You

Now let us examine something else that might poison you.

Did you know that **listening to the news and reading newspapers is one of the most destructive things you can do to start or end your day**? It is a recorded fact that more than half of the unpleasant news you are bombarded with **does not serve your life in any way** other than to provide you with information you do not need anyway. For the most part, the news only causes stress and raises concerns and feelings of weakness in most of its viewers.

Do you see any benefit in that?

The common argument is, "Well, what if they announce something I have to know about?" Do not worry, you will hear about it soon enough from fellow coworkers, family members, your neighbor, at the barber or beauty shop, etc.

More advice: If your job entails much travel, invest in good taped seminars and audio books – those that **open your heart** (not give you more information; **we have way too much information about God, Love, happiness... and much too little experience of them**). This way you can make the best and most efficient use of your travel time.

The Next Step: Self-Acknowledgement

In the next chapters, we will do some exercises that will bring us closer to our true self.

Exercise: Dealing With Others Versus Dealing With Self

Make a list of people who you feel have offended you. Write down all the events that connect you to them that have ended in disappointment. Now taking each event separately, answer the following questions:

Why was I so disappointed and why did I respond with such anger (sadness, rejection...)? Were my expectations too high, and thus was I disappointed only because he or she did not fulfill my expectations? What criteria within me led to these decisions? What needs were my decisions designed to fulfill?

For example, you failed to land a great business deal because your business partner – who worked side by side with you for years – reacted inappropriately at what proved to be the most critical moment and set too high a price.

Who is to blame? You probably feel your partner is to blame, but the question is, is that true?

Have you not known him and his shortcomings for years? **You should have known how he would react.** Why did you depend on him to close the deal when you knew that he has reacted this way in similar situations?

With that question, you can check your reaction and assume responsibility for the situation.

But be careful. This way you can easily feel guilty for the situation, and that is not to your benefit either. The right attitude is like this: "I put my all into this situation and did everything I knew best. Everything else – including the outcome of this situation – **was not in my domain.**"

You can learn a lot from this simple practice of **accepting responsibility for the decisions you make** and **freeing yourself from the outcome that follows when others step in.** We must not forget Jesus' promise: "Are not two sparrows sold for a cent? And yet, **not one of them will fall to the ground apart from your Father.** But the very hairs of your head are all numbered. So **do not fear;** you are more valuable than many sparrows." (Matthew 10:29-31)

If you can truly accept it, you will feel that there is **nothing that can happen that your Creator is not aware of**... and that is not in your higher good.

When you assume responsibility for events that happen to you, you discover that there is no one else to forgive... because it is you who are responsible for the reactions you have to the situation you find yourself in. That way, you will turn away from blaming others ("He doesn't respect the time we agreed to meet."), and will take responsibility instead: "I didn't consider all the variables like traffic, his previous engagement, etc. I expected him to live up to my expectations and give up everything else – just to be at our meeting on time. This has brought me to my current state of anger and disappointment."

Here is something else interesting that happens: When your **identity** is not linked to always having to be on time, you do not expect others to be the same – and you will **drop these expectations very easily**; not because "it is right to do so," but because you will simply find out that treating **yourself and others this way does not work in your favor.**

But when you see yourself through that identity ("I have to be on time so that people will respect and like me"), it will be hard to stay indifferent to your activities regarding this identity... and even harder to disconnect from the **disappointment that follows when you – or others – do not perform perfectly** (read: when you or others are late).

Exercise: Disconnecting From Your (Not Genuine) Self

This next exercise is both fun and enlightening. **Observe yourself for a day, and write down the emotions and the reactions you have to any situations that arise.** A tape recorder helps a great deal. The number of times you are jealous, malicious, angry, unfair, or helpless in a single day can surprise you. But this is not an exercise about feeling guilty, but about **recognizing what is going on**. It is simple, but very effective.

When finished, put your reactions, thoughts, and emotions into categories (pleasant: supportive, enlightening, etc.; and unpleasant: greed, jealousy, anger, worries, etc.). Then **choose an unpleasant one**; something that appeared repeatedly or was the strongest (what you see as the root of many other lower energies).

Work on it. First, **stop the automatic response** by consciously observing yourself: When you want to respond the automatic way, **choose to do something else** – anything – **instead**.

Next, **accept and embrace this energy with love**. At the same time, direct your energy into something that will **replace the old pattern**.

Exercise: Rewriting Your Present Views

We will – again – use affirmations in this chapter.

Divide a sheet of paper in two. On the left side, write down the affirmation. On the right side, **record your reaction to saying the affirmation aloud**. Then repeat the exercise: Write the same affirmation down, and again write down what you hear in your mind.

Always write thoughts in the same manner you would speak them and always include your name. Doing so will reproduce, as closely as possible, the true state of affairs.

Keep repeating this until it seems your response is **real or definite** to you, or until you encounter a specific reaction (below) to it in your response, which would indicate that an essential obstacle has appeared.

Such a reaction would look like this:

Affirmation   **Reaction:**

Affirmation	Reaction
I, Peter Green, become richer every day.	No way.
You, Peter Green, become richer every day.	I don't believe it.
Peter Green becomes richer every day.	It would be nice to hear it.
I, Peter Green, become richer every day.	I've heard that before.
You, Peter Green, become richer every day.	You're jealous, aren't you?
Peter Green becomes richer every day.	Yeah, yeah, the situation has changed boys.
I, Peter Green, become richer every day.	Finally the time has come.

And so on. Towards the end, you can see how your subconscious overcomes the unpleasant thought and stops fighting it. (This usually takes much more space and time than represented above.) The stated goal (affirmation) is achieved when your written response to your affirmation is positive on the first attempt:

The Millionaire Mindset

In this way you have succeeded. But it can also happen that the reactions bring you to an unsolvable obstacle that looks something like:

I, Peter Green, become richer each day.	I have waited a long time for this to happen
I, Peter Green, become richer each day.	It sounds like a cartoon.
You, Peter Green, become richer each day.	Who would say that to me?
Peter Green becomes richer each day.	You would say that to make fun of me.
I, Peter Green, become richer each day.	It sounds nice, but it is impossible.
You, Peter Green, become richer each day.	Even friends make fun of me now.
Peter Green becomes richer each day.	I will be the laughingstock of the town.
I, Peter Green, become richer each day.	Even if I did, I wouldn't tell anyone.
You, Peter Green, become richer each day.	Nobody would notice because he or she is too self-occupied.
Peter Green becomes richer each day.	Who even knows me?

You can clearly see that this person (above) lacks confidence, both in himself and the world around him. In this case, it becomes **necessary to change the affirmation to something his mind is able to accept**. As he gains self-confidence, the affirmation can again be altered.

Such an affirmation might be:

"I, Peter Green, become more popular every day. Every day something wonderful happens when I meet people."

Once this level is achieved, Peter would return to the previous affirmation or higher level.

As often as possible, engage the support of others along the way; **their faith in you will give you the extra courage and enthusiasm you need to succeed in tipping the scale in your favor.**

The Right Path

No matter how technically complicated all these suggestions (recording your thoughts, affirmations, self-analysis, etc.) appear, **every true solution happens in the same way and always occurs in two stages**:

- Disconnection of the existing (harmful) relationship, pattern, or energy.
- Replacement of these conditional energies with **unconditional ones**; therefore, listening to the heart and following this energy at every moment in all situations.

The majority of books, seminars, suggestions, etc. address only the **first point**. However, if you only replace one energy with another – which is not based in the heart, soul, and intuition – and continue the same way as you have till now, you will only replace the packaging, while the very heart of the matter will remain the same. You will not come to happiness that way.

So we can summarize every path described in this book (and others): **It is necessary to just turn away from the energies that poison us, open our hearts, and accept the energy of the heart**. For this to happen, it is necessary to **turn away from the identity (recognition) built on the energies of the physical/external world** (and material and other similar values that accompany it, which separate and categorize people).

As we said, we can get material wealth. However, if we want everything, and we want to be happy at the same time, it is necessary to **go into the heart**. The path always ends in the heart, where it also began.

This is Jesus' promise, as we have already mentioned. When the Apostles asked Him to describe the end, He said that we will **return to the beginning**, and this will be the end of searching and the return to Paradise.

The Primary Cause for Self-Deceit

Let us move a step ahead. **What is the basic reason** that led us into this situation?

The primary cause for self-deceit is a **lack of love** – for yourself, others, and life in general. If you want to move forward, you have to **establish the energy of Love in yourself and then proceed from it**; your thoughts, words, and activities should express this energy.

> *If you do not love yourself enough, then you will try to prove to yourself and others how good you are with every deed.*

Here is a common question that follows: "But how can I love me... if I know that I'm not good because I did these horrible things in the past... and therefore (maybe even) **don't deserve Love**?"

The simplest way to establish self-love is this: **Do not love your actions, emotions, titles, and images... love the God within you**. He is there, because **you are made in His image**. You also have (the vibration of) Christ, Buddha, Mohamed, Krishna, etc. within.

They all have dedicated their lives to show us that **the right path is following our hearts**.

You have your heart, intuition, and soul with an enormous amount of wisdom, love, peace, and joy that you can connect to every second.

You are God inside. Can you feel it? **Your Father wants to give you a Kingdom** – just ask for it (read: hit that vibration and preserve that energy) and **it is yours.**

If you can think of nothing good or nice about yourself, these are things you can love every second and all the time. **Everything else is not the real you – it is just luggage.**

So when you think of you, try to think that way; this is who you really are.

Love this, your True Self. And when you build the critical mass of the energy of Love, embrace your shadows – or other/lower self – along with it. (Read the step-by-step process in *Charisma, Self-Confidence and Personal Power*.) This is the path that anyone can use.

If you do not love yourself enough, then you will try to prove to yourself and others how good you are with every deed – as in the exercise at the beginning of the chapter (with the pencil and circle) – as well as in almost everything you do daily. Until you overcome those obstacles, you will not take a single step towards success, and you will even take several steps **backwards and away from true success**, which is always connected with raising your vibration.

When you are confident about yourself, your knowledge, experiences, and abilities, you will know of your many good attributes, and thus scoring below average on a single test **will not influence your self-image at all**. Love yourself enough, and you will forgive yourself a few missteps, and you will never have a problem acknowledging and owning up to your mistakes. You will be able to say, "I made a mistake, and I apologize for it. Can I do anything to make this situation better? Please, let me know." And you will mean it.

The same is true of successful businesspeople. If they are professional in their work and successful in their field of expertise, they can afford to not know everything without tarnishing their reputation as experts.

Now we will move ahead – to **connections with others**. Namely, we often use other people for our growth.

Distinguishing Yourself From Others

Day after day, something happens… something that you probably are not even aware of: You demonstrate to the world that you are not like everyone else – **you are different.**

How?

If you are like most people, you do so externally, through **the choices you make in material goods**. Some people buy designer clothes, others frequent expensive or fashionable restaurants, while others buy expensive cars and prestigious real estate and homes. Some people even distinguish themselves by refusing to buy these items or frequent these places.

Those that cannot afford the lifestyle they long for try to get it by **associating with people who can**… or at least by socializing together with them (and that way are "energetically connected" to that prestige).

People join various clubs, groups, religions, sects, and so on for similar reasons; **they are looking for some teacher or guru who will show them the way and lead them to happiness**. Such socializing is very supportive at first because this is the way we can break old patterns and arouse the energy to form something new. The problem is when we, as a group or individual, surrender our power and give it away in the sense, "Tell me what to do, you know what's best for me."

This indicates complete denial of one's true self, especially if the person is prepared to do what others suggest. Clearly, we are talking about things that this person **neither feels in the heart as joy nor perceives as a step** forward; as long as everything is in harmony with his or her internal image, and he or she is cultivating joyful expectations towards everything, he or she is on the path of development. But when he or she silences the part of himself or herself that says, "Watch out, this may not be as good for you as you want to see it," he or she is walking on thin ice.

In the end, we will have to **return to the heart and look inside**; it is just a question of how many teachers and gurus we will need to recognize this. The sooner we come to this decision, the sooner we will come to true contentedness.

The final guru and teacher will always be your heart. That is why – when you realize this Truth and feel the wisdom of your heart – you **do not have to search any further** because everything else from this point on will only distract you from your true goal. You just have to **claim that energy and work with it**.

Here is another interesting question. How do we know that we are in the heart or on the vibration of Love? **When we notice, accept, and express Love all the time, everywhere, to everyone.**

This can be a cruel fact for someone who is closely linked to only one philosophy, religion, person... because **Love does not separate**. If you really love, you are no more in favor of anyone or anything. So if you are, for example, a devoted Christian, you will love **Jesus Christ as well as** everyone else – Mohamed, Buddha, Krishna, Guru Nanek, boss, neighbor, strangers, etc. – with the **same spirit**.

Why Do We Want to Be Different?

Let us get back to our subject – distinguishing ourselves from others.

People who want to be noticed as special, extraordinary, or even as the cream of society all have the same problem – **they do not see themselves as who they really are inside, and for that reason seek a supplement that will raise them to an above average level in the eyes of others**. They usually think that a person is what he or she possesses, how "in" he or she is, or how he or she matches the latest fashion – in all areas of life.

Like we said before, they can see special values – gifts or talents – when they look at others, but they refuse to see them in themselves. Or they see them but compare them with those of others... and feel that **their gift is not as good as someone else's talent**. They now have an urge to

prove how good they are because they strongly believe people do not see the treasure that lies within them, but value and esteem them according to what they show outwardly.

Have you ever thought about the attributes of those that others hold in such high esteem? **They are people that follow their own path, unconcerned about others' opinions regarding their choices.** They do things their way, and that is what sets them apart from those around them.

The rest, who try to follow, never reach their level because they do not derive from their self, but **copy someone** – by following their external activities, not by following their heart and passion.

The saying, "Every copy is less than the original," describes this perfectly.

Personal Growth

We often think that we will be able to reach our own happiness through someone else's happiness, but the truth is quite the opposite: If your goal is to make others happy, you must make yourself happy first.

You will never succeed any other way **because you will be searching for either what you do not have or what you want (more of) – in others.**

As long as they behave this way – and please you – you will be **very happy and act lovingly toward them,** but when they no longer behave this way, you will point your finger and say, "We are out of love. And it's completely your fault that we're not having a nice time anymore."

The true path only begins when we learn to accept life and not feel that we are sucked into it and have no other choice.

Pleasure, which comes from expectations or the specifically defined reactions (responses) of others, is just a moment between two evils, says Sai Baba. "Today you are happy, but you need only one phone call to make you unhappy," added Stephen Turoff.

This will continue to happen **until we build satisfaction on the basis of what we carry within, which can neither be taken from us nor changed.**

In other words: **The true path only begins when we learn to accept life and not feel that we are sucked into it and have no other choice.** Until then, we are going around in circles and will be dependent upon the reactions of the surroundings.

> *You cannot help a beggar by becoming one of them.*

How to Please Others

A lot of people also think that their happiness is connected to serving others by **sympathizing with their emotions and the positions** they are in... no matter what these emotions and positions are.

Well, if your goal is to add to the happiness of others, this is the way to do it: offer them **an environment for their resonance with your (true) happiness**. If you are just sympathetic to their (unpleasant) emotions that come from lower vibration, think again.

You will not get to higher vibration – your goal – if you resonate with others by having sympathy for their bad moods. Brian Tracy once wrote that **you cannot help a beggar by becoming one of them**... this way you only get two beggars instead of one.

The first step to help others is to **remain within your (high and powerful) energy, focused on your goals**; thus, you can help others by **being a role model**. Secondly, **offer your help** – based on getting them out of lower vibrations into higher ones – unconditionally... when you are asked.

People firstly need **trust and proof** (role model) that something can be achieved; they need someone to show them that taking that first step is not as difficult as they imagine. Additionally, and most importantly, they need someone to show them that this **actually works**.

Contrary to what you might think, **when people ask you for help, they are not usually looking for you to express your empathy about their state or position**; even if they express the energy of wanting to hear something like, "Yes, you really have had a run of bad luck... such a good person and now this has happened."

Well, even if they think they want resonance on this lower vibration they are stuck in, they really **do not need it**.

Actually, this energy of empathy could help them **momentarily**, or in **the short-term**, to get **some fresh energy to make a start**. This way, they can find trust in you because they will know you **understand** them, and therefore **know what they are going through**, and also **what they need to get out of this state**.

But soon after that moment of resonance, you should **show them the way to get unstuck**, if you really want to help them.

Offer them **help getting out of their current situation and back on the right track – high vibration**. If you engage in the sympathy game with them (telling them how good they are and how tragic their situation is), they will **drag you down into their lower energy state**.

So persist in your energy and **offer only energies of higher vibration**: love, peace, power, trust, faith, hope. If they do not want your help – but just someone to understand their misfortune and a shoulder to lean on (read: someone they can release their tension on) – reconsider whether engaging with this person is part of your path.

You do not help people by being who they want you to be. **You help people most by living your higher potential so that you can offer them a positive role model, giving them the permission they seek to do the same.**

Imagine this situation: You are in pain and go to see a doctor. After writing a prescription for you, you ask him or her, "Do you really think I need this? Maybe I can get through without this… or you can give me something else instead?" And the doctor replies, "Yes, you are right. **What do you suggest?**"

Will you trust that doctor? No… The doctor **must remain detached from the patient and his or her illness** and offer the help he or she is trained to provide to assist him or her back to health. **Integrity counts.**

It is the same when you come into contact with someone who is on a lower vibration and asks for help. But be careful, integrity does not mean playing God before the other person and making him or her small.

Taking a Stand

Let us clarify another thing that will let you claim your power – **eternal indulgence**. If you have a problem with that, the next few lines could be helpful.

Have you ever said, "I'll wait another five minutes and not a minute more"? Of course, you may even say or think it often. But what happens when the five minutes pass? Your attitude changes if the person you were waiting for has not arrived, but is important enough to you to wait longer. "Now, really only ten more minutes, maybe something has kept him."

You read in the preface how much easier it is to think with a clear mind if you are not involved in something right now. So you can do something to prevent falling into temptation to wait longer than you planned:

When you agree on a time to meet, decide up front how long you will wait.

At that time, you are not yet emotionally involved in the situation. When you stand waiting somewhere and the time you promised you would wait passes, do not be tempted to comfort yourself by staying another ten minutes, telling yourself the extra ten minutes will not change anything or that you have got nothing better to do anyway.

(But again – **this is only a suggestion** if you find that this is your serious problem or that you have developed a pattern that you do not know how to handle. So that does not mean you are not allowed to wait for a friend a little longer!)

If you cannot take such a hard stand, or if it seems too cruel to whomever you are waiting for, ask yourself **how you could have spent this time in the most useful way**.

Perhaps you will discover that you **did not really want to go at all**; maybe you were just going as a courtesy to your partner or friend. You may even discover that these meetings mean no more than another obligation to you or that you are giving up something more pleasant and important to you to go.

If nothing else, **use all this waiting time for something more productive**. For instance, when you predict you might have to wait, take some good reading with you.

Standing up for you shows that you have respect for yourself and your time. **If you respect yourself, others will, too.** By telling people upfront how long you will wait for them, you remove the anxiety associated with the feelings of guilt you may have when you begin to exercise your assertiveness.

Getting and Offering Love

As we see, people attempt daily, in various ways, to **buy love**: with compliments, gifts, money, agreeing with someone, donating time, etc. Unfortunately, what they are giving and getting in return, **is not always (unconditional and pure) Love**.

The same is true with accepting love from someone else – **it is impossible to allow someone to love you more than you love yourself**. How much

The Next Step: Self-Acknowledgement

you love yourself is directly tied to how much love you allow yourself; how much you feel you deserve.

Even a compliment cannot exceed what you think you deserve: If someone's opinion of you is higher than yours, you will **reject the compliment** at some level.

That is to say, **inside you feel how much you are worth, and that is the limit of what you will accept about yourself from others**. You open the door as much as you think is right – as much as your zone of comfort will allow.

> *It is impossible to allow someone to love you more than you love yourself.*

This can be illustrated with a simple math model.

If you like yourself at a level six and someone else likes you at a level nine, you will only allow yourself **to accept love up to the sixth level** you are comfortable with.

Anything above that seems exaggerated, inflated, and unacceptable to you, and you reject it.

This extends to all areas of your life. For example, if you have a bad opinion of yourself, low self-esteem, etc., acquiring wealth is an unbridgeable problem simply because you do not feel that you are worthy or deserving of it.

So the more you can love yourself, the more love you will allow others to give you... and allow yourself to give them, as well.

Perhaps emotions that express loyalty, admiration, or even indifference are slightly different. As we said, by admiring someone to the point of putting them on a pedestal to the stars, you **deteriorate your own value** accordingly.

When you are able to just embrace everything, "good" or "bad," you will neither have enemies nor be attached or chained to anyone; **you will control your own energy**. This is the only way you will find happiness.

Do not search for excuses to postpone giving your love to yourself and others! Keep in mind also that people who least deserve love need it most.

Just love and you will be doing the best and the most that you can do.

In fact, **one way to know when you have accepted life is that you will not have that urge to change the things you have no real influence over,** or even the things you do have the ability to change. Instead, you will just experience life.

The quality and steadfastness of a relationship with another person arises from the love you give yourself... you experience what you express (remember?). For this reason, you can enjoy a good relationship with another person, allowing them to enjoy a good relationship with you, only if you have achieved a true state of love for yourself.

You Cannot Give What You Do Not Have

We can also say this another way: **You cannot give what you do not have.**

If you are not happy, how can you possibly add to the happiness of someone else? **If you do not have happiness within, how can you give it?**

How can you help others in realizing their desires if you cannot manage to realize your own? If you cannot love yourself, how can you give love to another? How can you accept someone else's love when you cannot accept love from yourself?

Directing energy into others is a lot of times yet **another trick of our conscious mind to take us away from contact with our soul**, our true self.

Exercise: Ten Minutes With Yourself

Here is another exercise.

You will need an alarm that you can set and a quiet room. Turn off all sources of sound, remove all things that could disturb your isolation, and set your alarm for ten minutes.

Sit down and do not do anything. **Just be with yourself.**

For people who lack respect for themselves, this test is disturbingly hard and will seem to last forever. Unpleasant and disturbing thoughts will short circuit relaxation, and instead of feeling comfortable and being able to quiet their minds, their conscious gatekeepers will be ever-present and filled with "not nice" self-talk.

How do you feel about taking ten minutes for yourself to complete this exercise?

Can you even afford ten minutes of your time just for you? When you consider how much time you spend each day doing for others, taking ten minutes for you should never be a problem – if you find it difficult, then you surely need to learn to love yourself more.

This is also a test that reveals what vibration you are in.

Do you think you have a problem with self-love? Many people do. If you are not sure whether you fall into this category, the test below could help. Answer the following questions by **writing down the first response your mind gives you**:

- Do you have a feeling you were hurt as a child?
- Do you have difficulty trusting those around you?
- Do you suspect people use you for their own purposes?
- If you hear laughter behind you (like in a crowd, bus, classroom, restaurant, etc.), do you suspect they are laughing at you?

If most of your answers are "Yes," then you need to engage in some exercises that will build your self-confidence. Your self-confidence and self-approval have an essential meaning for success in all areas of your life.

If we conclude – **the way you act towards others is a consequence of your feelings about yourself and vice versa**; the other person only engages a part of your energy – the part that **resonates when this person approaches**.

Therefore, **it is only when you are able to love this energy in yourself that you will be able to love this person**.

Dealing With Others: Continued

As we can notice, we went through many interesting situations and **never indicated any of them were bad for us or negative**. They could be unpleasant or unusual, but – in the long-term – always **supportive for our soul's growth**. Well, if we perceive them through the eyes of the ego, they are devastating. But we try to reach beyond that step.

So **a bad situation does not exist**.

We do sometimes experience unpleasant emotions, but that is not because of the situation itself, but because of our (mind's) **expectations** and our **reactions to various circumstances**.

That is why we can be miserable even when we see something beautiful.

For instance, when you see a colleague who has finally found his or her soul mate and is happy – is that a bad situation for you? Or maybe someone you know locally wins the state lottery – how does that make you feel?

We sometimes do react unsupportively when we see or are told about such situations.

Although we can react in hundreds of ways, the problem occurs the moment we start thinking about and **comparing ourselves to those who are happy**.

Actually, there are only two types of responses: pleasant (acceptance) or "not so pleasant" (comparing)… and a myriad of alternatives that fall under each.

As we said earlier, others have nothing to do with our emotions – they are just triggers for them.

Do not forget that **karma is the unfinished act of managing our own energy**. When we find ourselves in a situation where someone has irritated us so much that we lose control over our energy (giving it up to the person, object, or situation that triggered our emotion) then **this event becomes a true gift**: It shows us **an area where we need to make some changes**. So the **energy of the situation** is what knocks us out of balance, not the particular person that we seem to be connected to through karma – he or she is **just the initiator**, the catalyst for bringing it about, as we said earlier.

How can you tell?

Think about an event – involving someone else – that would normally make you lose it and go crazy. Now **think about the same situation happening with a different person**… but one whom you see in the same way you see the first person (that is if the first person is a good friend, think about another good friend).

See? The feelings may not be identical, but close enough; so it was not about a specific person, but a **situation** and our **expectations**, as well as our **response** to it.

Is there anything we can do about it? Of course, and you already hold the solution; it is simple – like everything else – inside you: **Forgive yourself for whatever made you take such a position and for insisting that everything has to be your way**… and move on with your life.

The Next Step: Self-Acknowledgement

Do not blame others for being who they are – **nobody needs to apologize to anyone for being what he or she is**. It is our choice whether we think something is wrong.

Keller described a common story from his marriage counseling practice. A lot of times either the husband or wife finds it difficult to **forgive the spouse the way he or she thinks and acts**; Keller's answer to him or her is, "There is nothing wrong with your partner, so he or she does not need your forgiveness. **You should forgive yourself for taking the position that you are right about something and he or she is wrong.**"

So the next time you think, "How can I change my husband's (wife's, child's, friend's) mind, so he or she will accept my decisions?" recall to mind: **There is nothing wrong with him or her; the challenge is with your expectations and the need to be right and have control over everything.** (The problem is probably in an **unharmonized common vision**; or maybe, you even **do not have a common vision that** will **unite both of you around the same purpose,** bringing **resonance** and an **energy boost**. If this does not happen, you search for energy, identity, purpose of life, etc. **through your partner.** You can read more about this in *Charisma, Self-Confidence and Personal Power*.)

This simply happens because all of us take positions of what is right and wrong... and then **treat others according to these, our personal rules**: If they follow these rules, we "love" them and see them as nice people, but if they do not, we hate them and find them disobedient, stubborn, or even rebellious.

Giving Our Power Away

The following example is a situation that demonstrates an incapability to claim our power and take responsibility for our actions and our selves, putting our destiny instead into the hands of (unpleasant) destiny.

It is seven in the morning, and you are just beginning to wake up. Slowly, you become aware of the new day and the tasks that await you. You think, "First, I need to speak to my boss about yesterday's unpleasant event. Then a dissatisfied client will be at my desk demanding a refund. I have to take the kids to their dance class, but I have such a busy afternoon at work that I don't know if I can get them there on time. Gosh, what a bad day."

The Millionaire Mindset

It is now two minutes past seven, and you are already in a bad mood. However, **nothing bad has happened to cause these unpleasant emotions** – maybe quite the contrary: The sun could be shining brightly, your husband or wife could bring you breakfast in bed... but you hardly notice or appreciate either because of the sullen mood **you chose**.

The only event that has taken place is the one you just imagined in your mind. Nevertheless, look what happened.

Your dread of the bad day that might be ahead of you has already played out in your mind. You have already decided that it is a bad day... and from moment to moment you build this energy up by relating to it (justifying it), thinking about it, talking about it, etc. **It is not the event itself that caused such a state – nothing has happened yet... it is your reaction to the event you only imagined.**

Other people's fault? It all came from you...

In the next few chapters, we will discuss things that are related to others, but are strictly ours.

About Envy

Everyone has a skeleton or two in his or her closet. You have probably experienced the uncomfortable feeling of having people know something about you that you are not proud of, or are at least embarrassed about.

Well, be glad... because there is nothing wrong or bad about that.

Here is why. Think about what the relationship is between the person who is being spoken badly of and the one doing the talking.

Often, these emotions are mostly a reflection of them – the people doing the talking. More precisely, about **their desires**. For example, they discuss your new car, saying how stupid it was for you to buy it. Remember, a lot of times **it is not you** and your seeming stupidity. What they are concerned about is **themselves and their desires** (for a new car, for the need to be right, or the most intelligent), **which they reflect in their comments**.

Everything a person says is an expression of his or her energy state or vibration, as we already know. (We said that if this person were to live in the heart, **it would never**

> *It does not matter to whom a person is speaking – absolutely everything he expresses speaks of his very self.*

even occur to him or her to criticize someone... because he or she would only see God's light and unlimited beauty in every person.)

As you also already know, **it does not matter to whom a person is speaking – absolutely everything he expresses speaks of his very self.**

In other words, **nobody kicks a dead horse.**

So be proud of being the subject of small talk and do not expect their comments to be nice. People who engage in such activities rarely consider or like to admit there are people doing better than themselves.

People prove themselves in the following ways:

- The most successful prove themselves through their **actions**. Good or bad, they are always talked about.
- Those that fail to prove themselves by their actions try to **prove their value with words** (self-praise).
- When nothing else works, people try to **force others to see their value** by trying to prove they are right and using strength and aggressive behavior to aid them in their goal.

As long as you belong to a group of people that others talk about, do not bother/worry – **you are part of an elite society.** Being noticed, praised, and criticized by others should never deter you from your goals; rather, it is a sure sign that you are on the right track if you just keep going... and are listening to your heart in doing so, of course.

Disappointment

Let us say a word or two about another situation linked to others: disappointment.

Who have you listed as people who have disappointed you? Were they enemies? No. How about a neighbor down the street that you simply greeted occasionally? Not likely.

The people you are closest to are the ones that let you down. Of course, you blame them. How can you take responsibility for such situations you find yourself in? Simple, **do not demand and expect so much from others.**

If you only depend on yourself, nobody can dissappoint you.

If you only depend on yourself, nobody can disappoint you. Should you find yourself in a situation where another person fails to fulfill their promise or puts you in an awkward situation, remember:

Most people act with the best intentions. However, their goal is to convince you that **what you see is not what you get;** so they **pretend to be someone else.** Often, and even though they may not be consciously aware of it, this is the root of the action they seek to accomplish.

If their task is not completed in a satisfactory manner, it – in most cases – does not mean that they intended to harm you... and they are probably **more disappointed with themselves than you are. They just did not know how to deal with the situation...** or they overestimated their talents and abilities.

The last thing that people in such situations want is the disapproval of others.

Friendship is priceless. If you crash your car, you can buy another one just like it. **But if you lose the trust of a friend, you may spend the rest of your life seeking another person who even comes close to what you lost.**

Imagine buying an expensive stereo. You put in a CD and do not like what you hear. Does this mean the device is no good?

People are like stereos in that they have many tapes to play. The solution to listening to a bad tape on a tape player is to push the record button and tape over it with your favorite music – not to throw away the stereo.

But in practice, what do you do instead? Most people **reject the person whose tape does not suit their ideas.**

Besides, we know that **nothing happens by mistake, by coincidence, or by accident.** This is how you should perceive your life events.

Reacting Poorly Toward Others Is Most Often a Cry for Love

Speaking about others, they may react poorly in certain situations, but the reason may be more important than we realize. For the most part, arrogance, envy, hate, etc. are just a **cry for love and help and the final step in acknowledging one's weaknesses.** When someone attacks you in this way, the fear of losing something is behind it.

A different way to look at it might be: How do you feel when you see someone who is disabled? Can you be angry with him or her for things he or she may not be capable of doing? Probably not.

Imagine the same with the person with whom you are involved in some unpleasant emotion; he or she is also disabled, in a way. Because –

to put it mildly – he or she is not very accomplished with his or her perceptions of life… and this is probably his or her way of crying for love, attention, and help.

That way, it will be easier for you to **feel compassion** for him or her, and a **desire to help**. Try to understand it this way (if nothing else helps).

Further, if someone is not interesting to you, you do not need to expend any energy at all for him or her; especially by being angry or disappointed. **Just forgive.**

That is why we do not look for a way to win this battle, but just **surrender all of our worries and fears to love.** (And we may discover that this is actually our biggest fear.)

"Positions make forgiveness difficult; needing to be right makes forgiveness almost impossible." (Thomas Keller)

Acceptance Is the Highest Point of Understanding

Total and complete acceptance of life as it is shows the highest point of understanding. It ensures you never blame others for your destiny and saves you from disappointment with people and events in your life.

To understand why a person acts a certain way, the Indians say, "You must walk a mile in his moccasins." **Circumstances often look much different from this point of view,** so when we judge someone, we really do not have the complete picture. (We also often find out that they are just acting out of fear.)

Here is something important to consider: **Acceptance, and even understanding, does not mean that you agree with a certain activity – that comes from the low vibration of others – much less that you support it;** like wanting to understand a dictator does not mean you have to be on his or her side.

It is more about getting into a **higher level of consciousness** that accepts, and looking at the situation from there. If we want to understand and thus accept someone, these are the necessary steps we should take:

1. We have to know – not just in our minds, but in our hearts, as well; actually, we have to live the fact – **there is an Eternal Light (the highest vibration possible, or God) inside everyone.**

2. **We all have to go through the five levels** to get to this light's realization (or activation).
3. Move your consciousness in high vibration and integrate it with your true, divine self.
4. **Understand and also accept however a person behaves** because you will notice that whatever he or she does is just a step that he or she must go through to reach his or her divine self.

That way, you will not judge anything. A perfect example is the story of Jesus. He knew that Judas would betray Him, but He understood and accepted that fact... and so He **did not interfere in the process.**

Everything less is not genuine understanding and acceptance, but an attempt to please someone (and deny yourself – or lose your integrity – in the process). We can also say that everything less is about trying to **resonate with a person's personality**, not with his or her true self.

And when we slip into the vibration of personality (duality), we **automatically begin to judge, compare, and "be smarter than God,"** which causes all kinds of problems to arise.

So we have to know that **there are basically two kinds of understanding and/or accepting**: One is related to a person's higher self – and this is the only genuine form of it – while the other is related to a person's personality; like his or her activities, thinking, habits, etc.

When our consciousness is in a higher vibration, we do not even have to know what is going on because we **automatically understand and accept everything.** So whenever we have to even mention (and separate) these energies, we are likely in a lower vibration and thus **judge and compare** a **person's activities.**

And this is not true understanding, but just **being nice to the person** (and expecting something in return).

Help With Acceptance and Understanding

A lot of times, having a **complete picture** helps us instantly distinguish – and thus, disconnect from – all the unpleasantness we project into the situation and the present circumstances. Namely, when we notice that that person **did not do something with the intention to hurt us or to act recklessly**

The Next Step: Self-Acknowledgement

toward us, but actually cared – unsuccessfully – the **energy of compassion is activated** inside us. Here is a story.

Last year, we went to Austria by car on a skiing holiday. While driving slowly on icy roads, another car suddenly came from a side street into the intersection and drove over the sign right next to us. We had to thank our experienced driver for avoiding the accident. Because there were several people in the car, it was easy to see by their reactions to the incident (accepting the situation versus blaming the driver) what level they were at in their personal growth.

Some waved with their finger, others cursed, but one friend said, "We don't know what was going on with that man at that moment. Maybe he could not stop in time with the ice being so heavy and driving into the sign was the only alternative that saved him from going off the road. Perhaps if we would have stopped and talked with him, **he would have jumped for joy and thanked us profusely for reacting so quickly, saving him from trouble, and all of us from an accident.**"

These words sounded significant and convincing – and people's anger transformed into compassion in seconds.

Here is another interesting concept to consider. Think about how long you have been living with and learning about yourself. A few decades, and still you and I cannot say with complete confidence that we know every part of ourselves, can we? We spend a lifetime learning about ourselves, and in the end, die without knowing ourselves completely.

It is remarkable that, after knowing people only a few hours, we can even form opinions about them – but we do. **Moreover, doing so labels them and places them in drawers, which it will be difficult for them to ever emerge from.** The names on the drawers say things like, a bad person, a good mother, an unprofessional businessperson, a good dancer, a rogue, a kind person, a hypocrite, a flatterer, a complainer, a success, greedy, etc.

Sometimes we have not even met a person yet, only overheard something about him or her – but that does not stop us from thinking we know everything about him or her… or stop us from quickly placing him or her into a drawer anyway. Even worse – **we repeat all this stuff about him or her to others.**

Dale Carnegie, in his book, *How to Win Friends and Influence People*, quoted a Dr. Johnson as saying, **"God Himself, sir, does not propose to judge man until the end of his days."**

Why should we?

As we know, **anger, jealousy, and other similar emotions are energy-guzzlers**. They steal your time, destroy your mood, and hijack your dreams and convictions. The more attention you give them, the more you put your consciousness into lower vibrations, and this highly affects your thought and actions. Any repetition of this stamps you with the "negative person" label in other people's eyes. And even worse, it will be true because all you will do is criticize others and complain about your lot in life. **You are the one most hurt by your unpleasant emotions and thoughts of revenge.**

> *God Himself, sir, does not propose to judge man until the end of his days.*

People you associate with will respond to you according to the vibration you are in. So do not be surprised if that picture is not nice. And do not bother to break the mirror because you do not like the image you see reflected at you – change the image instead.

When we accept ourselves, others, and life, we no longer have to fight for kindness. That is when we can look into our hearts and truly choose what we want to do with our lives because we are not burdened anymore; **we choose the path that fulfills us**.

It probably will not be activities in which we laugh and have a good time, but through which we **contribute a lot to bettering ourselves** (raising our vibration to the fifth level), and thus, others and everything else. Some people call this **serving**, which has a negative connotation because it carries in itself the source of **denial** and **suffering**, which is not true. Like everything else, serving also represents a voluntary dedication, or feeling of fulfilling one's mission, which is accompanied by joy, peace, and so on.

The common factor of serving, as performed by all the saints, is recognizing that in every person there is a light, which represents the greatest value and the origin of the Creator. Then they behave toward that person according to that energy... and nothing else about that person is important to them.

The Next Step: Self-Acknowledgement

My friend sent me this interesting e-mail when we were talking about the greatest values. "**Serving is the greatest principle which follows accepting.** Truly unselfish serving is possible only when we've either freed ourselves of all our wishes, or have satisfied them and realized that there are other things that are more important to us. A feeling of love towards people, animals, plants, nature, and ourselves guides us and helps us in this unselfish acting."

Christ, Buddha, Gandhi, and many other Saints illustrated this highest value to us with their example.

Once we have come this far, our internal expression is more important than the external. If we go a step further, we can ascertain that every individual has a will to decide whether he will act inwardly or outwardly.

For example, we can decide to become a successful businessperson, regardless of everything. In this case we have completely devoted ourselves to this goal. We could – as permitted by the (Sub)Law of Free Choice – **decide to turn inside ourselves and awaken Love within**, setting outward working in second place. That way, our goal is getting to the highest vibration possible, and as long as our exterior expression (for instance, the performing of a profession) allows this, we **follow it**. When it no longer permits it, we replace it – and choose an activity, which **supports our internal values**.

We see that we have now put the physical manifestation in the outside world in second place. **Our identity is connected to the energy state of consciousness we experience in ourselves**, and not to the expression of energy in the outside world.

This can be easily exhibited outwardly as **rejection** because we are not pursuing the prizes (power, money, fame, prestige, etc.) offered by the physical (external) world, but are working from inside and just accepting what happens outside.

This way we can also become famous and a household name – as the Saints experienced it – but it is not our intention, just the result; in these cases, **others make us famous**.

To summarize – serving derives from **performing our life's mission** (on the ladder of the five levels) when we turn inwards. And in this way, we discover that we have **a special mission and that the Light within us** especially flourishes if we perform work that arouses unconditional **Love within us**.

And in so doing, we will feel **fulfilled, complete, and liberated**.

People Are Egotistical

Read the title again. Does it throw you out of balance?

Without a doubt, this thought never fails to deliver audible gasps and visible shock; as if being egotistical – or, better said, standing for your viewpoints – were something bad. But this only means that **everything we do in life, we do only for ourselves**... if we dare to admit it.

Whatever the benefit, be it material spoils or moral satisfaction, there is some benefit to us in everything we do.

An elderly woman once said to me, "You see, everything I do is **for my son**. It is more important to me that he is well-dressed and not hungry than it is for me to be either." However, on further conversation, two things became obvious that support our previous point.

First, not only is it important for her son that he be well provided for, but it is also important to her that he be well cared for, **so others do not think she is a bad mother**. Second, it is **her son** anyway – not the neighbor's son, and thus it is beneficial to her to be concerned about him and his welfare **for her own peace of mind**!

De Mello pens an interesting dialogue in one of his books:

Two friends are talking. The first one asks the second one:

"If you had only one choice, which would you choose – me or luck?"

"Luck."

"You are selfish."

"Maybe you are selfish for **expecting me to choose you over luck**."

Joseph Kirschner, an Austrian author famous for his thoughts on manipulation says, "Manipulators will tell you that you are egotistical, simply because **they won't be able to exploit you anymore**." In doing so, they attempt to manipulate you by making you feel that **standing up for yourself is egotistical** and a bad thing.

The Next Step: Self-Acknowledgement

If you doubt "being egotistical" is a good thing, or are angered when you are identified as such, answer the following questions:

- When a good friend leaves or moves away, **who are you sad for – for your friend, because you worry how he or she will manage, or for you, because you will miss his or her company**?
- When you are filled with jealousy towards your friend or spouse, **who is it you are concerned about – you or your friend or spouse?**
- **When you look at a group photo that you are in, who do you look for first – you or someone else?**

Although the sentences above were a joke, there is some truth in it...

> Dale Carnegie said that **each day, from morning until evening, people are interested only in themselves**. It is natural and right. The only thing we should consider is **whether we are interested in our internal or external expression**. Namely, **if we are interested in our internal destiny and stand up for it with all our heart, we will do the best we can – for ourselves and others.**

Also, if you want to get from the first level (or first phase), where you are a doormat, to the second, **standing up for yourself is the most you can momentarily do for your development**.

For example, if you want to succeed financially – and every other way, as well – in life, in a big way, you should not be ashamed of what you have done. Taking responsibility for your actions does not mean just for the things you have done wrong, but for the things you have done right, as well.

Actually, **the person who is not certain that he is better than others in some specific tasks never even begins to tackle more important tasks**.

But be careful. Here is a "fuse" that will prevent you from surrendering to your ego; or in other words, how you can **separate an overwhelmed ego from being glad for your success**:

When you – or anybody else – achieve something, **do not give the credit to your** (or someone else's) **personality, but to God's nature**. That way, you do achieve this success, but **with the help of God** (that is inside of you and also everywhere outside you).

As suggested, **take a similar stand when you observe the success of others**; it will protect you from admiring or envying them. This energy will **link you together** rather than separate you.

Also, such a standpoint makes you confident and brings you **closer to the Creator,** or even **unifies you with Him,** because you now know that **whatever you, or others do, He is always with you.**

About Health

Maybe this is an appropriate time to say something about health.

"Without your health, you have nothing," is not just a phrase. It is true, and many do not appreciate this until their health fails.

> *Without your health, you have nothing.*

It is important to be aware of it... and be grateful for a sound mind and body, for arms, legs, hearing, and sight that deliver such pleasure through experiencing the beauty of the world. You can do whatever you like with these gifts intact. Take a few moments periodically to imagine what your life would be like without one or several of the above. **Then find ways to celebrate and receive joy from all the gifts your Creator bestowed upon you!**

Do not burden your body by overeating – it is a bad habit, and a lot of times a flight from reality – and give your body the rest it needs to preserve and repair itself.

Appreciate it and you will notice its appreciation of you. In other words, **listen to your body – and act the way your body is asking you to – and it will listen to (support) you.**

Even if you have an ailment or a handicap, try to embrace it... not fight against it. Sometimes it represents the **closest link to your soul** and **the fastest way to your spiritual growth** – if you allow the energy of Love in.

But a lot of times, **we are the ones exploiting and terrorizing our own body**... as though we could buy another in the store around the corner when this one wears out.

Perhaps your health is challenged by the decision you have made to **succeed in business, no matter the price.** For someone, the following advice may be the most important offered in this book:

The Next Step: Self-Acknowledgement

> Do not risk your health through bad eating habits, no exercise, a stress-filled environment, lack of sleep, workaholic habits, or not enough contemplation time – just to earn as much money as you can. If you do so, **there will likely come a day when you will gladly trade everything you have earned to have your health back.**

What is more is that this does not apply to health alone, but to other things, as well, for example, free time, peace of mind, friends, family, hobbies, etc.

In addition, there is another strange expectation people hold about themselves: **thinking they can fix in a second what has taken years to build.** Like eating too much for years and then expecting to visit a doctor – when they now have many problems – who will prescribe a "magic pill" or something to fix the problems they have spent years acquiring.

Life is not that simple. Nothing that took years of abuse to obtain can be cured overnight – not your health, weight problems, relationship crises… nor your financial woes. (But you can make a decision to work on them in a second.)

All of that is your goal: time for the things you enjoy, peace of mind, friends, family, hobbies, health… combined with money will make you truly wealthy and happy. You will never achieve the success you strive for by giving all of those up just to have more money.

One who is truly wealthy and successful has a balance of all the above.

You Can Think Yourself Sick

Recall our discussion on the subconscious mind and you can easily see the part thoughts play in influencing diseases and illness. Louise L. Hay, a world-renowned counselor, therapist, and author of *You can Heal Your Life*, *Sana Tu Cuerpo*, and many other books, describes how **thoughts are the source of almost all disease**. Here are some examples from her books:

Acne is a consequence of not loving or accepting ourselves enough. Alcoholism is a consequence of vanity, self-blame, self-dissatisfaction, and denial. Overeating is a consequence of fear, insecurity, and self-blame. Headaches represent self-criticism and low self-esteem.

Her books contain a table that lists roughly three hundred diseases and the correct thought process that must occur to eradicate them. All the "cures" are based on positive affirmations because **if your mind can make you sick, it can also destroy the sickness, heal you, and make you well**. Ms. Hay is **living proof** that this is possible because she herself has cured many serious illnesses in this way.

Health: A Step Ahead

Let us dwell on the topic of health a while longer and look at what medical treatment is actually about.

In the opening chapter, we discussed what brings about recovery and **what illness is about**. If we can successfully answer why illness even occurs, it will be easier to undertake treatment.

If we recognize that we are spiritual, energy beings – whose **energy is expressed through physical form** and that **we ourselves create the world in which we live** – we discover that certain illnesses only **reflect our care for our life force energy** and give us messages about it.

So illness is one of the **"learning tools"** through which we recognize **our consciousness** and through which we become aware of **where our life's energy is currently located**. We can even say, like Paul Solomon stressed, that the **symptoms we have are the language of God**. In the same manner, Keller says that in this way **our body becomes a roadmap of what is going on with our energy**.

The fact is that illness is an **energy disturbance expressed in our physical body**. Sometimes this disturbance can express itself differently, for instance, in our **environment**.

Is it possible to prove that the cause of illness is **an energy disturbance** and not something else?

There exists a whole series of evidence; perhaps the best proof is the **way we heal a certain illness disturbance**. If we look at a more serious illness, which we believe cannot be wiped out easily – for instance cancer – we discover that **a lot of people cured themselves so completely that there is not even a trace of the illness left in their bodies**.

It is very unusual when we discover that the methods of treatment, which gave **similar results** (complete curing), are **completely different**.

The Next Step: Self-Acknowledgement

Throughout the world, there exists **medical evidence** that people cured this illness in different ways, more or less miraculously. Let us list a few:

- **Special teas or healing herbs.**
- **Vitamins** and various health or natural **additives.**
- **Fasting** (drinking only water).
- **Diet** or special **nutrition.**
- **Meditation** or other **spiritual techniques** without the use of anything else (like Louise Hay practices or like Joseph Murphy who healed himself of skin cancer).
- **Classical operation** or classical therapies and drugs.
- Even **the book you are holding** in your hands.
- And so on and so on.

What can we establish? The methods are totally different, but **the result is the same**. This can only mean one of two things.

- **We did not search deeply enough** and were not able to determine the common factor, which unites all recoveries.
- We will **never find the common factor** as we imagine it – for instance some chemical compound or something similar – because these recoveries have **entirely something else in common.**

Presumably the second opinion is the right one; it is about "something else," and the factor, which influences recovery, is known. It is **the energy inside of us**, which sometimes with the help of outside assistants **enables the body to begin to produce healthy cells** or reestablish energetic balance.

All of this outside treatment (i.e., remedies) can help us, but it often happens that **unless we change a certain way of thinking, feeling, or behaving within,** the experience will recur and we will not even be able to solve it.

In other words, we have to **remove the blockages that our mind created** and thus **establish an environment for the life force energy to express** and take care of the body.

How many times have we heard that the disease came back because they were not able to remove all of it successfully and it has now spread? The surgeon who operated on this patient knows that he or she did everything the same way as with another patient, yet somewhere the disease recurred and spread, whereas in the other person, it did not.

Sometimes it even seems that the **surgeon and patient were completely incapable of influencing the course of treatment** and both just waited to see what would happen... like everything is left in God's hands. (And this is literally true.)

An old saying is **"God heals the wound, the doctor changes the dressings."** If we recall the (Sub)Law of Life's Mission, we can heartily agree with this. That is to say that if "even the hairs on our head are counted" as *The Holy Bible* says, it is not likely that we would remain **unnoticed and alone** in this experience.

The supplemental energies, which heal (or create the proper environment), are faith, hope, and trust in recovery. And when we cannot find this in ourselves, we turn to doctors or healers for help. Because **they believe in our recovery, we can abandon fears, release the energy that contracted us, and surrender ourselves to the doctor or healer.**

We will reveal some interesting facts here, but first we should take a quick look at the difference between healers and doctors.

Doctors and Healers

We will **generalize the matter,** so this description **does not apply to each and every doctor and healer,** but is only the general picture.

Let us first describe what distinguishes them. Doctors use their grasp of **classical medicine,** whereas healers are more employed with eliminating the **cause** of the problem with **energy and vibration** (and not so much with surgery or the precise diagnosis of what is happening on the physical level).

So doctors' advantage is that they are able to **diagnose the "damaged" parts of the body with extreme precision.** But they **are not involved enough** with the patient. That is, they do not come into resonance with him or her spiritually and **do not pay special attention to the patient's energetic balance or the wholeness of the mind, body, and spirit.** They are, however, very good at **removing or operating the affected tissue.**

Healers on the other hand usually do not succeed at giving such a good diagnosis or removing (or operating) affected tissue. (Again, this does not apply to all of them, just as not all doctors can excellently diagnose or are not involved enough with the patient's energy state.) But they direct a lot of attention towards **establishing a state of energetic balance in the**

The Next Step: Self-Acknowledgement

body, and they are much more **caring** and **loving** towards people (read: they establish greater **resonance** with patients, especially on the energetic level). That way, they **unselfishly focus on the diseased body part**, and with that absolute devotion, **they show great care.**

This is important... because in an experiment, which was carried out in the '70s in New York, Dolores Krieger, professor of nursing at New York State University Medical School, while working on her dissertation, discovered that the **decisive factor in treatment was the genuine care of a patient – or Love – received from a doctor, healer, or anyone else.**

In other words, it is about the **patient's openness** (through the energies of **faith, hope, and trust**) to some **other person** from whom – through resonance and the release of his or her own tensions – **the patient receives enough energy to abandon fears and worries and allow the burden of the experience to be transferred to the other person.**

And so **trust** and **mutual relationship** play an important role. If we look through history, we will find that miracle cures are often linked to faith, hope, and trust. Even Jesus talked about this saying, "...your faith has healed you." (Luke 18:42)

Sometimes in addition to, or even in place of, people's assistance, other **external resources** help recovery – because they help us, as said, establish a harmonious relationship in ourselves with their special **vibration. Or we discover in them the needed energy onto which we can project our faith, hope, and trust.**

The fact that people often cure themselves with an imagined drug, the so-called **placebo effect**, or without taking anything chemical into their bodies, indicates that **the root of their recovery is not in changing the chemical structure of the body**, but was more about abandoning fears and worries.

This is – energetically – similar to cooperating with a doctor or healer: We convince ourselves that **something will heal us** and delegate to it responsibility over our health. **The more we believe in it, the less worries and fears remain.** That is when we loosen the pressure and constrictions... and allow our mind/body/soul unit to **take care of itself.**

And so it could even happen that the illness is terminated the moment we decide on a certain method of treatment, which we strongly believe in, or when we connect to a doctor or healer in whom we firmly believe. All that is necessary for success is the maintenance of this faith, hope, and trust. Of course, if our **life's mission does not oppose it**... if it does, nothing will help us.

The Game of Energy

Here the human characteristics of the doctor or healer can play a big role. That is to say that with every contact with him or her, the patient will **seek confirmation of his or her faith** in the doctor or healer. As long as the patient is convinced that the doctor or healer is taking good care of him or her, the experience will continue. When he or she **begins to doubt**, the chain will be broken and the **condition may worsen in a moment**. This doubt may also be induced by **other people** – who express doubt with their observations – or even by other things: articles, statistics, TV shows, which do not support the patient's decision.

So it is about **finding an object of trust** with which a patient then resonates.

It is also known from history that the first medical treatments took place to get the **body into a state of harmonious balance** with sound or color, with herbs, prayers, etc.

Common to all recoveries is **the (renewed) establishment of the state – or vibration – in the body prior to the illness**. Keller says that **every illness is a neon sign**, which clearly and loudly says, "You are doing something wrong in your life. Notice it and **change it**... quickly, or you could even die!"

Illnesses are therefore help on our path and lead to performing our life's mission... and are not a punishment. That is why it is good to find out **what every illness is telling us**.

These are just some of the basics about treatment. You can find much more about this in the book, *The Health Is Within*. **It is a new approach to health care and healing, which will mark the new millennium.**

Healing in a Modern Society

Just a word about today's health care trend. Today many people decide to consume various teas, vitamins, and/or food supplements. The fact is that many people are **healthy without these things**, and many have **improved their health** in this way. So what is the right approach?

In any case, it is recommended to **take vitamin G**, advises Stephen Turoff. It is a vitamin, which is inexpensive, even **free**. It is available everywhere and can be taken in **unlimited quantities because it has no side effects**. It is miraculous and **cures all illnesses** – physical, psychic, emotional traumas, etc.

It may be taken by all – children, expectant mothers, the sick, and the healthy. It is **the fountain of both youth and happiness** (not just health).

It is vitamin G… or God.

So **enjoy God without worry and in unlimited quantities** – and everything else will work itself out.

Food as Energy

Here are some more thoughts about **food**. After all, this is unintentionally an area that often occupies us. Is it possible to say some truth, which would be useful for everyone? Today, in this age of information, there are more and more people who defend a **certain diet**. There is especially a lot said about **vegetarian and unprocessed** (uncooked) foods. (The fact is that ancient religions ate meat only once a week; on the other hand, a close friend of mine, who for decades ate only unprocessed foods – raw vegetables and fruit – was advised to convert back to a classical diet **because of serious health [stomach] problems**.)

Another truth says that the essence is **moderation**. We eat – and do everything – **according to our own feelings**. If someone else says that something is not healthy, and we do not eat it for this reason, we are **denying ourselves the experience**. A suppressed wish is never the solution.

Our body tells us what it wants and accepts, and what it does not… and it even tells us when and in what quantities. We just have to observe it and listen to it. And so often, a bigger problem is that we are so accustomed or even **addicted to food** that we **cannot give up certain dietary habits**.

Well, the fact is that, besides its psychosomatic influence on a person, food represents one of the more important causes of illness, feeling badly all around, and so on.

In my fifteen-year athletic career, I came to have some of my own experiences – which **work for me**; this does not mean that they will also work for you. I was in a situation where I had to lose weight very quickly (even up to twenty-two pounds in three weeks). I read and tried almost everything written about diets. I consulted doctors and experts in this area and tried all kinds of different dietary preparations; during all of this, my main concern was health.

The problem was that everyone who had prescribed their dietary method or food was certain that they were right. They even believed that their way **was the only right way for everyone**.

When I researched various methods of healthy eating, I discovered that each author's method really was best suited to him or her, but it only applied to him or her. Even when it comes to food, the golden rule applies: **No exaggeration is good**. This would also be the best general solution, which applies to everyone – **look for your own path**. We have to find out when we feel better, have clearer thoughts, more energy, and so on.

I felt best when I was consuming only fruits and vegetables. It was the most efficient diet I had ever had. You might consider trying this yourself by replacing one meal – whatever the easiest one is for you to give up – with your **favorite fruit**. Try this for a week, and if you find it makes you feel good, make it a **part of your daily menu**. You can gradually replace another meal with your favorite fruits and vegetables, but only if it makes you feel good.

It is interesting that a good majority of overweight people try to lose weight only when their friend or spouse points out how fat they are. A successful weight loss plan can only be achieved when the decision to lose weight is **yours alone**. Even the best plan is almost guaranteed to fail if your decision is based on someone else's desire for you to be thinner. Like bodybuilding trainers say, "The most important muscle you have to work on is your mind." This muscle plays the biggest role in nutrition, as well.

It is also important to be aware that you gain physical energy by eating. However, for your body to truly accept, absorb, and use the nutrients that produce the energy, **you need to respect the source – the food itself**. From this perspective, a prayer or some ritual before eating is most welcome. This is not just an expression of giving thanks, but rather a **holy ritual that forms the basis on which your body receives more qualitative energy**.

We can go a step further and – like ancient wisdom claims – **see God is in everything**; in this way, for example, my friend **gives thanks to God** before a meal, for **allowing him to partake of Him** (because God is in food, as well).

Here is some final advice that might help. Even if you have no desire to change the substance of the food you consume, at least **try to limit the quantity of food you consume daily**. Also, **the older you are, the less food you actually need** (and the more exercise). Many people agree that it is best to eat your last meal early and consume no food after 6 p.m. This way, your body will get the rest it needs to maintain and repair itself at night. A late dinner will cause your digestive system to work late into the evening, and it is therefore not surprising that you would wake up tired instead of feeling refreshed.

Your Body

This chapter is devoted to your temple – your body.

You can learn a lot from animals if you watch them. Animals live a natural life of resting, eating, breathing, etc. People, on the other hand, live a far more unnatural lifestyle. Since we are no longer consumed with having to spend most of our days foraging for food, we no longer get nearly enough exercise. Because of this (as well), the **body is unable to rid itself of disease**.

The body is really a temple of the soul, and that is how it must be understood. The body **is not the means, the basis on which we should build our identity, but the "vehicle" (resource), which serves the soul's growth**.

But do not go to the other extreme – worshipping our own body and forgetting its essence – the soul.

Stephan von Stepski – Doliwa in his book about Sai Baba (*Sai Baba Speaks to the West*) says, "Look at the body as God's word that became flesh. See it as God's temple, which must be cared for lovingly to be worthy of Him. But do not substitute the temple with its visitor – the soul. You see how impolite you are when you equate the body with God or the soul. First, you replace the house with its owner, then with its renter. So it is no wonder that instead of the owner, you see only walls."

The body is also **a map through which we can observe our habits, patterns**, and of course, our **own development**. It can also be evidence of neglect, addictions, or conversely, care, consistency, and respect.

Sometimes the body is also a "material" that serves as the soul's means of expression. For instance, Jesus was asked who sinned that as a consequence the child was **born blind** – the child or his parents. He answered, "It was neither that this man sinned, nor his parents; **but it was so that the works of God might be displayed in him.**" (John 9:1-3)

So the birth of an imperfect body can also be intended to **bring people, through faith and greater trust, into contact with God**; and – again – not to punish them, make them suffer, etc.

The Plan for Achieving Wealth, Success, and Happiness

1. **Return to the chapter, "Learn to Enjoy Yourself,"** and do the exercises thoroughly.

2. If you are not successful, take thirty minutes and work through the procedure of self-discovery, described on page 230 ("Ten Minutes with Yourself"). The primary advantage of these exercises is to **have fun and relax**, not to add stress, etc.

3. Reflect on yourself and your life by asking, **"When and in what areas of my life do I feel the need to be right?** How can I overcome this need and forgive myself for past mistakes?"

4. Think about your **principles, values, and points of view that you have had in certain situations or toward other people or objects**. Combining a rigid outlook and the need to be right is a powerful alliance, one that is difficult to change, but needs to be changed for you to love unconditionally.

5. Now consider and become aware of situations that **tip you out of balance**, where you react too strongly or shrink from a challenge, etc. Let them come out to a conscious level so you can observe them (and therefore embrace them with love).

6. Do you ever wish that you could **change other people**? Try to remember that nobody needs permission to be who or what they really are. Whatever you would change about them is a clue to something that you need to work on and change within yourself. Allow others to be whoever and whatever they are and **forgive yourself** for thinking they should be who you want them to be, and not who they want to be.

5. If You Want to Change Your Life, Make a Different Choice

Every choice we make has consequences that come along in the package.

Imagine the following. You are driving your car, and the fuel light comes on. Luckily you pull into a gas station before you run out of gas. You tell the attendant, "I'm on empty, and the fuel light has been on for a few miles. Can you please take care of it?" Taking a screwdriver from his pocket, the attendant **unscrews the dashboard panel and removes the warning light.** Oblivious to your obvious surprise, he says, "You don't need to worry about that coming on anymore."

While a peculiar story – because everyone knows that when the fuel warning light comes on you need to **fill the car with gas**, not just turn off the light, this kind of situation – working on consequences instead of causes – is not so rare and demonstrates many situations in our life.

For example, this is no different from **taking pills to cure a headache**. Your body has its own safety mechanisms to keep it in balance, just like a car has warning lights. Pain in your head is a signal that **something is wrong** – that something harmful is happening to your body. Whether it turns out to be stress or a tumor, paralyzing your nervous system so it ceases to send you the signals cures neither… nor does it bring you any long-term benefit. **You cannot cure the problem by treating the symptoms that warn you of it.**

This is as if something smells in your house and you constantly buy new air fresheners, open the windows, and try to cover the annoyance. Would it not be simpler to just remove it… and be **free of it forever**?

The Millionaire Mindset

Or we can take a look at a situation at work: If two colleagues in a company do not get along, **do you solve the problem by altering their schedules so they seldom meet?**

Well, all this could bring you temporary relief, but considering the damage caused by dealing with situations in this way, is it worth it?

Let us think this way the next time we encounter a problem: **Will we solve it at its cause or its effect (consequence)?** Solving a problem at its root usually requires **a lot of energy**, but is **final** and permanent.

Solving the consequences takes less effort, but never ends, and the situation could be getting worse. These are short-term solutions and only give the illusion of improvement. **The real essence of the problem is in its cause.** When you improve the cause, the results will show in the consequences:

- When you fill your car with fuel, the warning light will go off.
- If you have a headache caused by stress, decreasing your stress will relieve your headache.
- If you are working under unbearable conditions, discuss the situation with your partner or employees and resolve the problems that are making it unbearable.

Conflicts are resolved by facing the conflict, identifying the issues, and improving whatever does not work in your favor; but do not forget: If you want to have real closure, **you must do all this from the vibration of Love.**

Dealing With Problems: A Step Ahead

As we said before, we need to be careful that we do not **lose our way and begin looking for a scapegoat** for the problem or the **reason why the problem arose**.

Usually, we simply do not see the reason for the "problem" – we may perceive it to be a problem, but it is often the **mercy of the Universe** that brings the **seed of the soul's growth** inside – because **we do not know the soul's plan**. We see only the results in physical action, which often **does not coincide with our expectations** of how our daily life should be. That is why we perceive them as problems for which we must find the guilty party and punish him or her. It is not just about people – in the same way, it is a pattern: **We look for a culprit to punish when it comes to the energy within us.**

If You Want to Change Your Life, Make a Different Choice

Let us say a few more words about solving problems. When it comes to problems, let us first ask two questions, which are very helpful in problem solving:

1. "Do I have any **influence** over the situation?" or "Is it in my power to change something?"
2. "Is it about the **cause** or the **effect** (result)?"

We use one of three approaches to solve the problem:

- Solving it **at its cause**.
- Solving the **effects**.
- Neither of the above mentioned can be done, but we decide to **maintain the energy of high vibrations**.

The first two are quite clear, and we know when we will use them.

Solving it at its cause: We know that if we do not want the situation to happen again, we have to solve it at its roots. We can also verify if we are really solving the matter at its cause. (Sometimes we believe we are solving the cause when in reality we are addressing the effect. For instance, we do not get along with our partner, so we **change partners**.) The following question will indicate whether we are solving the matter at its cause or merely remedying its effects: **"Will this problem recur if we solve it in this way?"**

Often, we will see that it will; perhaps not in the same form, but it will… as in the case of changing partners. If we do not **change our vibration** – the way we look at ourselves, others, our life, our standpoints, patterns, and limits within – and come to new knowledge, we will attract a **person of a vibration very similar** to that of our current problematic partner, with whom we will go through a **similar experience**. This also means that we can even sometimes attract his or her **exact opposite**, who will bring **similar results**.

For instance, if we attract weak individuals like a magnet, it could very well happen that our next partner will be **power personified**. Yet, the experience with him or her will be very similar to that with our weak partners – **we will feel lonely, and no one will understand us**.

And so we often move back and forth between the two extremes until we realize that **this is not our goal**. We do not achieve balance by living in one and then another extreme, but by **accepting ourselves, accepting life, and**

allowing ourselves to choose the reaction closest to our heart at any given moment. This way, we gradually discover that extremes really are extremes and do not help us. In this way, we withdraw energy from the whole situation and only **experience the situation** – without expectations. This happens when we stop identifying with this issue and redirect our energy somewhere else.

We usually become aware of this repetition of the same experience over and over again by asking ourselves, **"Why does this keep happening to me?"**

Solving the consequences/effects: We cannot always solve the cause of the matter. For instance, we are a salesperson, and our boss buys items at high purchase prices. The reason for the poor sales is the item's high price. Because we cannot lower it, we will try to do whatever can be done at that moment. And so we will be solving the **consequences**: We will offer a free service or some other benefit which does not cost much, but means a lot to the buyer, for example. (It would be good if our boss would solve the problem at its root – buy only quality items at attractive prices.)

Maintaining high vibrations: Sometimes a situation comes along where **we can solve neither the cause nor its effects**. Often, we are not the ones controlling the situation, but have just fallen in (into the effect). Many times, the problem is related to **other people**. They could be ordinary (life) situations, or very complex and complicated situations.

For example, a family member orders something through the mail, from a TV shop or catalog. When the mail carrier delivers the package, the cash on delivery price is suspiciously high; but we pay it, saying, "Who knows what this is all about. Well, if something's wrong we can always send the packet back. Let's pay it anyway!" And all members of the family agree.

When we open the package, we discover that we received something other than what was ordered. "Oh well, we'll send it back," to which we again agree. But because it is Saturday, we will do this at the beginning of next week; after all, we have around eight days to do so.

The following week, we are all so busy and occupied that **we all forget about the package** and only remember it ten days later. We call the company, but they cannot help us – they have a complicated computer system, which is very strict and consistent. So we have no choice but to **keep the product, which cost a lot and which we neither need nor want**. (So we – again – throw money out the window.)

Before we say some more about dealing with the problem and consequences, let us take a look at quite a similar situation that happens at work.

The supervisory manager determines that sales of a certain item were very bad and did not meet expectations. He or she calls the sales department, which tells the supervisory manager that they did everything that could be done – even additionally advertising the product. The problem is the high sales price of the product, which is **considerably more expensive than that of the competitor.** The supervisory manager calls the price-setting department and asks why they set such a high price. "We didn't! We set a price with the lowest possible profit margin – and only cover costs," says the employee, "because we knew it would be a problem. If we were to offer it at a lower price, we'd be losing money. It's not our fault – **the original purchase price was too high.**"

So the supervisory manager calls acquisitions to find out why they ordered a product at such a high price. The department manager replies, "Sir, it wasn't our decision. We got the products in a package deal when we signed the contract for another item, which **we sold in advance and got at a good price.** But **the supplier didn't want to sell us the product if we didn't take it in combination with another – this one – item at their price.** They didn't want to negotiate the price. We realized that we would have nothing but problems with this product, but no one knew for sure what would happen. If I draw the line under the contract and take into account the sales success of both products, I'm not even sure if it was all worth it. I'd like to remind you that this was a **collective decision.** We even consulted you beforehand, and **you said to do what we think best.** Perhaps the salespeople should put more effort into selling the other product."

Common to both situations is that we found ourselves in a situation, where obviously something – that is not in our favor – happened, and we are left with the resulting consequences. Even more, we cannot do anything to deal with either the cause or consequences.

Now it is time to **decide** (choose) how to react to such a situation.

What do we usually do after realizing that there is nothing we can do to better the situation? Since we cannot **express creativity**, we often direct our energy into **releasing the tension**, which arose after the discovery that we are in trouble and that nothing can be done to improve the situation. **We begin to look who is to blame and express our ill will, pushing the problem away from us so that we will not be associated with it.** Because we are not to blame, or we at least want to show this conviction outwardly, and we do not want to be connected to this problem in any case.

The third way to approach problems, when we cannot influence the cause or its effects, addresses this very issue: **We do not allow our vibration to fall, but maintain a harmonious and motivational atmosphere.**

Maturity and **wisdom** are necessary to maintain high vibration and deal with situations **constructively** and **creatively**. But more often than not, this is not likely to happen.

When we find ourselves in such a situation, we often do not even think about solving the problem at its root or consequence – we save that for later – but we **move directly to releasing tension and finding a culprit**. Naturally, if we focus energy into finding the troublemaker, we will have less energy for problem solving; or we will solve a problem in a very troubling (lower vibration) energy.

You Choose Your Own Path

Of the many available paths, it is your choice which one you take. At any given moment, there are at least two paths before you – **being active** and waiting until later. **Choose the first path and you direct your efforts and energy in achieving your goals**; choose the other and you can become just a passive passenger on the river of life.

> *Fill your mind with solutions, not problems and obstacles.*

As a proverb says, **"If you don't know where you're going, any road will get you there."** (But sometimes – even in such situations – it is **good to wait for a while**... if your intuition says so.)

It is always more productive to view situations as challenges or opportunities rather than problems and obstacles – to always be thinking how to make it work instead of why it is not possible.

Fill your mind with solutions, not problems and obstacles.

Often, you will face a gap between what you have and what you want. **Your view regarding these challenges, more than the challenge itself, controls whether or not you feel well.**

In his book, *Think as a Winner!*, Dr. Walter Doyle Staples says that **you can choose to focus on the 10% of things you cannot do well, or on the 90% of things you master**. In the first case, you will be unhappy and in the second, the situation will be completely different.

What Is Necessary to Succeed? Intelligence?

It is often felt that, above all else, success is hindered by a lack of intelligence.

But who has the better chance of succeeding... the person with above average intelligence who is burdened with doubts and tries to tackle matters with hesitation, or the one with average intelligence who has a clear focus and is a person of action?

More than intelligence itself, your thoughts and patterns of thought are the decisive elements that guide your intelligence and lead you to success.

Research conducted in the United States shows that a **positive (supportive) mindset**, rather than intelligence, is **the most essential element of success**. Similar research at Harvard shows that students credited 85% of what they achieved to their mindset and **only 15% to their abilities**, skills, and innate talent.

In *Think as a Winner!*, Dr. Staples also wrote that Allan Cox, researching the leading men of the Fortune 500 companies in 1982, discovered that 94% of them believed that their success was a direct result of their mindset. In the same book, Charles Swindoll said that he is sure that **10% of his life is the result of the events that happen to him and 90% depends on his reaction to those events.**

I can say with certainty that this is true in my life, but I cannot say the same for yours. Why? Because **your truth is the one you believe in**. It has always been this way and always will be this way. For example:

Those who believe that life depends on reactions to a situation will think and say: "**When I experience disappointment again, I'll understand it as a lesson and take whatever it has to teach me.** If I am disappointed because I relied too heavily on or expected too much of someone, **I won't be mad at that person**. On the contrary, I'll be glad I was taught a golden rule that will prevent future disappointments, and it will be a small price to pay for seeing my life in a different light. From this day onwards, I know that I can only be angry with me, not others, because I allowed myself to be misled."

Those who do not believe that is true will think and say: "No way! If you think that I am going to just forget that someone broke his promise and let me down, you are sadly mistaken! **He'll get his dues for doing that to me – if there is no one else, I'll take care of it!**"

(But there is **something very uplifting** about the second approach: This person **admits and expresses his true emotions**. In this way, he or she will most likely **stay healthy** and will not hide or bury anything deep inside – **all his or her lessons are visible and within a few seconds' reach**. It is much more serious if a person feels that way, but **does not want to admit it to others or himself or herself**, much less show it. So the second response takes courage and strength to express – this is good. In this way, the second person can even grow faster spiritually than the first person – if the first person is **not sincere** and just wants to please himself or herself and others by acting. Well, in our case, we will assume that both people are honest.)

Just think how the two people above will behave when a similar situation occurs in their lives or when they consider their own truths?

The first experiences a small failure simply because the matter did not end as it should have, or as he or she would have wanted it to. However, he or she remembers what he or she promised himself or herself and focuses on the uplifting things that can be learned from the situation. **His or her disappointment is temporary and of short duration – he or she moves through the situation and is soon balanced, and in a good mood.** Besides, now he or she knows whom to rely on in the future and to what extent.

The second person experiences the same situation and becomes extremely agitated. He or she wonders why people do not regard him or her as they should. He or she spreads his or her poison, "Nobody can be trusted these days," The person refuses to help others because he or she believes that nobody helps him or her.

This person is in a bad mood for a few **days or even weeks**, trying to protect others from the same misfortune by **advising them not to have friends**, etc.

This situation has unpleasantly permeated the second person's entire psyche. When faced with new, but similar situations, he or she responds in the same way, repeatedly. He or she does not realize it, but **because he or she believes it to be true, his or her subconscious now makes him or her** seek out the very people that will only disappoint him or her, and the situation repeats itself in an endless cycle.

In the end, the second person is certain that the world is evil and that people only look out for themselves (which is whom the second person is now concerned with as well – himself or herself) and **finding a real friend is impossible.**

The only difference between these two examples was each person's reaction – derived from the **vibration** their consciousness is in – **to their own thoughts, to their individual truths.**

This is influenced neither by education, intelligence (in the classical sense – IQ), nor emotional intelligence (EQ), but by the **awakening of the heart's energy.** When we cross the border into unconditional energies and stop judging, not only does our view of the world change, but the **world's relationship toward us** does, as well.

Edward DeBono, author of more than twenty books and founder of "DeBono's School of Thinking" in New York as well as the concept of **lateral thinking,** gives a good description of the connection between thoughts and lead intelligence and intellect itself.

He says that **we can think about intellect as the horsepower in an engine** – increasing the horsepower does not necessarily ensure peak performance of the engine. **If your ability to drive (thoughts) is (are) good, you can get the most out of the car.** However, if it is bad, then more horsepower will not help. In fact, the results are far better if a good driver drives a car with less horsepower than a bad driver driving a car with more horsepower.

Of course, intellect is one of many advantages, but it has to be guided with thoughts of a high vibration.

Beyond the Q's

In the debate of all types of intelligence, a problem arises because the approach everywhere is very mental and polar. **People are judged, compared, and categorized in advance.** The heart, soul, and intuition **never judge, but only accept and honor life as it is.** "When you take a strict position – positive, negative, or anything in between – it is a clear sign that you closed your heart," said Keller. And this is true... because **when you support something,** you reject – or at least make less important – everything that does not coincide with what you support.

Does there exist a label, when we are talking about IQ and EQ, for people **who work from the heart and feel only the energies of respect and gratitude toward everything**? (These two energies are a sign that we live in the heart and are usually accompanied by faith, hope, and trust. That is to say that we express Love.)

How would we classify people who are involved in the mind and emotions? **How "smart" was Mother Theresa? What was Jesus' EQ?**

We already talked about the world of conditional energies (the world of duality and polarity) and the world of unconditional energies. We also talked about the five levels in which a person's consciousness is situated. We said that after the third level, where we release tension, we move into the fourth level where we begin to open our hearts, direct our attention inwards, and start building our identities on the basis of the internal world.

All classifications in the sense of mental and emotional intelligence or empathy (the ability to notice, understand, and vicariously experience someone else's emotions) mark the first three levels, which describe the world of polarity.

Here vital roles are played by the **mind and emotions**, which as we discovered are also the products of the mind, by **attaching certain explanations and meanings to neutral feelings**.

When we move into the heart, **intuition** takes the place of the mind and the **heart** takes the place of emotions. That is when we are no longer "very smart" because we are no longer acting according to the principle of the mind, which derives one thought from another to come to a logical conclusion. As we already know, typical of intuition is that an **intuitive thought often does not follow existing thoughts** and can suddenly come out of the blue, representing a realization, which has **no relation to our logical thinking up to that time**.

This is also the reason very successful people do not attribute such importance to intelligence – **because they build on intuition and a certain feeling inside**.

So in order to evaluate all these people on the basis of mental and emotional intelligence, in terms of IQ, EQ, and all the other Q's, we would need **an** additional description, which would include the energies of intuition and the unconditional energy of the heart or soul.

Here are a few more words about experiencing other people's feelings or empathy.

It is actually all about **getting into resonance with another person**. As we know, this only proves effective if **the majority of our energy remains in our heart or soul** in each life situation and each moment, regardless of what we are experiencing.

If we vicariously experience others' feelings, so that **we put all our energy into this empathy**, it could happen that **we take in all of the other person's fears and worries, as well**. This happens according to the Law of Resonance: When we widely open to the surroundings, we **accept the entire spectrum of energies from the object we are open to while resonating with it**.

The result is that we will feel exactly the way this person feels, but in so doing, will **lose our own integrity** – integration with our heart and soul, or with our true self.

Even more – if the person we resonated with was in a lower vibration, now instead of one unhappy wretch, there are two.

As said before, we can comfort this person, but this **will not help in the long run**: This person does not need comforting, but **assistance and a role model to move from a low vibration into a higher one**.

Here is another important question: **Why should we feel another person's energy… if our goal is to always be integrity personified, expressing our heart's and soul's potential?** What do we get by attempting to resonate with another person – at any cost – and by feeling what this person feels?

Some say this is important because if we know what the other person feels, **we can present an idea to that person in such a way that he or she will understand and – easily – accept it**.

Well, this will not bring us to our long-term goal either because we will **always be adapting to someone, trying to accommodate him or her**, while we will be trying to understand him or her, presenting things to that person in such a way that he or she will accept them.

The Millionaire Mindset

In this way, we put the **result of a successful conversation and sale**, or making the other person enthusiastic about our idea, etc. – **before our heart**. So this **result becomes more important than everything else**, including the vibration we are in.

When the result becomes the only goal, we can **easily excuse all (lower vibration) activities**, such as, "I had to do it, if I wanted to achieve this goal." This is the easy way to **close our heart** and direct our consciousness into achieving (only) wealth, fame, admiration, and so on... at any cost. And our mind has now a good excuse to do so.

We will solve all these problems when we are on the fifth level (the realization of life's mission) or in the third phase, if we use the shorter scale. That is, when we look at others and ourselves **unconditionally** with the energy of the heart, intuition, and soul. (If you recall again – the first phase is the "Doormat," the second phase is "Sticking up for one's self," and the third phase is "Acting out of Love.")

Everything else represents **lower stages**, which can help us reach some – material or in every case conditional – goal, but **will not include the heart's energy**.

> **This is the energy of the previous millennium. The enlightened millionaire works from the heart** and is not burdened with the response of others, nor does he or she care what others feel. **The enlightened millionaire's goal is to express unconditional love to everyone in every moment... and is not dependent on how people receive it.**

You have to know that many people do not want to accept this energy because in this energy all people are **alike** and no one is better or more capable, nor are there any secrets – you are what you are... and everybody else is **as good as you are**. There is **no more comparing, proving, affirming, or judging**.

And this is too hard a nut for many because here the identity they have built on the external world's goods – (solely) money, fame, position, etc. – means no advantage at all.

But it is the **only path, which will lead others and us to happiness**.

What Follows From a "Negative" Mindset?

Unfortunately, too many external events offer more reasons to be in a bad mood, worried, and dark-sighted rather than uplifted. The media takes the prize here because they discovered long ago that people are more interested in bad news and even horrible tragedies than in good news and uplifting events. Does a newspaper that only delivers **good news** exist? If there is one, you will have a very hard time finding it.

You and I live in a world that is primarily **focused on the "negative"** (that is, unpleasant and unsupportive). All our lives we hear things like, "Be careful you don't make a mistake," "If you don't win, all your effort has been in vain," "Nobody remembers who came in second," "If you don't get a raise, you're a loser who is soon to be in the throes of financial trouble," "If you don't get a good education, you'll never find a good job," "If you don't get good grades, you'll never amount to anything."

Given that we are raised to manage our lives from a worst case scenario perspective, it is not surprising that most people lean – because of fear – toward the unsupportive. And so the more time they think about fear, the more their consciousness is getting into that vibration. The final stage is, as we know, looking at one's whole life – inside and outside of a person – **from that vibration and therefore with that energy.**

It is because of the overall unsupportive picture that their subconscious, in seeking to realize the result their picture dictates, brings about the very circumstances that ensures their failure.

A few years ago, I read somewhere how Thomas Watson, Jr., founder of IBM, reacted when he discovered a mistake that one of his employees made that cost the company several million dollars. The employee was devastated and wanted to know what he could possibly do to correct the mistake and what measures would be taken against him for making it. He asked Watson if he intended to fire him, to which the wise man replied, "Be smart! Why would we fire you now... after we just **invested ten million dollars in your education?!"**

Fears: A Detour on the Road to Success

If you are like most people, you are often confronted with fears that hold you back – consciously or subconsciously. Although you were not born with them, you are under the

Fear is death...and Love is Life.

strong influence of the environment that implanted them. You might even be tempted to think that worry and fear make up the primary base from which your actions stem.

As said before, fear is an **emotion**. That means it is not something real, but only a **fantasy of something that could happen**. When we see in our mind a picture of that unpleasant event, we **identify with it, direct our life force energy into it**, and by doing so, **support its existence** and even **make it bigger**.

So **fear does not exist until we decide to bring it to life**. Therefore, if we put a lot of energy into it, it can even **look like it is stronger than what really exists**. Because…

Fear is death… and Love is Life.

Life exists if we want it or not, if we (consciously) support it or not, and if we are aware of it or not. Here is proof that we are Masters of creation: We can easily create something from nothing, only with our thoughts – we can **make something that is unreal** (fear) **seem real**.

So we just need to **disconnect from that fantasy** – or dream – and **claim the energy that always was and always will be: Love**. That way, we will automatically move our consciousness into higher vibration (or into unconditional energies), where **fear simply does not exist**… because **fear is conditional**; on higher vibrations, **only what is real can exist**.

We all know the powerful influence of fears. **Whether it is a fear of losing something good, or getting something bad, fear is often a driving force.**

And this is happening in all areas of our life. For instance, why does someone behave rudely or arrogantly?

Because the person is often **afraid of losing his or her authoritative power**, which would destroy or undermine his or her position in society. You already know where jealousy stems from – out of fear that someone else will get what you feel belongs to you, or out of fear for you, wanting or losing something you think you cannot have.

New situations in life force you to confront a new set of fears. You may even comfort yourself by saying, "It isn't so bad." Have you ever made a doctor's appointment, a dentist appointment, or a hairstyling appointment only to arrive in the respective waiting area… with no pain or the best hair day you have had in a long time? Now you want to go home. **Fear is a powerful motivator.**

Some of the more common fears are:

1. Fear of the Unknown.
2. Fear of Failure and Rejection.
3. Fear of Loss (losing what you have).
4. Fear of Facing Reality.
5. Fear of Disapproval.

You have to deal with all of these fears – and others, as well – if you want to succeed.

You cannot deny them or banish them to your subconscious; that will only add fuel to the fire that will probably and suddenly burst out beyond your control. Like fires, fears are easiest to put out when they are still small.

Confront your fears and overcome them forever!

Two Ways of Dealing With Fears

Actually, there are two ways to overcome fears.

When our consciousness is in a lower vibration, we **confront the fear directly** because we cannot direct our consciousness elsewhere, i.e., in a higher vibration. But what we do here is **not dealing with the cause, but with consequences**... because **the primal reason for existence of fear is the vibration that our consciousness is located in.**

Namely, **every vibration resonates with some particular energy.** You have probably found this yourself: **When you are in a bad mood, unpleasant memories and emotions from the past arise.** Actually, all energies that accompany that lower vibration arise – like fear of the future, past regrets, shame, or guilt.

So if we want to overcome fears, a much better way is to **lift our consciousness into higher vibration.** That way, we automatically redirect our energy – by focusing on something else that this vibration supports – and thus literally **take energy away from all illusions** (or fantasies or daydreaming); so all energies of lower vibration vanish.

That way, we **deal with the cause.** As long as we are able to maintain that high vibration, fear will not come back.

In the next few chapters, you will get some advice for how to deal with fears easier. But never forget, **if you want to be free of them for good, you have to permanently raise your vibration.**

The Millionaire Mindset

Fear of the Unknown

It would be hard to find a person who is not apprehensive, nervous, or even fearful of entering new territory, wandering into the great unknown. What will it hold? How will it change you? Will you be able to handle the situation or complete the task? Will you know what to do and have the ability to do it? Will you be laughed at? Will it be worth it?

One way of confronting the unknown is to **recognize that, without action, you will never escape mediocrity**. We have already covered that the primary difference between people who fulfill their dreams and those who do not is action – the former move from words to action, the latter never get beyond the words.

Or in other words: **Your motivation for gaining something (achieving your goal) must be greater than the fear holding you back**.

Here is how you can get started. Ask yourself, **"What would I lose if I begin to act... and maybe make a mistake in the process?"** Answer frankly. Typical answers are **time, pride**, and so on; a lot of times we will not lose money!

Then ask yourself, **"What would I gain?"** If nothing else, here is a good one: an experience that will, without a doubt, make you richer – maybe even financially – and one that will **bring you closer, above all, to success**. Also, you will gain **self-confidence**, the **skill to overcome your fears**, and a new **habit of discipline, determination, perseverance**, and the like, which will all bring you a step closer to attaining your (other) desires.

Here is a story that will illustrate this. I remember a case where a young entrepreneur was taking an exceptionally long time to decide whether or not to start a new business that excited him because his mind told him that he would not succeed. After a conversation we had, he decided to start the business because he felt this was his path. **He did not succeed**; in fact, the results were pretty awful at first.

I was surprised a year later when I received a **kind letter from him thanking me for the time I had spent with him**. He wrote that he has been a changed man since then and that he is enjoying what he is doing for the first time in his life. In the beginning, he was not doing well financially, but he gradually built a firm foundation and is now doing well.

"If I hadn't made **the choice** and taken that first step," he added, "I wouldn't have known that there exists work that can bring both money and pleasure. My first financial failure was a small price to pay for such awareness. More importantly, it enabled me to identify the fear that had been present in all my business and personal decisions in the past. **Today I laugh at the limits I was living under then.** Now I'm happy to meet new challenges and have been succeeding in everything I do lately."

In 1991, my partner and I started the construction of a large corporate building. We put all of our savings into this project. During that time, there was a war here in Slovenia (previously Yugoslavia), and alarms signaling a bomb attack often interrupted our work. People asked me several times if there was any point in continuing construction while the war lasted – what if the building were destroyed?

We decided to continue with our project. Had we stopped construction, then maybe our building would not have been finished until today, if ever. However, by following our own instincts and remaining true to our vision, the building has been serving the purpose for which it was intended for more than ten years.

Is it worth it to miss an opportunity? Think...

If making a decision appears too difficult, complete the test that you are familiar with: Take a piece of paper, divide it in half and write out the **pros** and **cons**. More often than not, the "against" side is filled with circumstantial objections, like a **lack of self-confidence**, or excuses such as, "I don't have enough money or time." The substance of these objections cannot compare to the reasons "for" doing something.

Chase your fears away and consciously decide to take a chance in life. It is usually well worth the trouble!

Of course, **the decision – as always in life – is still yours.**

Fear of Failure and Rejection

People who do not face and conquer their fear of failure and rejection can never really work successfully with other people; they will not dare to express their opinion ("Will I be laughed at?"); they will not dare to approach people ("Will they accept me?"); they will be unsuccessful in their careers,

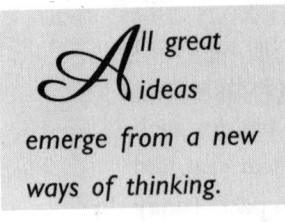

> *All great ideas emerge from a new ways of thinking.*

and so on. For example, they will be too afraid, and will not dare to sell, thinking, "What if he or she says no?"

Nevertheless, you know that everything you do in life involves other people. No man or woman is an island. People are everywhere, so we cannot just turn away from them and live in isolation.

How can you deal with such fears?

In addition to the methods already mentioned in the previous chapters (writing affirmations, visualization), use the method of writing out the "pros" and "cons" as described above.

Ask yourself, **"What do I stand to gain or lose if I accept the challenge?"** Do not let yourself be stopped by excuses. Instead, **awaken the energies of faith, hope, and trust** inside of you.

Besides that, we have to bear in mind that **no one in the world has always been successful**, or performed nothing but actions that brought success. We have all had our share of ups and downs, failures and successes.

One of the most important things to remember is: **When dealing with people, do not take rejection personally**. If, for example, you are a salesperson and your prospect decides not to buy from you, you must not allow this to affect your self-confidence.

It is important **not to identify yourself with the subject of the negotiation** (a product or service, your idea or opinion, etc.). Rejection only means that the other person has a different opinion than you do, not that you are wrong or even bad, stupid, or otherwise.

The same principle also applies in other situations. For instance, if someone you are interested in turns you down, it does not mean that you are a bad person, but simply that you **do not match the current image that he or she has in his or her mind, comparing what he or she wants with the information he or she has about you.**

Let us look at another example that involves jobs. We will again consider salespeople because they deal with many people – who are in all kind of moods – all the time.

Salespeople often have a problem with rejection because **it affects their self-confidence**, their **attitude towards the product and the company**, and their relationship with future customers, as well. After several unsuccessful trials, noticeable in the voice and physical behavior of the sales representative, such a person **completely loses the motivation to negotiate further.**

What can they do about this?

Here is one instance, but simple and effective, method you can use if you desire. When you – if you find yourself in such a situation – experience rejection (of the product, business, idea, meeting, etc.), engage your prospect in the following discussion:

"Are you aware that you may be refusing an outstanding offer?"

If the person is sincere, he or she may admit that he or she does not know the topic, product, or business, and thus rejects your offer because he or she is deciding for or against, based on **limited or incomplete information.** Therefore, maybe you have not presented your offer in a way that fully considers or answers his or her needs.

If the person answers "No," then you may have to accept that you **did not present the subject to your prospect in a sufficiently attractive or informative way.** Maybe you thought too much about yourself and did not focus enough on finding out just what your prospect was looking for. Remember, **the whole idea of sales is finding the prospect's need and filling it with your product, idea, business, etc.** But the most important thing is – and always will be – to **listen and follow your heart**... even if everybody else tries to talk you out of it.

All great ideas emerge from a new way of thinking. The person who does not try, does not succeed. Unfortunately, the educational system, family, and society in general foster a notion of what is right by telling you things like, "A bird in hand is worth two in the bush" or "The higher you fly the farther you fall."

Great encouragement... Isn't it?

If all people stuck to what they already knew, or already had, instead of trying something new, there would be **no development at all.**

Each rejection is another step closer to your success – if it does not hold you back – so you can persist in your genuine intent. **If you do not try, you will not achieve anything.** If you were successful one out of ten tries, earning a thousand dollars, then you can calculate that each try brought you $100 even though you did not realize the $100 until the last attempt. If there had not been the first nine tries, there would have been no tenth attempt and therefore, no money at all.

Most important in all of this, as said, is what **your heart tells you**. If you are following your life's mission, you do not even think about rejection or success: Most important to you is to **continue spreading the idea** and not how others will react to it. That way, you did your part; everything else depends on the individual.

For instance, if you are a salesperson, your task is not getting money for the product, but presenting the offer to an interested prospect, and expressing your enthusiasm with it, while in high vibration. You do not know what this will bring because **you can no longer influence it** – now it is the buyer's turn.

Actually, this kind of selling **brings much better sales results**, long-term and even short-term. This is because salespeople are working from and with the energy of **respect, gratitude, and joyful expectation**, and not from fear, which is typical when we perform various techniques; for **everything that is not love is derived from fear**. Also, do not mix this energy with **the fear of asking the customer if they want to buy a product** at the end of a presentation; these are two completely different things.

If sellers were to look at customers in this way, there would not be any pressure. The problem is that **making a profit is often more important to the sellers than maintaining high vibration within**. The reason that drives them is fear of not earning enough commission (money), if they **do not put enough pressure on a customer**.

This is – also – the energy of the old millennium.

Today **maintaining a high state of consciousness**, and not persuading people that they agree with us, is highly important. The time has come to bring, even to the workplace, the **vibration of love and begin experiencing work as the fulfillment of creativity and an opportunity to open our hearts** and not primarily to make money; the paycheck will follow as a **consequence**. That way, earning a lot of money will not be a primal motivational factor, but the **reward for maintaining the energy expressing creativity and love**.

Anyone who has a job can do this! (More on this in the book, *The Enlightened Salesperson*.)

A good example of believing in your own goals is the legendary Walt Disney, the father of cartoons. Disney faced **a thousand-plus rejections** while raising money to finance his ideas, before he received the positive response that allowed him to create the dream project that millions of people, from all over the world, now enjoy. What if he had allowed a fear of rejection to deter him from his goal?

The enlightened millionaire mindset is: **"(Only) The one who flies high... has a chance of staying at those heights!"**

Fear of Losing What You Have

The next thing that will hinder you is the fear of losing what you have. This fear is demonstrated in displays of **jealousy, possessiveness, disapproval**, and similar feelings and behaviors.

> *If you choose love (living in higher vibration), all fears will vanish.*

If you think about it thoroughly, you will see that you cannot act in a supportive way if you are afraid. Will the situation improve if you worry a lot? No, of course not. The only thing that you can expect by worrying is a change for the worse in your mental state – suddenly you will be filled with doubt, mistrust, and worry. Your performance of other tasks will **deteriorate**. Your life force energy will be used for destructive thoughts and maybe even for destructive deeds.

How can you help yourself overcome this debilitating fear?

You can ask yourself (from the heart) **what you are running from**.

What is it that worries you most... and what is your driving force (fear) from which worries and concerns are derived? Sometimes things can be solved quite simply; for example, if you are afraid of losing your money – like being robbed, losing your house in an earthquake, fire, etc. – you can insure your property or install a security system.

We should keep in mind that **a chain is only as strong as its weakest link**. By identifying the core of the matter that worries you, you can fix the root cause and thus fix the whole matter. This approach is effective in both your private as well as your professional life.

Again – the permanent solution is in developing attributes of faith, hope, and trust. **Learn to trust life, yourself, and God.**

One of the greatest questions ever is: "What am I so afraid of... that I **don't trust God to run my life?"**

We have to choose: **We can either trust God or our (rational – conscious) mind**.

If we trust God, we will never be afraid again – because **trusting God means living in permanent Love**. "There is no fear in love; but perfect love casts out fear," said the Apostle John. (1 John 4:18)

Like we said before: **If you choose love (living in higher vibration), all fears will vanish** – without any effort and without using any techniques – like when you light a candle in the dark; **where there is light, there is no darkness.**

So **open your heart, and you will scare fear away.**

Fear of Facing Reality

Sometimes we are prisoners of the fear of facing reality. We do not want to see the truth because it seems too cruel. We close our eyes and find excuses, escape to another world (through alcohol, adultery or other destructive behavior), and thus the cause of our fear remains undiscovered, untouched, and unchanged. Why? **Because if begin by facing reality, we will look at our pain and deal with it.**

Thus, we would rather not do that.

If you fall into that trap, you will **remain passive** and rely more on others (the state, doctor, lawyer, spouse, superior at work, etc.) than yourself to solve your problems. Also, you will find **a lot of excuses not to deal with the situation**.

The best example of being afraid of reality – and this plays out when decision-making is postponed – is people who are **afraid to see the doctor** because they are afraid of hearing the news that they may be seriously ill. They wait and wait... and their little problem grows into something that cannot be fixed easily, if at all.

Where is the solution? How can you make the right decisions and set priorities for you?

When it comes to making a decision about a subject we are not familiar with – but it would be good to be – a lot of times **faster is better**. But this does not mean that you should do something hastily. First, **disconnect from your fears** and personality (identity connected to this issue) and **connect to your heart**. Then, when you get an answer, **immediately act according to that answer**.

If you want to live the life you want, you have to make these decisions yourself.

However, if you do allow others to choose your path, then you lose out in two areas. Firstly, because you are forced to live with the consequences, and secondly, because you neither reap the full reward nor learn the lesson that making the choice or mistake yourself would have delivered. Therefore, if you do not make your own decisions and learn from your own mistakes, you will be living according to somebody else's wants and desires, shaped by the choices of someone else's vision.

Here is another approach to this fear.

We sometimes overcome fear by **energetically connecting to the situation**. For instance, if we are afraid of the dentist, we can decide to go to the dentist's office just to check his or her hours. The next time, we step inside and look at his office. And so on. (This approach can also be used to eliminate other kinds of fears. It is about building an energy line step-by-step, or the **gradual energetic linking to the new energy**.)

Oftentimes, we discover that once we **decide to do something**, it is more than half done; problems arise when we listen to the opinions of others. We are usually looking for **added energy** from these people, but get **reproof**, which takes our will and motivation.

That is why we discuss the things we feel in our hearts (and decide to act) **only with people who support our heart**. In such discussions we will – according to the principle of resonance, when we are both excited over an idea – get the extra energy we need to reach critical mass and take **action**.

Urgent or Important?

We have to separate **urgent** and **important** matters. It is **urgent** to be at a meeting this afternoon, but it is **important** to take a car to the mechanic, otherwise you may have a breakdown that could cause even more problems. Or it is urgent to be on time for your job, but it is important to drive safely in getting there.

The Millionaire Mindset

Do not let the important things become urgent.

I have noticed this in myself, as well – it is urgent to make some afternoon phone calls or to attend a meeting, but it is important to prepare for a seminar that I have in the evening.

Because I was doing the urgent things, I felt there was a lack of time for the important things – and I got into trouble.

Now I ask myself first: "How urgent and how important is it? What consequences does a delay or failure to complete a task have? Am I neglecting something important because of what I'm doing now?"

If you want to know whether you are deciding in favor of an urgent matter or an important matter, ask yourself: "**What suffers because of what I'm doing now?** What do I miss in this way?" If your answer is "Nothing," carry on. But if your answer is "Something," then you need to ask yourself **which of these two is more important**. Follow this with acting in a manner that focuses on the important thing first.

Oftentimes, **urgent tasks are connected to our short-term goals**, while **importance derives from long-term and strategic decisions**.

As you will see, urgent things are not usually the important tasks, except at a really critical point. For instance, it may seem urgent to buy a new car or new furniture, but it is important to save money for taxes. If, at a given moment, money is not available (for taxes), a matter can become both urgent and important at the same time… and then a **crisis occurs**. This can be a financial, family, or business crisis.

Do not let the important things become urgent.

Be focused and be aware of what is going on in your life, especially when it comes to a crisis. If you tell yourself the truth about what you see and are able to do something about it, you will seldom have a situation that will escalate into a crisis.

> **A problem that is very small and relatively simple to master at the beginning can easily become a major catastrophe, if left unattended**; a small fire can be put out with a glass of water, but it will not take long to develop into a raging inferno, which not even three fire brigades can put out.

So when a challenge appears, tackle it **immediately**… because – presumably – it cannot solve itself, and there is even less of a chance that someone else will solve it appropriately (at least not without some disadvantages for you). As we have said before: Change the root causes, and the consequences will change, as well.

Fear of Disapproval

Fear of disapproval is an essential fear for most people.

Here is some background. Every decision you make is assembled from several elements. In general, you could say that every decision made is a compound of emotional and intellectual elements.

Well, if our consciousness is in a very high vibration, we are detached from both emotional and intellectual elements because the heart (instead of emotions) and intuition (instead of intellect) leads us. Until then, **emotions and intellectual "facts" mostly influence us.** (We will presume the latter and explain further.)

Usually, **the emotional (imaginary) side overrules the intellectual**, as we discovered in the chapter about the subconscious. If you still doubt it, complete the following exercise.

Remember the last three things you bought in a store. **Did you spend your money wisely?** Were all of them **essential for your life**?

The answer is probably no… you could have bought **something cheaper instead** or **not bought these things at all**. I also assume that you probably do not have enough money to buy everything you wish. So why did you buy those things then?

You bought them **because you liked them**. Therefore, they were more emotional than intellectual purchases.

This kind of emotional decision is usually closely linked to a fear of disapproval, which is related to the **need to show ourselves in the best possible light**. The latter is a consequence of having bad feelings about a person's true (internal) self, so the person wants to influence others with external beauty; like clothes, hair, makeup, car, reputation, and so on. (On the other hand, emotional purchase decisions are often connected to **tension releasing activities**.)

The next division (of our decisions) could look like this: Each decision you make is influenced by **your relationship to the object** of your decision and also by **the opinions of those around you**.

The Millionaire Mindset

I live in a small town where everyone knows everyone else. This makes the news about the neighbor's new car spread fast. Does this news influence the decisions others make? Certainly!

Some time back, I had the opportunity to try this same test in my neighborhood; a friend and neighbor bought a brand-new, expensive, midsize car. I watched the reactions of others in town, in response to my friend's (very visible) purchase, and discovered the following:

1. Some neighbors **bought something**, even though it was cheaper and not a car, during the following months. They did not need a new car, so they bought some other luxury item.
2. Most of them did not buy anything new, but were saying, **"Buying a new car is just getting a lease, and everyone can afford to do that."**
3. Some of them announced that **they had heard how buying a new car was in fact throwing money away**. They also announced that they would prefer to renovate their house, buy a condo for their children, spend money for education, take a vacation, or buy something that would enable them to live a more comfortable life, etc.
4. Some of them were **enthusiastic** and visited the car's owner on Sunday afternoon. The only reason they were there was **to tell their friends the next day what a great car they had the chance to drive**.
5. Only a small minority did not begrudge their neighbor, who they felt worked hard for the car, and were **happy for him**.
6. Two neighbors **bought new cars** – one the same model and the other an even better one.

Only one event occurred, and yet so many changes took place in the immediate environment. I thought it would be interesting to ask each of them why they made these purchases... so I did. The person who bought the first car told me that he had wanted such a car for ages and had been intentionally saving his money for it. When his neighbor bought one, his wife urged him to buy because if his friend could afford it, so could he. She even chose the color.

What does this tell us? The opinions of those around us influence the decisions we make.

Think about your decisions. Do you always make them according to your needs and desires, or does the approval of others have an impact on your decisions?

(Of course, we all have to conform to some basic rules of society... but take a look at your **most personal choices and decisions**.)

The trouble is that **too many people depend too much on the opinions of others**. "He or she drives a Mercedes, but at home he or she eats potatoes and cabbage every day," is what others notice about this person.

This description is typical for someone who **places too much value on what others think about them**. Are these people, who feel the need to create an illusion of success, happiness, health, and wealth, really happy? **Not on the inside.** They must surely feel a great lack of self-confidence and love, so much so that the **approval of those around them serves only as a substitute for their own missing emotions and the approval of personal values.**

These people first ask themselves **how those around them will react to the decisions they make.** They will never do things that might be viewed as inappropriate and will never step out of the idea that others have about them; inside they will suffer because of it.

Here is a story that perfectly describes what we have been talking about.

Years ago, I spent a Christmas holiday on the coast where we stayed in a fancy five-star hotel. Most of the guests were strangers, like us. All of them, without exception, were well-dressed and well-mannered.

On the last night of the year, we attended a New Year's party with other guests in a large, beautiful hall. Everything was exquisitely planned, polished, and arranged in advance – like it should be for a special party. No mistakes.

I watched the guests throughout the evening. **They were all interested only in themselves.** (Well, it was a little different after a few bottles of champagne.) On the other hand, they behaved according to their rules of etiquette, speaking quietly among themselves, elbows away from the table, children staying in the seats they were placed in – forbidden to run around and play.

The group I was with behaved like we always do. Actually, we did not choose this hotel because of its five-star status; we were quite aware of all the rules that usually come in a package with class. We chose it because of the beautiful setting and beautiful rooms. Back then, my friend and I were involved in tourism, and we were given a very good price – one I just could not refuse (an advantage of all management people who work in tourism).

Although it was expected at the party for people to sit at the separate tables they had set up, we pulled them together. **We laughed all evening, told jokes, and happily relived moments of the year that was ending that evening.** We toasted several times and even sang some songs.

After midnight, we had intended to leave because we had an appointment with some business partners who were staying in another hotel, but something unexpected happened: Instead of being relieved that we were leaving – to further enjoy the evening in their perfection – the other guests **asked us to stay**. They even **asked us where we were going and if they could go with us**.

We were – obviously – the ones who awakened their suppressed feelings of playfulness, joy, and relaxation. They said that we were **the reason they were finally able to relax**; until then, all parties, shows, and other meetings were all a **kind of obligation**, where you had to be careful not to do something which would cause others to see you in a different light.

If you are one of those people who stay rigidly within the boundaries of other people's expectations, you have to **start loving yourself**. You have to discover that people will not love you less because you do not accommodate them by adjusting yourself to their expectations. As far as being different goes, always remember: **You are unique in all the world. Being different from others does not mean that they are better than you.**

You can find the cause for these feelings that urge you to fit in and make you feel different in your rearing. You have been taught, since early on, to be average. In kindergarten, you heard, "Can't you play nicely like the other children?" In school you were told, "If you've already finished your work, find something else to do so you do not disturb others." At home, your parents said, "Johnny's parents say that he always behaves. Why can't you be the same?" It is the same in other relationships.

When you trust yourself, you will know that **you can afford some mistakes** without having any effect on the people who love you. Begin your transformation with something small by acting differently, delivering an unexpected response. What will follow? Maybe astonishment, but **the world will go on** – and you will be a step closer to finding your true self and **"fulfilling your own personal legend."**

Acknowledge that you can live a different life. Many people are like actors, who take their masks off only when they are certain nobody is watching. That way, **all their lives are a game** that someone else directs.

I listened to a young couple a while back. They were very much in "love" (unfortunately, this word is overused and used too often for many forms of addictions and attachments). I soon realized, however, the young woman quite cleverly manipulated the young man's views about the opinions of those around them by saying things like:

"Well, I don't mind, but I don't want to see how others look at you."

"You just do it your way. Do what you think is right, no matter if he loses his temper."

"We can't arrive there looking like we fell from the sky."

You have to decide whether you are the director of your life or if you are just playing a role – even if it is the main character – in your life while allowing others to direct you. Are you going to fulfill your dreams and desires… or the dreams and desires of other people?

Here is another thing to remember: It is quite common that the more you respect, admire, and "love" someone, the **easier you fall under this person's influence** and the more you allow him or her to overpower you. Why is that? **Because you believe that by fulfilling the other person's expectations and desires, your importance to them rises.**

This could have started very early in our lives – when we were young and strived for the attention and affection of our parents. And this continues… until we resolve it.

The Family Disapproval Syndrome

Let us take a look at family matters a bit closer.

The basic cause of the family disapproval syndrome is thinking **you have to earn your parents love** and the notion that **they will stop loving you if you do not please them**; the effect is thinking like, "The easiest way to please them is to satisfy their wishes instead of my own desires."

For example, many people complain that one reason their personal relationships do not last is because of the disapproval of their parents. When something like this happens, you imagine that you are faced with the choice of **deciding between pleasing yourself** (continuing your personal relationship) **and disappointing your parents**, possibly even losing their love.

On the other hand, parents experience their own drama: They want to **give their children the best, but often want to turn them into copies of themselves**. Why? Because the greatest recognition for many people is the knowledge that **someone has adopted their views or their beliefs**.

The other reason for wanting to turn children into their copies is: **to educate children the way they think is best for them**; or in other words, to **give children the best they can**. And this is what they (parents) have and live, or what they always wanted, but did not succeed at. (Do you know parents who force their children to fulfill their wishes?)

Yet, parents are also afraid of **losing their children's love** or that their children will give their love to a third person instead of them.

All this reflects together in the special relationship between the parent and the child, which was formed during childhood, when he or she was dependent on his or her parents, and in which **everything ran according to the rules set by the parents**. The child is told, "You'll dress this way and learn to respect this rule," "I'll praise you when you do as I say, otherwise you'll be punished," "You'll respect this neighbor, but you won't speak to this one," etc.

In time, children discover that it is **easier not to resist**; at least not openly. Rather, it is better to give in to rules when circumstances demand it. So they do not contradict their parents, though they may respond differently behind their backs, harboring the fear that their true thoughts may be uncovered.

Said in other words – **in front of their parents, they do not say what they think, if their views are in conflict with their parent's principles and values**.

If, and when, this is embedded in a child, it is hard to imagine that he or she will **ever be able to express his or her opinion (when different) openly**, even as adults – in love, profession, or social life.

What is the solution?

First, **forgive yourself for being cruel toward yourself. Then forgive your parents.**

When you **understand the reason behind this syndrome**, it is much easier to wipe out the cause, and thus disconnect yourself from the consequences. First, **learn to express your opinions when you talk with your parents**. If this is challenging, begin softly and then gradually increase the frequency with which you express and defend your own feelings and personal truth.

One way to tread lightly is: Imagine your parents are ten years old – now **tell them everything you have on your mind** (and that you were always afraid to say and express). Another way is to **write a letter to your parents** – sharing your thoughts and ideas openly. Then put the letter into a drawer.

After that, **imagine mailing the letter and seeing it in your parent's hands**. They open it, are surprised or even shocked at first, but after finishing the letter, they understand you better and later apologize. You understand them because you know that they have always wanted the best for you. Remember, there is no formal school for parents, where someone teaches them how to raise happy children – they probably tried hard to do their best, however unsuccessful they may have been at times.

When you visit them the next time, **imagine that they have read your letter**, but are unable to change themselves (so fast). Inside, they **admit** everything you wrote, but they are still only human – prisoners of their old habits and a bit dependent on the opinions of those around them. You understand that they cannot show any changes outwardly, but you know the greatest change happened in their hearts.

You could send the letter – but this could result in even more stress in you because this letter could mean a tension releasing for you, with them as the target. (Actually, the letter itself is meant for releasing your tensions and thus uncovering your [hidden] emotions.) **You can communicate such things only when both parties are in a higher vibration (with open hearts).** If you can seize that moment, while standing in front of your parents, you can openly communicate your problems.

A woman who used this technique – without sending the letter – shared her successful experience with me. When she arrived at her parent's house, they gave her a friendly reception. **She could not resist embracing them and telling them how much she loved them.**

This was the first time that she had done this in twenty years. She was surprised when her parents responded the same way – they told her how **they missed her warm hugs and nice words**. During their conversation, she

The Millionaire Mindset

told her parents the whole story about the letter, from beginning to end. Her parents insisted on seeing the letter because **they had never imagined they had made things so difficult for her, thinking they gave her all the best**.

When they read it, **they both apologized with tears in their eyes and promised her it would have been different had she had told them sooner.** In the end, they agreed to spend the upcoming holidays together. She and her husband decided to prepare a special room for her parents and told them it would be at their disposal whenever they wanted to visit.

When you have finally set things right with your parents, move on to other people who are important to you and share your thoughts and feelings with them using the letter method. It will not take long to realize that **resolving the situation with your parents exposes the core of many of your challenges**. The ripple effect throughout your life, resulting from uprooting your fear of their disapproval, will be phenomenal.

Thomas Keller taught one of the quickest and most efficient techniques for clarifying issues with (or forgiving) parents.

"Inhale through your nose and exhale through your mouth. Imagine one of your parents standing in front of you. Remember all the things that bother you about him or her. Those things appear as a dark cloud spreading around your mother or father. Now start to inhale this dark haze through your heart. When you exhale, imagine exhaling light instead of darkness.

"Do this every day until the parent you have standing before you, in your mind, is surrounded only by light."

You may ask, "Why should I inhale someone else's darkness?" I asked the Angels, and they told me: **"Because this is the only way to learn true love."**

"Then repeat this technique with both the other parent and **with you, as well.**"

But careful – even in this technique the same Laws apply as with all other energy matters: We must **pay attention to critical mass**. So if we are in low vibration (resentment, sadness, desperation, etc.) and look at our parents' shadows from this energy, according to the principle of critical mass, we will only **reinforce** this energy, which is quite the opposite of what we want.

The only way we will be able to embrace our parents shadows is to **first create a very high vibration of pleasant, supportive, and uplifting energies within**. These energies will then embrace the unpleasant energies, which we imagine in our parents. So be careful, because if this pleasant energy is not strong enough, our consciousness will **fall into low vibration**.

On the other side, if the energy is significantly **stronger** than all the fears, worries, thought patterns, and everything else we do not approve of in our relationship with our parents, our consciousness will **remain in high vibration**, and in this way we will now be able to look at our parents from this vibration outward (**from love** and **with love**).

Let us explain the statement that the only way to recognize real love is through the absorption of the darkness that surrounds your parents. It stressed that **until you settle your relationship with everyone, you will not recognize true love**.

In other words – as said many times – if you do not "love thy enemy," you **do not know what love is**… because you are probably just **responding to the reaction of the surroundings**: If someone is kind and accommodating, you in turn are also kind and accommodating to him or her.

In *The Holy Bible*, this is described as Jesus giving two new commandments that are the greatest of them all: **"You shall love the Lord your God with all your heart, and with all your soul, and with all your mind. This is the great and foremost commandment. The second is like it, You shall love your neighbor as yourself. On these two commandments depend the whole Law and the Prophets."** (Matthew 22:37-40)

When they asked Him whom he meant by neighbor, He pointed to **a stranger on the street**.

He later combined these two commandments into one new one: "A new commandment I give to you, **that you love one another**; as I have loved you, that you also love one another." (John 13:34)

So all that must be known about the commandments is as follows: We must love God, ourselves, and all people the same. Even more concisely: **We just love – everyone – in all situations**. This is the final answer to every question.

Or as Sai Baba stresses, "Start the day with Love… Fill the day with Love… Spend the day with Love… End the day with Love. **This is the way to God.**"

Just Love

If you clarify the relationship with your parents, you will become aware of a new feeling. You will begin to love your parents (and others), not because you have to, but **because you want to, and it makes you happy to do so**. When you feel this, it means that you have forgiven them for all their mistakes and that you no longer carry any unpleasant emotions about them inside you. **Now you can start to live a new life.**

On the outside, your solution to various kinds of attachments to your parents is represented by removing your parents from the rigid parent role and into the more flexible friend role, or just people role. Once you do this, they will **never embarrass you again** because **you will not be attached to them** in the same, dependent way you once were.

Maybe you could use this technique with your children? Doing so will define where you end and where your children begin, which can often be a challenge.

Worries

Many good books have been written describing ways you can spare yourself from, or learn to live with, worry. One such book is Dale Carnegie's *How to Stop Worrying and Start Living*.

The next time you are worried, or filled with the feeling that you are no longer in control of your life, and things are slipping out of your hands, use this method:

1. Ask and answer, **"What's the worst thing that can happen to me?"** Leave nothing out of your answer, even the things that seem least likely to happen.

2. **Spiritually accept the worst that can happen.** Doing so greatly affects your subconscious. Before accepting the worst, you are subconsciously afraid, and your fear paralyzes you from responding positively as well as blocks you from finding any favorable solution. However, now that you have grown accustomed to the worst that can happen, it does not bother you anymore. You are not burdened with that fear, and you can say to yourself, "If it has to be this way, so be it." Through doing this, you give up the desire to avoid the worst, and the subconscious can find a solution.

Usually, the final solution is much better than you accepted as the worst thing that can happen in your thoughts.

3. Now be calm and solve what can be solved. Start with the most important affairs, the ones that cannot be delayed.

How to Act

Action is necessary and is always the best cure for worries and fear.

First, you **have to know exactly where you are**. Too often, situations are viewed through unrealistic eyes and the more you think about them, the larger they appear in your eyes.

Do this five-step procedure:

1. **Write down what worries you.** Define your thoughts about what worries you, anything that bothers you about what you are worrying about, and the roots of your worries, if you know them. If you can solve the challenge at its cause, it will be solved forever.

2. Write down all possible **solutions** that come to you by yourself or with the help of others. Sometimes you have to **ask for help** – I know it may be hard – especially if you are not used to asking for help, but if this is a key to the solution, you will survive. Do not forget to carefully choose the time for doing so: **ask for help with your heart open** (as much as possible).

3. Decide on **one solution that fits you best**, from the merits of what you have listed. Consider your abilities and current circumstances.

4. Decide on the necessary steps that will lead to fulfillment. **Set a deadline for the activities** and insert them into your schedule.

5. Take action and follow your schedule.

The Plan for Achieving Wealth, Success, and Happiness

1. Do the exercise about worries from the **"Worries"** chapter.
2. We talked a lot about meditation and worries. We mentioned once before how Keller defined worries – **as a negative meditation**. Therefore, he proposes the following to those who do not know how to meditate: "Focus and process your thoughts the same way as you do when you worry, except have in mind what you do want, not what you don't want."

> *Action is necessary and is always the best cure for worries and fear.*

3. Another very useful technique to solve worries is this one (also from Keller): Make two lists – the first list should include **worries you can influence**, like your schedule, diet, relationships, etc. The second one should include things that you **cannot do anything about**: other people, unpredictable situations, etc. **Burn this second list and trust the best will happen.** By worrying about, or for, other people, you build in your mind an unpleasant picture followed by unpleasant thoughts, and you therefore transmit lower vibration energy. This does not help much. We said before that thought is the strongest energy; so **think about people with love and care, not worry**.

Solve any outstanding issues with your parents through the practice of inhaling the dark cloud, as described in the chapter, "Fear of Disapproval." They need not be alive to do this. Repeat the same procedure with you and your children, if necessary. (But **stay in very high vibration while doing this.**)

6. Living a New Life

If You Do Not Know Where You Are Going, You Will Never Get There... or You Cannot Hit a Target You Cannot See

Imagine you are sailing on the open sea. Suddenly, you become aware that you are lost. You look around, but there is nothing but endless sea as far as the eye can see. You do not know where you are sailing to and therefore you do not have any support to find your way back home.

What is the likelihood that you will turn the boat in the right direction and land in your home harbor?

For a sailor who does not know where to go, no wind is good enough. In this situation, his only real choice is to let himself go – knowing the situation and chance will bring him somewhere.

Here is another example. What if you are lost in a forest and want to go home – which direction is it and what path will take you out of the forest and deliver you to your front door? It is not easy to find the answers.

Is the situation with people not similar?

They allow the outer world to lead and direct them beyond their thoughts. But when they become aware that they are not traveling the road they wanted to be on, they simply trust that circumstances will bring them back to the right track. This happens because they have not defined their goals and therefore have no knowledge of what the right track would be.

It is not enough to identify the goal... you have to also define the path to reach it, as well.

> *It is not enough to identify the goal... you have to also define the path to reach it, as well.*

This is where things begin to get complicated. It is easy to become overwhelmed and think that such a step requires too much effort. Is life leading you where you want to go? Of course, it is... **if you allow it to**. We mentioned before that there are several paths available to you, and everything depends on which one you choose.

We also said that life was like a river, and it helps to swim with the current; but this does not mean that you allow the stream to do whatever it pleases with you, like carry you out to sea, for instance.

Ask any millionaire and other successful people if they allowed life to bring them what they have achieved. No way! **They all set their goals, defined the paths necessary to reach them, and were ready to pay the price for their dreams to come true.** This means they **gave up everything that would block them on the journey to reaching their goal**. They avoided everything that attracted unnecessary attention, decreased their motivation and will to succeed, or tried to pull them away from their goal in another direction.

Here is another recipe to use for success:

1. Listen to your heart and make sure your wish, goal, or desire comes from it (not from personality). Then set a clear goal you want to reach.

2. Mark your path to it; you can achieve a large goal easier if you divide it into several smaller goals.

3. Give up everything that hinders you on your way or tries to lead you away from the goal, at least for a while. On the other hand, find the help and support that will help you maintain high vibration and all the necessary energy.

4. Insist on your way – actively or passively (that is, stay focused and listen to your intuition) – until you fulfill your goal.

We said before that people who talk – or dream (which is often the same) – about their goals are different from those who achieve their goals. Many of the dreamers just are not ready to invest in their success. But does reaching a goal demand that you sacrifice everything and "walk over dead bodies" to get there? **Not at all.**

If you enjoy life, the path to achieving your goal is an adventure and not torture. You already learned how to motivate yourself to be able to do each task with joy. As Paulo Coelho, traveler and best-selling author, advises in his book, *The Alchemist*: You can **"...choose between thinking of (yourself) as the poor victim of a thief and as an adventurer in quest of his treasure."**

Sometimes self-doubt will try to block your path. You learned how to overcome it through changing your thoughts. You also learned how to overcome your fears.

What then still stops you?

The only thing left to do now is to **make the right choice, plan your goals accordingly, and motivate yourself to persist in following your (original) decisions**. This chapter will teach you how to do this.

Above all, (still) have in mind that **financial success is not your only goal**. Without health, friendship, love, a social life, free time, peace, personal growth, and the like, your financial success will be an empty victory. As we said before, do not neglect the things that are important. Otherwise, the time will come when you will gladly give up all your hard earned money just to get them back.

The Truth About Motivation

On the CD entitled *The Evolution of Opportunity*, the company Network Twenty-One announced that **experts discovered that most people spend more time planning their holidays than planning their lives.**

From this, it is clear that most people are, **out of five levels**, located on the **first or second levels** (denial of one's self or searching for identity), which are followed by **tension releasing activities** (vacation).

Because these people perceive their tension releasing as the greatest goal in that moment, the future does not interest them as much because they have a **bigger problem** (they are overwhelmed with stress, pressure, worries, and concerns), which must be solved beforehand. That is why vacation often represents the climax of the year's activities for them; goals have to wait.

We, as people, function so that we usually **have solutions to current problems on our minds**. Hardly anyone thinks strategically or long-term. That is exactly the point: If we can think long-term and have a **clear, long-**

term vision, we will get energy, inspiration, and motivation from it in times when things do not go smoothly, as we have already mentioned.

Let us look at a practical example. **Sometimes we get a very clear and direct intuitive impulse about what to do.** This impulse is often very strong and the answer to our wishes. (Although it may be expressed in a way we had not expected.) At the same time, it **shows us a clear path** how to reach our goal. For instance, we could get a very clear flash of wit to **write a book**.

However, we must know how to understand the impulse: **It often comes only once** (in a very strong form – like a flash of wit). As you know, if we do not decide to **actually do something** with this energy at that time, it vanishes. Inside, we ordinarily feel that it would be good to do something about this. But at the same time, the strong energy, which carries or carried with it very strong motivation, is **no longer there**.

What is worse is that if we, for instance, ask ourselves again in a couple of days if we are in the mood to write a book, **the mind serves up a slew of reasons why now is not the right time (and it is a question if it ever will be)**.

Does this mean that we have just missed the opportunity? Or that this flash of wit overwhelmed us, but **did not hold us long enough**? No.

This flash of wit comes from intuition and always carries within it the seeds of motivation. Even if – after the first or initiating energy fades – the mind tries to tell us that we do not have the energy, knowledge, or so forth, this is not the case.

The secret is **going back to the initial energy to get the motivation**. So we will not get inspired by asking, "Am I motivated to write a book at this moment?" but by **re-experiencing the initiating energy and feeling the power and motivation of that moment**.

Of course, if our mind does not stop us beforehand in the sense, "Now you have a lot of other important tasks, don't fantasize about a book."

If we can manage to acquire a strong will to hush the mind long enough that it does not stop us at this phase, and we can repeatedly come back for the energy from the first moment, we will **always find enough motivation, strength, and inspiration in this energy**.

Herein lies the secret of long-term motivation. (You can read [much] more about this in the book, *Charisma, Self-Confidence and Personal Power*.)

Wanting What Others Have... or What Your Personality (Not Your Heart) Wants

When we are motivated, we are nearly ready to fulfill our goals, wishes, and desires... but **not yet**. We should clarify something else beforehand.

It is important to find out what we really want; that is, whatever suits our personal growth and makes us happy at the same time. Namely, more often than we think, we **want something that pleases our ego or personality** (external destiny) **instead of fulfilling us** (internal destiny).

And most of the time, we do not even know this is happening.

We can grow much faster if we look at ourselves – our goals, wishes, and desires – with a **detached mind**.

In the following chapters, we will take a closer look at **wanting something that we do not have** – but would **like to** – and about **wanting something that our personality – not our heart – wants**.

There is an interesting thing going on in your life (and everyone else's life at some time or other) when you desire something you do not have.

Example: A businessperson drives a brand-new luxury car – worth a small fortune – in the countryside. He notices a farmer plowing a field and thinks, "I would give **anything to trade places with him** this moment: no stressful meetings, no depression about losing a big contract, no rushing constantly from one place to another, and no financial pressures. **What a life**; breathing in the fresh air, surrounded by the beauty of nature, and above all, far away from the crazy pace of the busy world."

The same farmer watches the businessperson driving by in his luxury car and thinks, "What a car... and what a lifestyle the owner must be living. He or she must have important meetings with important people discussing important topics. I bet he or she has cocktail parties and vacations in cities all over the world. His or her closet is filled with Armani suits and he or she has a bank account that would allow me the peace of mind to never have to worry about how to pay my bills or what my family will eat. I have been working hard for thirty years and my whole farm isn't worth as much as that car. Compared to that person, **I have nothing** – living only from day-to-day. A successful business entrepreneur... **that is out of my reach and only a dream to me**."

In this case, it is quite easy to see that each one of them is located on their own level. As we recall, the first two phases are connected to the **tension within us** (the first to the denial of one's self, and the second to searching for opportunity and identity); the third is about **releasing tensions**.

The farmer is probably on the first level because he has the feeling that he is **left to mercy and displeasure** and has **no possibility for change**. And so he wants to become Mr. Someone and taste wealth (the wish for a new identity, or the second level).

The businessperson is on the second level (searching for identity on the basis of expression in the physical world through material goods, wealth, etc.) and aspires for the **release of tensions**. When he or she sees the farmer, this person does not see him through the missing identity prism, but thinks instead of **carefree relaxation**. Namely, everyone sees that which matches (or is in harmony with) **his or her vibration** and **the current wishes** that are derived from it.

We can see in the previous example how we are often **attracted towards what we are (momentarily) missing**.

You can also conduct your own simple test regarding wishing for what you do not have. Choose a book, tape, CD, or something else that you do not listen to or use very often, and lend it to a friend.

Within a few days of lending it out, it is highly likely you will begin to think about it and want it back. Why? Because your thoughts are now focused on that thing and not on the other things you have. **The more you think about it, the more you miss it and want to have it.**

So why do we find it difficult to enjoy what we do have, rather than longing for what we do not have or wanting what others have?

A big part of it is because we are taught to **compare ourselves with others**. Unfortunately, that leaves people constantly feeling that they are lacking something or that others are far better, and it is also why people are not satisfied with their achievements once they do reach their goal.

How does this play out? Let us say that you set a goal, like buying your first car. You dream about it; you give up little things to make the necessary sacrifice to buy your car, all because you have a burning desire to own your own vehicle. You say things to yourself and others like, "Once I get that car, I'll have everything I want."

Finally, the great moment arrives and you buy your car, sit inside, and start the ignition. It does not bother you that the car is used and not new. All that is important is that it is yours and **you have finally achieved your goal**. What a great feeling of freedom and satisfaction – nothing on earth could make you happier!

You spend the next few weeks doing all the things you imagined you would do while you were dreaming about getting your car. When you are not driving it, you clean and polish it lovingly, repair the small defects, and enhance some of its better features to make the car look even better.

Sooner than you might imagine, however, something happens: A friend invites you for a ride in his brand-new car. The leather interior has that new car smell... the shine on the car's body has the beautiful depth that only a new car can have and you can see. It is the latest model with the fancy new driver's console and dashboard.

This is a nice car!

Not surprisingly, you are no longer as thrilled with your used car. **You begin to dream about your friend's car instead... and what it would be like to own that car.** You still take care of your car, but now the extra effort to try to make it look better does not really seem worth it. You even feel a little embarrassed to drive it, especially to places you know your friend will be with his new car. Now you tell yourself and others, "It's only temporary." Or you try to raise its value by saying things like, "It doesn't look like much, but you should see the engine – it looks brand-new and runs like a dream. It would have been a sin not to buy it because I got it for such a great price."

In many ways, you are now seeking confirmation, from yourself and others, that you made a good purchase and buying it was a good decision. However, the seeds of what your next car will be have already begun to take root in your mind – a new car with power windows, remote locks, etc.

Everything starts again, right from the beginning, except now you are comparing yourself to a higher standard: with the used car, you compared yourself to those who had no car; **now you compare yourself to those who have a better (new) car.**

Setting new goals is a constant and necessary process. **However, when you do not acknowledge achieving your goals, and instead immediately**

The Millionaire Mindset

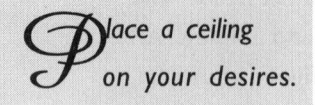

Place a ceiling on your desires. set a new one without pausing to just enjoy your accomplishment, **it wipes out all the credit for what you have just achieved**, and that is dangerous. Many simply do not know how to enjoy their accomplishments in life – constantly feeling the need to compare themselves to others has beaten them down to where greed has overcome them.

Often these things are an **escape from one's self**, as well as a **search for a new identity, which would make him or her better**. This is something completely different from, for example, goal achievement in sports or studies. It is one thing if the goal comes from the heart... and something else entirely if others or **outside surroundings** motivate or persuade us that we aren't good enough and so we must try differently.

If you are going to compare yourself constantly to others, you are going to be unhappy forever... because there will always be many who have better lifestyles, more money, greater opportunities, and heightened success. Sri Sathya Sai Baba says, **"Place a ceiling on your desires."**

Is This What You Really Want?

So **write down your wishes, goals, and desires, and then write what will happen when you achieve them**. If your goal has been a motorcycle, write that down, and then write **how your life will change** – what you will do, be, feel – and what will be different by enjoying your motorcycle. Be aware of your desire, both the price you pay for it (in the sacrifices you make to achieve it) and the enjoyment you receive from it.

Do not allow some new goal to appear and take its place too soon after realizing this goal, or it will rob you of all the joy the achievement was meant to bring. You will be **back at the beginning** – a new desire, more longing, more sacrifice and dreaming, instead of taking the time to enjoy what you have achieved.

Let us clear up another secret. These kinds of wishes, which quickly come and – even more quickly – go, are **wishes of your personality** (or ego) that are usually driven by comparing, proving, and affirming.

But when it comes to our heart's wishes, we **do not get tired of them**... and they are the ones we should strive for!

So how do we know if a wish comes from our heart, or if we have assumed it from someone else – according to the principle of resonance – or maybe it arose in our personality (as a result of comparing or competing)?

We can find out in the following way.

A wish that does not come from the heart **usually forms very fast – practically immediately – and completely takes over us just as quickly.** It is accompanied by extremely **aggressive energy**, which urges us to **fulfill the wish immediately** – tomorrow would be too late! So there is also the fear that we might miss out on something. In addition, wishes of this kind come **in waves**: When they are present, they are extremely strong, and when we forget about them, they disappear.

Then something will remind us of these wishes, and the aggressive energy will flood us again. Such are desires for new clothes, cars... and even jobs, for instance, in network marketing.

This is why **time is of the essence**.

If we were to wait a few days, we would go into a different energy and the wishes would go away. Here is another mind game that is taking place at the same time: If we do not fulfill this wish, we will have a **bad feeling**. But after a while, we are **glad we did not throw ourselves into it**.

If we think of a situation where we aroused energies of low vibration (for instance anger) in ourselves, we will notice something similar: The energy was very strong and aggressive, and inside **we felt a great need to give this energy out of ourselves**. But this energy also **drops very quickly**, and if we channel it by releasing it onto someone else (read: snapped at someone or blamed them for our problems), we soon, when our heart reawakens, **become sorry**.

Wishes that come from the heart or soul are much different. **They are present practically all the time, even if they are in the background.** With them, we have a kind of **feeling of fate**. We may even feel – perhaps secretly – the release of large quantities of energy, and we also feel growth. These wishes are not very aggressive, but show themselves as a **revelation**, such as, "How come I didn't notice this sooner?"

Even when we change our field of thinking or acting, or after some time passes, this wish **accompanies** us and suits all life areas and circumstances. So **no area of our life excludes this wish**.

We may also feel that kind of wish and **suppress** it in ourselves; the mind is a real expert at this.

Write Down Your Goals and Acknowledge Their Achievement

Let us go back to acknowledging our true wishes and **letting them make us happy**.

As a young man, I once had a conversation with an older man I had just met. Somewhere during the conversation, we discovered we both had the same make of car; only he had a model that was more prestigious and a very rare collector's car. My eyes lit up as he offered to show it to me. Sitting in it felt like being in another world. It was perfect in detail and condition – indeed, **it had everything a man who appreciates cars could ask for**.

You can imagine what that experience meant to me, especially with me being at an age where the car you drive is one of the most important things in your life. I was filled with excitement and admiration for the owner of such a fine specimen and searched his eyes for the sparkle of joy and pride that surely he must feel to own and drive such a collector's piece.

What I saw instead surprised me because a **dreamy and near absent look filled the eyes I thought should be sparkling with a playful, prideful, boyish joy**. Oblivious to my obvious disappointment, he soon began telling me of the experience he had on his friend's yacht the day before. His eyes sparkled as he told me the millions it was worth. "That yacht," he said, "is the kind of lifestyle that I would like. I cannot get that beautiful boat out of my mind. I dream about it all the time."

In that instant, I wondered **if people would see the same expression in my eyes when they came to admire my new, but used, car now that I had seen my friend's brand-new, luxury car**.

What stops us from being happy and carefree, like we were when we were children? Is it right that higher goals immediately displace what we have just achieved and weaken the value of what we have worked so hard to accomplish?

Think about it.

If you are honest with yourselves, you will see that you are likely still the same as the children you once were – it is just that **your toys are becoming increasingly more expensive**.

So what is different?

As a child, you did not think so much about the consequences of your actions or how others saw you. You did not have to think about behaving a certain way to keep up appearances. You jumped in a mud puddle because it was there, it was fun, and you did not worry about muddying your shoes – what your mother would say was always an afterthought.

Many adults long to play the creative games that childhood offered them – but now they worry about what **others will think**. So **they play the adult version of their childhood games**; having a better car is now just a substitute for having a better toy in childhood. The "Don't mess with my wife, or I'll embitter your life," replaces the "Leave my girlfriend alone, or I'll break your bike," etc. A lot of adults are **the same inside** as the children they once were, but **it is not fashionable to admit that**.

Make room for some craziness in your life and see how much it adds to your adult life; play hide-and-seek with your kids and do not worry about what the neighbors will say. How you feel is important – **it is your life**. Let a little joy in.

Enjoy each moment and do not allow those who do not have the courage to be joyful to discourage you.

Whether you realize it or not, a lot of those people **want to be as happy and carefree as you are, but they are either afraid or have become so out-of-touch with their inner child** that they have simply forgotten how.

When you decide to enjoy life, **the road to success is as sweet as the goal itself**.

Self-love is the all-important catalyst that enables you to enjoy your life and your accomplishments. Without it, you will be striving forever to prove a self-worth you do not feel – by buying bigger and better things in an attempt to increase your value… in your eyes and in the eyes of those around you.

That way, nothing is ever good enough, which is the **exact reflection of your feeling that you are never good enough**.

But it is so easy to surrender to life… and reverence every minute of it.

The line between life and death is so thin. Often, we walk on the edge and play games instead of turning inward and enjoying life. **Is it necessary** to stare death in the face before you can appreciate the miracle of life? For some people it is.

It should not be.

How to Set Goals

There is a well-known and expanded method of setting goals, which also includes motivation; if there is no motivation, your desires are not strong enough to carry you through paying the price for achieving them. We have outlined this for you step-by-step below. (It is a process similar to what Brian Tracy laid out in his book, *Maximum Achievement*.)

Step One: Identifying Your Desire — How Big Is It?

Does the thought of achieving your goal excite you and awaken feelings of great joy and/or contentedness? Do you see in your goal the same essence as what you are working and living for?

When you feel a burning desire to answer "Yes" to all these questions, then you are ready to travel your path, which will bring you to the successful realization of your goals. Sometimes, if you are not led by a pure and burning desire, but rather by greed, comparison to others, fulfillment of ideas that others have about you, etc., you will not progress further than this point. **Until you have a pure and burning desire to achieve your goal, you will find obstacles and make excuses that will direct you to other paths, away from your goal.**

Let us say a word or two about **passion**.

A burning desire does not mean you have to be passionate about your goal. For instance, if you are a surgeon, you presumably are not passionate and do not jump to the ceiling when you see a patient with an open wound and in great pain.

This burning desire relates more to your **life's mission** than the passion and enthusiasm that you express when you, for example, see your new car (you fall in love with it) for the first time, which is more about **searching for identity** and **tension releasing**.

Said another way, passion mainly refers to **external achievements** – acceptance from peers, material possessions, social status, etc. – while the desire we are referring to relates to **internal destiny** (or internal contentedness).

The following example is from the business world. An average, but mildly successful businessman was striving for success.

He was in the real estate business and did everything necessary to succeed. He invested in marketing, conducted his business according to the successful standards laid out by his predecessors, and was always in the right places, mixing with the right people. He also had a clear goal – to sell X amount of real estate by Y date and to keep and cherish his existing customers. He seemed to have everything needed to meet his success.

However, his challenge soon became obvious. For him, **working was not fun... it was only an obligation.** Business was a necessary "evil" that brought the money he needed to afford a few pleasures and to forget about painful moments in his business career. (By the way, most people are caught in just such a cycle – work is painful, you earn to be able to rest, and when the money is gone, you have to work hard again to earn more. Do you remember the chapter about your subconscious mind? As long as you harbor unpleasant thoughts within you, the results will be unpleasant, as well. And when you try to force positive changes from a negative mindset, you presumably will not succeed.)

I asked this executive a seemingly innocent question:

"Which newspaper or magazine do you look for first at the corner stand?"

"A car magazine," he replied.

I told him a story about Socrates.

One of the philosopher's students asked him, "How can I become as wise as you are?" Socrates took him to the fountain, pushed his head under the water and held it there. Caught off guard and nearly gasping for air, the student started to wave with his hands; he never expected something like this to happen!

When he was really desperate and near the end of his breath, Socrates released him. When the student started breathing again, the wise man asked him, **"What was the most important thing to you, when your head was under the water? Money? Success? Honor? Tell me, what were you thinking about, and what did you want the most?"** The student answered easily and without hesitation: "Money, success or honor? No way... Air! Air was the only thing I wanted more than anything."

"You see," remarked the teacher, **"when your desire to be wise is as strong as your desire for air was a moment ago, nothing will stop you."**

I told the businessman, "When you find the satisfaction in real estate that you do in cars, you'll have all the success you want."

He understood. I asked him why he chose this profession. His primary influence was his uncle, who was successful in the real estate business. He was a role model for success and the most respected person in the family. The uncle told everyone how this business was the best business and that he would not change his profession for anything in the world.

Well, **this was his uncle's way to success, but selling real estate is not the absolute path to success or the one that is right for all people.** His nephew copied his external actions, but **he could not copy his uncle's passion and mindset for real estate** – for this reason he was not even close to obtaining the same success as his uncle.

A Focused Desire Assures Top Results

We decided to invite the businessman's uncle over for a conversation to learn more about his underlying attitude toward his profession. The following week, they both visited.

First, I spoke just with the uncle. I asked him why he decided to get into the real estate business. "Since I was a little boy, I've been fascinated by it. I always imagined myself in this role. Whenever I watched a movie that had such a scene, I stored it in my memory. I still remember actors who played real estate brokers and even the scenes in the movies that fascinated me the most. I can even tell you what they wore! Once, I sat almost six hours in a cinema and watched the same film three times just because of one scene. I think this was the one that tipped the scale for me, when I had to decide what to do with my life. In my day, it wasn't so simple to convince my parents that their son would like to be a sales agent, one who shows and sells houses. Nobody believed in my success, but I persevered."

Then I asked him which magazine he looked at first at the corner stand. "I used to buy many magazines about interior decorating and architecture, now I am a subscriber to most of them. I don't go to the newsstand often because I think that reading the daily gossip is a waste of time."

I looked at the nephew. **It was clear to him now.** His uncle continued. "Well, I don't have any trouble with literature, but I don't usually have enough time for these magazines. You see, I read every one that is connected to my work. There I make new connections, renew old ones, and continually study how the most successful people in this business make their sales. I bring back so much literature from each real estate fair that I need several weeks to read it and incorporate the ideas into my work."

After some months, I bumped into the nephew at a fair. He told me that **he finally became successful in his business.** I asked him what he did to become so much more enthusiastic about real estate. "What real estate? **I sell cars!**" he answered happily.

Your desires are not the same as those of other people; if your actions are not in harmony with your true desires, you will never be successful in your business or as happy as you could be otherwise. Everyone has his or her own way, which is the right path for him or her. These are the things that you have to do yourself, and nobody else can do them for you.

But there are situations that exist where mimicking a certain person is successful.

When Is Copying Somebody Else Successful?

To begin with, it can only happen when **your mind is clearly focused on your goal and all you are lacking is the last step – the appropriate action to achieve it.** This means that your desire and the accompanying thoughts are known to you and have come from you and not someone else. All you need now is the experience – a technique, described step-by-step, to get the best result.

In this case, you study what other people have done in the same area to achieve their goals. For instance:

- If you want to raise **happy and healthy children, you would copy the child-rearing actions of a parent** who is famous for it.
- If you want to **buy a car and get a good price, copy a professional car salesperson** who is active in this field and has above average success.
- If you want to become an expert in your chosen business, **copy the most successful people in it** and then surpass them with your own ideas and success.

Whenever you want to copy someone, the big secret is to **adopt the other person's thinking and feeling about the subject**, not just mimic his or her actions. Of course, this must be **your own wish**; that is, the initiative should proceed from your heart and not from comparing and proving yourself to others.

Step Two: Become Certain You Are Going to Succeed

Your desire can be great, but if you do not believe in a positive outcome, there is no point in it. **Trust yourself even, and especially, when nobody else does**... because you know yourself best and you know what you are capable of, or willing to put in the effort to learn.

Follow your heart and listen to your inner voice.

Here is an example from my life. I grew up in a poor working family. After finishing school, I went abroad, and then I got a job in a big company back home.

This was back in the days when the socialist regime was still strong in our country, so salaries were very small. On the other hand, I worked much less productively at home than abroad – you just had to be there eight hours and you got a (miserable) salary. The biggest irony was that even if you wanted to work better and harder, you could not earn more money.

Anyway, I felt that I could find my happiness at home, not abroad.

In terms of numbers, my salary was approximately ten times lower than what I could have been earning abroad. It was then that I learned something very important, which later became the basis for my further development: **Perhaps I did not know what I was looking for in my life, but I knew what I did not want**. Sitting in an office for eight hours from day-to-day, earning a bad salary, living an empty, aimless life, void of all creativity, was not the way I wanted to live.

I was looking for better work that would give meaning to my life. I had had enough and had reached the level where I was ready to give up a regular income in exchange for personal freedom and growth.

Sometimes people have to suffer long enough in some relationships before finally reaching the point where they hit the table with their fist and say, "I have had enough!" When this happens because of self-realization, the decision to change is powerful and right.

Maybe I could call what happened next intuition. I simply knew that with my knowledge and experience, I could earn a lot more money. I went to my boss, gave him my resignation, and headed for the unknown. **Only one person believed in me – my (higher) Self.**

When I look back at it now, it is obvious that this was **one of the best things I have done for me in my whole life**. Because of this decision, I was able to begin building a new path for my life. Since then, my business has been abundantly successful. Of course, I occasionally experience things that do not turn out as I imagined they should, but most of the time, I live according to my desires.

However, I learned some things along my path. First of all, **be careful not to set your goals too high in the beginning**. Setting an unrealistic goal – like becoming a millionaire from scratch within a year – will not do you any good.

But now that you know how the subconscious works, you also know that if you set your goal too high, not achieving it will become the repeated pattern, and that is what will stay in your mind. This will cause your failure at even menial tasks, which you have performed successfully up till now. Be aware of various manipulators who will try to motivate you to force yourself, even if you do not feel it in your heart, by saying, "A person is only unsuccessful when stuck in the mud, if he does not pick himself or herself up and try again." **Follow your heart and listen to your inner voice instead.**

Only you know your path and nobody can force theirs on you, if you do not allow them to.

The other thing I learned in a big way is: **Do not set unrealistic timeframes**. When I look back at my wishes, I can say that I fulfilled my desires, but my timing was usually off.

I would like to share with you another example from the business world. Years ago, I was working with various dealers and representatives of companies to whom I teach effective sales methods, motivational methods, and the secrets of successful salesmanship and communication. I always come to the same conclusion:

Whoever has found himself or herself in this business, and is fulfilling his or her personal dreams through it, does not need motivational seminars to raise his or her motivation for work.

Motivation is needed for those who do not believe "this is it." Answer the following question to check if you have chosen the right path:

Can you imagine yourself as super successful – such as one of the best in the world – in the business (or task) you are in (or you perform)?

If not, then do not ask why you have not succeeded. You have limitations buried in your consciousness that prevent you from reaching a higher level.

Let us dig a bit deeper into our careers. Even if you already have a career, it could help you realize how much potential you have in it.

Here are some questions, which will help you **discover the ideal profession for you**. By that I mean the profession you have the best chance of succeeding in **with the greatest amount of happiness**... because you can only be successful in a business that your heart – or life's mission, which you also feel in your heart as a goal, wish, or desire – confirms.

When you enjoy – that is, when you are connected through your heart with – what you do, you will educate yourself and keep abreast of the current news in your field. It will not be hard to stay up late watching an interesting discussion among people in your field. You will talk about it, and pass further information along to your customers or coworkers, with passion and a firm belief that suddenly you will find out you are a step ahead of others in your chosen field or profession. There is only one more step to your goal now – **turning this knowledge and wisdom into money**.

A Test: What Is Your Ideal Profession?

You can help yourself by practicing the following exercise, which is a combination of advice given by Staples, mentioned before, and Michael LeBoeuf, a self-made millionaire and counselor.

Imagine you have so much money that you are financially independent; this means you can buy whatever you like, whenever you like. For instance, let us just say you have $50 million, enough that you do not have to work for more money. Now answer the following questions sincerely:

1. **What are you now doing that you would stop doing if you had enough money?**
2. What would you carry on with?
3. **What would you like to study, and in which area would you like to become an expert, if money were no object?**

4. What should people remember you by, and what would you like people to say about you and your life achievement(s) at your funeral?
5. **What would you start doing today, if you were absolutely certain you were going to succeed?**
6. What are you better at than other people?
7. **If you had only one year left to live, how would you spend this time?**
8. Imagine you are doing your chosen work. Now answer sincerely: Do you see yourself working in the same place, doing your chosen work, **in twenty years**? What do you feel when you think about this?

Generally, your hobbies are what you occupy yourself with in your spare time, things you **love to do the most**. So answer the next questions, as well:

1. **Which hobbies consume you so much that you forget the time?**
2. What attracts you about your hobby, i.e., the subject, the craft itself, etc.?
3. **With what things were you occupied as a teenager? Do you still have the same desire for them deep inside?**
4. What can you do or talk about for a long time without getting bored?
5. **How do you imagine a perfect day?**

Because every person's work is different, answer these questions, as well:

1. **Do you want to work at home or abroad, traveling, or in an office near home?**
2. How much contact with people do you want to have?
3. **How much privacy do you want?**
4. Do you want to work physically or creatively (brainwork)?
5. **Do you love to set goals and realize them, or do you prefer doing steady, repetitive activities?**
6. Do you want to be independent, or do you prefer that someone else have the final responsibility?
7. **How can you combine all the desires you quoted above into a business, or in other words, how can you transform your desires into money?** For instance, if you like sleeping, this will not help

you find your ideal work; it can help you only if you are looking for a job that offers you enough sleep or maybe promotes good and restful sleep (i.e., selling mattresses).

Do not censor your thoughts, but allow them to land on paper. Do the analysis at the end. Find common points, and you will find your theoretically ideal profession. Do not be amazed if you do not want to become a great businessperson or a leader. According to the estimations made by experts, only 5% of the world's population is capable of working independently (like a self-governing businessperson or manager).

You must be careful that the profession you are looking for now will not just express your wish for freedom, desire to be like someone else, or even a desire to get even with someone.

Your profession should not be based on just tension releasing activities because sooner or later, when you have released the tension, it will be evident that you will no longer have the motivation for performing this trade. The profession should provide you **the opportunity to express your own creativity** and the **awakening of love inside** (opening of the heart), as we have already mentioned.

In this case, you will never be bored, and you will never get sick of it. Considering that every person has a specifically defined life's mission – which he or she feels while in the heart – it is recommended that **the profession at least coincides with and supports this life's mission, if it does not directly express it.**

If you have children, or you are in the phase of choosing your profession, take this test because your happiness in life could depend on it.

Realizing Your Dreams and Desires

Once you know what you want to do in your life, you have to make a plan for how to bring it about. Let us imagine that you want to become a mechanic because this is the business you are dreaming about.

You have to produce a plan that will tell you **how to move from the first point**. So define – in writing – **the possibilities for how you can start**. For instance, you can start by reading literature, taking classes, asking questions of those who are already in this business, and maybe even asking them to teach you a few basic things. Choose the options that are **realistic** and **suit you best**.

Now comes the most important step, fixing the deadline by which you will earn your first $100. Say it like this: **"I'll earn $100 within a month (or so) from now, doing minor mechanical repair work."** Of course, you will not open your own shop right away, but maybe somebody you know needs help in theirs? Think and begin the task. When you earn your first hundred dollars, repeat the whole process, or maybe even **increase your goal**. If you like doing this work, you will educate yourself gladly and quickly, so challenges will be limited and temporary – all you need to do is take the first step and begin. Also, better and better opportunities will appear. Just **follow your goal with your heart open**, adjust the timeframe, and do whatever it takes.

Step Three: Define Your Goal and Your Current Starting Point

Here is your next assignment. **Specifically define your desires and the time it takes to achieve them.** Write them down, draw, and use newspaper clippings.

Let me tell you how I bought my first motorcycle.

Many years ago, I saw a beautiful motorcycle in a magazine and said to myself, "I'll buy one of these one day." I tore the page with the picture on it out of the magazine and kept it. I totally forgot about it. But sometimes, whenever I cleaned my desk drawer, I found it again. Each time I saw it, I was overcome with the same excitement I felt the first time I saw it, and I always put it back in my drawer with great care.

Years later, I spoke with my friend by phone. The discussion was about motorcycles. "I sold mine," he said. When he told me the model and year, I smiled.

"Listen, did the buyer take it already?"

"No, he doesn't have enough money yet. I expect his visit in a few days."

"Tell him not to bother, if he doesn't have the money. Give his deposit back, and I'll buy it instead."

My friend was surprised and I knew this bike was mine. I do not need to tell you what happened; **the buyer could not raise enough money.** The day I was supposed to pick up the bike – a few hundred kilometers away – an acquaintance that was in the transport business had to go to that town to make a delivery and would return with an empty truck. So we made a deal, and he brought the bike back to me.

And I also bought the motorcycle far cheaper than I ever imagined I could.

Setting a Deadline

In the whole procedure of defining your goal, you are in confrontation with one essential question – **whether to fix the time of realization (set a deadline) or just wait for a good opportunity to appear**.

The answer is not so easy. **The worst thing you can do is fix a final due date, which is not realized, and then repeat the procedure of not meeting your due date.** When I was buying a motorcycle, this date would not have helped because the situation just was not right for the purchase.

But often, the **time factor has to be determined** because this is the only way we can **define daily activities**. This especially applies in the case where the opportunity is already here; so when there are no "ifs" (unexpected events or things over which we have no influence), or other decisive factors that could **drastically change the course of events** between us and the goal.

Below is an example illustrating how to set a deadline.

Buying material goods is often one of the goals you will want to achieve, but this goal is conditioned by your wages and a finite sum of money. For example, image that you want to buy an item that costs $2,500. So ask yourself:

When do I want to buy this?

The answer is, for example, in six months. You have a savings of $500, so you need to gain another $2,000.

Assume that you are a salesperson and you earn a commission from each sale you make. Also, assume that you need at least $470 for monthly expenses.

So you should be earning roughly $333 more than your monthly expenses, which means you must earn $800 (expenses plus investment) each month to be able to afford the purchase in six months.

If you want to make $800 each month, you have to sell forty products because you earn $20 on every sale.

Here is your success plan: On average, you make a sale to **four out of the ten prospects you contact** (you have to know this from your sales experiences, do not just assume it).

You want to succeed forty times, so you need to contact **one hundred prospects to sell those forty products**.

To get in touch with so many customers, you need to make **twice as many phone calls**. Because only one out of two calls, on average, results in an appointment – you will have to call two hundred people each month or nine people every day. However, because you spend most of your time away from the office, you should call roughly forty people on Monday, and then you will have more time during the week to make visits.

One hundred visits, divided by twenty-five days, means **four visits per day**. You need less than an hour for each visit, so this is achievable. Now you have to consider customers that you have to visit a second time, because they could not decide whether to buy on your first visit with them. This will take an additional 30% of your time. It is still achievable with all variables covered.

When you determine everything necessary to achieve this goal, only one question remains: **Are you prepared to invest so much effort and energy into the achievement of this goal**?

Sometimes it is that simple. And sometimes it is far more complicated.

Having Dreams

It is good to have dreams. For instance, while desiring the motorcycle, I let my dream flourish (it was impossible to realize it sooner because only two models of that type existed in the entire area of our state).

Having a dream means gradually harmonizing with the vibration of the goal, having a certain set of circumstances growing in your subconscious and allowing it the time to show you the ideal chance to realize it. Sometimes things do go slowly.

Here is a case about an apprentice without schooling who wanted to become the owner of a drugstore. He had no real possibility of achieving such a high goal. But he persisted in his dream and **each night before falling asleep, he put little bottles on shelves – in his mind**.

To make a long story short, he soon began working in a drugstore as a regular worker doing various tasks. At the same time, he began formal schooling, after which his career began to climb. Ten years later, the day came when he became the owner of a drugstore. **He fittingly named it "Dreams."** (This story is taken from Murphy's book, *The Power of Your Subconscious Mind*.)

Step Four: Define and Deal With (Remove) Possible Obstacles

It is necessary to use the proper method in defining and removing possible obstacles from your path.

First, discover what obstacles hinder you the most. As you improve on and remove each obstacle, move onto the next one and do the same. Be careful **not to neglect your primary advantages**, nor **decrease your performance in the process**. If you reduce all of your steps to average – because you have overcome the obstacles and thus improved in these areas, but have neglected to grow your most important assets, which are now only average – you will be lost in mediocrity.

> *Believe in yourself and your abilities – all the time.*

Believe in yourself and your abilities – all the time.

Here is another thing we have to be careful about: While defining obstacles, we cannot allow ourselves to invest too much energy in them (read: resonate with them too much) because their energy can absorb us. So during this process, **our consciousness must, the entire time, be in the achievement of the goal and not the problem.**

If we identify with the problem too much, our strength, will, motivation, faith, hope, and inspiration will drop – and this could be the end of our dreams.

Step Five: Ask for Help and Find More Information

When you come that far, be open to what is going on around you.

Often obstacles, as well as solutions, will pop up **along the way**. That is why, although we cannot always plan ahead, we must be focused on action the whole time and not simply automatically performing an activity. We have to **observe life around us**; or we have to be **harmonized with time and space**.

So be aware of all the current events in your chosen profession, seek out the necessary information and people who are already successful and on a similar path as you are now, copy their actions, etc. Become a **detective for opportunities**.

Do not push the situation, but at the same time **be active. Go with the flow**, and adjust all the time. **Do not subordinate yourself, but adjust yourself.** Several paths lead to the same goal; the single straight path is the shortest, but it could be very demanding and may require you to sacrifice in ways you cannot or are unable to commit to. The second path is indirect, but may be a much more pleasant journey. Which one is best? I do not know. Only you can decide which road to take.

Be open to new information. If you do not know about something – and have not tried it – how can you know if it is useful to you or not?

Also, be ready **to ask for help**, even if you are not used to doing so. Sometimes good advice can save you a lot of stress, time, and money.

But **take care not to be diverted from your path. Ask for help, not opinions** – or even permission – to achieve your goal. You have dealt with this decision (whether to take your path or not) before when you were in your heart... and that decision remains.

Step Six: Work Your Plan

You now have all the information to help you create the scenario for reaching your goal. **Prioritize your tasks;** give up all the unnecessary little things, associate with people who support you, etc. Redefine your plan, if necessary, and improve it as new information becomes available, adding or removing elements as needed.

Remember, **your plan is dynamic**, so you need to be as flexible as circumstances dictate.

Step Seven: Belief, Persistence, and Realization

Live in the belief of achieving your goal, enjoy the feeling of realization, and be persistent until the end.

Use all the methods you have practiced (visualization, affirmation, meditation, etc.) to increase your self-confidence and direct you towards achieving your goal.

Persist until you succeed or consciously decide to change your goal – if you decide to alter or abandon it, make sure you acknowledge that you are choosing to do so, and recognize that sometimes plans change midstream.

Namely, sometimes, for whatever reason, you will **no longer want to achieve a specific goal you have set**. There is no shame in abandoning the goal, but you have to close that energy in a high vibration. That way, the subconscious will not **identify changing your mind with failure**.

Actually, altering your decision regarding your goal can be **the wisest move you make**.

For instance, you wanted to buy a luxury car, but you decided that saving money for a new house was a better investment. **This does not mean that you did not realize your goal**; it simply means that you changed your plan.

Sometimes "swimming with the current" means a **temporary withdrawal from the active pursuance of your goal** – this also is not failure; it is a change in your plan, a realization that the time was not right, etc. You will most likely reap a greater success because the delay may bring you the greatest profit in the end.

You have to be aware of this and acknowledge it, so this move does not rob you of your determination and drain your energy.

Therefore, it is important to **acknowledge when you achieve your intermediate goal**. Some of your goals may be small, but do not be embarrassed to share the victory of achieving them, if only with yourself. Celebrating your victories, at least by acknowledging your success, is the only way to be certain of their reality and gain added confidence.

Here is another important question that could help you along the path. Sometimes you may not know if your choices are right or where your actions are taking you. If this is the case, stop for a moment and answer this question before you resume your activity:

Will doing this bring me – not temporarily, but more importantly, strategically (long-term) – **closer to my goal, further from my goal, or will I remain where I am now**?

If the action distances you from your goal, you need to revise your plan and come up with some other way to get you closer to your goal, or at least keep you where you are now and prevent you from going backwards.

Losing the Battles, Winning the War

Sometimes it is worth losing some… or maybe even all the battles to win the war!

There will be situations in which you will be required to take two steps backward to move one step forward. **Always have your long-term goals in front of you.**

You sometimes have to give up certain things for a short while in order to generate long-term profits. To illustrate this, here is a story about a boy from America. It is taken from DeBono´s book, *Tactics: The Art and Science of Success.*

It is common knowledge that older children often make fun of the youngest one in the group. In this particular situation, they **made him choose between two coins,** one larger and one smaller. Of course, the nickel coin is larger in size than the dime.

The youngest boy always took the larger coin, and the boys laughed at his stupidity. They repeated this game every time a new boy joined the group.

After a long time of making fun of a young boy, one of the boys felt sorry for him. He met with the boy alone and told him: "The other boys are just making fun of you. When they offer you a coin, the smaller one is worth more. **You should always take the smaller one."**

The young, seemingly stupid boy looked at him and said: **"Of course, but once I do that, they'll stop offering me money."**

Who was the "stupid" one in the story? The boy had his long-term goal in sight and gave up the short-term goal – momentary respect and his ego – for it. In the end, he was the winner.

Think about using the moral from this case in your daily life.

Above All, Act!

Once again, let us reemphasize the real essence of achieving success, without which nothing can succeed, even if you have everything else.

Here we reiterate: **Successful people distinguish themselves from others by taking action.** They do not waste their intellect or time by looking for excuses to be idle or by finding confirmations to support the position of how difficult a goal is to achieve, presumably all aimed at finding a reason to quit. They **think less** and **do more.**

Think Less Sometimes

Years ago, my friend Thomas told me about an event that happened when he was a boy. He was on a holiday with John, his schoolmate, whose father was a professor at a university.

The headlight on John's bike burned out, and John called his father to help him replace it. His father, a man of deep consideration, first evaluated the bike from top to bottom, then lit his pipe and began to **ponder the best way to accomplish the task** efficiently and thus with the least amount of effort. John joined him, and they thought and discussed the situation: what tools they would need, which screw to remove first, and so on.

Thomas, who was used to performing practical tasks, asked them for a screwdriver and the spare bulb. He replaced the broken bulb in two minutes – as he had done on his own bike many times before. John and his father looked at him with **astonishment** – they were not used to handling such a menial task so fast and with such ease.

Exaggerated think-time is not recommended.

If the centipede had to think about which leg to lift first to take the next step, it would immediately entangle itself and not be able to move forward at all. The same is true with people. If you start thinking about walking while you are walking, it takes you a lot longer to get where you are going.

Engaging in such exaggerated thinking happens when you either do not want to do something, or in any way doubt what you are doing. So you look and look for new excuses to delay or avoid the task, "Do I have enough time?", "Is it necessary?", "Where to start?", "Am I trained enough to handle it?"

You can easily destroy your enthusiasm and the meaning of your goal through these seemingly innocent thoughts because you are focusing on the obstacles. If enthusiasm grabbed you, no task would be too difficult.

Do the following exercise. Take a sheet of paper and write the following at the top:

What is stopping me on my path to success? What is it about this path that scares me?

Now write down all the factors that truly hinder you. Listen to your mind's answer and record it.

By doing so, you may discover that all your real reasons are **just excuses**. OK, perhaps you really cannot do everything at once to move forward... but nothing at all?

The Cup of Life

The process for realizing your goals can now be simplified to a short, but powerful, recipe for success. Staples illustrates this nicely:

Imagine having a few cups placed in such a manner that the next one will start to fill after the previous is full and its contents are spilling over the edge.

The first cup is **belief**. When you fill this one, belief activates the cup of **capability**, and it begins to fill. You have to use it completely – fill up the cup – to reach **action**. When you fill up this cup, the cup of **results** begins filling, and when this one is full, the contents start flowing into the cup of **life**.

If the process stops at any stage, the chain breaks, and you remain in the middle of your path and without the desired results.

Love

"There is no road in the mountains. Sometimes people tread in high grass, leaving footprints. If more people do the same and more often, a path arises. If these paths have not been used for a long time, weeds grow over them. And your heart is overgrown with weeds." (This is the thought of a wise man whose name I have forgotten.)

One of our goals is love. We are going to look at it closer because it is a very specific area.

Several books have been written that were inspired by love or the lack of it, many nights spent crying, and many wonderful moments created. Love has caused wars and even created heaven on Earth.

This is, without a doubt, the most powerful and uplifting force that exists.

The highest form of love is total **understanding, acceptance, and surrender to Life**. We call it pure or unconditional Love. No limitations, no need to turn others into copies of yourself. No attachment, just sheer joy in each move of the beloved person and what makes him or her happy, while being happy for a person who is on his or her own path.

As we said, Love is a force that does not set any conditions. **Love is not needy or fearful; if you are afraid for someone, or you cannot live without him or her, then you have not yet reached unconditional Love.**

Maybe you are not (really) aware of the meaning of these words. Just think of what people have done in the name of love! Jealousy, for instance, is a completely egotistical feeling. **If you truly love someone, you do not envy him or her or force any conditions on him or her,** but accept him or her with all his or her attributes, good and bad.

Love brings the highest freedom.

When you really love someone, you encourage and help him or her on his or her path, **though it will not be the same path you are on**. You will be happy because he or she is happy, with or without you...

If you are afraid of losing someone because you doubt your ability to hold his or her love, and perhaps are even afraid that your beloved will find someone else, you might be tempted, because of your fear, to **deny him or her freedom and you might seek to hold him or her in all possible ways**. We discussed this previously in the chapter on subconscious; when you try to reach a goal by force, the effect is always the opposite of what you wanted to happen.

Here is a case that describes a dialog between an immature (A) and a mature person (B):

Immature (A): "Why didn't you go to the theater with me?"
Mature (B): "Did I disappoint you?"
A: "Well, you know how much it means to me for us to go together."
B: "Do you really love me?"
A: "Of course, I couldn't love you more."
B: "This means that you wish complete happiness for me?"
A: "Yes, of course, why do you ask me such obvious things?"
B: "Did you consider that, at the time, it was more suitable for me to act as I did?"
A: "Well, what about me? Didn't you think about me and how I would feel? Why do you act only for you?"

This is not love... it is a trade based on certain expectations: **I will support your positions and rules as long as you support mine.**

So as long as these **expectations are fulfilled, both are happy** (and "in love"). When one of them does not follow the other person's rules, the "love" ends.

This is how disappointment is born: Someone can disappoint you only when **your expectations are not met**.

Today people even get married **out of need** and not Love; they need someone to **fulfill their emptiness**. If people took **responsibility for all their own actions**, such situations would not happen.

If we are more precise, we soon discover that a lot of notions we connect with "love" have an **egotistical orientation and one-sided benefit** (when we have the possibility of choice or influence on goings-on). Most often, we are not even talking about love but **attachment**.

Now let us go back to the dialog above and analyze it. The immature person could simply say, "You are right. How could I have been so selfish to envy your happiness and think only about myself and my own feelings?"

The dialog shows that immature people are much **more egotistical** because they try to own a person and search for their happiness through them – which is **impossible**.

Immature people use sentences like: "You are all my life is worth living for." Or "Life is empty without you." Or "I love you so much, and I think about you all the time." And so on.

We have to know that infatuation is consuming… while **Love brings the highest freedom**. If you really love someone unconditionally, you will even allow him or her to leave, and you will be happy with it.

It is easy to see how people search for themselves through someone else. They subordinate themselves to someone else; become dependent on them – like an addict is to drugs or a smoker is to cigarettes – and **tie their identity and thus personal happiness to others**. Such people are often disappointed because it is enough that the ideas in their minds go unrealized.

"People who need love from others are dangerous people. Because only God knows what they are prepared to do to get it!" (Thomas Keller)

The Main Purpose of Intimate Relationships

We have to know that our spouse or partner is a **great teacher**, and that is why we are attracted to them – **they awaken certain energies in us, which for whatever reason we need for our development and growth.**

Keller says that the person who is right for you will fulfill two criteria:

- His or her **image suits you**, and you feel good when others see you with this person.
- He or she is a partner who can **show you patterns that can help you develop further** – through triggering special responses, i.e., anger or worry, in the areas where you are not in control of your energy.

Do you remember the old legend that told how a man and a woman were once one and then separated, and since then each of them has been looking for their other half?

The other half we are searching for in other people is our own heart and soul. Or we can even say – it is God.

Do not forget, **you are here – in Earth's Mystery School – to learn**. One of the greatest lessons is to **learn to love, not to be loved**, because **we are loved all the time**: by God, Mother Nature, people who care about us, etc.

Searching for the love of your life ends when you find inside what you were looking for outside. We all have both energies, male and female, **inside us**.

The male energy has the **power** to do the task, and the female energy has the key to the solution – **intuition and wisdom**. When both principles unite and work in harmony, you can act in perfection. When you achieve such a state, you can unconditionally love everyone because you know that you can depend on no one but yourself for your own happiness, and therefore you do not need anyone for your fulfillment and happiness.

And when this happens, it is the right time to establish a relationship with someone you want to live with... because **you will build your union upon your true life's mission** – and goals, wishes, and desires that derive from it – and you will (still) direct your energy into fulfilling it. And your partner will **support you, while you will support him or her**. That way, you will not be dependent on each other, but will **share a common vision**, multiply each other's motivation for going there, and **revere life in the process**. This is Love.

Marriage (two energies – male and female – working in harmony) shows us the symbolism of a process, which everyone needs to establish in himself or herself.

It is fair to warn you about a few things. The ideal partner – who will always be ready to fulfill your **wishes and act the way you want (all the time) – does not exist.** There are only adjustments to people who more or less suit your idea of the ideal partner.

"God has forgotten to create him or her... and then He has also forgotten to tell us that," says Keller.

In time, you may see the qualities you were searching for in your youth (beauty, popularity, approval of your friends) diminish in value when the time to build a life with someone arrives. That is when you start appreciating other qualities: support, understanding, comfort, help, sincere friendship, unselfishness, responsibility sharing, and so on.

> *You have to first be independent to be able to accept and give true love.*

There is another interesting theory described by James Redfield as "The third recognition" in his book, *The Celestine Prophecy*. When two people are in love, they are connected to each other. But because of that, they abandon the fundamental essence – the source. In the absorption of their union, they become sponges, one to the other, feeding off the energy of each other. Because they are unplugged from the basic source, there is no flow of energy coming in, and they cannot avoid the complications in their life together. **Everything transforms into a fight for energy**, which can be seen in escalating arguments and disharmony.

The solution is nonattachment and mutual independence. **You have to first be independent to be able to accept and give true Love.**

The same natural principles are true for Love as they are for other things: **What you give is what you get.** We have described how impossible it is to love someone else more than yourself, but you cannot allow him or her to love you more than you love yourself either.

So if you want to receive something, you have to be able to give it first (which shows that **your consciousness is on that vibration**).

Partnership

A business partnership is similar to a marriage or a love relationship. People with a common goal, and similar ways of reaching that goal, join forces because they feel they are stronger together and have a better chance at realizing their goal as a team. An added advantage is that **their enthusiasm and energy are passed between them, keeping each motivated and uplifted** in the face of challenges. Often, partnerships are formed between personalities seeking strengths in their partner to make up for their own deficiencies.

Problems arise when **the relationship becomes unbalanced and the flow of the unconditional (supportive) energy, between two (or more) of them, ends.** When this happens, a partnership gives way to supremacy and exploitation of one partner to the other's benefit. This is very similar to the problems in intimate relationships already described.

Problems also arise when one **partner takes advantage of the other to create his own interests through common energy.** For instance, he or she launches a new project with a mutual acquaintance, who cooperated in some previous project, or even uses the first initial project led with his or her first partner as a "diving board" for bigger and better things, forgetting all about the first partner who stood by his or her side and helped him or her.

Besides that, it is also important that **each partner finds his or her life's mission in his or her contribution.** If not, he or she will compare, prove, and affirm himself or herself to himself or herself, the partner, and others, which will block his or her creativity and turn energy in the wrong direction – instead of focusing energy on work, he or she will focus it elsewhere.

Here is more good advice that greatly helps me time and time again.

It is very useful for partners to **take notes on mutual agreements as they go along**. These notes can later be used as **minutes** as a lot of things become forgotten. The minutes also continually harmonize you with your **initial intention**, vision, or goal. If it no longer suits you, you can – if both parties agree – change it.

If all parties are mature individuals, the challenging situations can be used for personal growth and learning. Of course, it is a different situation if one (or more) of the partners is not at a level that enables him or her to respect the other person(s) or himself or herself, to take responsibility, to admit mistakes, and acknowledge the good qualities of others.

The prevailing thought is that partnerships do not work well or equally for everyone involved, and further, that everything grinds to a halt when it comes to challenges about money. I would say, however, that **two reasonable partners who can divide tasks and business areas in a manner that allows both to have the greatest profit possible and the deepest contentedness are priceless to one another in business**.

In this way, they both have much more. Instead of the first partner getting X amount of profit when he or she works alone and the second partner getting Y amount of profit when working alone, they can together make Z amount of profit, where Z **is much, much more than the sum of X and Y**. That way, they both gain more in comparison to acting alone.

I have been in a partnership for many years. I have learned a lot during this time, and I believe that I can be more successful in business this way.

I have learned the following truth, which I stick to firmly:

A partnership is successful as long as each party has the feeling that he or she is gaining more than he or she gives. In a good partnership, just like a good marriage, the partners almost compete for ways to help each other or make the other person's work easier.

But this is actually only feasible when **spiritual visions unite partners**. If something lesser unites them, there can be discord. But if (similar views on their) the **meaning of life unites them, everything else becomes less important** – that is why the relationship can only become **stronger**.

And now a warning: The following chapter is about money. It is not about hoarding as much as possible, but about **establishing a loving and harmonious relationship** with money. That is why it is highly recommended reading for everyone, even if you do not plan to become wealthy; because if you do not resolve your relationship with money, your spiritual development will stop at this phase, and as we have mentioned, you **will not be able to move any further**.

The Plan for Achieving Wealth, Success, and Happiness

1. **Make a list of your current goals for your life.** Then determine all the areas of your life that are important to you, such as family, free time, money, business, friends, personal growth, health, etc. If you have difficulty identifying those areas, think about how you would

spend a perfect day. Write these areas across the top of a paper. Now divide the areas with horizontal lines, so you divide each column into three parts again. That way, you create a column, for example "family," which is divided into thirds.

Now write **all of your short-term goals** (everything you want to achieve in the next twelve months) in the upper third. Below these, record your middle-term goals (three to five years) and below that, write your long-term goals (ten years and beyond) at the bottom. (See the table below.)

Using this, you can **direct your daily activities**. Check which areas you have progressed in each day. When you achieve your goal, check it off the list and move to the next goal. This method can be useful in learning to apply balance to your life because you instantly know where you spend too much time and energy and where you need to spend more.

2. Follow the procedure on "How To Set Goals" according to the steps described there. Regarding the broader, total direction in which you are moving your life, think about and answer the question, **"What am I afraid of in allowing myself to act on my inner voice?"**

	FAMILY	FREE TIME	MONEY	BUSINESS	FRIENDS
SHORT TERM GOALS (Within next twelve months)					
MIDDLE TERM GOALS (Three-Five Years)					
LONG TERM GOALS (Ten Years and beyond)					

7. About Money

Money Rules the (External) World

This chapter is designed for – besides giving very concrete financial advice – **the harmonization (establishment of a harmonious relationship) of our conscious mind and subconscious with the energy of money.** Why is it important that we are harmonized with money's energy? You might think there are people who simply do not yearn for great wealth. **But that is not to say that their relationship to money is balanced, which is the goal, if we want to get to the point where we master our life's energy.**

In fact, most things in our material world are directly or indirectly related to money itself or to what money represents. Taking an even broader view, money is involved in every form of crisis in the world today: wars, social injustice, national and class oppression, crime, and the destruction of the environment, to name a few.

One of the basic challenges of most people today is their search for material gain. It seems that whenever they have enough money or material goods, they do not have the time to enjoy them and vice versa.

Here is a thought to think about: "Give a person power (money), and his or her **true character will be revealed.**"

Money as God's Energy

However, something is sure and certain: **Money is God's energy, and that is why it must be handled like every other energy.** There is nothing evil, corrupt, or snobbish about it. What is even more interesting, some of the greatest spiritual people are – and were also in history – materially very rich. Others donated a lot of things, even money, to them. For instance, **entire buildings** were donated to Mother Theresa. Is that not exceptional material wealth?

> *Money is God's energy, and that is why it must be handled like every other energy.*

It is our **relationship to money and materiality** that is important and not the money/materiality in and of itself.

Here is a good question. How do we determine if our relationship to money is balanced and in harmony?

When a loving and joyful energy always arises within us, whenever we think about money or anything related to money's energy (purchases, rich people, bill-paying, etc.), our relationship with it is harmonized.

If this does not happen, we have not yet resolved our relationship to money, and are probably **avoiding solving – or are even denying – this relationship**. As we already stated at the beginning, if we want to grow spiritually, materiality is one of the areas in which it is necessary to establish an unconditional relationship.

This does not mean **being apathetic or shunning away** from money and prosperity. **If we deny, resist, suppress, or in any other way refuse money's energy or materiality, we are generally blocking our spiritual growth.**

As we know, if **we do not succeed at harmonizing through it** – which always happens with the help of the energies of loving and accepting – **we will remain at this level.** That is why this chapter is especially earmarked for everyone who gets a knot in their stomach when a thought, feeling, word, or event refers to **anything related to money or materiality.**

Also, this chapter does not talk about how to become egotistical and rake in loads of money, but how to recognize in money an **infinite teacher who never lies** and **lovingly shows us where our energy is unbalanced.** It also shows us how to notice this energy in ourselves and how to accept it unconditionally.

In other words, **money always follows an individual's life energy and symbolically shows its flow or deadlocks.**

Of course, everyone who wants a harmonious relationship with money, by achieving financial and material prosperity, will also find useful pieces of advice for **increasing his or her wealth** and more confidently and prudently **earning, spending, and investing money.**

We are going to look at some basic ideas, which we should master if we are to design our own fortune. There will also be some practical pieces of advice, which, if you follow them, will help you and bring you to greater material wealth.

But let us not go to extremes thinking that **everyone can earn a million.** Well, they could, but they will pay the price somewhere else. The essence – again – lies in the "(Sub)Law of Life's Mission." **If someone has chosen the experience of being rich, he or she will not have to try very hard to get wealth.**

Some people's missions are even to **show others how to become rich by his or her example.** However, it is necessary to realize that this is only their path. Their material wealth is probably also linked to their identity, which is why these people will be **happiest** when they increase their wealth.

If we remember the five levels in which our consciousness is located, we understand that the goal is not just material wealth, but **all kinds of wealth** and **freedom**, as well. However, it is necessary to know where we are and which experience is before us at this moment, not what we will have to perform at some time in the future.

In this way, we will discover that some of us want to **count money at the end of the day**, while others want to **"count" their vibration**; that is, their vibration (internal world) is most important, not external gain.

And so someone, for instance, may have chosen as this life's experience **developing a sense of perseverance, discipline, and group relations through everyday work habits.** If he or she were to come into great wealth all at once and stop working, his or her **whole concept (life's mission) would be destroyed.** That is why he or she is destined to endure in the work place and systematically build, enforce, and maintain these habits.

Two important questions arise here:

1. **Can this person earn great wealth anyway?**
2. **Will the person be unhappy if he or she does not have great material wealth?**

The answer to the first question is yes – it is possible (in most cases) for this person to come to great wealth. But this is not his or her mission, which means that he or she **will not be happy and will have to endure remarkable, difficult ordeals**. If this person remains in contact with his or her intuition, he or she will constantly realize that he or she is encountering certain signs or signals, which show him or her that his or her happiness lies elsewhere. Also, he or she will **hardly keep his or her money, which** is likely to be slipping through his or her fingers.

So if the person decides not to listen to intuition and perseveres in the accumulation of material wealth, there will be a lot of sacrificing or even suffering, but material wealth – in most cases – can still be reached. Anyway, it would be good if this individual would realize that **material prosperity and having a load of money is not the final goal**, but merely a stop along the way.

Our true happiness is always linked to our soul's growth. If we listen to our heart and intuition, we can always realize our next step.

But sometimes it is hard to follow intuition, especially if it dictates a path that is not aligned to what people perceive as **external power** (closely linked to **sexuality** and **money**). We live in a society where many people's priorities are material wealth at any cost, and where many of them also **appreciate others based on it**.

And how can we come to know what our heart is telling us? **We can learn everything necessary for our happiness and satisfaction in meditation or moments when we are really alone with ourselves and have turned inward.** What is more is that we also come to know the path, not just the goal.

The answer to the second question also follows from this. For instance, **the person, who in this life chose for his or her path an experience that is not related to exceptional material wealth, will not feel any heartfelt desire for it**. The desire can **come from his or her personality (ego) or from outside** – if this person falls under the influence of the surroundings. If the individual remains in the heart, the person will understand that he or she was very happy without three cars, a yacht, a vacation house on the ski slopes, and so on.

So **if we have within us a heartfelt wish for wealth, everything inside and outside us will guide us – eventually – and will help us on this path** to exceptional prosperity... we just have to listen to our intuition and wait for the code to be unleashed. If we understand these messages and impulses, and allow them to motivate us to action – and if the fears within us do not dominate – we will be literally led to wealth.

If we do not have this deep desire within us, we can force the experience, but will have no happiness.

All that we need for our happiness is available to us at every moment; we just have to turn inwards and look around ourselves – to harmonize with the conditions we are living in – and **unconditionally accept life**.

But again, it is not about the happiness of the personality or ego, which always compares, proves, and affirms itself before others, but the **happiness of our soul**, which strives for growth and ensures that our whole conscious comes to a state of unconditional energy in **all areas**, as soon as possible. This brings us to the goal where we **master our life's energy**.

So the basic question is: "**What is your identity linked to?**" Internal happiness (your heart and soul) or external wealth (personality, comparison, approval, etc.)? This is, as you know, the **driving force of everything you relate to**.

A Truth Behind Making Money

There are a few basic ideas that you should master to be your own lucky horseshoe, as well as some practical advice that is guaranteed to make you a wealthier person and in time maybe even a millionaire. This is good news for those who are yet to reach it.

Money, love, and life are three areas for which none of us receive an (external) "Owner's Manual." But luckily, we have the heart, which always knows all the answers. Also, people rarely, if ever, go to experts for advice in these areas. You probably have your hairdresser, mechanic, dentist, personal doctor, etc. to advise you, but if you are like most people, **you do not have the most sensitive areas of your life, on which your very happiness and well-being depend, covered.** Is this not, to put it mildly, strange?

What this means is that some things, which you are uncomfortable talking about, have to be personally acknowledged and then accepted and discussed with those who are qualified to help. For example, to ensure the smooth operation of your car, you go to an auto mechanic... **but for advice on how** to solve a crisis in your family, you probably go to your best friend – who has or has not established a good relationship with his or her own spouse – **instead of the specialists that can help you.** Where money is concerned, most do the same thing: They look only for tension releasing and not for changing the cause (or at least the consequences).

This is one reason this chapter about money was written. A lot of us have fallen, at some time or other, for various tricks and schemes that have resulted in the loss of our savings or prevented us from being able to save anything at all. Given these circumstances, it is both understandable and prudent that we do not trust everyone. Unfortunately, too often the really great information is not written down or spoken about, but simply "done and followed" by those who know it. Too often, this information comes, if at all, when it is too late. Writing this chapter is an attempt to correct this situation.

"It is logical that losses to one individual are a fantastic gain for someone else. Businessmen and women make a living from people being ignorant, not well enough informed. In fact, lack of knowledge and ignorance is the cheapest material from which money can be made." (Hans Dieter Meyer, The Association of Insurance-Holders in Germany)

Here is another thing to consider: If you want to resolve your financial problems, you should **lay your cards on the table** (and seek advice, if needed). What would it look like if you sought the counsel of a doctor and answered his questions about your pain with, "Mind your own business, this is my life!"

So let us take a close and honest look at our wallets.

If Money Is the Energy of God, Let Us Start Treating It That Way

Money is not its own objective, but plays two very important roles in our lives:

- It is a **teacher who, with inestimable accuracy, shows us what is going on inside of us** (the wallet never lies).
- **Money is given to us to finance our own creativity**; that is why some people should have more and some less; nevertheless, everyone should have enough to settle their bills and fulfill their heart's wish – of course, this is only possible when we know how to restore a harmonious relationship with money.

So let us start behaving that way towards money and begin accepting and loving it. If we can truly feel the divine side of money within us, we will suddenly stop squandering it and restore a respectful, but playful and joyful relationship with it. And respect does not mean that we must "pinch pennies" no matter what – quite the contrary. **If we want money to serve us, we have to use (spend) it**, but on the things that **support our soul's growth**, not, for instance, to buy things to compensate for our lack of love for ourselves.

What Is the First Thing We Must Do When It Comes to Money?

When we think of money, we first think of earning (acquiring) money. However, there is one thing that must be set in order before – we have to **protect what we have already earned**.

If the bottom of a dish leaks, we will not pour more water into it hoping that sooner or later enough will accumulate. First, we **patch the hole** and then increase the flow. This is, obviously, the smartest action to take at that moment.

We can think about money in the same way: We first **protect ourselves from losing it**. This is where the following things come in:

- **Protecting existing property.**
- **Protecting everything that brings us money** (for instance, our business or abilities so that we can continue to earn money).
- Examination or **analysis of what we spend money on**: how much of it slips through our fingers, how much do we use to finance our own creativity, and how much we use for other purposes.
- Examination of **all money-related fears** and their elimination.

Let us examine some of these more closely.

Protect What You Have

If we do not protect what we have already acquired, it could very well happen that **our new income will not cover our outflow of cash from day to day**.

This refers to two things:

- The purchase of goods, which **reduce our property and wealth**.
- The very concrete **protection of existing property**.

The first point refers to purchasing things whose value depreciates with time. The best example of this is **an automobile**. If we buy an expensive car, we could be systematically reducing our property with this purchase – even if we work and save money the whole time!

Let us look at an imaginary example. We buy a car that costs $25,000. In a few years, it is worth only $12,500. That means **we lose up to $6,250 every year**. That is more than $500 a month... but we have not even finished. Since we took out a loan to buy it, instead of $25,000, it likely cost us around $32,500. That is an **extra $7,500** that we will have to earn in that time – not to invest or use for our own interests, but to pay back to the bank.

When we sell the car, we will probably **repeat the procedure** all over again with a new car.

The next point – protection of property – refers to very concrete activities **to insure that the property we have already created does not fall into ruin**. That is to say, if we buy real estate whose value increases annually, we still have not done everything necessary; what happens if there is an accident – flood, fire, earthquake, theft, etc.?

We often say, "Sure, but the odds are stacked against something like that happening." If we were to ask people, who have lived through this, they will say the same thing, "I knew this could happen; but I never thought that it would happen to me."

The Protection of Property

Here is something else of interest: Many people have comprehensive (collision) automobile insurance, but **think very carefully about insuring their real estate**. If a car is something that we cannot live without, living without a roof over our heads is even more difficult. For instance, if we lose our car, we would find a solution very quickly and easily, but if we were to lose our home, it would be much harder.

Besides, a car costs much less than a house, yet its insurance is much more expensive. For instance, if a car costs $25,000, comprehensive/collision vehicle insurance costs **more than $400 dollars**.

A home, which is worth several times as much, can be insured against almost all accidents for around $150 (these prices are valid here in Europe). **So we should insure what we have already acquired.**

Protecting Ourselves

(**Warning**: In this chapter, we talk about the accidents that we could encounter and how to protect ourselves from loss of income in such cases. If reading about this does not suit you right now, skip this section and come back later.)

Something even more interesting happens when we think about ourselves. That is to say that people insure their material wealth, but not their **greatest wealth – themselves and their family**. Why, and in which cases, should we insure ourselves?

That depends on the individual. First, it is necessary to insure one's **capacity to work** or **the ability to earn money**. We often hear about a model insuring her legs, face, etc. for a large sum of money, or a famous musical virtuoso insuring his or her hands.

In essence, it is a simple principle: **It is good to protect whatever helps you acquire wealth**. No, we cannot protect ourselves (at the insurance agency) from losing our job – that must be done with **good, consistent work**. But we can, however, ensure that **we will not lose our job because of other factors**, for instance, **the inability to work due to health reasons**.

What would happen if you were a secretary and permanently damaged your hands? You probably would no longer be able to perform your job. If you were insured for such an accident – for permanent injuries and disability – you would receive monetary compensation to cover your financial loss.

That is why it is a good idea **to protect our work capacity/ability**. And this goes for every member of the family who contributes to the family budget, or whom illness, injury, or disability would deprive of cash inflow or activities that make life meaningful. That is to say that such an event drastically changes one's life and often requires **more money than before** – for treatment, rehabilitation, lifestyle changes, etc. Besides that, the person is no longer capable of earning in these new circumstances. In this way, **we can insure that in such changes we are, at least financially, less handicapped**.

Also, it is good to ensure that the financial well does not completely dry up. In other words, if the head of the household, who is the family's main provider, dies, the family's safety is also gone. That is why it is so important that the family is covered for such situations.

About Money

Such insurance used to be very expensive and like collision insurance, something that you invested in, which, unless you died, did not give very good returns. Today the offers are so good that we can even **earn or enrich our capital with this insurance** (in combination with investments). What is more is that now we can even **borrow against** the money we have invested (combination of insurance and remunerative insurance, such as mutual funds).

> *We insure ourselves against everything that could dry up our income.*

If we take a broader perspective, we will realize how elegantly we can cover our backs, in business partnerships, for instance. Consider the example where we work with a business partner who is of strategic importance. Let us say that he or she is a manufacturer, who produces the products we sell. **If this manufacturer has an accident or dies, our business will fold because we will have lost a key link in our chain: If there's no manufacturer, we have nothing to sell.**

That is why it is wise for us to protect our business partner and that **we – not his or her family – are the beneficiary in the event that he or she loses his or her ability to work.** (The family will take care of itself by insuring him or her so that they are the beneficiaries.) With this money, we will cover our current expenses and "buy some time" to look for a new partner or form a new agreement with his or her successor.

As we can see, we are not just talking about insurance, but the systematic protection of both property and the influx of future financial resources. The rule is: **We insure ourselves against everything that could dry up our income.** Usually this insurance is quite cheap in comparison to its return.

But we do not bite the bait immediately, choosing the first insurance agent or brochure we receive, but rather we look for someone, who will work **for us and not strictly for the insurance company (and therefore, against us).** This means that he or she will understand us and offer us what **we need, not whatever brings him or her the greatest commission.**

How will we recognize such a person?

It will not be his or her years of service or experience alone that are decisive, but rather his or her **heart and life's values, as well.** If we get along with someone and feel that we can trust him or her, that is a good sign. Then we should **put our cards on the table, trust that person, and**

present things to him or her as they truly are... because this is the only way he or she will be able to help us.

It is also a good idea to **sleep on things** and not decide in the moment we are attached to the agent's energy – through the process of resonance – and **seeing the situation through his or her eyes**.

Also, it is good to think twice about dealing with anyone who scares us by saying things like, "This offer is valid today, but may not be tomorrow," or "I'm here today, but I won't be in this area tomorrow!"

If this person – the agent – appreciates his or her work, self, and us (as a customer), the agent **will come to us whenever we ask**... if at all possible. Also, he or she will not forget us after we pay the premium; that is when **our relationship begins, not ends**. Just like a mother does not abandon her child after giving birth to it, but begins to establish new energies, which **grow into a relationship**.

The best agents are those who really **care about us** and onto **whose shoulders we can shift our worries**; in other words, those whom **we trust more than we would trust ourselves in such situations**. This is important because when we can free ourselves of worries and all responsibilities derived from a relationship or activity, we can direct our attention and energy elsewhere – where it is needed most.

So our goal is to find a person **whose life's mission and joy is taking care of us** while being professional, consistent, and qualified. That way, we will trust him or her so much that we will simply forget the situation and **feel good about it: There is someone there who thinks about me and cares for me professionally and lovingly**.

To summarize, our goal is like this: **When we think about our family's financial protection, we are filled with very pleasant feelings**. In this way, we can completely **direct our energy into work and other activities**, and can **permanently resolve financial worries** (regarding the protection of our values).

Sometimes it is worth investing some money in yourself for this feeling alone. As far as product choice goes, the following applies (even more so everyday):

Considering that the services of financial institutions (banks, insurance companies, exchange companies) are becoming **more and more alike** –

and, in the future, will probably be even more uniform as far as terms are concerned, **the agent/person has never been a more important factor in choosing an institution or offer.**

Gradually, all institutions will offer similar policies or contracts; for example, investing in mutual funds in general or even the same mutual fund. Then we will decide based on **feelings** and the **additional services**, which are not in the contract, but hidden behind – or along with – the offer; that is, **the agent's heart will be the decisive factor.**

So if at all possible, choose **someone who likes himself or herself, his or her job, and you.** Because if this is the case, the individual is also a **great expert** because this business obviously represents **his or her life's mission**, which he or she performs with Love.

This was **one look** at gaining wealth by protecting what you already have. If you resonate with it, it would be good to consider these steps. Nevertheless, if you trust life, God, and yourself – and feel that you do not need any protection at all, or if even thinking about protection provokes fear inside of you rather than worry-free energy – **take steps in accordance with this energy.**

But as always, you are the one who will live with the consequences.

The other thing we should consider is this: Try to take these steps **not out of fear** (of losing something, for example), but out of love. That is, do not decide (too much) emotionally or mentally, but allow your heart to help you decide.

The Principle of Income

The concept behind any form of wealth is creating income. Are you satisfied with your current income?

Probably not...

Have you ever wondered why this is so?

I believe that you have read the book carefully, and so you understand that the reason may be in the **lack of love for yourself** – so you forbid to treat yourself to deserve and have more – in **envy, spitefulness**, and other unpleasant emotions, various **fears** ("I'll have to work more, if I want to get more money."), in **disobeying the heart** (not following your life's mission), and so on.

The Millionaire Mindset

> **Money itself does not mean anything - it is just a piece of paper, a tool that can be used to trade for material goods.**

A typical example is a person who has constant challenges with money but **disapproves of accumulating wealth**, implying that it is dirty and that it spoils and changes people. He or she is carrying around a mental image that says, for example, "If you have much money, you'll be ruined by it, and you don't want that. So it's better to remain poor than seek wealth. **If you had money, you would encounter all kinds of problems.**"

The consequence of such thinking is, not surprisingly, a lack of money.

You have to overcome these thoughts and **become a friend** to money if you want to be free of financial worries someday.

Also, you have to be clear about the following fact: **Money itself does not mean anything – it is just a piece of paper, a tool that can be used to trade for material goods.** Money is only a stand-in for the things you want to buy. Does this mean that all the things you buy are bad and rotten? Imagine your job pays you in food instead of money. Would you now say that food is bad and rotten?

A Wealthy Self-Image

The Principle of Income says that wealth is first created in the mind.

People who cannot imagine themselves wealthy are not yet ready to become wealthy.

Everything begins in the mind as a thought. A lot of times, life is just a game that is directed from between your ears (your conscious mind). So if you cannot see yourself with money, then your subconscious still does not have a clear picture of how to act and therefore cannot help you get there.

Why You Are Not Wealthy Today

There are two reasons why you do not have as much money as you desire today:

1. **You did not think about or plan for today before it arrived.** Had you been more aware – then – that you would always need money, and acted on that awareness in the past, you would be wealthier today than you are right now. Why? You would have intentionally

saved – perhaps even by making small sacrifices over the years – or invested money (even small amounts), and would therefore have more money today.

2. **The work you have now is not bringing in enough money.** There are many ways to increase, even maximize, the financial and monetary rewards you earn from your job.

Increasing Your Income

You can get money in two ways:

- By **saving** (more) and/or **investing** (more).
- By **earning** more.

We will discuss the first option in detail later. Let us focus for now on the second option. If you want to get more money out of your work, consider these possibilities.

1. Change jobs.

What was the basic motive for you to take this job? A lot of people choose a job that gives them a satisfactory income and that is their only – or at least major – motive and condition. They think that they made a good decision: They will not be satisfied, but they – at least – earn a decent salary.

Well, the truth is **if you are unsatisfied at work, you will create tension inside**: Instead of developing and expressing creativity while working, you will express energies of a lower vibration… eight hours a day, day after day.

The consequence will be **a need to release that tension** – which can be satisfied by **changing that vibration**; so you will feel a great desire to buy something nice for yourself, take a vacation, etc.; all of which take money.

What follows is that **you are likely to be short of money all the time**.

So if you want to have more – after satisfying your needs and desires – you will have to change your present job for one that brings you not only more money, but also **more pleasure**.

You have probably heard the saying, "Do what you love, and the money will follow." **Successful people concentrate on their best work – the business – while unsuccessful people focus solely on the money.**

If we go a step further, we can discover that a lot of times this represents only an **intermediate level on our path to spiritual growth**: If – or when –

your vibration is high, **you can do anything and you will be content**... because you will see God everywhere and will be expressing Love and literally cocreating **with God**. That way, you will treat your work as service for a higher good (not just for money).

That means, you will no longer choose tasks you enjoy most, but **you will communicate with – or relate to – God while doing whatever**.

Sai Baba says that then everything will change; **instead of never seeing God anywhere** (that is to say that God is **nowhere**), you will see **God now – here**.

2. Take on an extra job.

Perhaps your primary job gives you great satisfaction, but does not yet provide a sufficient income. Taking a second job may be a better solution than changing jobs. Like everything else – it depends on the individual. You know best. You have to consider the consequences; working two jobs means added pressure and less time for everything else. Ask yourself if the increase in income is worth the additional taxes you will pay, the time you will spend, etc.

3. Invest more time in your present job.

Another possibility is to put more time into your present job. Since you are probably paid according to time or efficiency, your income will probably rise with more time invested. This alternative is similar to the one above – increasing your workload; except **it does not require acclimating yourself to a new job**, and therefore you need not concentrate on (and master) two different jobs.

However, the work may be **monotonous**, whereas adding an extra job might allow combining mental and physical work, a possible advantage. Besides that, you now (still) solely depend on one job, whereas by adding an extra job, you have two irons in the fire.

4. Be more efficient in your present job.

One good variation is to be more efficient at your present job, which often results in higher earnings. **Think about how you can save your company time and money or increase productivity.** Search for bottlenecks in your work process and fix them. Consider the **"Pareto Principle" – 80% of your income comes from 20% of the work done.**

So **concentrate more on effective tasks and less on auxiliary ones** that do not directly bring in money (like preparation, cleaning, etc.); nevertheless, you have to perform all preparation and other unproductive tasks very well. This means trying to do them in less time and with less energy – if possible – but **not with less quality**.

5. Learn to enjoy your present job.

You will move towards your goals faster if you organize your present job so **you enjoy it more**. Make a list of things that make you happy at work or bring you satisfaction from your job. The list might include: what you have, what you have always wanted, where your advantages are, how tasks can be done in a pleasant and fun way, and so on.

You will find that the job itself probably is not so bad; it is **just that you have been focusing more on the things that bother you**, rather than the supportive ones. Be optimistic and **start taking interest in your field of expertise**. Associate with people who do similar work and enjoy doing it – allow them to pass their enthusiasm on to you.

Maybe you will not get a raise at first, but you will be much happier. And not just at work. If I asked you which you would prefer, money or complete happiness, what would you say? Well, there you see.

Over time, **you will be noticed** – if not by your superiors at work, business associates, or partners, then by others (competitors). **There are always plenty of jobs for a worker who is conscientious and an expert in his or her field.**

Those who are the best in the business have doors opened everywhere, regardless of whether or not such a qualified person is needed at that time.

Wise employers employ someone the moment they realize that a person can benefit their company. They do not wait for an empty position where they would be forced into a feverish search for an appropriate candidate. And there is another reason – if they do not employ him or her, they may become his or her competitor.

The Principle of Supply and Demand

One other thing will influence **all your decisions connected with money**: the principle of supply and demand. Every price is set according to this economic law; it does not matter how much something costs at one time, but rather how much a particular buyer is ready to pay for it.

The Millionaire Mindset

More the buyers, lower the supply, and higher the price.

Less buyers, greater the supply, and lower the price.

You have probably experienced this yourself, especially if you have ever sold a car you have owned. A buyer arrives and says, "I can buy a car identical to this one, in better shape, somewhere else. Sell it to me for X dollars and I'll take it, otherwise I'll buy it there."

How did you decide whether or not to sell your car to this buyer? Economic law, the power of supply and demand, influences your decision: If there were enough buyers ready to pay the full price, you would politely reply that you do not intend to lower the price. But if other buyers are scarce, you begin to think and calculate whether you can accept and live with the offer. **You decide based on what you think the circumstances are or will be.** If you need the money, you sell; if you do not need the money, you may decide to hang onto it for a while – the market conditions are sure to change.

Harv Eker said that people know that supply, demand, quality, and quantity affect the success of selling a product. The supply equates to how many competitive products are available; demand – how many buyers and their interest in purchasing your product; quality – how well the product is made and performs compared to other similar products in the marketplace.

He continues with this interesting thought, "If you want to earn money, you have to sell the product. But if your desire is to become wealthy, **you need to sell many products.**"

So **quantity** is often the decisive factor. People who are employed cannot amass wealth because their employer **limits their hours**. Businesspeople whose business is organized in such a way that they have to be **physically present** to make money cannot amass wealth quickly; they literally do not have enough time.

> Eker says that the solution is in a **system** designed so that your work consists **of repetitive activities, which do not require your hands-on presence, but still bring you money.** The essence of the success of this system hinges on the word **repetitive** because it means the activity, which will bring you money, will occur repeatedly, **without your constant effort or vigilance** making it happen.

When you reach such a state, you can earn money even while you sleep – or are somewhere else... like the beach.

Myths About Creating Wealth

You have probably read or heard various myths (narrow truths that are only valid for a few specific cases, but not in general) surrounding wealth and wealthy people. All of which, if believed, hinder your quest for financial independence. Here are the most common and most destructive:

Myth No. 1: How much you earn depends on how hard you work.

We have already discussed this and learned that if this were true, the physical, blue-collar workers, who have been working hard for years, would be the wealthiest people on earth. Of course, this is not true. Instead, they form the bulk of the workforce and the vast majority of the middle-class.

If you witnessed your parents coming home tired from a long day's work in your youth, you probably learned that no amount of money is a sufficient reward for all the effort and sacrifices made to earn it. People who work just for the money are often deep in debt because they comfort themselves – for their long hours and sacrifices – with whatever they can buy; the material goods, becoming almost trophy-like, serve as evidence of all their hard work and sacrifice. Because they are surrounded by the drudgery of their workplace environment, they want to come home to all the beautiful things they lack when working.

Myth No. 2: Being paid for something you enjoy isn't work and you shouldn't ask for money for doing something that is enjoyable.

Check this with millionaires. They have so much money that they do not need to work anymore. Nevertheless, they work for other reasons: challenge, satisfaction, fullness of life (expression of their creativity), activity, fun, and all are connected to a **love for their work**. If there is no joy in doing a certain task, they do something else that makes them much happier and that enables them to realize their dreams.

However, just because you enjoy your work does not mean you should not get paid for it. In fact, that is the ultimate goal – **to get paid to do what you already enjoy doing**, so it never feels like you are at work.

Myth No. 3: You need to be in the right line of business to accumulate wealth.

Do you really think so? This would mean that all people involved in the same business would be millionaires. Of course, this is not true. In each business, there are winners and losers, even if the business consists of distasteful (to most) or **impossible** work, like sweeping the streets, collecting the trash, working in a factory, pumping gas, selling newspapers, etc.

On the other hand, there are losers in high-earning positions or businesses, as well, like real estate, management, medicine, or stockbrokers on Wall Street.

Myth No. 4: You need the right education to make a fortune.

Are the most educated people really the wealthiest? Not at all. If the right education were tantamount to acquiring wealth and achieving success, university professors would be the wealthiest people on earth. Ask them about their salaries, if you get the opportunity. The truth is vastly different – **the wealthiest people are those who can convert their knowledge** (or education) **into money** in the best possible way. They can be highly educated people (inventors, scientists, etc.) or almost ignorant. Being formally uneducated does not equate to poor performance on the job or the inability to form a vision strong enough to carry a person to his or her success – one can easily be an expert without having a formal education.

Myth No. 5: It used to be easier.

Statistics show an increase in the number of millionaires in the world every year. Talking about the good old days only offers comfort and a convenient excuse. If you look around, you will see there are people who acted the same way in the good old days as they do now, but their success has been recent.

With technology and progress come new ideas, desires, and needs, and there are even more business opportunities appearing daily.

Myth No. 6: I'm too old (young, short, stupid, etc.)

If you research the life stories of some of the most successful people, you will see that this is not true at all. Some become wealthy early in their lives – for instance, from the stock market – while fortune may elude others until retirement or beyond. Ray Kroc was more than fifty years old when he started the McDonald's restaurant franchise.

The same stands for every other physical attribute.

Myth No. 7: I don't have enough money to start.
This is no different from any other myth (or excuse). Like the others, it is obvious that this one is not true either. Many have made their fortunes starting from scratch, living in an apartment, or working out of their garage, and yet they developed business empires that are worth billions of dollars today. The other elements of success, discussed earlier, are far more important than having seed money to start a business.

But yes, often **money helps** and having it in the beginning certainly does not hurt. Like everything else discussed in other myths: Money could help, but **it is not always necessary**.

Myth No. 8: I'll begin when I know everything (or enough).
Do you believe that you will know everything someday? Or even that you will know enough to ever be really prepared? The more you learn, the more you can see what you still need to learn. Success and obtaining wealth is a dynamic process. Even if you could come out of the gate knowing everything there is to know, some of those elements will change immediately and many will change rapidly. **If you do not decide now, nothing will happen.** Live and learn.

Sometimes millionaires have even allowed themselves to go bankrupt and then – maybe even faster – reestablished their wealth; sometimes even greater than before. Money itself is not the obstacle that is keeping you from being wealthy. If you are really good in your business, do not worry because someone – a bank or business partner – who appreciates your talent and knows you are a good investment opportunity **will appear and make the money you need available**. And he or she will not do this for you, but for him or her. That is, he or she may ask you to let him or her invest in you because he or she sees a golden opportunity in you.

However, you cannot just sit around waiting for this – you have to establish such an environment and make it happen.

Build the habit of taking action – supporting your life's mission and leading you towards your goal – as much as you can. Make your workplace better or more efficient. After all, even if someone else signs your paycheck, **you really work for you**. Even if you are an employee in a large corporation, take good care of it. Well, it is not exactly your corporation... but it is the **only corporation through which you can prove what you are capable of right now**.

The Debtor and Poor Man Mentalities

There is a world of **difference between a poor person and someone in debt (or with no money)** – do not confuse the two. A poor person has **no ability, knowledge, or motivation and therefore no potential to make money**... while being in debt or without money can mean just a **temporary situation** (i.e., for someone with the ability, motivation, knowledge, or even wisdom to make a fortune).

Sometimes the obstacle in your path to wealth is **concentrating on money instead of business**. This always happens when you worry about how you will pay your bills. This is very dangerous if you are, for example, in sales or you work with customers because **your customers will feel that your priority is to make the sale** and **not to help them**.

Is there a way to alter this mindset?

This might help: Make sure that you always have at least $500 in your bank account. If you withdraw it, put it back at the first opportunity. Also, **always have a $100 bill with you**. Why?

First, you will know that **this is not all the money you have** because your account is not empty. So psychologically, you will not depend on the current sale because you will not feel quite so desperate to make it. This will help you think about something other than your bills and bankruptcy. The second thing is the bill itself in your pocket. How can you say or feel that you are poor, if you always have so much money that you carry a $100 bill with you everywhere?

The next matter of business is consistently depositing money into your account. In his book, *Money is My Friend*, Phil Laut proposes you **open a savings account and regularly deposit money in it, even if it is only $10 every week or every month**. Do this every time you receive your paycheck, or have it directly deposited, before you have time to miss it.

This way, your subconscious absorbs the thought that you usually – and probably always – have more money than you really need because you always have some left for savings and investments. Although you may only be depositing small amounts at first, they will accumulate in the account, earning a small interest, and in time, this will become a fair amount.

Try it; it could work like magic for you.

About Money

Programming Your Mind for Wealth

This is the best exercise for programming your conscious mind for wealth:

Take ten minutes and **write down everything that comes to your mind when you think about money and obtaining wealth**. Select the most unpleasant and most unsupportive thought you have – this will probably be the cause of all other "negative" thoughts – and **change it to a supportive affirmation**.

But make an affirmation that you **truly believe in**. Write this one several times – on your daily planner, on a sheet of paper you put next to your bed, in a visible spot in your car, and so on. Repeat it as much as possible, at least for five minutes each morning and five minutes each evening before going to bed.

Do this with dedication. Let the energies of respect, gratefulness, and joyful expectation be always present. **The transformation that usually follows is amazing.**

(You can find much more in-depth information about how to establish a joyful relationship with money's energy in Boris Vene's book, _Becoming Rich and Wealthy Through Divine Touch_.)

Bankruptcy Can Be Good

Edward DeBono tells the following story in his book, _Tactics: The Art and Science of Success_.

Having already had a taste of wealth, at twenty-six, Jim Rogers decided to visit an elder millionaire and ask him for advice. He was surprised by the old man's words. **"The best thing that can happen to you is bankruptcy,"** he declared.

"What?! Do you know what you are talking about? Who will take care of my family? Who will pay the bills? How can you propose something like that?"

"In fact... you're right. There is something better – **going bankrupt twice.**"

What would happen to you if you really went bankrupt?

You would probably discover that **the old man was right**. Bankruptcy is a good experience on the path to becoming wealthy. First, you learn that **it is all right to make a mistake**. Until that time, you may have believed that life came to you served on a platter and you just had to wait for it to arrive. Second, now you are **not as stubborn and capricious**; you begin to look around and expand your horizons.

Above all, the fall could help you take advantage of the **very next opportunity**, grabbing it with both hands and acting regardless of what anyone thinks because you have no other possibility.

In situations like this, when you are forced to act, your capabilities are tested and proven. Now **there are no excuses** ("I don't have time," "I'm too old," "I'd rather do it tomorrow," etc.), and **nothing seems too hard to perform**. The results will amaze you – because you will do things you were not even aware you were capable of.

Such an experience is worth its weight in gold to your future because you now know how to take action. You also know that you can take action, as well as what you can achieve, if you are sufficiently motivated in the right direction: When bankrupt, the motivation is usually a fight for survival… but as said before, you will **keep the wisdom** and **strength** that you gained from the bankruptcy and **make them available for dealing with future** (financial and other) **difficulties**.

It is important to acquire a belief in yourself through direct experience. **Knowing that you can depend on yourself to survive – that you can pick yourself up and move forward – is an incredibly empowering feeling and a most valuable experience.**

Welcome such experiences as you welcome success. Are you aware how much more conscious, glorified, grateful, and richer your life will be – or the much greater heights (due to material wealth and vibration) you can achieve – if you first fall on the ground and then resurface in all your glory… while **reverencing Life and being grateful for every moment, living in Love, peace, and contentedness?**

The Principle of Spending, Savings, and Investment

Let us go on. When we protect property and our ability to further create and succeed at earning more, it is time to **master money**. This is where spending, saving, and investing come in.

First a few words about **spending**. We have just found out that we usually **buy things that we do not really need, but just simply want**.

Spending is often related to **searching for identity, releasing tensions**, and **searching for resonance**. For example, a lot of lonely people, who do not direct their energy into a very concrete goal – i.e., some retirees or unemployed people – go to the bank for their money, even though they have to wait in line for ten minutes or more (complaining about it over and over again), despite the fact that direct deposit or home delivery is available.

This is not because of some principle or habit. Rather, they are **looking for contact with the outside world** – a resonance – or activities that keep them in contact with others, giving life a certain boost, spark, magic, and meaning.

On the other hand, we will discover that we often go shopping to **change the energy in which we have been situated for a prolonged period of time**. We use a visit to the store to unwind and disconnect from existing energy patterns. (We say that we need a change of scenery.) We do quite the same when we feel burdened and want to release that tension inside.

But the most common reason is searching for identity. We have already mentioned the **three phases** (or five levels) in which our consciousness is located. Let us recall the three phases and adjust them, so that we can describe them from the identity's standpoint:

Phase 1: Here people are the victims and spend most of their time being worried and scared. They believe that they have no influence over their lives and that they are at the mercy of their boss, country, mayor, etc. These are **passive people** who **observe life** and **strive to maintain the conditions necessary for things to continue to happen** never really intervening in their own lives.

Phase 2: Here **they want to be someone**. They direct their energy **outside of themselves**, searching for identity based on what they **have** (possess): material wealth, job and position in the company, social status, education, etc.

Phase 3: Here people turn **inwards** and discover that perfect happiness comes from the harmony they create within. That is why peace, contentedness, and the soul's tranquility mean more to them than outside status. Their identity is now connected to searching for balance and peace within. So they use outside circumstances only as a framework (or circumstance or condition) that offers them the chance to grow spiritually.

A lot of people are in the second phase where they are searching for their identity through material goods and status, which is **always related to income**.

The Real Reason Behind Purchasing Costly Goods

We mentioned releasing tensions and how purchases are connected to it. Let us go even deeper and clarify some myths regarding this subject.

Namely, we often notice that some people – who usually do not earn a lot – **resent** or even **envy**, for instance, doctors and lawyers, believing that they look down on others, stress elitism, and create a rift in society when they buy large villas and yachts, while some do not even have enough to survive.

Here is something interesting to consider. (This is summarized from the book, *The Beauty is Within*, by Boris Vene and Dr. Marjan Fabjan.)

As said, the more we live in stress and haste, the more energy has to be invested in releasing tensions, if we want to maintain balance.

These people, who look at highly paid professionals – i.e., doctors – often forget that these experts spent all week, sometimes even **ten or more hours a day, focused on patients' problems on which the very lives of their patients may depend**.

For instance, a surgeon has **up to fifty operations a day** and represents a father/mother, psychiatrist, motivator, priest (confessional and comforter), etc., to these people. At the end of the week, **it is urgent and important that this person relaxes, unwinds, and prepares for the next week – physically, mentally, and emotionally**. So that he or she is rested, focused, and full of energy on Monday.

The best way to unwind is to get away from it all, so that they can be in touch with themselves. That is why this person has, for example, a cabin in the mountains; which is actually the cheapest way to get peace of mind – in comparison to traveling every weekend, getting massages and similar treatments, taking trips, and so on. So he or she **has not bought the cabin or yacht to show off**, but quite the opposite: he or she **does not want anyone to know about the cabin** because he or she would no longer have the peace and quiet needed so much to rest.

When we look at purchasing material goods – which in essence represents a necessary instrument for tension releasing and therefore for the maintenance of high vibration – from this perspective, we are even grateful that they have them. After all, we, as patients, for example, are going to **reap the benefit when lying on the operating table**.

Of course, we are talking about experts who are **performing their life's mission, dedicated to their work with all of their heart and soul**. People who have material wealth merely to show off also exist, but their intent or purpose for buying the goods is quite different.

Spending More Than You Earn

Our wishes, which can **exceed our actual financial status**, often influence our spending. That is why it is very good, at least in principle, to **first lay out what we are going to spend our money on**. Then we leave a little something for free spending, which brings us joy and brightens our day.

Otherwise, some catalog or commercial could sidetrack us so much that we forget what we really need and had intended the money for, and **suddenly, we want the item** we saw in the advertisement.

A good exercise is **recording daily expenses** to determine where our money goes: if we have used it for the things we need (and had planned to buy) or if it just slips through our fingers.

Now let us list some basic facts that will be a big help in deciding how to wisely spend, save, and invest our money.

Statistical Inflation, Buying Power, and Real Worth

You have to distinguish between statistical inflation and the fall of buying power in general. In other words, between official statistics and the actual situation of how much prices rose in stores.

Although many people believe that these two concepts are the same in meaning, the truth is bit different.

Take Germany, for example. Its former currency, the Deutsche Mark (DEM), well known for its stability over very long periods of time, enables us to make a long-term comparison. You will notice that Germany had an average, statistical inflation of around 4% over a twenty-five year period, but prices rose even as much as twice that – like in real estate – and on average, **always more than the official figures**.

The Millionaire Mindset

Why was this so? Because the manner of calculation of statistical inflation is very specific – they put everything in one bag (everything that falls in price and everything that gets more expensive), mix it a bit, and dump out the result. It is true that some things became cheaper – but which ones? Are they the things Germans buy every day, the so-called **basket of life necessities**? No. Well, maybe some things, but they are things that affect them the least, like seasonal fruits and vegetables, which they already have in their gardens and which become less expensive in the summer months.

Seeing this, you can easily conclude that prices in stores went up more per year than was officially presented.

You do not believe this? Find some data on last year's statistical inflation. Then **count the goods that rose in price that were less than this figure**. For instance, if inflation was 4%, try to remember the things you bought, which rose less than 4% in price. There are a few difficulties, right? Now count the goods that became more expensive. I will bet you have no problem here.

You have to be aware that **inflation is also a political question, not just an economical one**.

Why are we telling you this when this is not a financial textbook? Very simple – to prove it is necessary to **enrich your assets through interest rates that are higher than statistical inflation**. That is the only way to retain the buying power of your money.

A Real Money Problem

You can preserve the value of your assets only if you put money into investments that have a profitability that is **higher than the growth in cost of living**. We will describe this case in DEM (former German currency), because Germany has, as said, long-term stability. The data has been taken from German economics.

The easiest way of calculating the growth of living costs is to take statistical inflation – for instance 4% – and **multiply it by two**, which brings you to 8%.

Put another way: The same 100 DEM that bought 100 kg (220 lbs) of bread twenty-five years ago (1 kg = 1 DEM) would only buy **14 kg (31 lbs.)** of bread today.

How about using houses for an example? According to statistical data from Germany, the price of an average house in the city then was 50,000 DEM, but today the same house costs ten times more – 500,000 DEM.

Let us see what would happen if we were to better invest that money.

If you were to put 50,000 DEM in a bank account twenty-five years ago with a 4% interest rate, **you would have had 133,290 DEM today – more than three times less than if you had bought a house instead.**

The following becomes your goal: **to be able to buy more with your money, rather than simply acquiring more money (paper).**

There are only two possibilities: Enrich your assets according to **monetary** value, or enrich them with **actual** value.

A Table Showing How Annual Inflation Reduces Monetary Values (Per 100 Units)

Before we review how to protect our resources from inflation, let us look at the table to see how inflation reduces the value of property.

What happens if we keep our money in a drawer at home? Let us assume that the average statistical inflation is 3%, which means that after twenty-five years, we only have **46.7% of our original purchase value**. That means that if we can buy 10,000 pounds of bread with that money today, after twenty-five years, we can only buy 4,670 pounds with that same money.

If inflation is 5%, the table shows that the value of our property after fifteen years represents only 46.33% of its original purchase value.

The question we should answer is: Do we allow the **3% inflation** to reduce our money's buying power from year to year… or do we obtain perhaps **3% profit annually** (which is very realistic and feasible)?

Monetary Value Versus Actual Value

Monetary value is the **money you save in cash** or at various financial saving institutions – banks, insurance companies, foreign currencies, the money you keep at home, etc. You do this **in the name of safety**. You have to be aware that absolute safety does not exist **anywhere**. Think about the possibilities of fire, earthquake, theft, etc.

What then is **actual value**? You can imagine these as things or materials that are tangible – **real estate, works of art, antiques, securities, precious metals, etc.**

HOW ANNUAL INFLATION REDUCES MONETARY VALUES (per 100 units)

TIME PASSED (YEARS)	3%	4%	5%	6%	7%	8%	9%	10%	11%	12%	13%	14%	15%	16%	17%	18%	19%	20%
1	97.00	96.00	95.00	94.00	93.00	92.00	91.00	90.00	89.00	88.00	87.00	86.00	85.00	84.00	83.00	82.00	81.00	80.00
2	94.09	92.16	90.25	88.36	86.49	84.64	82.81	81.00	79.21	77.44	75.69	73.96	72.25	70.56	68.89	67.24	65.61	64.00
3	91.27	88.47	85.74	83.06	80.44	77.87	75.36	72.90	70.50	68.15	65.85	63.61	61.41	59.27	57.18	55.14	53.14	51.20
4	88.53	84.93	81.45	78.07	74.81	71.64	68.57	65.61	62.74	59.97	57.29	54.70	52.20	49.79	47.46	45.21	43.05	40.96
5	85.87	81.54	77.38	73.39	69.57	65.91	62.40	59.05	55.84	52.77	49.84	47.04	44.37	41.82	39.39	37.07	34.87	32.77
6	83.30	78.28	73.51	68.99	64.70	60.64	56.79	53.14	49.70	46.44	43.36	40.46	37.71	35.13	32.69	30.40	28.24	26.21
7	80.80	75.14	69.83	64.85	60.17	55.78	51.68	47.83	44.23	40.87	37.73	34.79	32.06	29.51	27.14	24.93	22.88	20.97
8	78.37	72.14	66.34	60.96	55.96	51.32	47.03	43.05	39.37	35.96	32.82	29.92	27.25	24.79	22.52	20.44	18.53	16.78
9	76.02	69.25	63.02	57.30	52.04	47.22	42.79	38.74	35.04	31.65	28.55	25.73	23.16	20.82	18.69	16.76	15.01	13.42
10	73.74	66.48	59.87	53.86	48.40	43.44	38.94	34.87	31.18	27.85	24.84	22.13	19.69	17.49	15.52	13.74	12.16	10.74
11	71.53	63.82	56.88	50.63	45.01	39.96	35.44	31.38	27.75	24.51	21.61	19.03	16.73	14.69	12.88	11.27	9.85	8.59
12	69.38	61.27	54.04	47.59	41.86	36.77	32.25	28.24	24.70	21.57	18.80	16.37	14.22	12.34	10.69	9.24	7.98	6.87
13	67.30	58.82	51.33	44.74	38.93	33.83	29.35	25.42	21.98	18.98	16.36	14.08	12.09	10.37	8.87	7.58	6.46	5.50
14	65.28	56.47	48.77	42.05	36.20	31.12	26.70	22.88	19.56	16.70	14.23	12.11	10.28	8.71	7.36	6.21	5.23	4.40
15	63.33	54.21	46.33	39.53	33.67	28.63	24.30	20.59	17.41	14.70	12.38	10.41	8.74	7.31	6.11	5.10	4.24	3.52
16	61.43	52.04	44.01	37.16	31.31	26.34	22.11	18.53	15.50	12.93	10.77	8.95	7.43	6.14	5.07	4.18	3.43	2.81
17	59.58	49.96	41.81	34.93	29.12	24.23	20.12	16.68	13.79	11.38	9.37	7.70	6.31	5.16	4.21	3.43	2.78	2.25
18	57.80	47.96	39.72	32.83	27.08	22.29	18.31	15.01	12.27	10.02	8.15	6.62	5.36	4.34	3.49	2.81	2.25	1.80
19	56.06	46.04	37.74	30.86	25.19	20.51	16.66	13.51	10.92	8.81	7.09	5.69	4.56	3.64	2.90	2.30	1.82	1.44
20	54.38	44.20	35.85	29.01	23.42	18.87	15.16	12.16	9.72	7.76	6.17	4.90	3.88	3.06	2.41	1.89	1.48	1.15
21	52.75	42.43	34.06	27.27	21.78	17.36	13.80	10.94	8.65	6.83	5.37	4.21	3.29	2.57	2.00	1.55	1.20	0.92
22	51.17	40.73	32.35	25.63	20.26	15.97	12.56	9.85	7.70	6.01	4.67	3.62	2.80	2.16	1.66	1.27	0.97	0.74
23	49.63	39.11	30.74	24.10	18.84	14.69	11.43	8.86	6.85	5.29	4.06	3.12	2.38	1.81	1.38	1.04	0.79	0.59
24	48.14	37.54	29.20	22.65	17.52	13.52	10.40	7.98	6.10	4.65	3.54	2.68	2.02	1.52	1.14	0.85	0.64	0.47
25	46.70	36.04	27.74	21.29	16.30	12.44	9.46	7.18	5.43	4.09	3.08	2.30	1.72	1.28	0.95	0.70	0.52	0.38

Looking back in history, one of the best investments was **gold**. Today you can only buy 5% of the gold you could have bought with a dollar bill in 1940. **For an ounce of gold, however, you can get the same amount of goods as one hundred years ago.**

Investments: First Steps

In talking about monetary investments, it is important to be aware of something else – **the higher the profit margins, the lower the safety levels (the higher the risk).**

This simply means that you will not find an investment that is both highly profitable and safe at the same time. If one existed, then companies whose business it is to enrich your capital – make even more capital from the capital you already have – would just close their doors because no one would want to deal with them anymore.

Are investments profitable? Before you invest, make a comparison by answering the following question: **This investment is profitable and dependable… in comparison to what**?

If you immediately answer, "In comparison to investments in real value," you can easily say that investments are less profitable in general; but they have other advantages.

The Basic Principle of Investment

Everyone who decides to become financially independent in life should commit this to memory: **Assets can only be created out of what you do not spend from what you have earned.**

It does not matter how much you earn, but **how much money you have left from what you earn.**

Compare these two cases: You earn $100,000 a year and spend $98,000 for necessities that do not bring assets – you are left with only $2,000 for creating assets, savings, and various financial and capital investments. Or you earn only $28,000, but still invest $2,000.

In either case, you accrue the same amount of wealth **because your investment is the same.** That is to say, if you invest more wisely in the second case (earning $28,000) than in the first (earning $100,000), you will accumulate more wealth in a certain amount of time.

The Millionaire Mindset

> *Assets can only be created out of what you do not spend from what you have earned.*

The essential question is: **Where should you invest money to ensure the best conditions for creating profit?**

In the beginning, when you are still a novice in this field, it is smart to stick to this principle: **Do not bet all your money on one horse or put all your eggs in one basket.** Spread capital across several investments.

Also, **think about the risk you are willing to take.**

While it is true that profit can be above average in risky investments, the same can be true for the losses, as well. Who can guarantee you are going to profit? **If you cannot afford the loss, do not put your money in risky investments.**

The decision of how risky your investment should be also depends on **the kind of person you are**: either a gambler, who enjoys frantically checking the newspaper daily to see what has happened to his or her fortune, or a calmer person who wants to invest money somewhere and forget about it – knowing that it is (relatively) safe and (relatively) well invested.

Besides, you need to decide what other **terms** you want to have.

The terms we would use to define an ideal investment would probably be **safety** and **profitability**. Apart from that, some very important factors exist that the following examples demonstrate.

An Ideal Investment

A businessman invests money in a profitable and relatively safe material investment (i.e., real estate). One evening a neighbor drops by with a special problem: He is buying an apartment in the city. He does not have enough money, so he intends to sell his car. He writes an ad and several potential buyers answer. One of them is serious and says he will bring him the money that same day. But he later calls and cancels the agreement.

The due date for buying the apartment is in a few days. The neighbor knows the businessman is interested in good investments, so **he offers to sell his luxury car to him at 8% below the market value.** (Market value is the amount that potential buyers actually offered). The neighbor does so because if he does not get the money for the apartment in a few days, he will lose it, and buying it (over renting it) means he will save 20%. The point is, he checked with used-car dealerships and found one that will buy the car at market value, but not until the following week.

The businessman knows buying the car is a smart investment: It is safe and brings in several thousand dollars immediately. But what can he do about it – without available cash? He invested his money somewhere that does not allow immediate liquidation. With his good investment in real estate, he "forgot" one important fact: **liquidity – immediate possibility to convert assets into cash.**

> *Liquidity is one of the most important features that an investment should contain.*

What he would earn through monetary appreciation of his property over the course of a year, he could get almost overnight with this investment; but he is helpless now because he cannot get to his money.

Of course, this would not happen to a pro with experience in investments… or if he had **considered this kind of option**. It also would not have happened if the businessman already **had a lot of money to invest**. In both cases, there would likely be funds that could simply be invested for this deal (from a bank account, for example). But for those who do not have a good supply of liquid funds, this thought-experiment is a good exercise.

This situation – a businessman buying real estate and then having the opportunity for great, even better profit literally knocking on his door – is not common, but **it is common not to know when you are going to need money**. Can you imagine having your own resources invested somewhere at a 4% interest rate when some unexpected circumstances appear, i.e., losing your job, an accident, an urgent repair? Now you urgently need the money, but cannot get it because of the terms of the contract. What would you do? Well, you have to **get a loan at, for instance, a 6% interest rate**.

Liquidity is perhaps **one of most important features that an investment should contain**, especially if you do not have any more money available (for investments and unpredictable situations that would require some immediate expenditure).

Liquidity and Transparency

Being familiar with the meaning of these terms will inform you so that your investment decisions will be much better and more realistic. **Transparency means your money is in constant view**, which means you know exactly how much you have. Why is this important?

The Millionaire Mindset

> **If your investments are transparent, you will be able to see when the terms of the investment become unprofitable for you. If your investment is also liquid, you will be able to transfer the money to another, more profitable investment.**

This combination is powerful and gives you a high degree of flexibility, which you can see is very important.

Still, it must be emphasized that **we do not skip steps**. First, protect your property and everything you either have or that enables you to acquire capital. Also, make sure that you have some cash – at least, for instance, in the amount of one salary – somewhere on hand, and then begin thinking about enriching.

Often, we do not want to miss an opportunity, so we want to **enrich money first and then take care of basic security**. Sometimes this may even pay off… but what if it does not?

Here is another suggestion that can save you a lot of money in the long-term. Maybe the best thing you can do is to **purchase the space or equipment you are renting right now** (apartment, offices, garage, machines, car, etc.) Think about how to get to a **solid material basis quickly and easily**.

But, always move step by step.

Flexible Terms

Beginning investors tend to focus on the percentages that are written in the contract, but if you ask the experts what the most important characteristic of a good contract is, they will tell you it is the **terms**. The same goes for financial contracts, as well.

Problems occur when a contract demands, for example, that you **keep the money in an account for a predetermined time** – anywhere from five to twenty years, for instance. What if you lose your job, need to pay for your child's education, or fix a leaking roof before the contract time is up?

When you sign such a rigid contract, it could happen that an unexpected situation arises that you cannot handle without breaking the contract. Sometimes investment companies understand the momentary impossibility to pay – or the need to remove your investment – as a **violation of the contract agreement**, which they penalize accordingly. **Now you have created a huge loss instead of a profit**… because you did not pay attention to the terms of saving or investing.

Investment Possibilities

Today a whole array of investments are available that differ from each other in terms: savings deposits, term accounts, insurance with savings components, mutual funds, and other forms of investment in stocks, real estate, antiques, art.

An entire book is not enough to describe and introduce everything in an unbiased manner. Actually, there are two things that are important:

- You have to know **what kind of person you are** (as we have already stated): Do you either want a sound sleep… or the adrenalin rush of the chance of greater losses and greater returns?
- You also have to know **if you will need the money** or if you could afford to miss it, regardless of what happens.

Then, based on that, **decide which investment is best suited to you**.

Let us describe one investment, which we are likely (still) less aware of, but could be to our benefit. It is **stock investment**, where we **do not have to know anything about what is going on in the market** and are not occupied with buying or selling at the right time. We are talking about **mutual funds**.

The Advantages of Mutual Funds

Where do the companies that have your savings – i.e., banks, insurance companies, special investment corporations, etc. – invest that money? The answer is, in large part, in **real value** (industry, the economy, real estate) items.

So why invest through an intermediary, giving him part of your profits, if you can do it directly yourself?

Thinking like this will soon present you with two very basic problems – **lack of investment knowledge and insufficient capital**. Without knowledge and a sufficient amount of capital, you simply cannot compete with the buying power of banks, insurance companies, and other investment institutions. No reason to despair, however, because many solutions exist. Let us look at how you can help yourself if you want to invest in securities.

Several decades ago, special funds were established, which **put small investors together**. The result was that they gathered enough capital to compete with the big companies. (The fund is, above all, intended for small investors so they can indirectly trade in the stock market.)

They hired experts in their field to manage the assets, and the costs involved are divided among all investors, and are therefore an insignificant amount for each individual investor. Such funds can invest in various securities, real estate, etc.

The owners of mutual funds are investors – so a fund is not a legal entity, but a joint venture of investors who have invested their money in the fund.

The measure of success of a mutual fund is **growth of assets**, which is simply the return on your investment. Each investor receives X number of units (points) representative of Y dollars that they have deposited in the fund.

The most important advantages of mutual funds are:

Safety

The assets of an investor have to be invested into **many different securities**. This spreads the risk of the investment and decreases the effect of the rapid growth and rapid fall in prices of some securities on the market, which are in the fund.

The investor **knows the structure of the fund**. This means that they know which investments – stocks, securities, real estate, etc. – are parts of the fund, at any moment. With other forms of savings (like banks), investors are not given this information; therefore, the investor rarely knows what investments are included in the portfolio.

Costs

With each deposit or payment to a mutual fund, the fund manager charges you a **small fee** – this depends on the policy of each fund manager – that can be up to a few percentages of that specific investment.

This may sound like quite a lot, but you have to realize that being part of a larger pile of money, where the best experts will work to invest it, enriches your money. Considering this, the fund manager's commission is really minimal, however, you do have a choice – you can pay this commission and the fees to receive perhaps more than 10% each year… or you can opt not to pay and invest your money somewhere else with lower returns.

Profits

Profits are **not guaranteed** with mutual funds. Average returns on bank deposits are around 3% (and less) each year, but good mutual funds achieve an average of between **8% and 15% each year**, if you observe them over a long period.

Investing in mutual funds is one of the safest, most transparent, and profitable investments you can have. Above all, they are highly recommended for saving towards your pension, tuition, travel, car or house purchases, etc.

In comparison to other investments, mutual funds offer you **the possibility to see and withdraw your money whenever you want**. This means that you can actually see what is going on with your investment (whether it is increasing or decreasing), day-by-day, via the Internet or daily newspapers.

There is another advantage to investing in mutual funds in comparison to middle and long-term forms of saving. Monthly deposits are **voluntary**, which means there is **no prescribed amount**, which has to be deposited each month in the mutual fund (an advantage of the investment).

Moreover, monthly deposits are not a requirement; instead, you can deposit according to your desires and financial ability. Conceivably, you could make deposits one month and then not deposit anything for the next three months, invest heavily – maybe even multiple times – the fourth month, and nothing in the fifth month, etc. It is all up to you and your individual budget.

The Cost-Average Effect

There is a special method called **the cost-average effect**, which means: **The golden rule is to invest the same amount of money, regularly, over a few years** (a permanent, standing order is recommended). This kind of regular investing brings some extra profits because you are protected on both sides; when the price is **low** (the value of securities is decreasing), your money buys more shares. When the price is **high**, your money buys less shares; this method keeps you investing regularly, but protects you from buying a lot at expensive rates.

You can read a detailed (step-by-step) description of how to do this in the book, *Becoming Rich and Wealthy Through Divine Touch*.

Developing Investment Skills

It is time to look at some skills that will show you the truth of Rockefeller's statement that **it is better to think an hour about money than work for it all month.**

You want to buy a car. So how can you use your current situation to make your money work for you?

Today you can easily buy a car on credit or through a leasing program. As you know, you will have to have either a vehicle to trade in, or a deposit for anywhere from 10% to 30% of the value of the car, depending on your credit rating.

If you intend to buy a car worth $30,000, you will have to invest about $6,000 (a trade-in offsets this out-of-pocket expense) to gain the right to co-finance it with a certain company. You will pay the balance, plus interest, over three to five years of equal, monthly payments. To make the following example easy to calculate, let us say your credit rating affords you a 20% down payment and you have no trade-in. The price of the car you want to buy is $30,000.

The total payment is approximately the same as the present price of the car. So **you would pay $6,000 at the time of purchase and another $30,000 during the next three to five years**, to pay back the debt (this is only an example and not based on a concrete offer).

What does this mean for your financial portfolio? If you want to answer this question, you have to put yourself in the future, three to five years down the road, **when your debt is paid off.**

You have a car, for which you paid $36,000. While you were paying for your car, **its value dropped** to approximately $10,000 –that is only if you kept the miles low and the car in good mechanical and aesthetic condition. What is clear is that **nobody will admit to overpaying on account of this borrowed money**: Your car has the same market value, after a certain time, as someone who purchased an identical one with cash.

In three to five years time, you lost $26,000. The price of the car when you bought it ($30,000) less the price of the car today ($10,000), plus you lost your **initial investment of $6,000**, which totals a loss of approximately $8,670 each year (if your loan was paid over three years). **This means that you had to channel $723 of your earnings each month just to maintain the**

same asset level (just to remain at the same wealth level as before the purchase).

If you did not earn this much, you took a substantial bite out of your overall wealth.

How can you protect yourself from a situation in which your assets are dropping instead of growing?

Here, you will see two possibilities. One will be adjusted to a cheaper car and the other one to a more expensive vehicle.

How to Create Wealth When Buying a Car

John decides to buy a car priced at $9,750. He decides to purchase it with a lease. He makes a deposit of $3,500, and the rate over the next three years is almost the same as the car would have cost had he paid for it with cash. All payments combined, John will pay $13,250 (a deposit of $3,500 plus $9,750 of regular monthly payments) for it.

After a year, the company that made his car comes out with a new model, which will cause additional depreciation in the value of his car. He decides to sell the car at that time so that he will not lose too much money. Because the prices of used cars drop with years, his car is worth only $7,750 at that moment. If he does not sell it, he will get only $6,000 for it after two years, when his debt will be paid off. His loss would be $7,250, or **almost the very price of his car**.

In both cases the loss is huge.

Is there a way out of this mess?

Before deciding on the purchase, think about **how urgently you need such a car**. Perhaps you could be satisfied with a car that is a year old instead of brand-new?

Like most people, if you have money challenges, it is mostly because you do not make a purchase and investment plan that you stick to no matter what. If you had made such a plan for this one, two, or three years ago, you would have anticipated your upcoming purchase and taken a part of your earnings to invest in something with a good monthly interest rate. This would have enabled you to take out a loan for a lower amount now, or even make the purchase with cash. Yes, cash! But let us return to our example to see what can be done.

If you agree that you can be satisfied with an older car, you will pay $7,750 for it instead of $9,750. This is your first savings, but it is not the largest one. In the previous case, a lease would cost you $3,500. Can you avoid it? **Yes, if you think ahead.**

Instead of paying the $3,500 deposit outright for leasing the car, you **put this money in a good interest-bearing account instead, and leave it there for a year or two.** Besides that, you also put money in a special car account each month. You find out that by saving a few hundred dollars regularly each month, you can easily save over $7,000.

This shows that if you had thought about the purchase a year or two before, you would not have needed an expensive loan or leasing agreement, and you would have **saved $3,500** instead of losing $10,000 over the course of the year. You would buy a year older car and save an additional $2,000 (instead of paying $9,750 for it, you would pay $7,750). What you should do is **drive your old car for another year or two and save money each month.**

Solutions for Buying Expensive Goods

Here is another example of wise planning when buying an expensive car worth $75,000.

One of the possibilities is a cash payment. Popular opinion says **it is cheapest to use your own money and not to take out a loan or enter into a leasing agreement.**

This is true until you start to increase your profits by using borrowed money to earn more interest than the rate for paying the money back.

When you manage to do so, you will use the savings institutions – banks or others – to help you increase your assets.

Instead of paying cash for an expensive car, you decide to take out a loan or enter into a lease agreement. You pay only $25,000 upfront, and purchase a small house, condominium, or real estate for the remaining $50,000 to rent out.

What does that bring? **You pay the remaining installments (for the next five years) from the monthly revenues you receive by renting the place out.** Now look at how this affects the situation after five years, when your car loan is paid off.

In the first case, when you pay with cash, you have a car worth $25,000 after five years (presume the real price decreases two thirds over five years) – and that is about all.

So you would have created a loss of $50,000 from your assets.

In the second case, your car, worth $25,000, is also paid off, but in addition you would have had real estate that is constantly increasing in value. If you chose a good location and bought it for a good price, **value always increases**; if you put it in a profitable business as well, the price could have increased even more than 100%.

Suppose that value increased from $50,000 to only $60,000 in five years.

Now you have a car worth $25,000... and real estate worth $60,000.

And that makes a difference of $60,000 in comparison to the first possibility. If you look at it from the investment side – the input was $75,000 in both cases – you have a $50,000 loss in the first case and a $10,000 profit in the second case.

Such situations are possible **only when you invest in material goods**. The point is to use other people's money (if you do not have your own). The best examples are renting property because a renter is buying momentary advantages – but nothing tangible, the rest is yours – or investing savings so that your investments earn interest higher than the amount that you are paying for the loans.

Einstein's Secret

Which of his own discoveries do you think Albert Einstein thought was the most important? Nuclear energy? The Theory of Relativity? No. According to his own words, he considered his biggest discovery to be **the practical use of the compound interest rate**.

What you will now learn is the last stop on your path to building wealth – **the last, but perhaps most important, tidbit of all.**

Einstein's Rule of 72

There is a simple rule, which will help you calculate – in just a few seconds – how much interest and time you need to **double your money**.

- If the interest rate is 3% yearly, you need twenty-four years to double your money (72/3 = 24).

The Millionaire Mindset

- At the interest rate of 6%, you need twelve years to double your money (72/6 = 12).
- At the interest rate of 8%, you need nine years to double your money (72/8 = 9).
- At the interest rate of 9%, you need eight years to double your money (72/9 = 8).
- At the interest rate of 12%, you need six years to double your money (72/12 = 6).
- At the interest rate of 18%, you need four years to double your money (72/18 = 4).

Can We Appreciate a Good Offer?

Many people think that all investments seem pretty much the same, give or take a percent or two. Sometimes they even say, "3% or 5%, it is all the same." That is why **they do not appreciate the extra 1% they could be getting in some investment**. We also notice that these are often **people who have not tried saving at very low interest rates**. They usually **have never saved before** and now want somewhere between 20% and 50% interest per year. Everything less is of no interest to them.

But that is not the case. There is a big difference when deciding between **duration of the investment** and **percentages** or **profit** (interest). Even just 1% can bring us much more than we would expect over a long period of time. Leaving money to compound **a few more years** can increase our property immensely. Let us look at some concrete examples of this.

Interest Rate and Investment Duration

Let us say, for instance, you are **investing money every month for twenty years**. If you invest $100 each month at a permanent average interest rate of 9%, you would have $64,350 savings after twenty years. You put in $24,000 (twelve months x $100 x twenty years) and you would earn more than $40,000 in interest.

What would happen if you were to save **five more years**?

Instead of $64,350, an added $6,000 (twelve months x $100 x five years) at the same interest rate would result in approximately **$106,530 after five more years**.

The Difference of Two Percentage Points: A 40% Higher Payout

The difference of two percentage points in interest can equate to more than a 40% higher payout!

You decide to invest $10,000 at an interest rate of 7% for the next twenty years. During this time, your investment increases to approximately $38,700. You can calculate this yourself by adding 7% to the $10,000 the first year, then take this new amount and add 7% of this value; repeat this another eighteen times, once for each year.

What happens if you invest your money for the same period of time, but at a **2% higher interest rate** (9%)?

In this case, you have $56,000 at the end of the period, which is **more than a 40% increase** over the previous investment, with only a 2% difference in rate.

You can find these and more examples in the table.

How to Read the Table

Let us look at what we can make out from the table.

We have **$10,000** that we leave to compound for **twenty-five years**. If we look at the column under 3%, we can see that we will end up with $20,937.

If we have a 5% annual interest rate, which is only 2% more, we end up with **$33,863**. This means that **with 2% more interest, we end up with 50% more money**.

Let us examine this further. What happens if we get an even better offer, let us say 7%? We can see from the table that we end up saving **$54,274**.

An 11% interest rate yields us $135,854 or **more than ten times as much**. If we succeed at compounding our funds with a 20% annual rate for twenty-five years, we end up with **$953,962**.

The difference between investments with a 3% or 20% return is nearly **a million dollars**! And this was not using unrealistic profits with 50% or 100% returns per year. A Slovenian proverb says that **whoever is not satisfied with little things, is not worth more**. If we change it around, we could say that if you are not pleased with little things to start with, you usually will not even come into bigger things.

DURATION OF INVESTMENT (IN YEARS)	ONETIME INVESTMENT OF 10,000 MONETARY UNITS										
	2%	3%	5%	7%	9%	11%	13%	15%	17%	19%	20%
1	10,200.00	10,300.00	10,500.00	10,700.00	10,900.00	11,100.00	11,300.00	11,500.00	11,700.00	11,900.00	12,000.00
2	10,404.00	10,609.00	11,025.00	11,449.00	11,881.00	12,321.00	12,769.00	13,225.00	13,689.00	14,161.00	14,400.00
3	10,612.08	10,927.27	11,576.25	12,250.43	12,950.29	13,676.31	14,428.97	15,208.75	16,016.13	16,851.59	17,280.00
4	10,824.32	11,255.09	12,155.06	13,107.96	14,115.82	15,180.70	16,304.74	17,490.06	18,738.87	20,053.39	20,736.00
5	11,040.81	11,592.74	12,762.82	14,025.52	15,386.24	16,850.58	18,424.35	20,113.57	21,924.48	23,863.54	24,883.20
6	11,261.62	11,940.52	13,400.96	15,007.30	16,771.00	18,704.15	20,819.52	23,130.61	25,651.64	28,397.61	29,859.84
7	11,486.86	12,298.74	14,071.00	16,057.81	18,280.39	20,761.60	23,526.05	26,600.20	30,012.42	33,793.15	35,831.81
8	11,716.59	12,667.70	14,774.55	17,181.86	19,925.63	23,045.38	26,584.44	30,590.23	35,114.53	40,213.85	42,998.17
9	11,950.93	13,047.73	15,513.28	18,384.59	21,718.93	25,580.37	30,040.42	35,178.76	41,084.00	47,854.49	51,597.80
10	12,189.94	13,439.16	16,288.95	19,671.51	23,673.64	28,394.21	33,945.67	40,455.58	48,068.28	56,946.84	61,917.36
11	12,433.74	13,842.34	17,103.39	21,048.52	25,804.26	31,517.57	38,358.61	46,523.91	56,239.89	67,766.74	74,300.84
12	12,682.42	14,257.61	17,958.56	22,521.92	28,126.65	34,984.51	43,345.23	53,502.50	65,800.67	80,642.42	89,161.00
13	12,936.07	14,685.34	18,856.49	24,098.45	30,658.05	38,832.80	48,980.11	61,527.88	76,986.79	95,964.48	106,993.21
14	13,194.79	15,125.90	19,799.32	25,785.34	33,417.27	43,104.41	55,347.53	70,757.06	90,074.54	114,197.73	128,391.85
15	13,458.68	15,579.67	20,789.28	27,590.32	36,424.82	47,845.89	62,542.70	81,370.62	105,387.21	135,895.30	154,070.22
16	13,727.86	16,047.06	21,828.75	29,521.64	39,703.06	53,108.94	70,673.26	93,576.21	123,303.04	161,715.40	184,884.26
17	14,002.41	16,528.48	22,920.18	31,588.15	43,276.33	58,950.93	79,860.78	107,612.64	144,264.56	192,441.33	221,861.11
18	14,282.46	17,024.33	24,066.19	33,799.32	47,171.20	65,435.53	90,242.68	123,754.54	168,789.53	229,005.18	266,233.33
19	14,568.11	17,535.06	25,269.50	36,165.28	51,416.61	72,633.44	101,974.23	142,317.72	197,483.75	272,516.16	319,480.00
20	14,859.47	18,061.11	26,532.98	38,696.84	56,044.11	80,623.12	115,230.88	163,665.37	231,055.99	324,294.23	383,376.00
21	15,156.66	18,602.95	27,859.63	41,405.62	61,088.08	89,491.66	130,210.89	188,215.18	270,335.51	385,910.14	460,051.20
22	15,459.80	19,161.03	29,252.61	44,304.02	66,586.00	99,335.74	147,138.31	216,447.46	316,292.55	459,233.07	552,061.44
23	15,768.99	19,735.87	30,715.24	47,405.30	72,578.74	110,262.67	166,266.29	248,914.58	370,062.28	546,487.35	662,473.73
24	16,084.37	20,327.94	32,251.00	50,723.67	79,110.83	122,391.57	187,880.91	286,251.76	432,972.87	650,319.94	794,968.47
25	16,406.06	20,937.78	33,863.55	54,274.33	86,230.81	135,854.64	212,305.42	329,189.53	506,578.26	773,880.73	953,962.17
26	16,734.18	21,565.91	35,556.73	58,073.53	93,991.58	150,798.65	239,905.13	378,567.96	592,696.56	920,918.07	1,144,754.60
27	17,068.86	22,212.89	37,334.56	62,138.68	102,450.82	167,386.50	271,092.79	435,353.15	693,454.97	1,095,892.51	1,373,705.52
28	17,410.24	22,879.28	39,201.29	66,488.38	111,671.40	185,799.01	306,334.86	500,656.12	811,342.32	1,304,112.08	1,648,446.62
29	17,758.45	23,565.66	41,161.36	71,142.57	121,721.82	206,236.91	346,158.39	575,754.54	949,270.51	1,551,893.38	1,978,135.95
30	18,113.62	24,272.62	43,219.42	76,122.55	132,676.78	228,922.97	391,158.98	662,117.72	1,110,646.50	1,846,753.12	2,373,763.14
31	18,475.89	25,000.80	45,380.39	81,451.13	144,617.70	254,104.49	442,009.65	761,435.38	1,299,456.41	2,197,636.21	2,848,515.77
32	18,845.41	25,750.83	47,649.41	87,152.71	157,633.29	282,055.99	499,470.90	875,650.68	1,520,363.99	2,615,187.10	3,418,218.92
33	19,222.31	26,523.35	50,031.89	93,253.40	171,820.28	313,082.14	564,402.12	1,006,998.29	1,778,825.87	3,112,072.64	4,101,862.70
34	19,606.76	27,319.05	52,533.48	99,781.14	187,284.11	347,521.18	637,774.39	1,158,048.03	2,081,226.27	3,703,366.45	4,922,235.24
35	19,998.90	28,138.62	55,160.15	106,765.81	204,139.68	385,748.51	720,685.06	1,331,755.23	2,435,034.74	4,407,006.07	5,906,682.29

The Foundation for a Sound Financial Future

What is most important for long-term financial success? If we disregard quick instant profit, the secret is in the **regular and long-term deposit of funds**. Here, the same principle applies as in filling a pitcher with water: You either fill it all at once – and there has to be a lot of water to do this – or you fill it **persistently and consistently**, perhaps even by droplets, **for a very long time**.

Let us take a look at what this financial discipline can bring.

If we regularly invest 100 monetary units (let us say USD) each month for a period of fifteen years at a fixed annual interest rate of 4%, after 180 months, we have saved (principal plus interest) **$24,466**. During this time we have **deposited $18,000**, which means that we have **earned $6,466**.

What happens if we secure an **interest rate** just 3% greater (7% total interest) and **invest five years longer** (depositing an additional $6,000)? If we compare this situation with the last (a 4% interest rate, where we saved fifteen years and got $24,466), we discover that this "small" difference in terms yields **twice as much ($50,754)**.

We can see this in the following table.

Let us study another example (and learn to read the table). We again invest 100 dollars (or any other currency; we can also multiply or divide this number by ten, but we must then also do the same with the result) per month.

This time we have an 8% interest rate and invest for twenty years (240 months). We can read in the table that we **invested** a total of **$24,000, and saved $56,900 in total**.

That is why every (additional) percent of interest, and every (additional) month, is so important.

The Secrets of Saving: Turn $16,000 Into $1,000,000 – Anyone Can Do It

Here we discuss the value of saving when you are young, and the secret of **how you can become a millionaire with just a $16,000 investment and a little time**.

James and Mary are both twenty-three. They decide to save money for their futures. They each choose a different method of saving:

DURATION OF SAVINGS (IN YEARS)	No. OF MONTHLY INSTALLMENTS	FACTOR	TOTAL INVESTED	MONTHLY SAVINGS WITH EQUAL INVESTMENTS OF 100 MONETARY UNITS							HYPOTHETICAL UNLIMITED MONTHLY REVENUE						
				AMOUNTS SAVED													
				2%	4%	7%	8%	10%	15%	20%	2%	4%	7%	8%	10%	15%	20%
1	12	1.04	1,200	1,211	1,222	1,238	1,243	1,254	1,280	1,306	2	4	7	8	10	15	20
2	24	1.08	2,400	2,446	2,493	2,563	2,586	2,634	2,753	2,874	4	8	14	17	21	32	44
3	36	1.12	3,600	3,706	3,814	3,980	4,037	4,151	4,446	4,755	6	12	23	26	33	52	73
4	48	1.17	4,800	4,991	5,189	5,497	5,603	5,820	6,394	7,013	8	17	31	36	46	75	107
5	60	1.22	6,000	6,302	6,618	7,120	7,294	7,656	8,633	9,722	10	22	40	47	61	101	149
6	72	1.27	7,200	7,639	8,104	8,856	9,121	9,676	11,208	12,972	13	27	50	59	77	131	199
7	84	1.32	8,400	9,003	9,650	10,714	11,095	11,897	14,170	16,873	15	32	61	71	95	166	258
8	96	1.37	9,600	10,394	11,258	12,702	13,225	14,341	17,576	21,554	17	37	72	85	114	206	330
9	108	1.42	10,800	11,812	12,931	14,829	15,527	17,029	21,493	27,171	20	42	84	100	136	252	416
10	120	1.48	12,000	13,260	14,670	17,105	18,012	19,986	25,997	33,912	22	48	97	116	159	305	519
11	132	1.54	13,200	14,736	16,478	19,541	20,697	23,239	31,177	42,001	24	54	110	133	185	365	643
12	144	1.60	14,400	16,242	18,359	22,146	23,596	26,817	37,134	51,707	27	60	125	152	214	435	792
13	156	1.67	15,600	17,777	20,315	24,935	26,727	30,753	43,985	63,355	29	67	141	172	245	515	970
14	168	1.73	16,800	19,344	22,350	27,918	30,109	35,082	51,863	77,332	32	73	158	194	280	608	1,184
15	180	1.80	18,000	20,942	24,466	31,110	33,761	39,844	60,923	94,105	35	80	176	217	318	714	1,441
16	192	1.87	19,200	22,571	26,666	34,526	37,705	45,083	71,342	114,233	37	87	195	243	359	836	1,749
17	204	1.95	20,400	24,234	28,955	38,181	41,965	50,845	83,323	138,386	40	95	216	270	405	976	2,119
18	216	2.03	21,600	25,929	31,335	42,092	46,565	57,184	97,102	167,369	43	103	238	300	456	1,138	2,562
19	228	2.11	22,800	27,659	33,810	46,276	51,534	64,156	112,948	202,149	46	111	262	332	512	1,323	3,095
20	240	2.19	24,000	29,423	36,384	50,754	56,900	71,826	131,171	243,886	49	119	287	366	573	1,537	3,734
21	252	2.28	25,200	31,223	39,061	55,544	62,695	80,263	152,127	293,969	52	128	314	403	640	1,782	4,501
22	264	2.37	26,400	33,058	41,846	60,671	68,954	89,543	176,226	354,069	55	137	343	444	714	2,064	5,421
23	276	2.46	27,600	34,930	44,741	66,156	75,714	99,751	203,940	426,190	58	146	374	487	795	2,389	6,525
24	288	2.56	28,800	36,840	47,753	72,024	83,015	110,980	235,812	512,734	61	156	407	534	885	2,763	7,850
25	300	2.67	30,000	38,787	50,885	78,304	90,899	123,332	272,464	616,587	64	167	443	585	983	3,192	9,440
26	312	2.77	31,200	40,774	54,142	85,024	99,414	136,920	314,614	741,211	67	177	481	640	1,092	3,686	11,348
27	324	2.88	32,400	42,801	57,530	92,213	108,611	151,866	363,087	890,759	71	188	521	699	1,211	4,254	13,637
28	336	3.00	33,600	44,868	61,053	99,906	118,543	168,306	418,830	1,070,218	74	200	565	763	1,342	4,907	16,384
29	348	3.12	34,800	46,976	64,717	108,138	129,270	186,391	482,935	1,285,568	78	212	611	832	1,486	5,658	19,681
30	360	3.24	36,000	49,126	68,527	116,945	140,855	206,284	556,656	1,543,988	81	224	661	906	1,645	6,521	23,638
31	372	3.37	37,200	51,320	72,490	126,369	153,367	228,167	641,435	1,854,091	85	237	715	987	1,819	7,514	28,385
32	384	3.51	38,400	53,557	76,611	136,453	166,880	252,238	738,930	2,226,216	88	251	772	1,074	2,011	8,657	34,082
33	396	3.65	39,600	55,839	80,898	147,243	181,473	278,715	851,050	2,672,766	92	265	833	1,168	2,223	9,970	40,919
34	408	3.79	40,800	58,167	85,355	158,788	197,235	307,841	979,988	3,208,625	96	279	898	1,269	2,455	11,480	49,122
35	420	3.95	42,000	60,541	89,992	171,141	214,257	339,879	1,128,267	3,851,657	100	295	968	1,379	2,710	13,218	58,967
36	432	4.10	43,200	62,963	94,813	184,359	232,641	375,121	1,298,787	4,623,294	104	310	1,042	1,497	2,991	15,215	70,780
37	444	4.27	44,400	65,433	99,827	198,502	252,495	413,887	1,494,886	5,549,260	108	327	1,122	1,625	3,300	17,512	84,956
38	456	4.44	45,600	67,953	105,042	213,636	273,938	456,530	1,720,399	6,660,418	112	344	1,208	1,763	3,640	20,154	101,967
39	468	4.62	46,800	70,523	110,466	229,828	297,097	503,437	1,979,739	7,993,808	116	362	1,299	1,912	4,014	23,192	122,381
40	480	4.80	48,000	73,144	116,106	247,154	322,108	555,035	2,277,981	9,593,876	121	380	1,397	2,072	4,426	26,686	146,877
41	492	4.99	49,200	75,818	121,972	265,693	349,120	611,792	2,620,958	11,513,957	125	399	1,502	2,246	4,879	30,704	176,273
42	504	5.19	50,400	78,546	128,073	285,530	378,293	674,226	3,015,382	13,818,055	130	419	1,614	2,434	5,376	35,325	211,547
43	516	5.40	51,600	81,327	134,418	306,755	409,800	742,902	3,468,970	16,582,972	134	440	1,734	2,637	5,924	40,639	253,877
44	528	5.62	52,800	84,165	141,017	329,466	443,827	818,447	3,990,596	19,900,873	139	462	1,863	2,856	6,526	46,750	304,672
45	540	5.84	54,000	87,059	147,879	353,766	480,577	901,545	4,590,466	23,882,354	144	484	2,000	3,092	7,189	53,777	365,626
46	552	6.07	55,200	90,011	155,016	379,768	520,266	992,954	5,280,316	28,660,132	149	507	2,147	3,347	7,918	61,858	438,771
47	564	6.32	56,400	93,023	162,439	407,590	563,131	1,093,503	6,073,644	34,393,464	154	532	2,305	3,623	8,720	71,152	526,546
48	576	6.57	57,600	96,094	170,158	437,359	609,425	1,204,108	6,985,971	41,273,463	159	557	2,473	3,921	9,602	81,840	631,875
49	588	6.83	58,800	99,227	178,186	469,212	659,422	1,325,772	8,035,147	49,529,463	164	583	2,653	4,243	10,572	94,131	758,270
50	600	7.11	60,000	102,422	186,535	503,295	713,419	1,459,604	9,241,700	59,436,661	169	611	2,846	4,590	11,639	108,266	909,944

About Money

- Mary begins to save immediately. She deposits $2,000 in the first week of the year, every year, until she is thirty at a 10% annual interest rate. After that, she does not invest any more, but just leaves all the money she has already invested in the account. She invests a total of $16,000.

- James decides on his thirtieth birthday to start saving. He also finds a 10% annual interest rate, and invests $2,000 in the first week of the year, every year, until he is sixty-nine years old. He invests a total of $80,000 (40 × $2,000).

What is the situation over the years?

Mary		
Age	Investment	The amount she has at the end of the year
23	$2,000	$2,200.00
24	$2,000 ($ 2,200 + $ 2,000) + 10%	$4,620.00
25	$2,000 ($ 4,620 + $ 2,000) + 10%	$7,282.00
26	$2,000 ($ 7,282 + $ 2,000) + 10%	$10,210.20
27	$2,000 ($ 10,210.20 + $ 2,000) + 10%	$13,410.22
28	$2,000 ($ 13,410.22 + $ 2,000) + 10%	$16,974.34
29	$2,000 ($ 16,974.34 + $ 2,000) + 10%	$20,871.77
30	$2,000 ($ 20,871.77 + $ 2,000) + 10%	$25,158.95
	She leaves the money in the account and does not invest anymore.	
40		$65,255.85
50		$169,256.86
60		$439,008.70
61		$482,909.57
62		$531,200.53
63		$584,320.58
64		$642,752.64
65		$707,027.90
66		$777,730.69
67		$855,503.76
68		$941,054.14
69		$1,035,159.55

The Millionaire Mindset

James		
Age	Investment	The amount he has at the end of the year
30	$2,000	$2,200.00
31	$2,000	$4,620.00
32	$2,000	$7,282.00
33	$2,000	$10,210.20
34	$2,000	$13,210.22
35	$2,000	$16,974.34
40	$2,000	$40,768.57
45	$2,000	$79,089.40
50	$2,000	$140,805.50
55	$2,000	$240,199.90
60	$2,000	$400,275.53
61	$2,000	$442,503.09
62	$2,000	$488,953.40
63	$2,000	$540,048.74
64	$2,000	$596,253.61
65	$2,000	$658,078.97
66	$2,000	$726,086.86
67	$2,000	$800,895.86
68	$2,000	$883,185.10
69	$2,000	$973,703.61

It is interesting to look at both investments according to time periods.

When both are forty, Mary has already invested $16,000 and earned $65,255.85. During this same time, James invested $22,000 (11 x $2,000) and currently has only $40,768.57.

At the age of fifty, Mary has invested a total of $16,000 but now has $169,256.86. James has invested $42,000 (21 x $2,000) and now has $140,805.50.

At the age of sixty, Mary has still only invested $16,000, but her investment is worth $439,008.70. James has now invested $62,000 (31 x $2,000), and his investment is now worth $400,275.53.

When both are sixty-nine, Mary becomes a millionaire with a total investment of $16,000. She has $1,035,159.55 in her account. On the other hand, James had to invest $80,000 (40 x $2,000) but still has only $973,703.61 in his account.

Mary has earned more than James and invested only 20% of what James had to invest at the same interest rate.

If you have children, share this example with them. The only advice is this: To be financially independent someday, **start saving today**. It is never too early. On the contrary, it does not matter if you are eighteen or fifty years old – make the decision to begin investing something on a regular basis, today. As you have just seen, each year you delay will cost you more and bring you less.

The Plan for Achieving Wealth, Success, and Happiness

1. Once again, read this whole chapter very carefully and pause at any place that seems strange and unfamiliar, perhaps even stupid or foolish. This is very important. Some people, certain of the dark side they think money should have, never allow such advice to sink in. John Gray, author of many best-selling books, says that money only **multiplies or emphasizes your inner condition;** If you are unhappy without money, you will be even less happy with lots of it.

   Without a doubt, money gives you a certain energy in life. Imagine winning a few million dollars – would you not behave a little differently? Besides, as Thomas Keller says, **"Money is clairvoyant and will do exactly what you think of it in your life**: if you think it's the root of all evil, for you it will be just that. If it is good and you feel right about having it, so it will happen." On the other hand, Sri Sathya Sai Baba said that **there is nothing bad if a person is wealthy because God gave them this wealth to manage; it is a person's free will what to do with it**. So do not close the door and do not hinder yourself on your path. Money is divine energy.

2. Let us **protect our wealth and the abilities that enable us to acquire (earn) money**, if this is what we feel inside. Also, let us **begin to deposit at least a minimal amount of money in a special account**, if we want to be financially independent someday.

The Millionaire Mindset

3. Do the **expense record** exercise: Record what you spend money on – down to the last penny – day by day for an entire month. You do not do this to feel badly at the end of the month, but to **determine if you spend your money on things you really need or simply buy impulsively**. Oftentimes, you will discover that you spend large amounts of money on things you had not planned on buying.

4. If you are not pleased with the state of your finances, **make correcting your finances your goal**, which means you will either **limit your expenses, spend wisely**, or you will **earn more**; or even better, you can combine two or all three of these suggestions. Read about the possibilities and choose the one that is best suited to you.

5. **Very important: Invest and deposit your money according to your intuition and inner voice.** Today there is more and more gossip about how the financial system is not based on a healthy foundation and that it is only a question of time before the big financial shock happens. Perhaps now, while you are reading this book, everything is different... but perhaps it is not. Whatever the case – lust for money should not tempt you so much that you would not listen to your inner voice. Above all, **diversify your capital**. There are many good investments available: purchase of land or businesses (to rent out), investments in new businesses, etc.

8. The Basics of Working With People and Why Learning the Basics of Selling is Vital to Success

In the forthcoming chapters, we will reveal some essentials about dealing with others. Also, you will get some guidelines where and how to put these skills in practice.

Whatever business(es) you are in, you always discover that one thing proves to be the decisive factor in the end: how well you **handle dealing with yourself**... and, consequently, **with the people around you.** If you want to offer something, recommend something, do something, demonstrate something, etc., you always need another, interested person to talk with.

A worker must converse with his or her boss or maybe other subordinate workers. A secretary is the coordinator between the director and other employees as well as external business partners. A man converses with his wife and children. A homemaker has to deal with the grocery clerk, neighbors, sales representatives, etc.

We all play different roles: salesperson, buyer, negotiator, manipulator, or manipulated person... almost all the time.

The Secret of Successful Cooperation

The better you understand and handle these relationships, the more successful you will be in all areas.

Still, we do not forget the basics: **This only applies in situations where your heart dictates this kind of work**, so you are not denying your true self... and you are not pretending and trying to be artificially kind.

> **The better you understand and handle relationships, the more successful you will be in all areas.**

On the other hand, **the other person has to feel the same way.** That way, you are united on the basis of **common goals and visions.**

The American Carnegie Institute conducted research on how much of an engineer's success is influenced by technical knowledge and how much by other things. The result: Only 15% of his success depended on expert knowledge and **85% on the ability to successfully communicate and work with other people.**

As a matter of fact, we could say it this way: Successful communication is based on **the ability to choose the right profession, search for your life's mission within it, and persist in following the heart** (read: remain in high vibration), no matter what.

If we act on this basis, we will automatically understand and successfully communicate with people.

If you recognize this, and make an effort to gain all the necessary knowledge, attributes, and effective habits in this area, **you are welcome everywhere** and have many friends and a distinguished position. Let us look at where each of these attributes is most effective – at work, home, and elsewhere.

You can look at all the advice that follows as sales advice or advice on dealing with people, but in fact, these are one and the same.

Encouraging Others

What do you do when you find out that someone performed in a way, or said something, that you know is likely not best (for him or her and/or others)? Actually, you always have two choices when dealing with people.

1. **Put them on solid ground**; show them that you know a better solution.
2. **Be understanding of their effort**; acknowledge that their intentions have been the best and then give them encouragement.

Choose the first possibility, and you will only prove **how right you are** and **how wrong they are.** Between the lines, you are saying: "I would have handled this differently. It's your fault. If you would have given this more thought initially, things could have been different. I can't help you at all; I can't even empathize with you because you made a mistake and have to suffer the consequences."

It might also happen that you start heated arguments with them, where everyone is compelled to defend themselves and their decisions. It is impossible to find common ground in such situations.

Do you remember the case about the IBM founder, Watson, and his reaction to his employee's mistake that cost the company a fortune? He viewed the money lost as an **investment in the employee's training**. Why should he fire him when he has now invested so much money in him?

All great people think alike; they encourage people who then become devoted to them. Benjamin Franklin once said that **he would not say a bad word about any person, but that he knew everything about them that was good**.

Let us recall some facts that we learned in the book. Remember critical mass? We will use that knowledge here to explain our relationship(s) with others.

We said that we are all in a specific vibration (or state) all the time. Vibration can vary, but we are in some state all the time.

The longer we resonate with a specific vibration, the more that vibration comes to us – and the more this becomes our personal truth. As we view life through this filter, we either fail to see everything that does not match this framework, or it becomes strange to us.

When we hit that critical mass, we begin to **identify with this state**, and the energy we transmit is a **literal reflection of it**. Other people – those who can resonate with the vibration we transmit – usually feel this as their energy.

Here is the reason why we sometimes have a hard time relating to others: **We do not understand others because we do not, or cannot, resonate with their vibration**. That means we are so much into our own world, and our personal truth becomes so powerful, it immediately overwrites (or holds or influences) everything else we want to look at. If we are even more locked into our world when we look at others, we **feel no energy about them** (because we find no interest in them), so we find them uninteresting and strange.

In both cases, the result will be no resonance and therefore **no energy**. We know that when we resonate with someone on the same vibration, we feel

more energetic because energy was built during the process of resonance. Therefore, we are attracted to that person: **We feel good and uplifted while with them.**

If there is no resonance, we feel a kind of **resistance**: We direct energy towards another person – to build a resonance – and **get no return**. The consequence is that **we do not feel good**... and we are not very motivated to see this person again soon.

What can you do if you do want to understand others? There is only one solution – you **need to expand your focus and awareness**.

Life is not only what you see – based on your **personal truth**, experiences, positions, goals, fears, etc. – but much more. **When you expand your focus, you will also see the truth of others, not just your own.** Also, with the expansion of your awareness, you also **raise your vibration**.

When this happens, you will not have challenges with understanding and accepting others because **you will be able to see their lives from their perspective, as well**. That will enable you to **feel compassion toward them rather than need for comparing, proving, and confirming**. That is, when they do something that differs from what you prefer, their energy will not throw you out of balance, but you will be able to remain in your vibration.

Another challenge is dealing with people according to the proverb, "Treat others the way you want them to treat you."

This is very useful when you are in a **very high vibration** (in your heart) or when you know what others want. If your awareness does not "cover" another person's truth, or give you the expanded awareness to have a better idea of what they might want, then you cannot know. That means you can do your best, and do everything that you want in that kind of situation, how you would like to be treated, etc. But people **will not appreciate, or even recognize your good work** simply because **they wanted something else**.

No seminar about communication, selling, or anything else will replace the lack of understanding that comes from your small picture of life. When your awareness expands – so you can truly **resonate with him or her on many levels** (physical, emotional, intellectual, spiritual), while **remaining in your (high) vibration – do what you feel is best** in that situation, and both of you will feel uplifted.

This is exactly what Jesus had taught centuries ago when he said, "Treat others the same way you want them to treat you." (Luke 6:31) And this is also the big secret of successful communication – simple, but very strong and everyone can use it.

This knowledge can be used in business, as well. A salesperson who cannot accept a different opinion will never be successful. **He or she wins the battle – proves his or her expertise – but loses the war (no sale will result).**

Do not try to find shortcuts in life. Do not expect you will be able to understand or assimilate the "perfect communications skills," i.e., using sales techniques, taught in seminars. **You have to work on yourself first**, then these techniques may help.

Anyone can be "wise" and criticize, and most people do exactly that. But if you can truly accept the other person with your heart open, **you will not need any communication techniques to make him or her love you**.

In his book, *How to Win Friends and Influence People*, Dale Carnegie quotes a thought by Thomas Carlyle: **"A great man shows his greatness by the way he treats little men."**

Emerson said this a bit differently: **"Every man I meet is my superior in some way. In that, I learn from him."**

Do Not Avoid These Words

You can easily check if you are in the vibration of comparing, confirming, and proving... or that your identity is not linked (too tightly) to the desire to amaze others.

When was the last time, in a serious conversation, you admitted that **you were wrong** or that **you had not mastered something** or **needed help** at some task?

These are the kind of things that sometimes, if your self-esteem is low, you can be afraid to admit. Why?

Because you think **they will lower your importance in other people's eyes and you will lose their respect**. But the truth is just the opposite – **those who understand will appreciate you even more** because you have been sincere and honest. When you admit these things, you save time, possibly money, and decrease the stress level for everyone.

Focus on Common Desires, Not Your Own

One of the problems in communicating with others is that it is easy to think too much about our needs instead of paying attention to **common desires** (ours and those of the people we are speaking with). That way we literally strive for their energy, and thus **use them** to help us achieve our goals and desires.

Do you like strawberries and cream? Let us assume that your answer is yes. But when you go fishing, what do you use as bait? A strawberry or a worm? Of course, the answer here is easy. But when it comes to dealing with others, a lot of times people focus on themselves… and are not even aware of it.

You will always be successful in dealing with others if you ask yourself these questions before beginning a discussion:

"How can I help this person? How can I assist him or her in solving his or her challenges, increasing his or her profits, bettering his or her reputation, adding to his or her health, increasing his or her pleasure, and making his or her life easier?"

Needless to say, **this should be your heart's desire**, not just a way of accumulating money. That way, you will **establish resonance in a common vision**, which is the **greatest generator of energy**.

If you try to impose yourself or your ideas on others, you will not get through unnoticed. **People feel your energy**; if you work in their (common) favor, they feel your care. But if you are only exploiting them – only to gain a profit – they can feel that, too.

My friend, the architect, is in very high demand. When asked what he ascribes his success to, he answers, "I listen to my customers carefully, then I transfer their dreams and desires to paper. This is the bulk of my work… and I enjoy it very much."

The most successful people are the best solvers of other people's problems (while doing it with love).

Here is another real life example. Mr. Clark was a car salesman. He visited all the automobile fairs to learn the novelties of his industry, he associated with experts, and he read magazines. He also made a list of advantages regarding the competition for each car: Sometimes it is the price, sometimes safety, or additional equipment. His advertising always pointed out these advantages. He was very consistent in doing this and expected huge increases in his sales.

When a buyer came to his car lot, he presented each car according to what he had found out during his comparison research. He justified his statements, and he even asked the buyer if he had convinced him that what he was telling him was true, and he usually got a positive answer. **And that was all he got from them**... the conversation usually ended with: "I'll think about it."

Despite having many visitors that he had treated with kindness and attention, he just could not get to the final step – selling the car.

Mr. Clark had a problem that he was not aware of: **He did not know how to listen to his customers**. He treated them as if they were copies of himself and had the same thoughts he had. However, because every person is a planet in and of himself, motives for buying differ for everyone.

I recommended he test the following sales method: Do not force your desires on your customer; instead, **imagine you are helping a friend buy a car**. So do not just push your opinions onto your customers, instead, focus your attention on some things you believe the customer forgot, but are in need of attention. You can do this by posing certain questions to him or her that will help you find out what your customer is thinking without uttering statements that do not elicit a response.

"What do you use now? Why did you decide to buy this particular one? Are you satisfied? What do you like the most, or what one feature would you change, if you could? What do you think it's missing? Why did you opt for the change? Have you ever bought from us and why? How would you like to do business in the future?"

Mr. Clark had another challenge – **he loved talking**. When he exploded with enthusiasm, he just could not be stopped. Well, it would be fine if he just talked about what interested the customer, instead of discussing special features and details that were of no interest to his prospects.

After he finally acknowledged this problem, we decided on a special tactic: **He would look at each customer who walks into his establishment as a person he really needs to listen to**. This would enable him to sense his or her desires and at the same time prevent him from talking too much. He would, of course, ask questions that would help the customer express his or her needs and desires.

After a week, we met again. He felt a bit embarrassed because he admitted that he finally realized he was acting like a horse with blinders, which prevented him from seeing left or right – just in front. He did not improve his sales during this time, but he succeeded in getting his prospects to come back. He said, "When I listened to what the customers were talking about, I learned, directly or indirectly, all the things I needed to get them excited about the purchase. It's unbelievable how easily I reached the goal by talking half as much."

We agreed he would let me know when he sold the first car using this method. I promised to take his family for a trip if that happened within a week. I did not have to wait long; it happened in two days. In less than six months, he achieved his sales plan for the year and exceeded it by 120% by the end of the year.

You will always be successful in business if you understand and concentrate on your customer's desires rather than selling your own. And if this makes you happy, you will be happy – and successful.

Here is another example from the life of Andrew Carnegie, a man who knew this rule very well:

One of his relatives complained that she did not get any answer from her sons who were studying at university far away. They were so busy working that they had no time to write back. "I am so worried something might be wrong," she complained. The cunning Carnegie knew where the problem was, and he offered her a bet for a hundred dollars that the boys would answer his letter without his asking them.

What did he do? He wrote them a nice letter and closed with a sentence telling them **he put a banknote for twenty dollars for both of them** in the letter, which he purposely neglected to put in. He did not have to wait long for a reply: "Dear Uncle Andrew, Thank you for the letter, but you forgot the money…"

Attributes Common to the Best

The first and most important attribute that successful people share is their **belief in themselves**. Without this, you can forget about success, even though you may be selling very good products or services. **Words do not sell, energy and enthusiasm do.**

The second attribute is **belief in the product and trust in the company (or in all the companies involved)**, i.e., producer or supplier, distributor, etc. If you know that the products you are offering are excellent – and the accompanying terms and logistics behind them are, as well – you do not need to be skilled in complicated sales methods to persuade a prospect about their quality or to make a purchase.

The next attribute, which arises from the first two, is **belief in the benefit inherent in the purchase**. Not for the good of the sale (because your pocket is in need of some monetary "stimulation"), but **for the benefit of the customer**. That is to say, you should be sure that the **customer is getting an incredible value for his or her money**.

If you have these attributes, you **will not have the feeling you are imposing something** on your customer – which is a big problem of sales representatives – but that you are **helping your customers out**.

If you have ever doubted in the goodness of your deeds, then you missed developing one of these attributes. This does not apply just to sales, but your personal life, too. The attributes can be described like this:

Belief in yourself, belief in your idea (product), and belief in the benefit received by the people you talk to about it.

How can you improve these attributes in yourself?

The Magic of Improvement

It is most important that you first **firmly decide to do something**... and then **stay motivated during the process**. But be careful that your desire for improvement does not drop. This mostly happens when your **expectations are too great** and **you want to achieve too much** (and) **too soon**.

Namely, you **do not allow yourself to change gradually**; instead, you jump to the top from the bottom stair.

For example, you want to strengthen your discipline. You decide to get up an hour earlier the next morning, so you set your alarm clock and fall asleep. The next morning, in the "middle of the night," the loud alarm wakes you up. If you are not firmly determined, thus your will is not strong enough, this is likely to happen: Once you remember the clock is set only so you can do more work during the day, you **start to bargain with yourself**. You begin to think about **how you could make a better effort during the day so that you would not need to get up so early**.

The Millionaire Mindset

You remember that you have some spare time for lunch, which you could use productively instead, and you could cut the time you spend reading the newspapers. Answering phone calls will not take up much time, and now you are wondering why you wanted to get up earlier at all. Satisfied, you **reset the alarm clock for the normal time and go back to bed**.

It did not work out because the temptation to stay in bed was too strong. Would it not be easier for you to get up **ten minutes earlier the first day** and reserve this extra time for some pleasant task? For example, you could read a favorite magazine, take a longer bath, fix a nutritious breakfast, etc.

Each day, you could make a bigger step – gradually setting the alarm clock to wake you up a few minutes earlier. That would easily bring you to success at the end, getting up an hour earlier.

How Ivan Learned to Sell

Ivan decided to sell machines that were worth a few thousand dollars. His challenge was similar to the challenges of his fellow sales representatives – he did not trust his abilities and understood each "I won't buy" as "The machine is not good. You are not worthy. Don't bother me by offering something like that." So he decided to begin with a different skill.

He ordered a package of **ballpoint pens**, which he has used for years and has been very satisfied with, from a wholesale dealer. His plan was to offer a pen to each prospect as he wished them well. He knew from experience why this pen was so good and the price ($1.00) would not be intimidating either.

He decided to do this for the next two months. He offered a pen to his friends with these words: "Look, isn't it nice? Not only does it write wonderfully and last long, it doesn't smear, and the price is good, too. Here, you try writing with it. What do you think? Fantastic, isn't it? I was surprised myself the first time I wrote with it. I can't believe they only cost a dollar. Do you want one?"

The result was unbelievable. First, he abolished his **fear of failure and rejection**, which was uncomfortable at first because a few friends rejected the offer. But he later used each rejection to **ask the reason and learn about people's needs and desires**. Then he got used to the fact that **people were not rejecting him**. He did not blame anyone for rejection and still considered the person a friend who perhaps just did not need to make the purchase at that particular moment.

Apart from this, his sales were going really well. Ivan's basic motive was to conquer fear and gain self-confidence, so at first he did not even think about sales success.

He improved his sales skills so significantly that after two months he could offer the pen to almost anyone in casual conversation, whether he was in an elevator or at the bank counter, and closed around 70% of the sales successfully. That does not mean that he sold to seven out of the ten people he met, but that he sold to **seven of the ten people whom he assessed were interested in the product and to whom he introduced it**. (That is also how he learned to distinguish a prospect from "someone to talk to.")

He learned that he had one particular challenge in the past – **he was afraid of whether the prospects would buy**, so he was also afraid of asking them, "Do you want it?" He expected that he would just talk (do the presentation) and the prospect would, if he or she were interested in the purchase, just **stop him and say: "OK, I've heard enough – I'll buy it!"**

Today he thinks differently. "If you don't ask for the sale at the end, you are not selling, but are just **having a nice and interesting conversation**. I call these salespeople **professional visitors**. So now I always ask. Although the answer is sometimes 'No,' I don't despair; I just ask for the **reason behind his or her decision**. I pose this question in such a way that his or her answer helps me with the next prospect, someone who might think the same way as this person."

"Without this knowledge, I wouldn't know how to offer the products to similar prospects because I wouldn't know their desires or needs. I learned that people love to express their opinions if only they have someone who will listen. I love to listen because this way I can learn everything I need to help me offer them **the same thing** in a different way – the way they desire – **and then they buy**. Lately, I love to ask a few standard questions up front – what do they currently use, why they use it, what they like or dislike about what they're currently using, etc. This way, I have all the information I need before I even make them an offer."

The Millionaire Mindset

Obviously, Ivan understood very quickly the secret of successfully closing a sale: to learn what the prospect wants or wishes and then offer the product in a way that fulfills their expectations.

One more thing needs to be considered here – sales ethics. The right salesperson can sell almost anything. But a successful and ethical sale is the sale where **both parties are satisfied not only for the first moment, but also tomorrow, next week, and ever after.**

When you help people, you do not feel guilty or have "a lump in your throat" when you meet customers again. In fact, it is just the opposite: You are glad to run into them and happy for the opportunity to ask them how satisfied they are with the products, now that they have had an opportunity to use them.

How does Ivan's story end? He is progressing steadily with his success in sales and is about halfway to his stated goal. He now has to transfer these newfound sales abilities to his basic business, which is selling expensive machines.

There were, in fact, no problems. He wrote down the advantages of his product in comparison to the competition and included all its good attributes. He developed a few versions of a sales conversation because he now knew that not all people have the same desires. Namely, you can buy the same thing for many different reasons: Somebody buys a specific car because it is fashionable, another for safety reasons, a third because of payment terms, the next because his girlfriend wanted it, another because his neighbor has one just like it, and on and on. But they **all buy the same model.** "The primary part of the sales conversation is done at home, in solitude, when you prepare yourself," he found out.

At this point, the one thing all his sales conversations had in common was that he listened most of the time and buyers talked about their problems, desires, and dreams. In the end, he showed them how his product could bring them closer to their dreams, which had almost lost their luster because of their daily burdens. Or he showed them how he could help them achieve greater success in business or as individuals. His sales pitch now depended on what was most important for the prospect.

Sometimes he came across a wavering prospect. He knew that he could make that sale, but at the same time, he also knew that his product was not what the prospect desired. **In such cases, he recommended what he thought was right.** He even gave out the addresses of his competitors if he saw that it was in his prospect's best interests.

"Sometimes this didn't seem right because I didn't know what I would achieve, but I feel that I can create the greatest benefit for the prospect and myself this way. The result came later because those same prospects are now **my best clients**. They told their contacts in business circles about my help – and they do the same today. Their friends and acquaintances come to me because they know that I'll advise what's best for them. **I have to admit that I have never enjoyed business as much as I do now."**

All the most important sales knowledge is gathered in this simple example, but this is not everything you can get from it. Because of your increased self-confidence, success, and general interest, you not only get better in sales but also in everything you do. Ivan described it like this: "I have always been restrained. Now I see this was the fear of being different or standing out."

"I ducked so everybody would just leave me alone, and I wouldn't have to defend myself. When, for instance, I ordered fish in a restaurant and got something else, I had my thoughts, but I didn't say anything. Today this wouldn't happen. I usually stand up for myself (if I feel it in my heart). Often, I take things as a joke and don't embarrass people. Or I express things gently and with love. In fact, **nice words from the heart are universal**, and I can use them in any situation. I also found out another communications secret: If I don't want to resolve a problem the moment I notice it, I wait for the right moment and everything goes smoothly."

It is essential for each person to learn the basics of trade because it is through this that most people can abolish their fears and prejudices.

The Secrets of Successful Interpersonal Relationships

There is a whole string of little secrets when it comes to really good interpersonal relationships. These are things that are useful not just in sales, but in our everyday lives, so it is good for everyone to know them. Let us look at one of them. The rest are introduced in more detail in other books.

Often, we succumb to temptation because we think **a certain product is going to create a demand by itself** – and that people merely need to know that this product is available.

And we are not talking about just the sale of products and services, but the demonstration of our **ideas**, which is also a kind of trade: We want to bring our side of the story closer to the person we are talking to so that he or she will be able to accept it and agree with it.

In fact, sometimes it is just the opposite; **the better the terms are and the less we explain them, the more suspicious it looks**. For instance, you intend to "sell" $100 for $5. Is the offer good? Of course. Does it mean that people will come in droves with their money? No way.

Sometime back, I came across a financial project, which was excellent. There was only one challenge – **there was no demand for it**. The product had good features and it did not have much competition in the market, but sales were horrible because prospects did not know the product and it was strange to them.

What is strange and new easily provokes fear.

How can you expect to present a person some novelty in the financial market in just two hours and expect the prospect to invest all his or her hard-earned savings with you?

For this reason, it is important to **make things more familiar, and give people more information, to get them enthusiastic about the purchase** (read: to create the critical mass of trust and resonance between the company, product, and prospects).

So how do salespeople usually overcome this challenge? With discounts? Well, this is a good and successful solution… if a prospect **likes the product**.

But when it comes to novelties, **money (usually) is not the biggest hindrance** – something else is. So even discounts would not help.

Here is an example. Let us imagine that a shop offers very strange trousers that you do not like… at all! The price for a pair is $100. You see them in the shop window, but you are not interested.

A week later, you pass by the same shop window, and the price is now **reduced to $50**. The shop owner thought the shop would be full of buyers, but **nothing happened**. Of course, if something you do not like is offered, **you are not interested… at any price**.

Usually, if you did not like something yesterday, you are not going to like it today, unless you get some new information or a different idea (like you want to **buy an opportunity**; or, said differently, you want to buy a discount, not a product).

What can you do in such a case? **Put yourself in your customer's shoes.**

People usually have their own ideas about most things, even a guide or a role model, especially when it comes to fashion. As a clever salesperson, identify your target market. Maybe they are teenagers. What do they wear? They probably follow fashion trends and imitate their music and movie idols.

Now you need to find out **what is the hottest thing to wear nowadays**. You find out, and then you may find a picture of a very popular music star wearing almost the same trousers you were trying so desperately to sell in your shop. Cut the picture out of the magazine, enlarge it, and point out the likeness: **XX is wearing them – and you can, too**!

In such cases, you have to think about **getting a product closer to your customers choice**, so you will need to **put additional energy into this process** and **wait some time until critical mass is built**. This could happen in days, weeks, maybe months, or never.

That way, you will not push people, but rather **establish an environment** for your customers to **resonate with your offer**. Said another way, you should **establish the conditions and circumstances for customers to come to you**.

Also, handle this problem (little demand) at its **cause**: If you want a quick return for your investment in the future, you should order products for which there is the **greatest demand** rather than those that you get at a **good purchase price** but no one wants to buy. Also, do not put mature, orderly ladies behind the sales counter, but rather **someone from your target group** who can **immediately identify with the buyer** and **is on the same wavelength**.

(If you want to solve such problems once and for all, you have to build your business on the **"5 Foundations of Successful Business,"** and all kind of troubles will disappear. You can read more about them in the book, *The Enlightened Salesperson*.)

Energetic Selling

This chapter is a special appendix from a forthcoming book, *Selling with Energy: How to Influence People without Saying a Single Word & Other Secrets*.

It is a complete guide that precisely explains how to motivate yourself to sell and act in any life situation to achieve maximum success so that everyone benefits.

It also gives very specific sales instructions, which have two common attributes: **They are very efficient** and are **beneficial for all participants in the sales process**. Because it is written for businesspeople, the book talks mostly about business situations, but if you change the questions a bit, the same things are valid in your personal life, as well.

Here we go.

What is the primary cause for each success or failure? Energy.

"Everything in life is a battle for energy," said James Redfield, in his book, *The Celestine Prophecy*. It is true!

Here is another interesting truth: If physical (mechanical) laws are valid for all material things, then they are **valid for people, as well**. This energetic influence of one person on another is called **"Energetic Selling"** – because it really acts subconsciously, and everyone can use it – without learning.

Let us look at some of the more important features of energetic selling.

Define Energy

If everything in life is a battle for energy, it is important to know what kind of energy people approve of and what kind they do not.

First, look at how this plays out in a sale, or what each customer desires to have.

Each person wants to have products, services, life situations, and people around that:

1. Offer a solution on **how to stop the drain of their life energy**.
2. Offer a solution on **how to gain more life energy**.

They do not approve of actions, which:

1. **Do not offer this solution,** or offer a solution that is **not effective enough in comparison to the price (energy) we offer for such a solution** (money, time, etc.).
2. Offer a solution that **hides other energies** that we do not want – pressure, dependency, too much work, or too much energy put into achieving particular goals – **in the background**.

It is interesting to look at which **mental states** take or give life energy, which people want, and those they avoid (if possible).

Energy is taken by:

- **Worries**, uncertainty, **a feeling that you have to do something or everything will be wrong**, stressful situations, **loss**, distrust in the future, **a feeling of dependence**, a feeling that you cannot influence your future, **a feeling that people do not acknowledge and appreciate you**, health and emotional problems, **expectations**, yearning, etc.

The consequences of this energy drain are tiredness, despondency, depression, loss of will and the power to work, loss of motivation, a feeling of inferiority, etc.

Energy is given by:

- **Success and positive results** (the solutions to situations) in general, **pleasures**, confirmation of your qualities and acknowledgment, **money**, gifts and prizes, **a feeling that life is turning for the better**, friendships, and a feeling that you are not alone (or that help is available at all times), **enthusiasm**, etc.

The consequences are a good mood, happiness, cheerfulness, peace, joy, love for everything, faith and belief, a feeling of fulfillment, etc.

Applying Known Facts

How does energy relate to facts already known?

You have probably heard that there are only two primary motivators that are most important for people:

- To **avoid pain**.
- To **gain joy and happiness** and have fun.

(The consequences of these are **trust, peace, and an open heart**, which we all want to achieve.)

Can you see how similar these primary motivators are to the facts of energy drain and gain? Actions that **drain energy are those that cause pain** (in the widest sense of the meaning); but if you overcome them or get rid of them, you have more energy.

And the same goes for your clients.

On the other side, actions that **supply energy are those that give you joy and happiness**.

The primary secret of successful interaction with people is hidden here. Everything else you have heard, up till now, was a **consequence** of this universal principle.

"Learning" Energetic Selling

Energetic selling can become very simple once you reach the following state:

- You are **conscious of it**.
- You are **living in your heart**, not amid grudges, doubts, fear, etc. Rather, you have a lot of energy that derives from a high vibration, which enables you to unselfishly help others in resolving their situations. This also means that you have raised your vibration to a level where **you see and respond to everyone from your heart**: No matter what the vibration of the person you talk with, no matter how he or she responds, you stay in your heart. So you have to be **strong** – have a lot of high vibration energy – and **come from your integrity** (integrated with your true self or God within), not allowing yourself to be dragged into another person's energy.
- You decide to **give** your customers this **energy of high vibration**, so they can do with it whatever they please.

This energy of high vibration is showed as **approval of life**.

How do you know when the person you are talking with has gained more energy of high vibration?

It is actually very simple: when they have a **better opinion about themselves** after they leave your company. Also, when they are – **after leaving your presence** – thinking about themselves and not about you. And finally, **when they are more content – and they leave in a higher vibration** – compared to the vibration they were in before the two of you met.

Getting Top Results With Energetic Selling Techniques

The easiest way to make sure you are engaged in energetic selling is quite simple. **Prepare yourself for every meeting** using the following list of guidelines, and check yourself throughout the meeting to make sure you are still on track. Evaluate yourself again after the meeting. This early vigilance will enable you to form a habit of energetic selling. Once you do this, you will always act from the energetic selling platform, and your business will record your successes.

You cannot lose if you do business this way.

In the beginning, it is good to cooperate with a friend, who will be able to neutrally judge when you have moved from the energy of the heart – unselfish desire for the satisfaction of all people's goals – elsewhere: into anger, fear, offense, violence, the need for recognition, concentration on one's own wishes, and so on; in short, into actions that take energy.

The Million Dollar Question
What is your big goal in life?

This may be the most important question you ever ask yourself and answer. Why?

Because the answer to that question is the **blueprint that your subconscious works upon... and everything you strive for** will **come about so as to match this blueprint.**

Here is the most common answer to that question: My big goal in life – or at least a fair part of it – is to **help people.**

Remember this answer. Now we will look at something else that will show you why a lot of people are not successful in business.

Your Search for Happiness Directs Your Mission in Life

Imagine the following: **You are standing on the street giving flowers to all those who pass by.** With no strings attached!

Well, maybe giving flowers to strangers, even though it would make a lot of people very happy, may not be something you can imagine yourself doing. If not, then imagine **giving each of your customers an extra product or service**, worth a lot of money, as a present, a thank you for his or her business – with no strings attached.

In addition, your gift is something the customer really needs urgently, but does not have.

What kind of feeling would this give you?

Probably, a great one. Moreover, you would feel warmth in your heart because you are fulfilling your life's mission of helping people, would you not?

The next question is:

Imagine an everyday situation at your current job. **When you intend to visit a customer to offer a new product or service, do you have a similar feeling of enthusiasm, joy, and happiness?**

Or even more directly: When you stand in front of a customer and are selling, **do you have the feeling you are imposing something on him or her... or unconditionally helping him or her?**

Also, when a customer makes a purchase, do you feel as if **you have given him or her a gift,** or that **you have taken hard earned money out of his or her pocket?**

Are you "stealing" his or her money, or does the purchase bring the customer a value, let us say, ten times greater than what he or she paid for it? (The point is, if you truly believe you give people something that is of much greater value than what they paid for it, you will have no problem offering the product or service at its original price.)

The questions you have just read are the most credible indicator of where you stand in the sale. The same goes for each personal situation whenever you talk or negotiate – just substitute "a customer" with any other person and "the product" with any idea in the examples above, and you will have the same concept.

Such a question that relates to your personal life would be:

Do I have the feeling I am imposing a certain idea on my spouse, or am I supporting him or her the way he or she wants?

Please, answer these questions sincerely because quite often the cause of a bad attitude toward the product, customer, or yourself, is hidden somewhere in here... and it is usually the cause of your lack of success in sales.

The Recipe for Failure in Life

You will not believe how many people have the feeling they are imposing something on someone when they are selling. How can you be successful if:

- You want to help people (your mission!), but you feel like **you are stealing their money.**
- You want to have a good time, but selling is **difficult and you do not enjoy doing it.**
- You want to do something completely different – that is more fulfilling, and because you have a feeling **that is your mission** – not what you are doing now (selling goods).

Do You Need Customer Confirmation?

There is another prevailing characteristic that prevents people from succeeding in sales:

Some people need the customer's confirmation during the sale just to continue.

If you have this characteristic, this is what it looks like when you try to sell. You demonstrate your product to the prospect that is standing in front of you and say:

"This function is unique to this product and is necessary to achieve the kind of quality in operation you should expect from a..."

You now **look at the prospect**. If the prospect nods and bends forward with enthusiasm, you explain further with even more excitement. However, if he or she is calm, or makes even the slightest gesture that might indicate he or she is not quite as excited, you **freeze and panic**.

In your head, you start to say things like: "Oh no! I'm not going to make this sale now. All of my presentation is based on this person being interested in what I am saying and showing right now! But this person doesn't think the way I was told that customers do! He or she is probably thinking of my competitors and their product right now, and what they can offer. Maybe I should mention them in my presentation and let this person know that we're better. What if my explanation of this feature is too complicated and this person isn't following me? Maybe I should repeat the explanation because it is important for me to get approval so that I know we are on the same level."

At this point, **instead of continuing with your presentation, you try to get approval from the customer.**

If you get it, you continue your presentation with relief. But if you do not, you **stop right there and insist on getting confirmation**. Or you continue, but with **less confidence**, enthusiasm, energy, and joy.

In other words – even if you decide to continue, you are stuck. The result that follows is obvious. By the way, this same process also happens when you introduce your other ideas to people, not just in business situations.

You cannot be successful if you cannot get through these and similar obstacles in your life. But the great thing is that you can overcome all of these problems without studying sales techniques, but by changing **energy itself**. It is very simple; everyone can do it, and it brings outstanding results – while **having fun**, not suffering.

(End of summary)

A Step Ahead: The Secrets of Successful Communication

Here is a short summary of the description of the transfer of energy that is used not only when we want the best results in selling, but in effective everyday communication, as well. Although it sounds unbelievable, it works.

We know that the main energy unraveling between two people is **not words, but life energy, which is hidden in the background**. Words can be an explanation and additional motivation for this, but are certainly not the deciding factor.

How can we verify this in reality?

- Has it ever happened that a friend was enthusiastically telling you about a project – for instance, network marketing – and at the time, you had the feeling that it was a **very good thing**? Then after a few days, you thought about it again, and it seemed **somewhat strange and it no longer interested you**?
- Or have you gone into a store where the salesperson showed you an article of clothing you loved... and bought, but when you got it home, **you regretted having bought it**?
- Or, for instance, you went to a football (or soccer, basketball, etc.) game where there were a lot of spectators and an unbelievable atmosphere. Even though you are ordinarily a quiet person, you

sometimes **reacted to the events on the field very impulsively** – like the people around you.

- Or you wanted very much to be involved in a business someone you appreciate and respect is involved with – and probably yields him or her a lot of money – but over time, you realized that this just **is not your path** and were relieved that you did not get into it? Or you even went in this direction, but soon discovered that **such work brings you neither happiness nor profit**, although you were very enthusiastic at the beginning?

All these cases demonstrate the **energy link between two (or more) people**. This is – most easily – possible when the following conditions are fulfilled in both people:

Transmitter (person who transmits a message, for instance, offers something, teaches, etc.):

- The message is **interesting, supportive**, and **up-to-date** for the other person.
- The message was relayed with a **joyful, relaxed energy** (so there is no concealed threat or pressure hidden within).
- **Intensity** is also important: how often the message was relayed – for instance, once a week or three times a day – how deeply it penetrated (how much the other person truly believes in what he or she is transmitting), and how long it lasted (one minute or half an hour).

Receiver (the person connected to the energy of the transmitter or accepting the information):

- How well he or she **comprehends the information** or energy. This is based on how much he or she **trusts the transmitter** and how useful he or she **feels this message** is for him or her at that moment.
- What his or her **existing energy state (vibration)** is: standpoints, patterns, general outlook on life and the theme at hand; that is, does this message **support his or her values, rules, positions**... or repudiate them.
- If all these steps **provoke a joyful expectation**, if all of the preceding conditions are fulfilled, he or she awaits the unraveling of events with a pleasant eagerness.

On the basis of the above mentioned situation, the receiver **more or less opens up to the other person**. If he or she does not open up enough, the message (energy or word) does not transfer from one person to the other, nor can the receiver evoke this energy by himself or herself.

Said another way, the **transmitter and receiver do not resonate with each other**.

Therefore, not only is a skilled and openhearted transmitter important; an **open receiver** is also a requirement for successful communication. When this is the case, they essentially **create an energy channel** by which the message can now travel.

Also, as long as the receiver is closed or unreceptive to happenings around him or her, this energy passes him or her. While the words can be heard, the energy is weak and does not usually stimulate the receiver because words normally influence only the **mind**.

If you want to influence something inside, you need the support of **feelings and the heart**. And this can happen only when a receiver is open and receptive to such energies, which are transported to him or her according to the principle of resonance.

The **energy of respect**, which inspires **trust** in the other person, is a must for this state of openness. In other words, **if we want great communication, both parties should feel the energies of respect, gratefulness, and joyful expectation**. This is the groundwork for successful communication.

Checking the Energy Transfer Hidden Behind People's Words in Everyday Use

We can verify everything mentioned above. For instance, a business partner, whom we greatly respect, calls us. He or she is a very successful, honest businessperson everyone likes, and is also our role model. He or she is known for associating with only the right people. Nearly everyone we know wants to associate with this person, so we are **very honored that he or she called us**.

He or she says, "Hi! I was thinking that you and I should do some business together, if you're interested, of course…"

How would we react? **These words would probably meet a very positive response.**

Let us take another example. An acquaintance that drives a fifteen-year-old car and is always talking about the millions of dollars and big deals that he or she is going to pull off – although he or she has not realized any deals yet – calls us. This person is employed as a driver in some company and has never bought us a drink, but always claims to have conveniently forgotten his or her wallet when the bill comes.

(This is not to underestimate or compare anyone because we must imagine the situation very clearly in this case.)

Let us imagine that this person says the same thing, "Hi! I was thinking that you and I should do some business together, if you're interested, of course…"

Now what would you say? Probably something completely different.

We can see that **the essence is not in the words, but in the openness or receptivity to the other person**; in other words, the essence is in **everything hidden behind the words**.

In the first case, we are very interested when a capable person invites us to do business with them. In the second case, we are not interested even though he or she used the **very same words, tone of voice, and even body language**.

A similar transfer of energy also happens when we are in someone's company and open up to them… **even if the transmitter is quiet the entire time**. (In this case, the person may not even know that he or she is a transmitter for us or that we are connected to him or her.)

The Easiest Way to Reach Fresh Energy, Strength, and Inspiration

In other words, when we energetically open up to someone, we create – as we said – an **energy channel** along which energy flows according to the **higher to lower potential principle**.

This means that usually the person who opens and accepts will drag the other person's energy onto himself or herself.

This can be unsupportive for us – if we connect to people of lower vibrations – or **extremely uplifting and supportive for us**. Let us take a look at the latter.

By establishing an energy channel with a person on a **high vibration**, a double effect is achieved:

The Millionaire Mindset

- **We fall into the energy state (vibration) of the person to whom we opened up**; therefore, we take on his or her outlook on a situation, his or her vision, courage, etc.

- **We simultaneously disconnect from the blockades, obstacles, and standpoints in which we had been located until then**; in other words, we disconnect from our vibration. In this way, we also feel the support on the side of the other person because he or she is providing us with an example and support, which encourages us to dare to think about higher, deeper, more important goals. In a way, we even transfer responsibility for the final outcome to the other person from whom we are essentially seeking confirmation that we are on the right path.

And so we find ourselves in a completely different energy that is fresh and inspiring. Perhaps the other person **did not even say anything**, but widens our horizons (raises our vibration) just by being there. He or she gives us good feelings and the strength to think differently like, "I'm going to think beyond my limits, if I get carried away, so and so will stop me."

And so we could also say that it is, to some extent, **looking for permission to dare to think in new directions** and looking for the outer boundary.

Or said differently, this person takes care of us while we are broadening our consciousness (by lowering fears), potentials, and viewpoints, and allows us to reach the final frontier where such thinking is still realistic.

This happens because inside we (subconsciously) say, "If this person is a role model in this area (i.e., business), I'll try to think as he or she does. How would he or she react now? What would this person do in this situation?"

That way, we can experience **huge progress** because:

- This person **protects us from going astray**.
- This person instills **strength and self-confidence** in us so that we can think differently and move on from our own way of thinking, feeling, and working to a higher level – **out of old standpoints and limits**.

- Finally, we can **connect to his or her vibration when, in his or her company, we feel the person's optimism and trust, and that he or she is not burdened**. (As we describe this example in medicine: We search for faith, hope, and trust in some drug or doctor so that we can let go of our fears and worries, and direct our energy from illness into something else... and therefore allow the body to release a healing energy). In this case, **we allow our consciousness to unleash our true potentials**.

So this person (transmitter), who we are building our new thinking and acting on, has a **very direct influence on us** and is oftentimes **a trigger for our ideas, movements, observations, and discovery (and release) of our past patterns, etc.**

And perhaps **all he or she is doing is sitting next to us, accepting us with his or her open heart, and nodding.**

If we look at how having the opportunity to be in the shadow of successful people changed people throughout history, we become aware of the **remarkable strength of this influence.**

The Easy Way to Learn and Practice This Knowledge

What we have already mentioned is a remarkable way of communicating with others. In this chapter, we will see one of the most appropriate possibilities to **learn and practice it**... and also gain many more benefits. This is especially recommended for those who want to **expand their horizons** and experience **private business firsthand**.

Many people are aware that satisfaction in business and the feeling of completing their mission is priceless. They want to be **free and independent**, and they are ready to invest their time and energy into it. They are also ready to take all the responsibility that goes along with it.

The challenge occurs, however, when you have to choose **the right business** – one that has a future that will bring money as well as enable personal and business growth and development. Well, even this could be done... if it were not for the **investment** that has to be made now!

However, it does not need to be this way. There is the possibility of collaborating in various systems that already have an established business that would not demand a large investment.

We are talking about multilevel marketing (MLM). But **do not be fooled or scared off by the name**. Regardless of whether you have already tried MLM, and are perhaps even involved in one right now, and regardless of how you feel about MLM in general – read this chapter; you might just get a new perspective on things. Besides, you can apply the information in this chapter to **other areas** just as easily, such as choosing your own private or home business.

What Does This Kind of Business Have in Common With Expecting More Out of Life?

As already said, when you decide you want or need to earn more money than your regular job pays, several questions arise: How, where, when, and with whom can I reach my goal – that of earning more money in an honest, pleasant, and effective way – as soon as possible?

In that moment, people need **unprejudiced, honest advice** and **support**. The problem is that many people live in an **unsupportive environment**. Namely, the people around them fill their heads with everything they think these people cannot or should not do. Therefore, a person's decision to earn more money is not well-received by their friends or family because **they know that it means they will have less time to spend together** and that **the business could separate them**.

Does this mean that multilevel marketing is – or is not – the right path for you?

If you do not really feel that kind of business, and especially if you do not feel the products or services you are about to promote, MLM – according to statistics – is possibly not the way you will become rich, happy, or even successful.

Still, **it has great potential to push you forward on your path of life**. We can say that even if this is not the final point of your business self-realization, it is a **great intermediate stage** that can **boost not only your career, but your personal development** (read: vibration), as well.

Multilevel marketing is recommended for the following reasons:

- To **build self-confidence**: Many people have challenges with self-confidence. If you want to be successful in an MLM system, you just have to gain it – willingly or not: The system itself forces you to take actions that will ultimately build your self-confidence.

- To **reduce or eradicate fears**: fear of rejection, fear of making new acquaintances, fear of public appearances, fear of selling, fear of change, etc.
- For a chance to **broaden your horizons and expand your perspective on life**.
- To **instill and develop a desire to work in harmony with others** and support their path – MLM is sometimes the easiest way to gain that feeling because you can only succeed if you support others in becoming successful.
- To **inspire the desire for independence**.
- To **develop and cultivate a desire for leadership and organization**.
- To **attract new, fresh energy** and therefore actively approach your (monotonous) life: New winds will blow into your life when you meet new people and work with them in a new business, helping you move forward.
- To continue to feed the ever-present **need for education and personal growth**: Many MLMs take good care of their members.
- To **learn to stand up for yourself and your ideas and not allow yourself to be misled**: Sometimes you learn just how much you allow others to lead you and how much you define your own life (this applies to MLM systems that impose their ideas on people and do not allow them to follow their own ideologies).
- To **develop and implement self-discipline**.
- To **learn how to be motivated for action**.
- To **learn about yourself** (perhaps even to discover what you do not want to do).

There are as many reasons as there are people who work in MLM systems… and you will probably find even more of them.

Dramatic Change

When you enter the world of sales, you are in for a dramatic change. Suddenly, you are surrounded with people enthusiastically telling you what **you are capable of achieving** (sometimes even with a "little" exaggeration) and who have a clear goal and are ready for action. Therefore, this is a good option if you want to **change your environment** or **break the patterns** of your daily routine.

Many people entered this world shy and without any self-confidence, but overcame these challenges with the help of education and by taking action – they became self-confident and independent links in society.

If we use "our language:" MLM is a perfect environment providing you a good opportunity to **grow from the first level** (doormat) **to the second** (standing up for yourself).

Which Company Is Right for You?

So the question is which MLM system is suitable for you? By the way, some people focus on a single, bad company and judge all others by that company's bad example. For instance, a real estate company goes bankrupt, and it is not long before people say that all real estate companies are bad. Or a bank mismanages the investments of its lenders, and soon people withdraw their money from other lending institutions. The truth is, however, there are good and bad companies in **every** branch and industry.

So do not be misled by the extremely bad – or conversely, the extremely good – performance of one of the companies in the branch.

Recognizing the Right Company

The first real question is, "What does the **right** MLM company mean?" The only fair answer is, **"It depends on the person asking."** Those who choose to work in multilevel marketing are generally divided into two basic groups:

- Those in the first group **seek a new vision of life** (new and creative ways of spending time), search for new goals in life as well as their own identity, want new acquaintances, etc.
- Those in the second group are primarily seeking an **additional or new primary source of income**.

Most people want a combination of both of these things, but are primarily focused on either the first or second goal.

Even the way MLM companies do business is divided in a similar fashion: Their goals are either to develop visions and improve the quality of life of their members... or **easy money**. Well, the truth for most MLM companies is mostly somewhere in between.

The first group **does not emphasize making money overnight**; it has a long-term vision, selected products, quality service, and cares for customers; the second group prefers momentary advantages that benefit the buyers.

Are You Ready for MLM?

So the first questions you have to confront are: **"What do you want to achieve in life, and how do you want to spend your days? What is your vision (goal, mission)?"**

It is important to join an MLM system that sells an excellent product or service – something you can be proud of – because **this product or service will accompany you day after day**, and probably even **become a part of your identity**: Either you will see yourself through the prism of this product or service, or others will.

So ask yourself a question, **"Am I ready to recommend these products and services to my friends, acquaintances, and strangers?"** If the answer is "Yes," then proceed. However, if your answer is "No," then try to look at this from a different – detached – point of view. Is it about your fear of rejection, fear of new things, and so on, or is it about **mistrusting the product (or service) and the company**? It is good to be cautious.

Another thing: **Be careful if you join an MLM system just because you want to compensate for bad experiences from other areas of your life.** The MLM will then become just an excuse and a "shoulder to cry on" (read: an environment for releasing tensions). That is why it is extremely important that you know what you want to achieve – with an MLM system and in life in general – and if you are not achieving it, simply and promptly **walk away**.

Also, **do not allow yourself to be absorbed by the system**. Sleep over all information.

There is something else that you should be careful about: **You can get stuck at that level** – in an MLM – just because you feel you are accepted… while in return, compromising your energy in a way you do not like.

We have already covered that you can only be successful in life if you do the things that make you content and fulfill you, and not by suffering because it's going to get better someday. **Suffering only creates more suffering** – because you are operating from a vibration of suffering, and every action on your part continues to contribute to the critical mass of suffering. As you know, **if you want joy, insert joyful attributes into your life**.

The Secrets of MLM Marketing Success

The main challenge that most individuals encounter in multilevel marketing is: "Why am I so uncomfortable recommending the purchase of a certain product?" We would do well to spend a few minutes with this one.

The answer is clear – you **do not believe that it is the best that can happen to your friends**.

It goes even further: If you cannot persuade yourself that a product is good, how can you – without feeling guilty – persuade others?

The first condition of success is **belief in yourself**, then **belief in the product**, which is offered by your MLM. This is followed by **belief in the company**, which is always in the background (producers, distributors, MLM system), and **belief in the benefits of the purchase for your customers**, of course. (We said all this a few chapters ago when we talked about success in selling; MLM is just another application of it.)

So ask yourself, "Will the customer spend his money wisely by purchasing this product? Is this the best decision the customer can make?" If you believe in the MLM system and the company you are involved with, the answer is going to be a resounding "Yes!"

Listen to your heart and intuition as well as your experienced sponsors (the mentors who are affiliated with you).

Gaining Faith

So you should choose an MLM that deals with products you willingly **use, like, and truly believe in**. For instance, if you are the kind of person who only believes in what you see and what you can hold in your hands, then you should not base your living on trading in securities or financial investments; you need a quality material product.

Here is another aspect to gain that faith.

If you polled a large number of people, who are currently involved in MLM, many will say **they did not completely believe in the beginning, but their perspective changed over time**. It is true, but more often something else happens: When these people became successful, they also earned a larger sum of money.

That way, this **success in selling and the money confirms to them**: "There are people in need (of this product). Now when I see this, I believe." And they, in the process, gradually develop belief in the business.

Therefore, belief in yourself, the product, the company, and the benefits for customers sometimes comes from that success (or from earned money) **as a consequence.**

In this case, it is important to **check if success is luring you in such a way that you will be content** – so that you will persist in a supportive and uplifting spirit long enough for the critical mass of success and faith to prevail over obstacles, worries, and fears. That means that you should **first clarify with yourself if it is even possible that you will one day be enthused about such work** and be content.

If your sponsors promise that you will retire after three years, earn big money doing nothing, travel around the world, and enjoy yourself, you better look at **how many** (the percentage) **of your coworkers**, who working in circumstances similar to those you will be working in, **have achieved this goal** in three years in the system.

Do not allow yourself to be led astray by words and promises. Nor is it good, on the other hand, to compare yourself to people who have not done anything for their success. As always, **your heart will provide the right answer.**

Throughout all of this, you should remember that perhaps **doing nothing and just traveling the world is not your life's mission**; it is probably just about **releasing temporary tensions**. That way, after achieving a big financial goal (that allows you to rest and enjoy earned money), you will – after some time – begin to miss spending your time creatively and constructively.

Asking the Right Questions

There is an excellent method you can use to evaluate and validate if MLM is right for you. We will demonstrate it with a practical example.

A friend invites you to try multilevel marketing, but you are not interested. However, he or she insists and shows you the calculations and pictures from collective travels, all of which you like. The only question you need to answer right now is: **"Is this compatible with my vision of life in every area?"**

Let us assume an answer: Money and traveling probably are compatible with your vision of life – there are not many who would disagree with that statement – but you feel that looking for customers and recruiting new business partners is less compatible with what your vision involved.

How will you decide? **Make another list.** Put all the hard work and everything that goes along with it on one side and all the pleasures, such as money and new friends, on the other.

Do you think you would enjoy such a life? If your enthusiasm does not rise to the level of joy, **is it at least bearable for you?** Could you wake up content while doing this kind of work?

If your answer is negative – and we do presume that you are going to achieve success, travel a lot, and make good money – this matter deserves real consideration on your part.

But if the answer is positive, then you have to ask another question: **"How will this change my life – will it make it better or worse?"** Do not forget the things that come along with the advantages, which your mentors sometimes "forget" to mention, i.e., **added burdens, erratic work hours, less time for friends, family, sports**, etc.

Even if all of this is acceptable to you, you need to adopt a realistic view. Are you **ready to learn**, adopt a new way of thinking, associate with and meet new people, gain the necessary self-confidence, speak in favor of the advantages of the system's products, and perhaps even speak in front of a large audience?

Another thing – **do not put everything else first and forget about the money**. Only you know best how important money is for you. The more important it is, the more time you need to dedicate to this question.

Here is what you can do. As said before, if money is important, **ask your friends and mentors** (before you join) **how much they are earning**. Not how much they will (someday) earn, or they wish they earned, or they have the chance to earn, but how much they are earning now, today.

Now **compare their appearance and presentation to yours**. What would you improve? How would you present the product? To whom would you present the product? If you perform similarly to your friend or mentor, the result will likely be similar; do it better, and the results will probably be proportionately better. Also, if you have a **better audience** (prospects) – for instance, if you know more people who trust you and follow your lead – you will have great chances to achieve more.

But how do you know **how much better** your success is going to be, if you perform better?

You do not. The only way is to try and find out.

Here is the last thing you should never forget: **your life's mission**. Some people have chosen the experience of success for this lifetime, while others have not. Ask your heart, and you will get the right answer.

So if you feel good about it, try it. As you know, **if you never try anything new, you will never get anything new.**

The Meaning of Education in Life

As we have said before, biographies prove that all successful people are, or were, **experts in their respective fields**. They all invested a lot of time improving themselves; and this does not only apply to professional or formal education, but to learning new philosophies, skills, and habits that expand your horizons and help you to grow personally, as well.

Many people have a kind of fearful respect for schools and an uncomfortable feeling regarding them because they remember the past when they had to learn various things they either were not interested in or disliked. This is not the true purpose of education; the point is **to learn things that you recognize as supportive** and as **helpful in building a good and happy life**.

When this happens, you learn with pleasure – or at least without resistance.

The most standard path of education leads people through elementary school, high school, university, and finally to employment – begins after high school or sooner for some – and often even unemployment.

We usually decide the kind of work – the specific position in a company and even the company itself – **we will be doing after this process of education**. It is not strange not find any good use for most of the things we learned in school. Also, professional seminars and courses (foreign language, computer programming, etc.) usually follow when you start working because your bosses want you to fit their picture.

Does this match your idea of an ideal day? Read the following case.

Jean's Story

Jean has always been a good student. After elementary school, she went to high school and excelled in economics. And because she had high ambitions, she continued studying economics at a university. She finished successfully, although a year later than she had originally planned.

She applied for a job. She was lucky because after only two months of interviewing, she was offered a position as the **purchasing manager in a pharmaceutical company**. During those two months, she saw that life was not turning out like in the movies. For this reason, **she accepted the job, although her idea of work was a little different**: a successful businesswoman with a laptop, cellular phone, and meetings where she would negotiate better terms.

Her company registered her for several evening courses. Her schedule looked something like this: phone calls in the morning, rushing around, tension, adjustments, improvisations, responsibility, correcting the errors of others, only two hours of spare time, and two courses in the evening.

We met for the first time two years after she took this job. She complained that this is not how she imagined her life would be. "But this is just the beginning, I'll get used to it in time... and it will get better," she added immediately, like she wanted to apologize for saying something that most people would have kept to themselves.

I asked her: "That's great Jean, but **what if you don't get used to it?** What if you'll still be haunted by desires from your youth and visions of your ideal work?" She didn't say anything, so I continued: **"Do us both a favor and think for a minute about living the next thirty years like this. Do you feel happy?"** She could not remain quiet any longer. "What?! Happy? **I'll go crazy if things go on this way!"**

Together we reached the conclusion that **she would have never accepted this job if she had been aware of the consequences**. But now she could not afford to quit the job because she had a car lease to pay off, rent for her apartment, and other costs.

She could, however, do something else.

The Basics of Working With People...

We made **a list of things she loved to do**. From the list, she chose four things that could **help her earn some money on the side**. Tennis was one of them. We **defined all possible ways** and discovered it would be easiest if she began as a tennis instructor for beginners, in her spare time (weekends). She checked around, and a week later, she had a job as a tennis instructor for children.

To shorten the story – a few years went by. **She married the owner of a big sports center.** She is now managing, organizing, and running the business, but sometimes she teaches, if one of the tennis instructors is ill or otherwise absent. Her husband handles most of the sales, and she makes sure things run smoothly, in harmony. "I'm not sorry for one hour I spent in the previous company," she says, "because if nothing else, I learned something very important: I discovered what was killing my spirit and what I really don't want to do in my life."

What about the education? "I use all my experience quite successfully in the business I am in now. **The university gave me a general view and a broad perspective.** But some things I had to learn in the moment, and I still do. In fact, I'm grateful to the university because **I also learned to be selective** – how to choose the most important information from what was available, as well as how to learn quickly and the ability to adjust to new situations."

All businesspeople and other successful people agree that **learning never stops**. Flexibility and constant adjustment to new directions and circumstances are necessary. If the opposite happens, and you lose your competitive edge, someone can pass you by and leave you behind like just a page in history. Like Ray Kroc, the owner of the McDonald's chain of fast-food restaurants said, **"People are like apples: While they are green, they grow... and when they are ripe, they start to rot."**

> **Find the areas in life and a professional field that you are interested in and enjoy.** Educate yourself, but choose only those subjects that please you and are not just required. If you persist long enough, you can become an expert, and you will have little trouble converting your knowledge into money.

This will be the business that will bring you both pleasure and enough money to live the life you have imagined.

How Do We Check Whether We Will Be Happy in a Profession

Jean, from our story, was lucky because she stepped out of a life she felt pushed into at the time. She found out soon enough that there are **urgent** and **important** things (remember these?) in life; she chose to do what was important, and in doing so, she did the right thing. It is easy to become so blinded by urgent matters that you do not see what is going on and forget about the important things.

Before you decide about your profession, you would do yourself a great service to ask yourself why exactly you want this and **how much you want it**. Do not choose something out of fear of criticism, a profession that is only more favorable to you because of what others think. Is it really something for you?

Take the simple test that Jean did. Imagine your profession. Now think about doing this for the following thirty+ years until you retire. **What do you feel?** Are you happy? Do you think, "It's fine, for a start, but then I'll do something else?"

Be sincere. Perhaps you still have time to avoid a big mistake – maybe the biggest one of your life.

Failing to Choose the Right Profession: What Happens?

If initially you did not choose a business you enjoy, this does not just reflect in momentary dissatisfaction, but everywhere. How can you be happy in life if you are in a bad mood eight hours every day (job) and bring that bad mood home with you? (It is difficult to just switch it off.)

This is – again – how the "Law of Critical Mass" works: The emotions, which we experience most often, will shape our consciousness. In other words – **the longer we experience certain emotions, for instance sadness, suffering, victim-like feelings, etc., the harder it will be to get out of them**.

Gradually, our consciousness will be so stuck in them that we will not be capable of experiencing anything else; or **no other vibrations** – such as beauty, peace, and joy. We will **perceive the world around us from these unpleasant feelings** (because we can resonate only with similar vibrations).

It will seem like the entire world is like this because that is how we will experience it inside.

That is when we really believe that there is no more beauty anywhere... and that it used to be – a few decades ago – much nicer, the people much friendlier, and so on.

> *Choose the kind of work you love doing.*

The secret is that **the world did not change (much) – at least not in the way that we see it – but we did.**

What happens then?

You might just be tempted to search elsewhere, like a pub, for comfort in the evening. Of course, because life is hard – due to your undesirable and stressful work – you will fall asleep worried, dreading the unpleasant tasks that await you tomorrow. Once more, you will take a look back as you have many times before and ask, **"Why me? What am I doing wrong? Why does luck always turn away from me?"**

Such people despair, seek comfort, and complain for two-thirds of their lives, and sleep the remaining time.

What does such a person get from life? **What is the point?**

Even making great money in a business you do not enjoy does not compensate for this, because in the end, **you just buy things to forget about the torment it took to earn this money**. For instance, you reward yourself with a vacation to find rest from your difficult, day-to-day life and to forget your worries.

No matter how you turn the matter, there is only one solution – **choose the kind of work you love doing**.

The Future of Education

The future brings a lot of challenges. One of them will concern education; namely, **the whole idea of education will gradually change**.

This way, people will enjoy their jobs – and lives – much more because **they will be able and dare to choose the right workplace** (that will support their life's mission and therefore their heart's path).

So what will education be like in the new age? How will it be different from that which now exists?

First of all, every **individual's life's mission**, and therefore his or her **potentials and talents**, will be considered.

Each person will be given the chance and opportunity to **freely express himself or herself in accordance with his or her life's mission** – not by placing him or her in a mold, forcing him or her into the education of technique, tactics, and principles just because he or she is good to know because he or she once helped someone else.

Let us not forget that the **goal of all of our activities is to return to the heart, find God in ourselves, and live this energy every time we breathe in and out**. The heart does not need to know why someone else was once successful… **because it conceals the wisdom of the Universe within**. We just have to know how to listen to it (open ourselves to this vibration).

Besides, in the future we will **stop comparing, proving, and affirming**… even in the area of education. Our only goal will be to **begin to live in joy, happiness, and peace** – here and now, without fear of the future, survival, or what others think of us.

That is why the **grading system will also change**. There will be differentiation between whether a person learns by memory or proceeds from unconditional energies – intuition and the mind – and **complexly thinks from high vibration outward**.

In this way, the individual's **values and potentials** will be included in his or her grades. (Perhaps in this way, we will avoid silly mistakes… like when in his school years, Einstein was proclaimed a below-average student with an undeveloped mind.)

From this it follows that education will become an **activity that opens the heart** and **fills people with contentedness, peace, and trust**. Or we can also say: the activity that **establishes a supportive environment and conditions for expressing a person's true self**.

This is only possible when **individuals know their mission, choose it freely, and unconditionally channel energy in this direction**, which the educational system should support unconditionally. Also, the education process will **allow them to grow** – which includes making mistakes without being punished for them – and thus go through all the phases of growth.

For the same reason, students will **need someone with an open heart near them, who will also unconditionally support and help them on this path** (theoretically, and even more so, practically – by example) **so that they will reach their goals quickly, easily, and in the most supportive way.**

And so the critical mass of certain activities and (unconditional) feelings will be achieved quicker and unobtrusively; actually the whole situation **will not look like teaching,** but the **exchange of opinions and the pleasant association of people, who mutually respect each other.**

Also, the energies of **respect, gratefulness, and joyful expectations** will accompany the whole process.

With no intimidation, threats, obtrusive competitions, comparisons, and so on – **only things proceeding from the heart, intuition, and soul will matter.** (That is also why teachers will be **chosen very carefully** because these are people whose vibration – intentionally or unintentionally – conquers and lures students in. **An open heart and high vibration will be the first requirement for a teacher.**)

There will be no champions, or better and worse, because **identity will not be built on the basis of comparison with others, but on consideration of one's own heart.** And so, when tracking his or her growth, each person will be compared only to himself or herself, and will **respect and appreciate others, as well,** because everyone will know that **every person has a heart and intuition and carries God within.**

This is the energy that will become the most important.

This method of unconditional education and motivation is already in use in some new-age companies and among some individuals.

This system is called "Shadowing" and is based on the Five Universal Laws. It is not only the most pleasant method of motivating and educating, but also **the most efficient.** (The results, which we have observed to date with the use of this system, surpass all other techniques. More on how to apply this to your own life is written in the book, *The Enlightened Salesperson*.)

The main advantages of this kind of work are:

- **You do not have to conform to anyone,** study, or be or do anything that you do not want to.
- The system is even **useful for the education and motivation of those who do not want education or are not motivated to listen to or obey anyone.**

As said, the system is based on the unconditional support of the individual's life's mission, and for this reason it is **not understood as a struggle or suffering, but as unconditional help at all levels.**

The Plan for Achieving Wealth, Success, and Happiness

1. Ask yourself and answer sincerely: **"When I do my work, do I have a feeling of giving to people or taking from them?** Does my heart open up at work? Am I expressing my creativity, or do I have to perform this job? Am I adapting to the situation or denying myself?"

2. Ask yourself and answer sincerely: **"What am I doing that I know is not best for me? What should I be doing, but am not?"** Write the answers down on paper… and start taking action!

9. You Always Have the Opportunity to Choose

You always have the chance to choose – not just in your profession, but everywhere. If your decision is right, signs will show you that you are on the right path. You will easily solve challenges and receive help from unexpected people and events, and the thought of achieving your goal will fill you with pleasure and joy.

Do not get discouraged if near the end you get a feeling that something might not be right and you start doubting your decision, because challenges are going to start surfacing right at that point. It is almost always like this… **and you have to hold your own**. This is like the final test to see if you deserve to taste sweet success; if you truly believe, it will not be difficult.

A friend of mine has been working in tourism for many years. Suddenly, he got into severe trouble and was even considering quitting everything. Still, he held out and put a giant effort towards completing his plan. Today he is the model of a successful young entrepreneur, and he knows that he did it right. But at the time it was hard and seemed like everything was conspiring against him.

As long as you feel you are on the right track, **do not ever give up**. You might lose many "friends," but **the most loyal friend will remain with you**. This friend has always been there for you and will be with you to the end, whether you want it or not.

However, I hope that after all this time you became a good friend to it, as well. We are talking about…

The Millionaire Mindset

...your precious heart.

If you manage to win this friend to your side, you will never be lonely, depressed, or sad again. You will not need confirmation from others because you will have enough from yourself.

Be careful not to lose this friend.

Maybe you will feel, occasionally, that it abandoned you, but this is not the case. **Your heart is always there with you to show the way – if you let it.** But sometimes you abandon it so much that it moves to its solitude and lets you discover your own mistakes; however, **when you call it, it always returns.**

Do not try to change your friend to become like you (your intellect) – believe in your heart and give yourself to it. **It will not disappoint you;** you just have to allow it to lead you.

If you resist, you might confuse it: While you are constantly searching for it, you are turning away from it in the very same moment.

Be good to your heart, and you will receive even more love than you have given it.

> *Your heart is always there with you to show the way – if you let it.*

Learn to love all the time. When you learn that, you will not need anything else... because **Love is what you could use to describe everything supportive and uplifting you have learned until then.**

Sri Sathya Sai Baba says, **"There is only one cast – the cast of humanity. There is only one language – the language of the heart."**

Spread love wherever you go. Take it with you, and give it away to everyone. Maybe they do not know they need it... but you know you want to give it. In this way, you can do the most for them and yourself.

Now go.

P.S.: The Story of a Boy Who Achieves Everything... or Miracles Do Happen!

The Story of a Boy

This story is about a poor boy who did not have many chances to succeed in life, at least not from where he started in life. But still...

The boy, now an adult nearing his forties, was born into a family with poor and uneducated parents. His father finished four years of primary school and did physical work in a factory, and his mother was a cook in the city hospital.

Besides that, his father was very good at something else, as well: He was a master at finding some reason to fight with nearly everyone he came into contact with; he was like a magnet for conflicts. Or so it seemed through the eyes of the boy.

The boy grew up in this energy and assumed many of the patterns himself. Well, this is actually the purpose of the School of mysteries on Earth: **Parents are the ones who remind us which unsolved energies we carry in ourselves – but we have decided that we will balance them in this lifetime** and move forward in our spiritual growth.

That is why there were a lot of challenges in the boy's life. Among all things, he was not too enthusiastic about going to school and learning, and his parents just did not know how to teach or motivate him.

He barely made it through elementary school. In the seventh grade, he faced even more challenges when he was moved from a city school to a village school, where as the new kid in town he was the target of laughter and bullying from his stronger schoolmates, which greatly affected his self-image.

So he was living from day-to-day, waiting for better times to come. Although his parents did their best to make his life easier, they could not offer him many of the things he wanted. But inside he had something, which distinguished him from others: **He never succumbed and allowed sorrow or a lack of faith to get the best of him and cause him to lose hope for a better tomorrow.**

After finishing elementary school, he **decided to become a salesman.** He chose this profession because he was impressed by the capability of certain people to close the big deals with only one "tool" – their brains. The school was in a larger city, which also meant more freedom from his very strict father.

Searching for Identity... and Freedom

At the same time, there was something else going on in the boy's mind: **He began to see himself as an independent individual with his own identity** (and no longer an extension of his parents). But his self-image was not healthy... at all.

He wanted to correct his negative image of himself and the cruel world that brought him such unpleasant situations – which were the consequence of many physical strikes from his father and schoolmates – with cigarettes and beer. In so doing, he wanted to be different, but at the same time, he wanted to be included in the "in crowd," although cigarettes and beer were never to his liking. **He had hoped to gain the respect of those around him in this way**, but above all he wanted attention from girls, just like every other young boy who is not exactly the center of attention wherever he goes.

Soon after he had begun school, he made another drastic decision: He **gave up on school** because he was disappointed with the program. Namely, the tradition of the old school was such that the apprentice had to do all the hard work in the warehouse to harden up and become a good trader. So he mainly – as a part of school practical work – had to do hard labor in a warehouse rather than learning sales and working with people, which was his desire and goal.

And he did all the labor for free... no more! He thought, "If I have to do this hard work, I should at least be paid for it."

He became a physical worker without any education... at the age of fifteen.

The Story of a Boy Who Achieves Everything...

Day after day, getting up at 5 a.m. and going to work, **he knew that this was not all that he could achieve in life**. On the inside, he felt that he was born for something greater and not for the work that he was suffering through now.

But he also knew that he must take the first step if he wanted to change his life – he needed to **break the cycle he was trapped in**. He realized that if he **just waited and did nothing, he would miss something precious and his path would take him to the same inevitable destiny as his parents** – an undesirable workplace, lack of money, lack of time for himself and his family, unrealized desires, nervousness, stress, fears, etc.

And his parents and childhood clearly revealed that he had three main, very big problems (which outwardly showed themselves as his external destiny): **lack of money, problems in communicating and in relationships with people, and an inadequate education.**

He had the feeling that **most of his problems were derived from these areas**. He felt that if he could **successfully solve these three problems, he would take a big step forward in life** (and move forward in his primary destiny, as well).

A Big Turning Point

After thorough consideration, he decided to take his life into his own hands. As simple as that. Because he had a weak body, he **became actively involved in sports** – athletics, bodybuilding and martial arts. His self-confidence grew with his physical strength, and he was not getting beaten up anymore either.

His uncle, a professional sportsman working as a fitness and karate instructor abroad, helped him a lot. He had a very special approach for motivating the boy to train hard: He often **promised the boy a reward for his progress**. For instance, if he lifted more weight above his head or did an especially difficult karate move correctly for his uncle's next visit, he would be rewarded.

This was an excellent way to motivate the boy to set goals, which brought him to the seaside for the second time in his life, at the age of sixteen. (The first time, he had gone to the sea on a school trip.) He took the trip with his uncle, who awarded him for passing a test for a higher belt in karate.

There was also progress in the boy's thinking regarding his job; six months of toiling at physical labor after leaving the school of commerce were enough to make him realize that **he would not do well in life without education and knowledge.** So he registered at a vocational school before taking that trip to the seaside.

At the end of his first year there, his name was published **as one of the best students** in the newsletter of the company that gave him his scholarship. He completed school successfully and **began working full-time**, but new disappointment awaited him here: His new job was not much better than what he was doing before when he had no education. His salary was – as was appropriate for a beginner – especially small. **He started working two shifts** to earn more money, but was still making less than the average income at that time.

As far as finances went, he knew exactly what he wanted: **to earn enough money to at least live a good life and not be burdened with day-to-day expenses, as had happened in his youth**. The thought of living a life in debt, struggling to make ends meet, worried him. He had witnessed this at home all through his childhood.

In his desire to earn more, he made an agreement with his boss. He would continue working two shifts – sixteen hours per day – but instead of getting paid for his extra work, his boss would give him **the next month off**. He planned to use this time for some other work.

His request was immediately approved. He now had one month off. But how would he put it to good use?

A Month of Vacation That Was Not a Vacation

And so he decided to use this spare month to **work abroad**. He traveled to his uncle's place in Germany, where he performed odd jobs. He noticed that he could earn much more shoveling snow than he did working in the Slovenian factory where he was employed.

He mainly supported himself as an athletic masseur and personal fitness trainer. This way he also improved his command of the German language and learned about the different business habits of successful Germans. During his first month there, he earned more than he had earned in the factory with all his overtime hours.

Work and sports activities abroad enabled him to meet many successful people, who **taught him to think differently**. One of his great wishes was also fulfilled – he met Arnold Schwarzenegger, who gave him hope for continued work in the sports and personal fields.

With the help of his friends, he received his first well-paid contract as a sports model. **A poor boy from the country finally got lucky.**

This is how everything started. His dreams came true – fast sports cars, motorbikes, travel, expensive clothes, beautiful girls, admiration of others, etc. But...

Making so much money brought the poor boy, who had never before tasted the sweets of money, into a new world. **His lack of self-confidence, low self-esteem, and the opportunity to finally show who he was, uncovered other characteristics he was never aware of – conceitedness, arrogance, and self-centeredness.**

However, he began to live his dreams. His life finally got meaning, and the boy had the feeling that he was mastering his fate.

He was well on his way to completely losing his identity.

Life Always Directs Us to the Right Path

And so life, in all likeliness, probably would have continued. But when God has bigger plans for us, He will use all means to get us on the right path... despite the fact that we may think that we are the masters of our destiny. We **are completely powerless before God,** or the **life's mission** we are intended to fulfill.

The boy had been a big fan of fast motorbikes since he was a child. Now he finally had the money to buy the best one. And that is how it happened.

During an innocent Sunday drive towards the coast, a bus driver ran a stop sign, and **the boy crashed directly into him at high speed**. He was told that he was **very lucky to have survived at all**. Diagnosis: broken left knee, torn nerve in his right leg, and the prognosis of the possibility of a stiff left leg (because he may never be able to bend his knee), and a paralyzed right leg.

His left knee was operated on and the necessary screws and wires were inserted, as well. Doctors also tried to revive the nerve in the right leg with ordinary electrical impulses.

This accident changed his internal and external view on life. Because of his massive blood loss at the scene of the accident and other side affects, he literally lost about twenty pounds of body mass overnight. **Only a shadow remained of the athletic, decisive young man.** His sports career, clear vision, and path to Paradise (money, fame, women, etc.) – all vanished in a flash. Yesterday, he was living every young man's dream; now he found himself in a living hell.

His whole world had crumbled.

What would he do so powerless, with no significant education, money, or friends? What would he do with his life? Who would even like such a boy? He had every reason to withdraw, feel sorry for himself, mourn the beautiful moments he had lost, and look into an uncertain future in fear.

But he did not give up. He believed. With both legs in plasters, he conscientiously exercised every day in the hospital because **he believed that he would not only walk someday, but also do everything that people with healthy legs do**.

His health improved, and after a month and a half, he left the hospital on crutches. Hoping to heal his wounds faster, he went to the coast. He had trouble walking among people with his crutches, but that was not the worst: **He also had big psychological problems.**

Before the accident, he could beat most good athletes in running and do squats with four hundred pounds on his shoulders – now he could not even walk without crutches. **He felt useless to society.** He would have loved to hide and for this reason **felt even more hurt by the pitying looks from passersby, who were curiously watching a tall, unhappy muscle-man trying to act as normal as possible.**

After six months, he stopped using crutches and was able to bend his left knee a little. The long rehabilitation of his paralyzed right leg began. Every day for more than a year, he had physical therapy where he regularly exercised his knee and received electrical stimulation to revive the dead nerve.

Because of his pessimistic doctor's prognosis, the twenty-year-old boy had only two choices: to either **give up** or **persist**. He chose the latter… and chose to replace his pessimistic doctor!

We Should Never Give Up – Faith and Endurance

He began inquiring about the best neurosurgeon. When he found him, he tried to make an appointment, but learned from the nurse that the doctor was very busy and would not be available for several months and that there was no chance of being treated by him sooner. Disappointed, he opted for a desperate move: He went to the nearest payphone, searched for the doctor's number, and called him directly.

His endurance and belief paid off – the doctor himself answered the phone. The boy related his sad story and asked him for help. **The doctor agreed to see him right away!**

Immediately following his examination, he was admitted into the biggest hospital in the country. The nerve operation lasted six hours, but the surgeon managed to mend him. But this was only the beginning – it was a long journey to (possible) complete recovery.

Despite his efforts, although he could not live the same life he once lived – much less perform his previous job – because he had to use orthopedic devices, he did not lose his determination. **He continued to practice and registered to study further.**

After several years, his injuries partially healed, and he continued working. What is more, despite doctors' fears that he would never walk again, **he received the bronze medal in the national bodybuilding competition** just a few years after his critical traffic accident.

Finally, the sun began to shine for him in the emotional area, as well. Because of the suffering he had endured during the accident and his recuperation, **he changed his life philosophy and began to look at the world and people in a different light**. That is how he met his wife (from whom he has two wonderful children and still lives happily today), who **accepted him as he was at that time with all her love. A new chapter in his life began.**

Nothing Will Ever Be the Same

He began working in a factory again. Even though he had a newly acquired education, he could not get an acceptable job – just promises. After a few short trips abroad, where he earned extra money doing what he did before, **he made a decision.**

The Millionaire Mindset

One morning, he went to his boss with no previous announcement, thanked him for his understanding, and expressed his desire to **quit working there**. His boss was irritated and asked, "Are you aware of the consequences of your decision? Do you know how hard it is to get a job nowadays? Do you even know what you want?"

He answered with words that later became his motto in life: "You're right. Maybe I don't know what I want… but **I definitely know what I don't want!**"

He decided to try swimming in business waters because freedom was very important to him. He said to himself, "If I can earn at least as much as I from employment, and if I can do what I want, when I want, **I'll be satisfied**. If I am able to earn even more…"

Soon after this decision, he received a business opportunity that offered even better conditions than working abroad – intellectual work in **multilevel marketing**. With endurance and all the life experiences he had gathered, he quickly achieved **amazing results**.

He soon organized and led a larger group of people… more than a thousand. He gained knowledge from the fields of insurance, the stock market, banking, and finance. Above all, he acquired knowledge from management, communications, and sales, which he successfully used to train people.

> Because of those experiences, he had a great epiphany: "If you wish to be satisfied and successful in business, it is important to **do work you enjoy**. You can find such work by doing work you do not enjoy and gaining new wisdom with every experience. **The secret of success and advancement is to perform every job with love and dedication even though it may not be your dream job or the work you initially desired**… because this is how you get noticed and gain valuable experiences and friends who truly respect you."

Soon after, he and his friend constructed **their own office building**, **established a company**, and opened a fitness center, and **fulfilled some of their material desires**.

Despite all the challenges in his life, **the boy succeeded**. No family, circumstances, or health problems stopped him or weakened his desires. He proved that **almost anything is possible**.

If he was able to overcome such obstacles – with faith, hope, and trust – and recover to a healthy, happy, and settled life, then (under normal circumstances, when a person's life's mission makes it possible) almost **anyone** can achieve this. **You only have to follow your heart's desires and look to each new day with belief and trust.**

This is the advice of that boy. And I know his story very well...

... because I am that boy.

But the story does not end here; this is where it actually begins.

The Second Chapter in Life

I now had a new goal before me.

An inexplicable desire to learn more about myself unfailingly dragged me out into the world. I began to ask myself: "Where did I come from? Where am I going? What is the sense of my being on Earth, and what is my mission here?"

I had nearly traveled the world to get those answers until I decided to find the truth in a rare and beautiful place where I had never been – India. I heard an interesting story there, which brought me close to another great wise man.

Unbelievable Experiences – Miracles

In 1990, a wise man in the South of India decided to build a hospital specializing in the most difficult heart, eye, and urologic surgeries. The hospital was supposed to open a year later, in 1991.

Experts from Switzerland who were evaluating the possibilities of realizing this project shook their heads and had several concerns. They said the **climate was not appropriate for such a hospital**, and using the latest technologies they would need **at least seven years to build such a hospital** in Switzerland.

The first three months of 1990 passed and construction had not yet started. Everyone asked the wise man if he had changed his mind. No, he was still sure that they would start building soon and that the hospital would be finished in the agreed time. **Then miracles started to happen.**

The first one was that after five months of planning, **the hospital was built in seven months**. The second one is that it is technically well equipped to run for the next one hundred years. They perform between **3,000 – 3,500 surgeries each year** (information from 2005).

The third miracle is that treatment is **free – for everyone**. More than ten thousand people are on the waiting list for surgery, and some of them are from foreign countries.

The costs for building the hospital were well over fifty million dollars. Some of the distinguishing characteristics of this hospital are peace, serenity, love, and the respect of doctors – some are world-renowned experts. In addition, even the World Health Organization (WHO) recognized and praised this hospital for its successes.

The wise man who founded this hospital built another, even bigger (at another location). He also established several hundred **educational institutions** (primary schools, middle schools, universities, etc.). Under his direction, waterworks that **bring healthy drinking water into seven hundred villages or to about five million people in Southern India** were also built. Even today world-renowned politicians visit him, achieving significant economic results domestically afterward.

His name is Sri Sathya Sai Baba.

The School of Miracles

His educational program, Sai Education in Human Values, is already used in **more than one hundred countries** throughout the world. Some countries have even **accepted it as part of their educational system on a national level**. One such school, which is attended by problematic children who were expelled from classical schools, was established in Harlem, NY (USA).

In one school year, these children became not just good, but even excellent pupils under extremely harsh grading criteria. Again it became evident that **Love, mutual respect, and true care for humanity overcome all troubles**.

> Sai Baba says, "**What use is all the global knowledge, if we cannot establish values with it?** If there is purity in the heart, it is expressed as beauty in the character. If there is beauty in the character, there is peace at home. If there is peace at home, there is order in the nation. If there is order in the nation, there is **peace in the world**."

A great number of doctors cooperate with him. One of them is Dr. Aggerwal, who is well known for inventing a small device that uses

vibrations to cure. The device reads the magnetic record, which is the same as the sick organ's, and then creates the original vibration of healthy tissue, which is then consumed with sugar pills or water.

He has trained hundreds of people around the world under the condition that they would treat people as he does – free of charge. His vision is that **people could heal themselves in the future.**

The Time of Miracles

We can look at miracles in different ways. Some do not believe in them, others are enthusiastic, yet others worship such a person, falling on their knees before him or her.

My wife, Moksha, learned about miracles first hand when she was invited to a personal conversation with Sai Baba. He gave her a golden ring with three diamonds, which he simply **materialized**. (In addition to the ring, he also gave her the gift of his signature with which he blessed the first, shorter version of the book you are holding in your hands. The blessing may be found at the beginning of the book.) Or he took a ring from another dimension, as some experts say. This is not unusual for him. I know people who have golden or silver rings or other things such as chains, watches, and vibhuti (holy dust that has healing and above all transformational effects), which he donated to them.

But this is far from all that this wise man is capable of.

Here is an experience I witnessed. With an audience of over ten thousand people from all over the world, he materialized the smallest version of *The Holy Bible* ever known with gold plated pages.

Interestingly, people from various religions and cultures from the entire world were present at this event, which took place during Christmastime. **We were all like one big family.**

Sai Baba works at all levels. Besides the spiritual (nobody comes back the same after having visited him), which is most important, he also contributes very concrete projects (like the hospitals, water system, and educational centers already mentioned) **with which he improves the material world and cares for people's well-being.**

Miracles Happen at Every Step

This was not the end of the miracles on the journey to India. While on my way home one typical day, I made an incredible internal connection with Sai Baba (or with some "strange" energy that knows much more and much deeper answers than my mind does). Although I was sitting on the terrace of my Indian friend's house, I spoke with Sai Baba as though he were sitting in front of me. **Whatever I asked, I received the answer.**

Among other things, I found out that I would not be able to sell the business offices, which I had just begun selling intensively in Bled, Slovenia. Furthermore, he told me that my friend Rado, who was employed in another company at the time, would take the offices under management. This experience seemed really incredible, so I checked it out immediately after returning home from India.

I told Rado what I had heard, and he said with obvious surprise, "I've been thinking about that for quite some time, but did not dare mention it." So we soon agreed on the terms, and Rado began a successful career as an entrepreneur. He also made huge progress in his personal development with this step.

The second revelation I received during meditation was even more incredible. Prior to my departure to India, I had just begun negotiations with one of Slovenia's leading companies in vacuum cleaner sales. They wanted to expand their activities to neighboring Croatia and chose me to lead the entire project.

While meditating, I asked about developing this business and received an unclear answer: Things would unravel, but nothing like I expected. Nevertheless, I should keep the promises I had made to that point.

Upon my return, I did everything that we had agreed on, which was in my power, but something always went wrong. I had had enough – this was not the business for me. So I stepped out voluntarily.

Three months later, the general manager of the company called me and asked, "How did you know?"

"How did I know – what?" I replied.

"You mean you don't know what happened?"

He told me about the huge problems they had in Croatia because the vacuum cleaners had a defect – a malfunction of a vital part. A majority of buyers made a claim against the product, resulting in additional costs, negative business references, distrust, and dissatisfied customers in general.

The third disclosure I received, but did not understand then, was that I was to describe my life in a book. A friend reminded me about that a few days ago, when he suggested that I would best explain the experiences I want to share with people by telling my story.

Was it all just imagined, a coincidence, or something else? Whatever it was, for me, **this information was a miracle** that spared me many problems.

Exploring the Secrets of the Future

During that same journey to India, I experienced something else that has remained etched in my memory.

One of the many mysteries hidden in India is an ancient library in Bangalore. It stores 3,665 writings and some say it is 5,300 years old. Each of these writings is made of 365 palm leaves, which are 18.9 inches long and 2.4 inches wide. Writings are densely written with minute handwriting in the Tamil language. When these leaves become too fragile – which happens about every hundred years – the wise men recopy all the writings.

Thousands of years ago, in these writings, **mysterious writers wrote about the lives and destinies of many people who had lived before them or yet to be born.** The most important information was taken out of a lesson from an Indian wise man whose name was Shuka Nadi. The name "Shuka" means God's wisdom, and "Nadi," a certain moment in life.

Tradition says that this text is the copy of God's plan, and that all knowledge, which has appeared in the world from the beginning to the end of creation, is kept there. The most puzzling aspect of this library is that it does not store the data of all people ever born, but of those who come, will come, or did come to Bangalore to find their destiny. It is possible to learn the past, present, and future of people who visit the library.

The events revealed in reading the pages are important for the internal and external growth of the individual, even though they refer to very concrete, practical themes.

Discovering the Story Written About You Thousands of Years Ago

We announced our visit to Bangalore just before we left for India. When it was my turn for discussion, an elderly gentleman, who was reading the palm leaves, told me some information from my present life. Although we had never met before, he knew a lot. He told me some details from my previous lives and missions in future years, all the way up to my death. He asked me if I wanted to learn about the time of leaving the body, which he also told me about.

The information I got was very compatible to what I had received through past-life regression (explorations into previous lives through various techniques), astrological cards, and different wise men. I was even more impressed, when I discovered that my wife, who had had a conversation with the same man six months earlier, had been given the **exactly same information** about our future.

The aforementioned texts of Shuka Nadi, which prophesize the **future, are based on universal principles, written in Vedic texts**. These principles presume:

a) A Connection between thought and time.
b) An awareness of each moment in the present time.
c) Using a **mantra** as a seed for personal development.

Warnings of radical changes, which will happen on the planet in the coming years in consequence of our **disrespect for nature and natural principles**, are also written on the palm leaves. But even in the darkest moments, Shuka Nadi appeals to the **restorative forces that reside inside each of us**. This is the seed **of supportive and uplifting thinking**, which can bring radical changes and common happiness in **light of that, which today we call unconditional love**.

The fundamental message of the palm leaves is conquering egoistic visions because of which we are caught in regional, national, racial, social, and thinking molds/forms. We must overcome the limitations of our thoughts and think of all people as one loving family. This is easiest if we mutually help each other come to the destination of our journey – **back to Oneness**.

It is not about helping others at the expense of denying yourself or "buying love" from others, but not turning away from them and working unconditionally from high vibration for the good of all.

But we do not need to take the first plane to India or anywhere else to recognize our own destiny or find the information we seek. **All the answers are inside of us.** Well, if we are unable to help ourselves, or want the advice of an expert, we can still go to people who are already one step further and can successfully read our secrets.

A number of years ago, an astrologist named Zorina made an astrological chart for me, and it is incredible how everything happens, as with any well-prepared plan, just as she said and wrote back then. After Zorina, the astrologist, Katja, managed the same – differently, but still convincingly. I am always surprised how everything overlaps. Or the remarkable fortune-teller, Marta, who can forecast future events from coffee grounds with unbelievable precision… and gets everything right. (At least until now she has, and not just for me, but also for everyone I know.) **Miracles.**

Magic in Thailand

We experience all kinds of miracles – or magic – every day. We may view situations as more or less magical, but at the end of the day, we should be thankful for each and every moment.

Let me describe an experience that my friend and I are truly grateful as it brought unexpected relief in pain.

It happened on the island Koh Samui in Thailand.

My friend Jani, an architect who decided to travel to this warm place because he was overworked and had severe pain in part of his spine, was with me on that gorgeous island. The second day of our stay on the island, he read the book *Journey of Souls*. A chapter that discussed **not being afraid of strangers, who bring messages from the Creator's kingdom**, attracted his attention.

While he was reading that chapter, a man around fifty appeared. He told Jani that he was from Japan. Although he could not know anything about Jani's problems, he wanted to bless him in the sea. Jani complained that he could not go into the water because of the severe pain in his back. The stranger insisted and headed between the waves completely dressed. Jani remembered the chapter about strangers and followed him into the water.

The Japanese man showed him how to put his hands together to pray. Jani obeyed. In an unintelligible language, the stranger started to pronounce words, which Jani repeated. Shortly after, the stranger dunked Jani's head under the water and they prayed again. The stranger warned Jani never to repeat the ceremony. He took a small notebook and pencil out of his wallet and asked Jani not for money, but for personal information because he wanted to remember him.

After recording the information, he said good-bye and ran along the coast. Jani watched him and then turned away to look where I was. After a while, still a bit confused and surprised about the experience, he turned to look for the Japanese man again. Although the entire coastline was visible and you could see for miles, Jani could not see the man. He just vanished. Jani soon felt **that some of his pain was gone and the next day he was completely cured.**

Something More Than They Taught Us

Why do I describe stories about miracles? For me these miracles were only proof **that something else exists,** something more than our parents told us about or schools taught us. The miracles we experience every day are intended to make us **aware of the meaning and mystery of living** on Earth.

Do not let my personal experiences with miracles or Sai Baba mislead you. They meant a lot to me, and I needed them in a certain moment, so that I could carry on with my development. **All things are presented to us with a certain purpose, which is hidden behind the miracles themselves.** DeMello said that the goal is to **wake up** and learn that the Universe and human beings, as part of it, have a much more important meaning and task than we usually realize.

But people are too often **directed to the event itself rather than the message it brings.**

What Interests Us Most

This was clearly illustrated by an adventure that happened to me some years ago. I was invited to the introduction of a new book that described the secrets of the Resurrection of Jesus. With the help of the Cloth of Turin, which covered Jesus after crucifixion, **the 2000-year-old secret is revealed.** The editor of this book wanted to tell us how we could learn more unexplained things about this historical personality by using modern technology. (They created Jesus' picture according to the prints using radiocarbon-date research.)

The question of an older person followed: "Does that mean that modern technology will help us learn **what Jesus ate**?" Without waiting for an answer, another obviously enthusiastic lady said, "Excellent! So we can establish **Jesus' blood type.**"

Extraordinary questions. Suddenly what Jesus ate, his blood type, etc. became very important. **But nobody was much interested in what He was teaching.**

We often miss the point of a message because we want to be similar to big people in unimportant things – the way they walk, dress, look, their wealth, etc. – instead of being similar to that person for **what makes them great**! In *The Holy Bible* it is written that Jesus warned us how to watch for phony prophets, who are wolves coming to us in sheep's clothing: **"You will know them by their fruits."** (Matthew 7:16)

He also said something else very interesting. Namely, what a spiritual person who is trying to be close to God should be like, "By this all men will know that you are My disciples, **if you have love for one another."** (John 13:35)

This is very important for all who practice spirituality. **The goal is not in the performance of the technique, but in loving one another.** If we do not do this, we are distancing ourselves from the goal regardless of everything else.

We Do Not Have Time for Miracles

In this consumption-driven society, material wealth is often prized above all, and we do not have enough time for God or the Creator, who is **living in us, and everywhere around us**.

Still, we need so little to experience a new moment that directs our attention to the greatness of life and our important role in it. Because of my heavy schedule of professional commitments, I too find myself in situations where I **forget my path, mission, and myself**. But never to the point that I would allow events to deter me from searching for the Truth.

If you want to experience miracles, you first have to be open to them, and then recognize them in your daily life. The easiest way to experience a miracle is to **confront your life and lovingly accept each situation it brings as a gift**.

Like Paul Solomon said a while ago, **"Two life forces exist in the world – love and fear. Where real unconditional love is, there is no room for fear." One excludes the other. We cannot love someone and at the same time fear for that person because **unconditional love does not know fear**. The Apostle John said: "There is no fear in love; but perfect love casts out fear, because fear involves punishment, and the one who fears is not perfected in love." (1 John 4:18)

Karma and Destiny

I realized that all the experiences, which often **affected me on a personal level** – particularly the thought that I would be crippled – were gifts for which I am thankful today because they directed me to the **true guidelines of life**. Besides, I probably would not be able to understand other people or be in resonance with them without these experiences.

If I look back at life, I notice that **time and time again, I received opportunities for growth**; of course, at the time, I did not call this a miracle, but a problem. Today I am realizing how every problematic situation shaped me and **prepared me for the new tasks to which I otherwise would not have measured up**.

(Today when I encounter a problem, I still ask myself: **"Where does the gift await me? What must I learn from this? How do I ensure that this won't happen again in the future?"** Also, when tackling anything, I ask: "Is my work in harmony with the first [basic] intention? Am I doing my work happily, or am I denying myself? Am I working so as to 'spread the Light' in all people, or am I working unfairly and narrow-mindedly?")

But I did not embark on this path alone. Besides my family and friends, big-hearted people also helped me. Although they may not have stood physically next to me, I always felt their proximity.

I would like to introduce to you some remarkable people I had the pleasure of meeting on my path.

People Who Helped Me on My Path

The first is Stephen Turoff, an English surgeon, who is love personified. But he is also an excellent surgeon, who **operates without narcotics or instruments**. He lives in England and heals people around the world, and he also enjoys coming to Slovenia. He operates with the help of so-called psychic surgery, which is performed by Masters working through him. (Anyone who has not experienced this first-hand will probably have a hard time imagining the process.)

In the waiting room, where there are a lot of people from all corners of the world, one notices Sai Baba's photographs and the vibhuti, which simply appears on the photos.

My wife had serious problems with her spine. She went through all sorts of tests and examinations in hospitals, but the diagnosis was always a clean bill of health, although she suffered unbearable pain.

Stephen performed the aforementioned surgery on her while I stood next to him. I watched in astonishment as his fingers vanished into part of her spine. Without a drop of blood – and mostly without any instruments, just his hands – he **penetrated the skin and operated on her internal organs**. Finally, he sews (without any instruments) the wound afterwards, and you get a typical scar – for a few hours! After that, the scar is gone, along with all traces of the procedure.

After the operation, my wife felt relief, and the pain was gone. My experience of the operation is similar.

The second person I would like to introduce to you is the shaman teacher, Foster Perry. He has been a regular guest to Slovenia lately. At his group therapy sessions, he achieves outstanding results by **cleaning certain bonds and obstacles from the past** that have collected in the physical body, energetic body (aura), and energetic centers (chakras). The most amazing discovery is why someone has pain in a certain part of his or her body. He says that our energetic body still holds wounds from our previous lives (this is easier to understand if we believe in reincarnation, which means the soul is eternal and simply changes its "temporary home" – the human body). Although his work seems superficial, the **results are excellent and very deep**.

The third is Thomas Keller. His gift is in direct communication with the world of Angels and the Creator. He is a student and broadcaster of the knowledge of Paul Solomon, a nominee for the Nobel peace prize. Thomas emphasizes that every person has his or her own individual Truth, which must be respected. There also exists a **cosmic truth**, which Thomas calls **faith, hope, and love**. Individual discussions with him are outstanding because he answers all your questions with the help of Angels.

These are just some of the world-renowned healers I have had the opportunity to meet.

My path always crossed theirs when it was time for them to help me with life's turning points. I am going to describe a few that are related to my three big problems (communication and relationships, money, and education).

Challenges and Life's Turning Points

I remember one of my **first public appearances**. In those days, communication represented an exceptional problem for me, so I got a lot of tests (or opportunities for growth). Here, one of them is described.

When I got the opportunity in network – or multilevel marketing, I **attended educational seminars regularly**. They took place abroad in foreign languages. What was interesting was that the director appreciated and obviously had great faith in my rhetorical abilities from the very start.

Once, when he was stuck in traffic, from among all the old pros who had been active in the system much longer than I (and had attended many more educational seminars), he **chose me to begin the seminar instead of him**.

This is a very demanding task because if you do not lay a good foundation at the beginning, everything goes downhill from there. Although until that time **I had never really lectured** – and especially not in a foreign language – **I accepted the difficult task**. The auditors were mostly college educated, which was an **additional burden** for me because I had only had a secondary school education.

However, I gave it my all... and **in an hour and a half, told everything that I had remembered from the director's two-day seminar**; well, in slightly altered sequence, but nevertheless...

The seminar was a complete fiasco.

But it carried within it the seeds of growth: **I began to study things** because how everything turned out mattered to me.

I had the same obligations in similar multilevel marketing systems later. **Wherever I went, I was surrounded with people** with whom I was pushed into harmonizing relations through communication, and **I lectured everywhere**. In this way – whether I wanted to or not – I was improving in the area of my perpetual problem – communication and relations.

Later, the publisher of my first book gave me a book entitled *Public Appearance Skills*, which I was happy to study thoroughly. Shortly thereafter, a representative from a political party called, asking if I could prepare a communications seminar for him. This is another reason for devoting my attention to the topic.

Soon after I successfully completed seminar, **an esteemed institution from the capital of Slovenia asked me to take over their regular seminars on rhetoric and communications**.

Actually, life itself simply led me – because I never sent any inquiries or asked for work or for any of these jobs.

Through all of this I also grew in my relationships with others, both in the personal and professional areas. In my life, I have to this point done **nearly everything in tightly knit partnerships**: With one partner I have a family, with another an office building, with the third a book, and with yet another a fitness center. These relations also sculpted me through experiences so that I grew in these two areas (communications and relations) everyday.

Meanwhile, one of my greatest tests, which recurred many times, was **striving to help people so that they would not suffer**. Time and again, I received energy in return: "You are here to save only one soul – your own. Occupy yourself with yourself, and with others **only when they ask you for help**. If they don't ask you for help, **keep your heart open, love them, and trust that they will make it on their own**."

Even today I am learning to act on my surroundings with an open heart and trust. At the same time, I am aware and accept that I cannot always be in high vibration. Sometimes I fall down, and unpleasant feelings arise within me. I am finding, however, that this processing time from the point when I realize this and begin consciously filling the critical mass of high vibration, which brings me back to pleasant feelings, is progressively shorter. In this way, I am not ill-humored months or weeks, but only for a few hours or even minutes.

Where this will lead me – in all areas: partnerships, business, neighborly relations, and so on – I do not know. I want – and also work on – having an open heart most of the time; because for me, this is the only measure of success: **A successful person is someone who succeeds at maintaining his or her consciousness in high vibration**.

The Millionaire Mindset

Here is a note regarding my second problem – education.

Because I wanted to get to the bottom of things in terms of education, I enrolled in an elite educational program where I wanted to achieve **more than just a title**. After successfully completing my degree, I discovered that **the secret is not in the title, but in professional knowledge**. And so my desire for a classical education passed away.

> *A successful person is someone who succeeds at maintaining his or her consciousness in high vibration.*

Also, because I discovered that in areas related to my growth, I had been **educating myself all my life**, and will probably continue to do so until I die because this makes me happy and I feel that this is the right path – I just never perceived it as education.

Next Problem: Money

At eight years old, I first began earning money working on golf courses where I collected stones and golf balls and later pushed golf carts loaded with players' equipment. Because my parents were not able to offer me abundance and prosperity, I had no other choice, but to **provide it myself**.

I later earned enough money to buy clothes, a bike, a motor scooter, vacations, etc. by working in factories during winter vacations. But it was barely enough for living through the week, much less for saving or investing.

That way, I was able to afford the things that I never would have been able to afford otherwise, but this did not lead me to my goal: to **not be burdened by money** and to be able to buy whatever I like. As I grew up in material distress, my first goal was to be financially liberated. At the time, material wealth was my **biggest goal, and I would not have traded it for anything**.

I truly believed that I would be **happiest in life when I successfully acquired a lot of money**. That is why I constantly educated myself in the financial area. At the time, I was also working on different projects that brought a feeling of prosperity closer for me.

Both led to the logical conclusion that I began **earning by advising others how to settle their relationships with money** – while I, myself, was learning at the same time. On this path, I met people who were extremely wealthy. Some I perceived as role models, but for the majority, I became aware that **I did not see myself in their roles**... because some of them slaved night and day, others asserted their power and "connections" in their work (while damaging others, which was the last thing I wanted), while still others sacrificed – or traded – their free time, friends, and families for business success and so on.

Anyway, I came to the point where I could begin to **afford the finer things** – from little things to increasingly larger ones, and finally to luxury cars, exotic trips, and an office building. But this was not the stuff dreams are made of because money did not bring me ultimate fulfillment inside.

I began to wonder if money is really the best and the most one can achieve.

The closer I came to financial independence, the more I noticed that **money just multiplies one's internal state**, as John Gray says. Therefore, if you are happy without loads of material wealth, you are even more so with money. And if you are unhappy without money, then **money, in itself, will not magically make you happy, but will only allow you to afford more in your unhappiness.**

I began constantly questioning whether I really wanted to have (just) a lot of money – or if I **wanted everything**. In other words, I learned the real **purpose** or **mission of money**: It enables us to **finance our own creativity**.

That is why it is so important to harmonize our relationship with money. Then when we finally come to a certain stage of harmony, money **helps us perform our real life's mission**, which may or may not be connected to finances, expenses, and so on.

In other words: I discovered that **all the money in the world could not buy me a ticket to unlimited happiness, but that it can help make getting there easier.** Actually this path goes through money... but it does not stop there. (More on this is in the book, *Becoming Rich and Wealthy Through Divine Touch*).

If I look back and examine my life, I worked on rather different projects in my career. Often, I was successful, and sometimes I was not. I even went **bankrupt** in between, but this was the price at which I came to understand that there are more important things in life than just material prosperity.

Besides, an unpleasant experience **always brought a blessing with it**: When I was – after an unsuccessful attempt in business – back at the beginning and deep within asked myself what I wanted to do in life, I **always came back to my basic life's mission**, from which I turned away because of my appetite for money. I finally made the major discovery that **fulfilling my life's mission brings me the most... in all respects**.

Money Brings Challenges to the Neighborhood

In my village environment and during socialism, it was even more difficult to achieve harmony with money. I am not talking just about income, but the reactions that follow. Anyone who stood out from the average was considered a crook that came into money suspiciously.

From that there arose new challenges: **how to guarantee prosperity while maintaining good relations with the surroundings**, which will – most likely – announce that you are a cheat who earns money illegally.

I remember an illustration of this, from many years ago, which has remained in my memory.

It was a nice day, and through the window I noticed how our neighbor, an older gentleman, was repairing the low concrete border-wall between us. I was grateful and went outside to thank him for making sure that things are maintained; after all, the fence was on the border with our property, so his work benefited the view on our side, as well.

When I approached him, I noticed that he would probably have some material left over. So that it would not go waste, I asked him if it is possible to repair part of another border wall, which is next to our house, with the leftover mortar and that I was prepared to pay him; I explained that I personally did not have the motivation or experience that he did, much less the joy to attempt the work myself, but that it would be nice if it were done.

The neighbor immediately seized the opportunity and complained that young people do not know how to do anything. Yes, that is true – I would not attempt such work myself unless it were absolutely necessary, which I also told him.

I added that not everyone is good at everything and that **we would both benefit if we each stuck to what we knew and enjoyed**.

He looked at me seriously and said that he **did not even know what I do for a living** or where I got the money for such a prestigious car. Even though he had known for years that I owned an office building, which had always been occupied, he argued, "Sure, but you co-own that with that other guy."

Finally, he added, **"I hope you do honest work."**

I felt as if I had been doused with cold water. I did not know that the neighbors actually even thought about me or doubted whether or not I was engaged in honest work. I had always worked – and raised my children – **according to the principles of respect, justice, and love toward everyone**. Is it possible that my closest neighbor (still) doubted whether I had made wealth legally and ethically?

I told him what I do for a living and mentioned that at the time I was giving a lecture for the employees of the National Assembly. He commented, **"How can you lecture in Parliament, when you don't have a doctorate?"**

This was the second cold shower in the span of a few minutes – and, in practice, an **excellent opportunity for me to determine how much I actually trusted and stood behind my principles, and how much I allowed various comments to affect me**.

> *Fear is not overcome with arguments, explanations, rationalizations, excuses, and so on, but with love.*

These two comments – although I thought that I managed my internal harmony – **made me lose my balance**. (If I had completely believed in myself and everything I did and lived, I would have laughed off the comments and they would not have affected me.)

Again, I had seen that **money is still the eternal theme of village talk** and that people were still were not used to the idea that even a poor boy without a doctorate could make money and have something smart to say to highly educated people. **They still had put me in the same category that I had been in years ago, when I was, like most boys from the village, an average-Joe living from day to day.**

I became aware that **I have to remain strong – integrated with my Self – in such situations, and that I cannot allow the fears of the speaker to be transmitted onto me.** All that needs to be done, in such moments, is for me to remain in my energy.

Fear is not overcome with arguments, explanations, rationalizations, excuses, and so on, but with love. People are calling out for help, and every sharp word from their side, which does not come from the heart, is a plea for love, acceptance, and approval.

I have to finally **disconnect from the past and begin to live more in accordance with the new vibration** – in all areas. Even if it means not yielding and succumbing to fears — not even for the sake of good neighborly relations – but trusting and working to the best of my ability, from inside myself outwards.

The low vibration energies, which others feel toward me, or are left over from the times when they were not on speaking terms with my father, are **their affair**. My lesson is to **accept people as they are and to spread the Light**. That person may then decide if he or she will continue to play the game on his or her own terms, or allow us to build a relationship on a higher vibration.

I do believe that, sooner or later, there will come a time when we will be able to rejoice together lovingly with everyone. **I just do not want to wait for others to give me permission to do this today.**

The Mission of the Book, *The Millionaire Mindset*

During this time, my life had already changed dramatically. The first and second versions of the book, *The Millionaire Mindset: How to Tap Real Wealth from Within* – which was later supplemented and renamed *The Millionaire Mindset Awakening Through Divine Touch* – were released. Not only was it so "destined" because things evolved in the nicest way, but also because **I, myself, got a lot of confirmation that I was on the right path.**

I began to realize something completely new: **the power of expressing my true self**; or the power of **creation**. Up until this time, I had thought that life's goal was linked to activities for releasing tension, like traveling, enjoying the countryside, nature, etc. **In the last few years, I realized that there is no greater pleasure than creating without limit** (or serving, as some would call this).

This energy gave me the strength to start believing in yet other miracles. For example, when the book was released, I knew that it was a world's bestseller; I even talked to journalists and others, referring to it as a **world's bestseller, when fewer than a thousand copies had been sold.**

Besides that, the book – and Nikola and I as authors – **had appeared in nearly all the media, even on the most watched television shows.** We appeared alongside the most well-known Slovenians – and all of this happened all by itself; we never asked or paid for any publicity.

Soon companies also began ordering **hundreds of copies of the book as gifts** for their employees and clients (this is the case even today).

Today a Miracle, Tomorrow...

So I – as usual – saw Heaven's gates open: large quantities of books, travels, and introductions, America, the Balkans. "Well, it has finally begun," I thought, "all we need to do now is translate this into English, and we've won again."

I began looking for a good translator, which seemed simple enough. Well, it turned out that this presented two problems: **The first difficulty was in the transfer of energy** – no one succeeded in getting the exact vibration – and second, **nearly everyone wanted to make enough money (from this translation alone) to build a house.** At least, it seemed that way to me because translators asked for enormous amounts of money.

Well, I pressed on. If I had decided that the book was to go around the world, that is what it would do! **I actively and systematically checked the market to find someone, who would measure up to the task.**

After three years, I realized that this was not the right way. Something was not right because events were not unraveling the way they should have been. **The search was exhausting... and led me to no success.**

"We'll just sell here and forget the world for the time-being," I decided one day and **gave up looking.**

Not long after, two capable young businessmen visited me. The purpose of their visit was to release *The Millionaire Mindset* in electronic form, creating **the first Slovenian e-book on the market.** (To date, no book had presumably been offered in electronic form for sale, they were all available for free.)

During the course of the conversation, I learned that one of the gentlemen – Rok, who later brought more miracles into my life – had **already released a book in English,** which he had written and translated himself with the help of his team. He was ecstatic when I suggested that he translate *The Millionaire Mindset*.

The Millionaire Mindset

We, as authors, were even more ecstatic when we received his sample translation. It was so good that in a heartbeat, we knew the search was over... **the time had come.**

My lesson was – again – very clear: **to neither force nor withhold things, but just trust and leave them to the Creator to execute His plan.**

The Call From America

Rok did not just translate part of the book, but agreed to offer it to the world. One day, he sent an e-mail that **Joe Vitale, author of the bestselling book,** *Spiritual Marketing,* was thrilled with the book and wanted to have the entire book to read. If he liked it, he would offer it in America.

The Millionaire Mindset was translated, and Joe was so impressed that he decided that he would be the publisher and release it himself in electronic form for the whole world. He simultaneously **ranked it second on the chart of "The world's best books of all time"** for achieving prosperity, which was a special honor for me.

Besides Joe Vitale, today Mark Victor Hansen, co-author of the *Chicken Soup* series of books, also has the book and was greatly impressed by Sai Baba's dedication. Joe Sugarman, "TV shop wizard," named it **one of the best**. An Indian publisher, Mr. Padmanaban, who has been personally connected to Sai Baba all his life, also wants to publish it in India.

We are now preparing a copy for the legendary Isaac Tigrett, "the father" of the "Hard Rock Café" restaurants, who also cosponsored the hospital we already mentioned in India; during our meeting in India, he expressed his desire to read the book.

Readers from all over the world **compare this book to** *The Holy Bible*, calling it **"the word of God in the hearts of people,"** and so forth.

This year (2005), the new book, *The Millionaire Mindset Awakening Through Divine Touch*, got – with its new publisher – **a fresh impetus and even greater push.**

All this time, the book had a life of its own. This is without a doubt my life's mission because I often felt that I was in God's grace and that everything would turn out fantastically.

Yet, the huge success of the book remained in the shadow of another trial.

While this miracle was happening, there came another great turning point, which is not related to this book.

When You Decide on a Path, You Get Trials

It was the summer of 2003. At the time, I was (again) quite blessed because I could enjoy the release and excellent sales of my new book, *Becoming Rich and Wealthy Through Divine Touch* (in my country originally titled *Enjoy Life... While Becoming Rich and Wealthy*).

The title of the book itself carried **remarkable initiative energy**. As if God had said, "Enjoy life, and you will become rich, yeah? OK, let us just see if you really stand behind this: **I'm going to give you an ordeal during which it will never occur to you to enjoy yourself, then prove that you really live up to your assertion.**"

One of the standard trials of the Universe is that **upon each passage into a new vibration or stage of development, we get a final test with which we either confirm – pass the test – or deny the new vibration and fall back** until we really stand steadfast behind the energy. For that is finally the sign that we have truly conquered it and can move forward into new energy.

It is like a demanding test we take in school: **We will repeat it until we score 100%.** If we fail, we return to the previous level to repeat it.

Obviously, what followed was one of the most powerful ordeals I had ever experienced.

Enjoy Life... When You Are Face to Face With Death?

In winter, I had noticed certain changes in my skin, but did not pay them much attention. "It will go away," I thought, "like everything else up till now." Things did not improve with time, and I noticed that things began to progress. I went to see my family doctor, who after months of unsuccessful treatment referred me to a specialist.

When I heard the diagnosis, a chill ran down my spine: I have a serious illness, which is often terminal. But I did not take this seriously and perceived the whole situation like another trial that I would conquer and teach people about, providing them an example how to get through serious illness in high vibration.

I was not at all aware of the consequences of this disease. Well, it gradually hit me, and I realized that **my life could change drastically because of this**. After all, my father had died from a similar disease. That is why I began to nurture different feelings toward the illness.

The doctor told me all that had to be **removed immediately** and had already **set the date for the surgical procedure**. Although I had already had a surgery date, I did not feel good about it.

Make a Decision... and Stick With It Until You Reach Your Goal

And so again, I was faced with a trial. Would I follow my beliefs and stance – for instance, alternative medicine – or would I choose a **sensible goal**? On the one hand, I was a believer, or at least a fan, of alternative medicine; on the other hand, I believe in Oneness, or the **pooling of everything that unconditionally leads toward the set goal**.

At that point, I decided that **I would not neglect something by betting everything on one or the other** – for instance alternative medicine – but that I would use **all the knowledge of traditional and alternative medicines**. After all, my one wish was to **get well**, not to confirm something or reject and deny something else.

I found myself in a situation where I did not have a good feeling about the hastiness regarding the operation, and something kept holding me back. **I did not believe that I could do this so superficially**; after all, **the meaning of an illness is always internal change**. Illness points out an **obstruction in our life's energy**. At the same time, I was also aware that some procedure would be necessary. I decided to seek the opinion of another specialist.

And so the path, through various events and the help of a coworker, Maja, brought me to an exceptional surgeon, Dr. Marjan Fabjan. By this time, I had calmed down and had a completely **different attitude toward the disease and doctors**. Dr. Fabjan's entire staff was very professional and pleasant. No wonder – **the world outside of us merely symbolically represents the world within us**. There was something else that confirmed that I had made the right choice in deciding to see him: The first thing I noticed at Dr. Fabjan's were **Sai Baba postcards** on the wall. And Dr. Fabjan, a well-renowned expert, was also very respectful and showed me love and care.

The Story of a Boy Who Achieves Everything...

I sensed in him **the pooling of traditional medicine and deep spiritual knowledge**, which is why I **trusted him completely** and placed myself in his hands with a tranquil heart. Nevertheless, I wanted to solve this in a more spiritual manner if possible, without surgery.

Dr. Fabjan set about the issue professionally; he removed only a small portion of tissue and sent it for examination. There they confirmed his diagnosis and the diagnosis of other doctors I had seen – it was a very serious disease. When I again heard that this disease is no joking matter, **I adopted a completely different attitude toward everything** – the world, life, and myself.

I realized that **the mind is not always the builder**, as I liked to tell others and myself... because I never thought that I could become so seriously ill. No chance! If I had thought that I could become ill, I would have never exposed myself to the sun, visited tanning salons regularly, and would have taken much better care of my skin.

I convinced myself that people **do not have free will with which they rule the world** – regardless of how rich, successful, loving, etc. they are. **Everything is just part of the Creator's big plan. As long as our will comes from the heart and intuition, and is in harmony with our life's mission, we really have the feeling that we have an influence on it.** When it does not, the situation is quite different.

With this realization I actually began saying goodbye to this world.

Well, these are very special feelings. Within myself, I felt **gratitude and happiness for everything I had experienced**: my loving family, success, friends, material satisfaction, etc. In these few decades, I had experienced everything most people only dream about.

In this energy, I came to yet another big realization: When I looked at my achievements in this way, it **occurred to me that I had succeeded, and that I had experienced God's kindness, goodness, and mercy in this life.** For me, this was a great turning point: **I was finally able to stop where I was**, and I decided to **stop pushing for things that did not support my soul's growth**, like money, fame, and so on. I would disconnect myself from all these stresses and devote myself to the magnificence of life trustingly.

I still faced the dilemma about what to do regarding the operation.

Again, I met with a big test (as many times before in life): **Do I insist on my way, or trust and surrender myself to God to take care of me**? And so this phase of saying goodbye was also a **phase of surrender**, when I no longer forced the surroundings, but **allowed "His will to be done."**

It was then that I found out that the afore-mentioned Stephen Turoff was coming to Slovenia. **I decided to wait for him, which meant postponing the operation for two long months.** Still, I sensed that this was the right thing to do – let him try everything possible. Maybe in this way, I would avoid traditional surgery. Even Dr. Fabjan did not object to my decision.

My Second Encounter With Stephen Turoff

Two months had passed in an interesting mood, but in this time I never gave into desperation or sadness. Finally, the day arrived when I found myself in Turoff's waiting room.

His practice is to have you write your problems on a piece of paper. When you lie on the operating table, you place the paper – which Stephen may or may not look at – next to you. Then he begins operating. In my case, he did not look at the paper, so he **was not informed about what was wrong with me**, what part of my body was affected, or what illness I had.

While I lay on the table, three times over his assistant repeated to him why I had come and began describing my illness. He only nodded and said, **"I am sure God knows what needs to be done,"** while the expression on his face was not at all worried or frightening, but gentle and full of love. (He operates unaware of his actions and allows God to work through him via known healers. During this procedure Stephen even talks, sings.)

He poured holy water over the areas where I had the illness and began **operating on completely different areas**. While he did so, he looked at me very rigorously and **asked who wrote the *Kabala***. (I had looked at this book on the shelf in the waiting room shortly before, but he could not have known that.) I replied that I did not know.

His harsh tone surprised me because we had embraced, joked, and remembered old times just the night before at his seminar. Now there was a completely different energy speaking from within him.

After he finished operating on me, **he asked me if I knew how to write God's name**. He gave me a piece of paper and pencil, and I wrote something my own way. He wrote, "JHVH" and said, "When you understand this, you will be able to write your book." I told him that I had already written it (this experience happened, as mentioned, in 2003, the first edition of the book, *The Millionaire Mindset*, was released in the year 1997) and that Sai Baba had even signed it.

Stephen turned and left to operate on the next patient.

I stopped, dressed slowly, and thought. I began to understand the discovery to which he wanted to bring me: **Everything is done by God and not by us.** He also wrote the *Kabala*. **When we are in our hearts, we allow God to work through us.** And that is when we have the most strength and success. Mother Theresa said the same thing somewhat differently; she said that **she is just an instrument of God** or **the tool through which He works**.

And so **I did not write my book... God did.**

In the next few days, I returned to Dr. Fabjan. He again took a sample of tissue and sent it to the laboratory – it showed that the **disease was no longer there**.

That is when something completely different showed up. **Another serious degeneration was happening in a different part of my body at the same time.** We had not paid any attention to it until that time. Neither did Turoff, although he saw the place where the disease was growing.

My Experience With Dr. Fabjan

Dr. Fabjan decided to do an immediate biopsy of the newly affected tissue. It was discovered that it was a **much more serious form of the disease**; I learned that it had already happened that people with this diagnosis **died within six months**. That dealt the final shocking, sobering blow.

I found myself in a situation, where it was necessary to make a decision to either fear or trust.

The most important feelings I experienced at Dr. Fabjan's clinic were feelings of **relaxation**, which came from **boundless trust**. In this way, I was able to completely surrender to the experience. Despite everything, I knew that God was taking care of me. Deep within, I felt that **God was also working through Dr. Fabjan's hands and would save me**. Dr. Fabjan was – like everyone working from the heart – **just a tool in His hands**.

So it became evident that **everything is God**... and that there is no **separating between this or another kind of medicine. God and His will work through everything, regardless of the technique people may use.** In the end, we learn – if we can be honest enough with ourselves – that we are all only tools; we can congratulate ourselves or pat ourselves on the back only because **we opened our hearts enough to hear Him and had enough courage to unconditionally follow this energy.** Everything else is God's work.

When I learned this, I realized that **I had always been – and still am – in God's hands**.

In the end, everything turned out well with my disease. Today I still carefully observe and check for changes or pain, and in so doing, express respect and loving care for my body. But for now, everything is as it should be. I am conscious that if I repeat the pattern in myself, the disease can return, as Jesus stressed, "Go now and **sin no more**." (John 8:11)

With this experience, I realized that **the point of disease is change: Something must be changed, and you have to stick to that change.** Until then, I had only lectured; now I had actually lived and confirmed this experience.

In hindsight, I see that my serious health ordeal was a **test of trust and surrendering**, more than a test of illness. **It was about looking for God in myself and restoring my relationship with Him.**

Joy and the Continuation of the Experience

Dr. Fabjan and I immediately found a common language and became friends. The result was that we decided to **write a book, which would incorporate our knowledge**: professional health work (the reasons behind the appearance of illness and the mission of medicine), various experiences and learning, and appreciation and respect for God and everything in general.

That is how I knew that our meeting had a very deep spiritual meaning: **the union for a higher goal**, not just curing a disease.

Besides that, I experienced, in practice, the **importance of choosing the right energy at the right time**.

If there were ever an appropriate time to enjoy and be happy, it was during these difficult times; in this way, **I was taking in the energy of joy and peace** with which I defended myself against fear and worries.

I could have surrendered to pessimism, turned away from joy, and so allowed fear to devour me – but I would have completely missed the point. The essence is as follows: **When you want to find yourself in some energy, begin living (expressing) it.**

As feelings of joy and happiness were not usually my companions during that experience with illness, I took care to choose and perform as many joyful and uplifting activities as possible.

Often in life, **we do exactly the opposite: Instead of doing joyful things when we are in a bad mood, we lose ourselves in fear and worries.** (You can read more about this and the links between disease, energies, and the feelings we experience in ourselves in the forthcoming book – mentioned above – entitled *The Health Is Within*.)

Keller once said, "When you learn that you have a serious disease, the first thing you have to do is go to the zoo and feed peanuts to the giraffes… take in some fun!"

This is the point of free choice that is given to us – **to choose that energy when we are short of it**. In my case, I needed joy, faith, hope, and trust; that is why one of the best things I could have done was to **choose to do the things that bring these energies**.

This is the grace of the world and simultaneously a great lesson, which must be learned: **not to look for things outside of ourselves, but to turn inwards, trust, and choose and awaken – in ourselves – everything we want**. This is also the answer to the old myth about how to turn lead into gold, which symbolically represents the passage from a low or poisonous vibration to a higher one.

Once we begin to live this recognition, our life becomes nothing less than a chain of miracles. Because we no longer force nor hinder experiences, our life begins to unravel without the mind's influence. Therefore, **we are able to experience life's situations in a much happier, painless way**… while conquering the wisdom that the experience brings us.

My Vibration's Influence on People

I, myself, received a lot of help on my path. At the same time, during my employment with myself, I sometimes, intentionally or unintentionally, represented both principles to people, who found themselves near me:

- Sometimes I approached them **at the right time to tell them the right things**, so they had enough energy to take a step forward.
- Often, they also saw in me **the expression of the god Shiva**, who is known for **destroying everything that is not right** so that something better can be built on its foundations.

And so I experienced many interesting reactions, of one kind or another, which I triggered in other people. Here are some of them.

My energy can be very strong, even **disturbing** to people... if they do not go along with it, resonate with it and use it as a push for their own progress and growth.

One of the advantages I had was I made people aware of what I wanted in each project. And I also had **vast motivation**. This often proved to be an exceptional advantage; or better said, an advantage for me and maybe for some, but **never for all involved**.

Namely, some people liked my way of work, fell into my energy, goals, and desires... and **stuck to me**, while **forgetting their heart's desires** during the process. I knew where I was going, but they did not; they just **blindly followed me**, and it often happened that they found themselves at a dead end. On the other hand, if people knew where I was going, and they had similar visions, then together we achieved incredible results.

I was first quite surprised about myself when, after a motorbike accident, I decided to market the services of foreign insurance companies. I had very strong motivation – disappointment over Slovenian insurance companies and the deep conviction that I was doing remarkable work for people – and that is why I was penetrative and successful.

And so it happened that I, as a young boy and novice without any special education or references, walked into **people's houses... and they gave me their savings** – to do whatever I thought best.

I derived my motivation from a clear vision. Because everything was going as planned, and people actually had much better savings terms than those that were available domestically, I had even **greater inspiration**. This strength and confidence were very obviously felt, and so successes followed one after the other.

The final result was that I had set a sales record in the history of a respected insurance company that had been on the market for more than 150 years. I had not just exceeded the previous record by a percent or two – I achieved such results that **the CEO, himself, could not believe it and tried to persuade me that it was impossible to achieve something like this.**

To me, this was a clear sign from the Universe – or God – to **focus my attention on this area**. I sensed big potentials in myself, and this only progressed later on.

From that point on, I had – more or less – large groups of people around me. It was interesting to observe how my vibration touched some of them (those who resonated with it), but not others. My big realization was that I usually said the same things, encouraging them in a similar way, but **only some people accepted this and grew, while others did not**.

There is great strength in this... That is to say that I became aware that I am not the one changing people, but that **I am working like a lighthouse shining the same way on everything**. Only some people take advantage of this light to see the path more clearly, while others do not even notice it and for that reason cannot use it.

I later joined a project, which was the logical continuation of traditional insurance sales. This time, I moved into the area of **securities (stocks)**, but still in combination with insurance; only here we separated the savings and insurance components.

Essentially, my work was very similar to that of the past experience, except that now I had a product even better than traditional life insurance. Again, I organized my team and found people who either:

- Had **the same vision and accepted my energy as help** in realizing their goals.
- Did not have the same vision and **perceived my energy as too strong.**

With this group of motivated people, I also achieved a new sales record because I had **strong motivation, which I took from myself (my vision) and with which I "shone upon people."**

The Millionaire Mindset

That is what was happening nearly all the time and still happens today. Not so long ago, I had a consultation with a young man who was very decisive and dedicated, employed in the sales of insurance services. I told him – again – the same things I had told many people before him. (I know this branch very well, that is why I always introduce my vision for strategic development so that all – customers, agents, and the insurance company – will be most satisfied.)

I was surprised how closely the boy followed directions... and **drastically increased his sales** even though he had previously tried various techniques and none of them worked.

Later, I wrote in the introduction of his own book that I was not the one who brought this about, but that he was; I only **guided him so that he would see certain unexploited possibilities**, but he was the one who made the decision to take advantage of them and saw the process through. (Today he has expanded abroad and has exceptional results.)

I soon realized one more remarkable thing: I was often only physically (especially energetically) present at strategic meetings and **hardly said a word** – I was just there. But the results that followed were **remarkable**. When I analyzed the situation, I came to the following conclusions:

- **My presence was enough** for people to **open up** and, through resonance, perceive my confidence in them and their work; in this way, they came to have **better opinions of themselves and more strength**.

- At my side, they felt **confident** that I would stand by them if something were to go wrong, so they could afford to take some risky steps. If they were to exaggerate, I would stop them; as long as I was quiet, it meant that everything was within the limits of the acceptable. They already had clear ideas of what to do... they just **never succeeded in realizing them**, mainly because of a lack of trust, faith, strength, and courage.

Because they trusted me, they **transferred their worries to me**, similar to the way I did in my medical experience with Dr. Fabjan: **Because they were no longer burdened with problems – I was now caring for them – they directed their energy into achieving the goal**.

In this way, many companies have achieved amazing breakthroughs and growth; not just in the business field, but also in the establishment of better relationships. But usually both happened simultaneously.

It even happened that the Slovenian office of a respected international company, which operates in just under sixty countries around the world, **went from last place to first in its growth** – after only six months of our cooperation. The second benefit from our cooperation was better mutual relationships between coworkers: **People who were on bad terms with each other, and were not even talking to each other, began working together fruitfully.**

What did I do to bring this about? **Nothing.** Or, at least nothing special. I did exactly the same thing I had done in many, many companies that found themselves in a similar situation. (Some companies were not prepared to change and persisted in old processes, and are either at the same level today, or are even worse off than before.)

My Professional Path Today

Today when I overthrow taboos and move the limits of the possible in my work, I **enjoy myself immensely**. This is mostly because I use **ancient knowledge** that makes higher vibration possible for all participants, and in the end, **everyone feels better**.

The most joyful work with which I am engaged is probably helping **people, who have everything and are still unhappy, pass to a higher level**. These are people who have tried everything in life to find happiness, but are still stuck in the search.

On the one hand, they have influence, power, and the means to attain their goals… yet on the other hand, inside they feel that something is still missing. They are prepared to do whatever it takes to move further, and the experience of passing to higher vibration – as a consequence of our cooperation – is usually **so strong that these people want to transfer this happiness to others**. And because they lead large groups or organizations – either directly or because their opinion is so important that many people accept it – this is the means for the **fastest growth of a large number of people**. This represents a special contentedness for me.

The most important energies, which are shown (even more) when a leader decides on this path, are **trust, honesty, and fairness**. This means that people no longer pretend to be Mr. or Ms. Perfect, but that they **discover and accept their karmic tasks** and their **real life's mission**, and begin to look at life from this perspective.

When a leader begins to research his or her life story in this way and shares it with others, **many coworkers resonate and identify with it so strongly** because they can see themselves in it. This is because the Truth is always reflected in it, and there is no greater power than the Truth, or Love, which is the same. Therefore, people who open their hearts and resonate with the story feel **exceptional strength and faith in their own lives**, which is also where excellent motivation for further work comes from.

And so a leader's **forceful strength**, which sometimes hides a **desire for control and dominance that stems from fear**, often transforms into **trust and the desire for passage to a higher vibration for everyone**.

People near the leader notice this… and stop fearing authority, but with trust, respect, and gratitude, open themselves up to this (new) person… **and begin to grow themselves**.

This is the real strength. (More about experiences in this area, and the system for how to conquer it, is described in the book, *Charisma, Self-Confidence and Personal Power*).

The Most a Leader Can Do for the World

Recently, we have been discovering that **frank success stories, which speak honestly about every – pleasant and unpleasant – experience and coming from the heart**, are so strong that listening to them opens the hearts of everyone, not just those linked to the leader (or author of the story).

And so we were thinking about how to bring the stories about the Truth close to as many people as possible – and had a fantastic idea: **Let us write a book in which we "enrich" the life story of an influential and charismatic person with an esoteric explanation of his or her life's experiences.** We would add a description of the Five Universal Laws and how they appeared in this person's life, point out that person's life's mission, and therefore expose a **story about achieving life's vision – not just business success – which derives from karmically conditional surroundings**.

The Story of a Boy Who Achieves Everything...

In this way we achieve something big:

- **The person (leader) gets a personal map** – or drawing of the path, directions – how to reach higher vibration in all areas of life (or just the professional area, if he or she so desires), or how to free himself or herself from the karmic cycle.

- When the leader collects material for the book, and systematically thinks about his or her life, he or she becomes **aware of karmic tests and consequential problems**, which are often the cause for internal dissatisfaction.

- The leader gets a **review of life's turning points**, which serves as an example and reminder to him or her and others.

- As a consequence, he or she is exposed as a **person, who is close to others**, and not like someone who is above his or her subordinates... because when presented in this manner, **people perceive him or her in a different, gentler, more intimate light that links people** (because now they easily resonate with him or her).

- Also, the **new image** sticks to the leader because others (coworkers) begin looking at him or her differently and they **connect to the leader on the basis of the heart's vibration**.

- So the leader gets a **new identity** because he or she unleashes trapped energy and discovers completely new potentials.

- The book can serve as **learning material** and a road map if we decide on business cooperation (or personnel training, establishment of systemization, etc.).

- The book is also an **exceptional reference letter** with which people, who resonate with the story, feel the person, learn his or her potentials, and on the basis of this, decide on cooperation with him or her (with much less bureaucracy, verification, or ill trust... because from the very start resonance is established based on the heart's energies, which guarantee an **exceptional business relationship**).

- The book shows the author as an **expert in his or her field** and also as an **expert and respecter of spiritual laws**.

- **Everyone who reads the book can identify with it** at one level or another: The leader may represent an example to one person, to someone else the description of his or her own path (if he or she is in a similar situation), yet another person now finds trust in today's leaders and in this world and so on.
- And so the **vibrations of Truth, Love, and Light are spread around the whole world**.

However, I am very careful in choosing the individuals with whom I tackle this project. Like I stressed before, I only choose those who are really prepared to move a step forward in life; for example, people who have achieved nearly everything in their professional field, who want to further harmonize other areas, or **bring God's vibration into their work, which has a lot of influence on the surroundings as well as other areas of life**. These are, for instance, doctors, politicians, businesspeople, athletes, teachers, priests, statesmen, etc.

In this way, we **unite together in purpose on the basis of the heart**. And because "Jesus (the heart) is present where two (hearts) are joined in His name," such a book usually becomes both a **revolutionary textbook in this professional area** and sets new standards, which show **the development of the area in an unconditional, enlightened direction**, where all participants gain and nobody loses, and their consciousness is directed into the heart.

Clearly, I work closely with this leader, and I usually find myself in the role of his or her **personal adviser**, as we are constantly comparing the book's vision with the current situation. So we truly **unite vibrations**, and the result is a big step forward.

Today I am also deciding to **train perspective personnel** – people who have **desire and motivation as well as highly developed human values**, but may not be far enough to be opinion makers, recognized experts, or the like. They are diamonds in the rough, who will someday be the pillars of society; **why not direct them to the heart today so that someday they will lead the world from this vibration?**

The method for leading these people is very different in basic energy, but similar in vision: to **come to the level where you can perform your work out of love and with love for everyone – yourself, your colleagues, and all participants**.

Both systems of schooling – for the training of leaders as well as perspective youth – achieve top-notch results, and **great joy**. (The system for training perspective youth is described in the book, *Enlightened Salesperson*, where the revolutionary motivational system, based on ancient knowledge, with which I achieved all these results, is described for the first time.)

It is about a real miracle – one in a line of many – when you see the cocoon transform into a butterfly before your very eyes. Again, I want to stress that I am not the one changing people, but only have the grace that my life's mission is related to this. So when I am deeply enough in my heart, **I allow God to speak through me.**

This is the reward that means the most to me and why, time and again, I am enthusiastic when I get the opportunity to reveal to a new group of people the beauty of their hearts… while I, during the process, **connect to my own heart even more each time.**

Sai Baba demonstrated the aforementioned very clearly at the (very important for me) Christmas speech in 2003. He took a flower in his hand and said, "As long as you hold the flower in your hand, it is yours. When you release it, it is God's… and before you picked it, it was God's. So it is only yours in between; no matter how much you may want to hold on to it, **it will return to God sooner or later.**"

"**If you live in the heart, you are living God**… which means that **the flower was God's the whole time**; you were only working in accordance with His will."

So let us begin to live in the heart so that we will be able to surrender our experiences to God, who will work through us.

This is the biggest miracle: Sensing that we carry God within us, remembering this as much as possible, and beginning to live from this **unconditional vibration outwards**. In so doing, we will not only solve our problems, but **affect a great number of people with our example**.

I have often said at seminars that man dies in the evening and is reborn in the morning. Sai Baba enhanced this saying, "Each time we inhale we are reborn… and we die every time we exhale." (This also means that **we should have God in our thoughts with every breath**.)

And so we have **the opportunity with each new breath, at every moment, to pass into higher vibration.**

When Miracles Happen to Us

Miracles happen to us every day, we just do not perceive them from our mindset. We often think that the label "miracle" belongs to magic carpets, miraculous sudden recoveries, making diamonds appear out of thin air, and so on. In other words, we think that a **miracle is only something we have not experienced and cannot explain with our mind.** But this is not the case.

At one of his lectures, Turoff – apparently quoting Einstein – said, **"There are only two ways to live your life: One is to notice that nothing is a miracle... and the other is to notice that everything is a miracle."**

The whole Universe is a miracle, and we are part of it. Can we influence the weather tomorrow or change a season? No one – neither politicians, nor millionaires, nor other influential people – can succeed at this. Whether we like it or not, we are only **part of this creation.**

My life is undoubtedly a miracle. So is yours, if you look at it the way I look at my life.

Even **my story is the story of each one of you** – if you perceive it symbolically – **and the other way around,** because we have, in various areas, gone from **crucifixion to resurrection.**

Every life story – yours, too – symbolically shows the course of events from which each of us should learn that the **goal and sense of everything is to find God in one's self... and allow Him to express Himself through our hearts.**

In time, **human beings will exceed their limitations and develop further.** They will surpass personal egoism and begin intensively exploring eternal questions about themselves. They will find explanations for the sense of the evolution of life. **They will recognize their unlimited strengths.**

But it is not important what follows... because life is here and now – in us.

Let us be grateful for everything, even for each and every breath, because **we are experiencing the grace of the Creator at every moment.** It does not matter what was, what will be in five years, or what the neighbor was doing with a new car. **We are what is important... here and now;** the most we can do for others is to set an **example.** Let us become "prototypes" of happy people and spread this vibration to everyone!

The Story of a Boy Who Achieves Everything...

Do not be occupied with hard questions about your future because you will **forget to live**. Just trust that you will, when the time comes, understand everything.

Instead, find God in yourself today so that you will await the future with an open heart.

In other words:

Life is a game – **play it!**
Life is a challenge – **accept it!**
Life is love – **share it!**
Life is a dream – **fulfill it!**
Life is a gift – **be glad of it!**
Life is an adventure – **be part of it!**
Life is a secret – **discover it!**
Life is a fight – **give yourself to it!**
Life is beauty – **glorify it!**
Life is a composition – **compose it!**
Life is a chance – **use it!**
Life is a song – **sing it!**
Life is a goal – **achieve it!**
Life is a mission – **complete it...**

...and end the game!

Glossary of Concepts and Expressions in the Context Used in this Book

Often a particular word or expression is used to describe different things. For this reason, we have included explanations of some of the most frequently used concepts and expressions. These definitions are not general (professional), but are adapted to the content of the message. It is often difficult to find the right word, especially when describing energy.

Whenever such a word or expression is used in this text, it expresses the concept as explained in this glossary. This is especially true in cases where the meaning of a word or expression differs from that of its general use.

While reading, it is recommended that you refer to this glossary until you are harmonized with the energy hidden in the background.

The concepts that follow are not in alphabetical order. These concepts and expressions are placed in a sequence so that if we read them in order – which is highly recommended at first – they will expand our consciousness.

Truth (with a capital "T"): Refers to Universal Law, which has always held true, holds true today, will still hold true, and applies to everyone. It does not refer to a personal perspective of a situation, which we call an individual's (personal) truth, but rather is derived from Universal Laws.

Life's energy: The collection of our internal (spiritual) world and its expression in the physical world; everything that happens inside of us. It also represents a motive for acting outwards. These are all of our thoughts, sensations, realizations, relations to values, standpoints. It is influenced by past and future experiences, thoughts about the future, and the way we comprehend, process, and express everything around and inside of us in general. Often the word energy alone is used.

Charisma: The energy, which an individual expresses, that expresses self-confidence and personal strength outwards. People with charisma trust in and follow themselves – intuition and the heart or soul. The strength, which the energy of charisma carries within it, usually stems from the individual's life's mission and is strongest if this mission – or destiny as a consequence of karma – is related to the unconditional energies coming from Oneness (or Unity).

Consciousness: The concentration of a person's life energy at some moment and in some place. It expresses values, identity, integrity. This is the existence of the individual who in himself carries everything else. This is the point here and now, which is expressed on all levels – physical, emotional, mental, etc. – and is a direct result of karma. It shapes our future experiences (destiny).

In some literature, consciousness represents that part of the mind of which a person is conscious, as in the word association, conscious-subconscious. (In this book, we will use the term conscious mind for that part of the mind.)

Otherwise, consciousness is meant to be the total of the subconscious mind (or simply the subconscious; the part of the concentration of energy of which we are not aware), the conscious mind, and the superconscious (intuition and soul).

Vibration: Denotes a person's specific energy state or the stage at which his or her consciousness is located. It can be low (fear, hopelessness, worries, sadness…) or high (happiness, peace, freedom from care, love…). This state of consciousness can be momentary (momentary vibration) or may last for a longer period of time (general vibration) when the consciousness only occasionally descends or rises out of it. If a predominant part of the consciousness is located in a specific vibration, we are talking about the prevailing vibration.

Critical mass: The boundary value – in this case, of energy – for changing direction or aim. For instance, the critical mass of the energy of anger means that the person's consciousness has just reached the level where it may pass over into this vibration. This is most easily illustrated with a scale: When the critical mass reaches a certain level, the scale tips in favor of one side, which takes the initiative.

Resonance: Harmony (through energy communication) between two things; the method of transferring energy between two subjects, which are on the same wavelength. If, for example, we activate a tuning fork and place an identical tuning fork next to it, the sound from the first will expand and so – through resonance – be transferred to the second, which will also begin transmitting sound even though nobody physically touched it.

Resonance occurs in two phases: In the first, energy is transferred from one subject to another. In the second, when both subjects emit the same vibration and work in resonance (harmony), the invested total energy of both is multiplied or drastically increased.

Here is a typical case of resonance: If a group of soldiers marches across a bridge and matches the vibration of the bridge, they can come into resonance with it, which results in the bridge beginning to sway. If this energy lasts for a longer period of time, it may pass over into the second level, where the energy is increased and the bridge may even collapse.

Another case of resonance: If we want to move a rock off balance, it must be pushed forward and backward in precisely the right rhythm. When it moves a few centimeters forward, we wait for it to pass the point of equilibrium in the other direction (back), and in that moment we push it again and wait for it to move forward and then back to the (new) outermost position, when we push it again. Eventually less and less energy is required to increase the distance between the outermost positions until they reach critical mass, when only a slight thrust moves the rock off balance.

Energy is transmitted between people according to the principle of resonance. This is also the way we acquire energy.

Life's mission: The collection of thoughts, sensations, ideas, and expressions of all kinds (for example, activities), which arises from the soul's need for growth. It represents the consequence of karma and simultaneously denotes the destiny of this life. At the same time, it shows a direction, which is dictated by a person's deepest wishes originating from the heart, soul, and intuition. Performing their life's missions enables individuals to move forward and finally free themselves from karma's cycle.

Karma: The consequence of previous activities; responsibility resulting from previous decisions. Destiny represents for the future what karma represents for the past. The point in between is our momentary consciousness. Just as karma carries within it the seed of previous decisions, destiny carries the seed (source) of future decisions with the same intention. The goal of both is the same: to bring individuals to the point where they will manage their life's energy completely and without reservation.

Destiny: Life's mission, consequentially linked with karma (previous decisions) and the consciousness (momentary decisions); the "plan" by which we release ourselves from karma's cycle. Everyone's utmost goal is the same – to return to the beginning, to unconditional energies (this is not necessarily the goal already in this life). The paths vary from one person to another.

We use the term destiny for something else, as well. When we refer to the energy of the external life's mission (the energy that we direct from ourselves into an outside, material world), we will call it external destiny. And when we refer to directing life force energy into the building of an internal energy state (of thoughts, feelings, and other energy expressions within ourselves), we will call it internal destiny.

Identity: The collection of something we respect in ourselves and/or in others. It can be what we have, what we are, or what we are striving for. It is our highest value or the highest expression as we see it, and it is the basis on which we want others to notice and treat us. Also, it is our highest form of recognition, as we would like to portray ourselves to others and ourselves. It can be the things we possess (material goods), what we have in ourselves (values, abilities, talents, skills, etc.), what we approve of (philosophy or religions), etc. It is not necessary for us to already have this. We can simply point our consciousness in this direction and strive for it… or simply express energetic or physical agreement and support.

Integrity: Diligence in persisting in one's energy, in standpoints, actions, promises, etc., while the consciousness is in high vibration. It is derived from the phrase "integrated with (true) Self," which means staying in the heart (or being in very high vibration).

We are in the state of integrity when, for example, we are not focused on outside influences (obstacles, changes in the environment, etc.), but are coming from inside ourselves and bringing that energy of highest vibration outwards. If this is so, we can accept everything around us – because we are not attached to the environment and therefore have no expectations of it. But this does not mean that we allow everyone or everything – especially those who do not resonate with our consciousness – to influence us… much less avert us from our path.

The perfect examples of this are the lives of Jesus Christ, Mother Teresa, Gandhi, Sai Baba, and other enlightened people.

This is not stubbornness, defiance, etc., because these energies of lower vibration tie themselves to outside influences. So if we persist in our purpose while being in low vibrations, we do not accept the environment, but wish to control others... and deny and reject everyone and everything that does not agree with our desires.

Energy line: Directing the consciousness toward a particular goal or in a particular direction. Also, the connection of our consciousness with something – for instance, with an event, memory, feeling. Expectation is derived from this – when we direct our energy line toward some specific result – and also the attachment. If expectations are not fulfilled, there is usually the appearance of a low vibration feeling (fear, anger, fury, etc.).

Unpleasant energy: Low vibration energy. This is the term we use to replace the old concept of negative energy. Namely, it is very difficult to define energy as positive (beneficial) or negative (not beneficial) because energy just is. Additionally, what we feel as unpleasant does not always mean to be unsupportive of us. For example, low vibration energy – such as sadness, apathy, etc. – is usually unpleasant. However, it shows us certain useful information and the path forward.

The best expression to describe this energy is: the energy of low vibration.

Being open, openness, and being closed: The (dis)allowance of energies from the surroundings to reach us. Openness shows the wish and/or need for resonance – or at least its possibility. Whereas while being closed, resonance is not possible. Rather, we are avoiding or resisting it. A higher level of this state is the state of integrity.

Oneness (or unconditionality or Unity): The energy state in which we exceed opposites, judgments, and standpoints and only accept whatever is, without having any standpoint or tendency toward a particular energy – for instance, for some particularly defined expression or result.

In this state, we allow anything to happen and have neither good nor bad feelings because the outside world can no longer reach us. The energies of faith, hope, and trust are present.

The most typical representative of this group is the energy of Love. Oneness always expresses a very high vibration. We usually use Oneness to describe the heart, soul, intuition, and God. This is a state in which outside factors have no influence over us. (See also the descriptions for "Unconditional energy" and "Love.")

Duality, polarity, state of extremes or opposites: The energy state in which conditional energies are present. These are energies that respond to stimuli from the surroundings. (See also the description for "Conditional energies.") This is the typical state when energies of low vibration are activated.

Duality is always created in the mind and is then usually transmitted to emotions. It is indicated through extremes: left – right, good – bad, love – hate, etc. In such energy, it is impossible to create lasting harmony because the energy is dependent on support from the outside, which we usually cannot influence.

When we feel well in duality, it is really an illusion of happiness rather than happiness itself (because a change in the surroundings destroys this inner satisfaction).

Intuition: Unconditional mental energy (we hear or rather perceive it in the mind as an idea or flash of wit).

Heart (heart energy, also love or Love): Unconditional sensual energy; we feel it as an awareness and not as an idea or flash of wit. For example, the feeling when we take a baby into our arms. Active energy that is expressed. (See also "Love" and "Unconditional energies.")

Unconditional energies: Energies that have no opposites, do not set up any energy lines (pressures) of unpleasant energies, and need nothing to exist. Their specific attribute is that they maintain their vibration and strength in any situation and do not change. If they do change, they are not unconditional, but are obviously linked to outside influences. (We often confuse the term "changing energies" with "dropping our vibration" – which is likely to happen – and where a consequence is energy change.) These unconditional energies just are, and they do not derive their strength from the environment. For instance, contentedness, Love, acceptance always show themselves as active and creative energies expressing themselves, and are always derived from Oneness. (See also the description for "Oneness.")

Conditional energies: Energies that are formed from a certain energy line (expectations). They have their extremes and most often also opposites. They react to other energies and change depending on the events around them.

For instance, sadness can change into happiness with a particular event/occurrence and vice versa.

They usually need something specific to be created and to exist. For instance, anger needs a certain thought, feeling, or event in order to appear. Therefore, they are always linked to outside influences. Sadness does not appear of its own accord; something must evoke it – either in the person or the surrounding physical world. They arise from polarity or duality. (See also the description for "Duality.")

We can also say that we literally create conditional energies in our minds. While Love exists by itself and we cannot do anything about it, conditional energies are actually our imagination because they are consequences of how we interpret our current reality.

Love: General (generalized) or collective name for unconditional energies. It contains all unconditional attributes: peace, compassion, joy, harmony, acceptance, etc. True love – or Love (with a capital "L") when we particularly emphasize the attribute of unconditionality – is unconditional, so it does not react to outside influences and does not change.

That is to say, Love is an energy, not an emotion. But this energy is a base from which emotions originate. When we add "stuff" to that energy (i.e. our personal descriptions, explanations, worries, etc.), we get an emotion. Therefore, we cannot feel Love unless we let this pure energy – without any filters of the mind that distort it – come into our conscious awareness.

Gratitude: Unconditional energy, which indicates a link to and approval of some particular energy. It often expresses approval of openness or resonance with something, for example, one person to another. It is very close to the energy of respect. We may also describe it as respect to which has been added the energy of the joy of union and the return of energy. Very dynamic energy.

Respect: An unconditional energy, which expresses openness and affection (agreement) toward another energy, so giving it the possibility of resonance without wanting to change or influence it. A dynamic energy, although somewhat more passive than the energy of gratitude. If not harmonized or in balance – expressing an extreme – it may turn into fear-respect or idolatry (glorification of someone else at the expense of one's self, or self-destruction).

Feeling: The first sensual awareness. If we explain the sensual awareness in a certain way or add an attachment or mental explanation to it, it becomes an emotion. For example, if an acquaintance that owes us money greets us politely on the street and we allow ourselves to accept only the energy – without the mind adding some special meaning to the event – it is merely a feeling. If our mind says, "He only greeted me politely because I loaned him money," we have turned the feeling into an emotion. Also, the genuine and unconditional sensual awareness of situations (around us or in us).

Emotion: The conditional sensual energy; a feeling with a certain meaning attached to it. That means we add something (a meaning) to neutral energy (Love) and therefore change its meaning… and usually its strength, as well.

Emotion actually stands for *e*-nergy in-*motion*. The power of emotions is derived from the intensity of the meaning we attribute to the feeling. The more our situation can influence or hit (throw) us – which usually happens the more we identify with it – the greater the power of emotions is. Oftentimes, this power has no direct relation to the event itself, but only to the strength or importance of our explanation. We can also describe emotion as the perception of situations (in us or around us) through mental and sensory filters.

Five Laws: The Five Universal Laws, also legalities, principles, or however we refer to them. These are the **Law of Living (on Earth), Law of Vibration, Law of Resonance, Law of Energy, and Law of Critical Mass**.

These are the basic "rules" with which we can, in some combination, describe each and every event that has ever happened in the history of mankind or ever will happen. They describe the surroundings, energy, and processes of how this energy reshapes itself (in time and space, or on Earth).

They also contain some Sub-laws like the (Sub) Law of a Life's Mission, which is part of the Law of Living.

Personal strength (also just "strength"): In the book's context, this does not mean aggressive energy that sets conditions, intimidates, or frightens, but rather the strength within an individual that motivates the surroundings to open its heart and follow it because it so desires. Regarding relating to others, it comes as the result of linking common goals and visions from which such strength is derived (not out of fear or the desire to control or govern). It is always derived from the integrity of a person or a group.

God: Also, the Creator, nature, Father, He; refers to the concentration of all energies, which are present within us and outside of us. Everything that is.

Life, and everything else, evolves from Him. He is most often personified with the energy of Love and Truth. Jesus, a synonym for the conception of Living Love, is represented as His son. Jesus said of Himself, "If you chop a piece of wood, you will find me there. If you lift a rock, I am under it." (*The Gospel of Thomas*, saying 75)

Of God, he said: "In that day you will know that I am in My Father, and you in Me, and I in you." (John 14:20)

God is (located) in the "kingdom, which is found within us and outside of us." (*The Gospel of Thomas*, saying 3) And we are created in His image: "Has it not been written in your Law, 'I said you are gods'?" (John 10:34)

It is not an icon, but an energy – or experience, not to be confused with religion.

Perhaps the Apostle Paul best described God in *The Holy Bible*: "The God who made the world and all things in it, since He is Lord of heaven and earth, does not dwell in temples made with hands; nor is He served by human hands, as though He needed anything, since He Himself gives to all people life and breath and all things; and He made from one man every nation of mankind to live on all the face of the earth, having determined their appointed times and the boundaries of their habitation, that they would seek God, if perhaps they might grope for Him and find Him, though He is not far from each one of us; in Him we live and move and exist..." (Acts 17:24-28)

About the Authors and Their Works

Boris Vene devoted his life to personal growth, developing human potentials and achieving harmony in his mind and soul. His three youth's biggest problems – education, lack of money and poor communication skills – changed into opportunities and wisdom, with whom shows people the way to real-I-zing their soul's growth and thus to eternal contentment. He brings human values and "divine-touch approach" into many areas of personal and business life. The result is controlled growth and personal development: general success, happiness and peace. He also works as a coach and mentor to leaders.

Nikola Grubisa consistently works on awakening ancient sacred knowledge, based on "Universal Laws of the Universe", which consider soul's growth and karma of the individual. He systematically puts these findings into theoretical and practical models and systems, which represent useful tools for everyone who wants to return back to their roots – the heart.

INISA publishing house has already released several books by Boris Vene and Nikola Grubisa. The following new releases from the »Divine Touch Publishing« series will be available soon:

BECOMING RICH AND WEALTHY THROUGH DIVINE TOUCH (Boris Vene)
- Describes the symbolism of money, an esoteric look at money and the karmic relationship with money.

- Explains why and how nearly everyone can be rich, but not necessarily happy.
- Offers practical advice to earn more and enrich your money.
- Suggests how to handle debtors.
- Learn how to restore a harmonious relationship with money, recognize its divine energy and incorporate it in your life.
- Includes a special supplement for financial advisors, etc.

THE MAGIC OF 5
- 5 enlightened systems that help us harmonize and perform all activities in life so as to approach Oneness (with theoretical and practical instructions).
- Examples from personal and business experiences.
- Gives detailed explanations of enlightened systems in practice: the 5 basics of a successful relationship, the "System of Pillar Support" (a system of non-forcing motivation that brings exceptional results), the achievement of Oneness, etc.
- Describes the connection of all systems with ancient esoteric knowledge based on the primal strength of God, who is hidden in every individual.
- Instructions how to connect with God and how to work in relation to other people.

HEALTH IS WITHIN US: HOW TO RESTORE OPTIMAL HEALTH CONDITIONS WITH THE HELP OF DOCTORS, HEALERS AND THE PROCESS OF SELF-HEALING
- Dismisses the differences between classical and alternative medicine: offers a fresh look at medicine, illness, healers and doctors from all perspectives.
- Discusses the true cause behind the source of illness and recoveries (supported with examples).
- Describes how processes happen within the body and tells the reader how to use that knowledge to his advantage.

- States the facts about miraculous cures: when, for whom, and in what circumstances they can occur.
- Talks about the combination of modern medical science with ancient healing and esoteric teachings – the connection of classical medicine with healing along with a spiritual look at life and the personality of the individual.

SURGEON THROUGH DIVINE TOUCH: BEAUTY IS WITHIN (Boris Vene and Marjan Fabjan, MD)

- Talks about inner and outer beauty: how to recognize both, what is their purpose, how to combine them to express self-confidence, charisma, etc.
- Tells all about identity: how to acquire it, how to find strength within, how to harmonize your outward appearance with your life's mission, etc.
- Explains how to reestablish friendly relations with others according to the principles of Oneness.
- Includes a special emphasis on cosmetic surgery (with examples): who should decide on surgery and under what circumstances, what the success of cosmetic surgeries depends on, situations where the patient will almost certainly be disappointed with the result – regardless of the expertise of the surgeon, etc.
- Offers background behind the work of doctors: if we are familiar with their purpose, we can understand their processes.

SELLING WITH DIVINE TOUCH

- Reveals the secrets for successful sales and the establishment of an effective and pleasant salesperson-to-client relationship.
- Suggests how to lead and motivate people, uncovers the secrets of successful communication, and describes how to influence your peers without saying a word.
- Gives a detailed presentation of the "System of Pillar Support" and the "5 foundations of a successful business".

- Includes a questionnaire for self-analysis (and the analysis of other sales people).
- Shows how to establish an enlightened system of strategic sales that is buyer friendly and yet attaches the buyer to the company at the same time.
- Gives practical approaches and examples for the implementation of strategic sales in companies, etc.

MARKETING WITH DIVINE TOUCH

- The secrets of marketing and promotional success with details: what is essential to make people notice you and want to work with you. How to realize this without comparing oneself to the competition, working successfully and without worry – regardless of circumstances on the market, etc.
- Describes how to determine and develop your competitive advantage.
- Lists the 5 basics of successful business that ensure top-level sales and more business.
- Explains the esoteric influence of a director or owner on the development of events within a company.
- Debates whether to focus on strategy or tactics and the traps therein.
- Offers practical examples of enlightened marketing that is pleasant for all while producing excellent results.

CHARISMA, SELF CONFIDENCE AND PERSONAL POWER

- How to recognize one's life mission and talents as well as one's attachments, fears and worries.
- How to systematically harmonize one's relationship with all past experiences and other energies that obstruct people from completely fulfilling their potential.
- A practical review of the path through duality into Oneness or how to awaken the energy of God: how to establish a connection, relate to it, and use it in everyday life (applicable in any religion and not specifically attached to any of them).

- How to systematically regain all of one's strength and work from within regardless of circumstances (while still being pleasant or working from the heart),

  The power of forgiveness (practical instructions and a step-by-step description of the process), relations toward groups, power in the workplace, and the art of top-notch (energetic) communication, etc.